VOLUME ONE

ANCIENT AND MEDIEVAL RITES OF PASSAGE

A HISTORY OF
YOUNG PEOPLE
IN THE WEST

VOLUME ONE
ANCIENT AND MEDIEVAL RITES OF PASSAGE

A HISTORY OF YOUNG PEOPLE IN THE WEST

EDITED BY

Giovanni Levi and Jean-Claude Schmitt

TRANSLATED BY

Camille Naish

The Belknap Press of Harvard University Press

Cambridge, Massachusetts
London, England   1997

Originally published as *Storia dei giovani, 1: Dall'antichità all'età moderna,*
© Guis. Laterza & Figli Spa, Roma-Bari, 1994; and *Histoire des jeunes en
occident, 1: De l'antiquité à l'époque moderne,* © Éditions du Seuil, Paris, 1996.

Published with the assistance of the French Ministry of Culture.

Library of Congress Cataloging-in-Publication Data
Storia dei giovani. English
  A history of young people in the West / edited by Giovanni Levi and
Jean-Claude Schmitt ; translated by Camille Naish.
     p.   cm.
  Includes bibliographical references and index.
  Contents: v. 1. Ancient and medieval rites of passage—
v. 2. Stormy evolution to modern times.
  ISBN 0-674-40405-X (v. 1 : cloth : alk. paper).—
  ISBN 0-674-40406-8 (v. 2 : cloth : alk. paper)
  1. Youth—Europe—History. 2. Youth—Italy—History. I. Levi,
Giovanni, 1939–   . II. Schmitt, Jean Claude. III. Title.
  HA799.E9S7613   1997
  305.23′5′094—dc20   96-34751

CONTENTS

Illustrations follow pages 38 and 230.

ANCIENT AND MEDIEVAL RITES OF PASSAGE

A HISTORY OF

YOUNG PEOPLE

IN THE WEST

CHAPTER 1

INTRODUCTION

Giovanni Levi

Jean-Claude Schmitt

If there is a recurrent theme in the anthropological, psychological, demographic, and sociological studies that marked the 1970s and 1980s, it is certainly the theme of youth. Yet it has not really been treated directly, nor subject to a major synthesis; nor has it been viewed in a cultural-historical perspective such as that adopted by the majority of studies collected in the present work. That alone is sufficient reason for publishing this book. But this project is also justified by the concept we, as historians, have of youth and the place of young people in history. How then do we define our subject?

In view of the important work done by Philippe Ariès and the echo—still resounding—of the debates it gave rise to on the history of childhood, historians might well be content simply to extend these inquiries, following their observation of childhood with that of the age that comes next, in the hope of continuing in this way through the entire human life cycle. But such is not our intention, for to proceed in this manner, it seems to us, would be neither desirable nor even truly possible. On the contrary, we wish to emphasize the specific nature of youth, without electing to view it simply as one age among other ages. That is why the problem of a definition immediately arises. We have, however, no intention of providing one sole definition, valid in all places at all times. Like the other ages we pass through in life—though perhaps even more so—youth is a social and cultural construct. As such, it is distinguished by its "liminal" nature, being situated somewhere between the shifting margins of infantile dependency and adult autonomy, within the period—a period of perpetual change—in which adolescent potential reaches turbulent fulfillment. Youth occupies a borderline between sexual immaturity and sexual maturity, when the intellectual faculties are forming and beginning to blossom, when authority and power have not yet been acquired. More than any other physiological development, it depends on cultural factors that differ according to human societies and epochs, each imposing its own brand of order and meaning on a phenomenon that seems transitory, if not unruly and chaotic. Neither demographic quantification nor legal definition can provide a clear delimitation for an "age in life" such as this. Accordingly, it seems to us unprofitable to seek boundaries in this area, boundaries that others have tried far too often to define.

Instead, what we shall emphasize is the marginal or liminal character of youth, the perception of something that never attains a concrete and stable definition. For here we encounter both the wealth of symbolic meanings, promises, threats, potential, and fragility implicit in youth, and the subsequent ambiguous attention, composed of simultaneous expectations and suspicions, that societies devote to it. It is in this hybrid state of mind—a mixture of attraction and alarm—that societies always "construe" youth as an unstable social reality, and not merely as a fixed juridical or demographic fact. Better still, they see it as a cultural reality, charged with a horde of symbolic values and symbolic customs, and not simply as a social reality that can immediately be observed.

We should add that among the principles for classifying human beings, the principle of age has the particular capacity of defining impermanent conditions. Unlike the fact of belonging to a particular "social class" (from which individuals can hardly ever escape, except those who occasionally realize their hopes of "social mobility") or sex (a circumstance theoretically unequivocal and permanent), the fact of belonging to a particular age group—especially a youthful one—is a temporary state for everyone. Individuals do not really belong to an "age"; they simply travel through it. Thus the combination of its essentially liminal nature and the relative brevity of its duration is ultimately what characterizes youth (though in ways that vary according to societies) and subsequently determines not only the attitude other people have of youth, but also young people's attitude toward themselves. We should, however, stress that there is nothing immutable or universal in all this, since a society that is more rigid and static in its structures and representations will have different legal and symbolic procedures to emphasize the elements of continuity and reproduction in the roles allotted to youth. On the other hand, a society that is more flexible and better able to admit the value of change will more easily acknowledge the conflicts necessarily involved in passing from one age to another, and in handing the baton from one generation to the next.

These initial considerations in regard to our subject demand renewed reflection as to our methods. Readers of this "history of young people" may well wonder what has become of the classical questions posed by social history concerning the differentiation of groups or classes in societies. They may also wonder how valid, for a historian, is an investigation couched in such terms as "age cohorts" (since elsewhere the difference between the sexes comes first). Such methodological slippage obviously implies the adoption of other conceptual models, at the point where biological factors (age and sex) conjoin with the symbolic structures that make them socially effective and historically significant. Even then these new procedures should not be contrasted too artificially with older ones: the history of the contemporary world constantly reminds us, for example, that youth is a variable concept and that social differentiation and inequality in regard to wealth and employment weigh most heavily here. And so, without turning our backs on traditional social history, we wish only to help make the interpretive models more complex while simultaneously examining the ambiguity of social segmentations, solidarities, conflicts, and even the effectiveness of symbolic representations. In this regard, the history of youth appears as fertile ground for experimentation.

The authors of this collective work are fully aware of the theoretical difficulties implied by these questions. They had no thought of responding with one single voice. On the contrary, they decided to declare their multiple points of view, so as to avoid the prematurely reductive or too uniform concepts that a synthesis produced by a single author might propose or impose. Thus our historians bring to this project their knowledge of their own specific fields, by virtue of the sources they know best, and they have been able to refine their methodology in the course of previous research. Accordingly, readers will discover here not just one history of youth, but *several* histories, and histories of *young people* in particular. Each of these histories is reinserted into the weft of its particular social milieu and is also linked with different historical contexts.

Our refusal to indulge in any sort of premature generalization is also apparent in the historical fields covered by these contributions. These fields pertain exclusively to the histories of Western societies and cultures, from antiquity to the modern world. We shall, however, refrain from discussing the present period, for we would like our work to retain the character of historical (rather than sociological) research, in addition to being a collective reflection on the conditions and limitations of historians' methodology. The scope of our chronology will compensate for the relative narrowness of the comparativist perspective, as will be apparent when we inquire what separates a young worker of the industrial age from a Greek ephebe, or from a Medieval squire. Is not the distance between them as great as the distance separating either of them from a young samurai of the old Japan?

There is a further simplification we have tried to avoid: the illusion— which historians often give their readers, sometimes inadvertently—of a linear history unfolding on a continuous, rhythmically punctuated world, a history proceeding from some hypothetical beginning and pointed toward a conclusion already implicit in the premises. This would enable one to imagine a remarkably smooth evolution, from the youth of traditional societies, defined by their ritual functions and by custom, to the youth of today, "tuned in," ideally liberated from constraint and freed of all taboos, having eliminated all difference between the sexes in regard to behavior, fashion (the unisex blue jeans), and choice of a profession. Far from pursuing such an objective, we intend, on the contrary, to emphasize the multiple dimensions of historical data that cannot be reduced to a single schema not by simply tackling diverse eras, but by dealing with problems and aspects of the history of young people that vary from one era to another. In short, the texts collected here mean to convey an image neither of continual historical development nor of social and cultural homogeneity.

To write a history of young people thus implies a plurality of perspectives. Insofar as it is a phase of socialization occurring before adulthood, youth comprises numerous aspects of the "liminal" moment of a rite of passage (as anthropologist Victor Turner might say) or, as Arnold van Gennep might remark, of the "margin" that actually constitutes the core of the rite, between an initial phase of separation and a final phase of integration. What is true of rites of passage holds true for the entire process of socializing individuals, from childhood to adulthood. And as they develop, the rituals of youth specific to each area of social and cultural life logically constitute a privileged object of study. In each case we shall follow a particular sequence of events: in the Catholic tradition, for example, the progression from first communion to confirmation. We shall show how ordinary citizens move from military service to civic duties, assuming civil and legal responsibility, becoming legally empowered to marry, or to engage in politics, trade unionism, and so forth. Youth is thus punctuated by a succession of rites of entry and rites of exit, giving the impression of a process of solidification, through stages, ensuring the gradual definition of adult roles.

Youth must also be perceived in individual terms, as a crucial time of formation and transformation for every human being; a time when body and mind mature and decisive choices are made, leading up to the moment when one is definitively let loose among one's fellow creatures. In this respect, youth is a time of short-lived endeavors, of ardent but changing vocations, of "quests" (like those of medieval knights), of professional, military, or amorous apprenticeships, with all their successes and failures. It is full of ephemeral moments, notable for their evanescence and marked by ceremony, as when the young knight is dubbed or the novice takes the veil, when the aspiring soldier goes before his draft board or the freshman student is hazed. There are moments of crisis, individual and collective, but also of enthusiastic commitment: do we not find young people in the vanguard of revolutions and revolts?

Youth is also the focal point for a series of strong images, ways of imagining and representing both the self and society in its entirety. These images are fertile territory in the study of symbolic phenomena. Society creates images of young people, assigning them characters and roles and seeking to impose rules and values on them; then it observes with distress the seeds of disintegration latent in this period of mutation, the conflicts and resistance inherent in integration and social reproduction. Therefore, venturing beyond the more established taxonomies (such as the different ages in life, the age of political majority or of legal responsibility), we shall discuss the vaguer—though possibly more enlightening—representations of social roles. Some of these are positive (as when youth is glorified as the bulwark of the nation) and some negative (as when a diffuse sense of hostility toward young people allows them to be seen as the source of all manner of disorders and aberrations). All these symbolic projections play an effective role in the "politics" of youth, whether in attempts to exclude young people or, conversely, in the function of social control that certain societies grant them precisely on account of their liminal position. In the latter case, society turns young people into judges and censors, mediators between social agents or mediators between the living and the dead of a community, endowing them with the power to sanction social and moral disorders through derisive bursts of cacophony (the charivari)[1] or by initiating the mocking rituals of carnivals. But it also happens that society, for better or for worse, expects young people to break with the solidarity of class or family and bring about a collective renewal, dissolving the more rigid social concretions: heralds of inspired groups, charismatic or mystical, they become young saints in revolt against their fathers and the corrupting influence of money (for example, Francis of Assisi) or young prophets in the Camisard rebellion.[2] But in another setting or another time, the same young people can also succumb to the seduction of some providential leader, come to embody the New Order of their dreams.

Such is the profound ambivalence of youth and young people: it is this very ambiguity, variously perceived in different times and places, that has led to a wish for clearer identifications of young people's status, for definitions of age limits and corresponding rights and duties. The development of states disposing of vast territories, the effort required by homogenization and by social control—not to mention the demands of production, politics, education, and the military—have gradually resulted in organic forms of socialization and control, be they in a scholastic system that is constantly growing larger and more codified, in military service, or in the law.

Finally, we may fittingly inquire how young people view themselves and the society in which they live. Unlike children—history's silent masses—young people, even long ago, spoke of themselves and wrote about their circumstances. How is the historian to track down those feelings of individual and collective identity and group solidarity that turn young people into a ritually organized social body, or into a politically active and autonomous one at certain moments in history? Through individual cases, including cases of autobiography, we shall try to uncover the demand for autonomy or the sense of revolt that helps young people to forge their own personalities, simultaneously opposing the adult world and reinventing values originating in their familial or cultural milieu. We may even, with care, venture down the thorny paths of psychohistory, though without actually using—as we perhaps should—psychoanalytical tools, which are still a subject of debate among historians.

In short, what the authors of this work have in mind is to illuminate the liminal features that characterize youth, from biological realities to social roles and symbolic preparations. Let us take a further look at certain elements of their project, and at some results.

Youth as a social artifact: Nowhere, in any historical period, can youth be defined simply by biological or legal criteria. Everywhere, always, it exists only in a form invested with values and symbols. From one context to another, from one era to another, young people assume different functions, and diverse sources define their status: the city or the countryside, the feudal castle or the nineteenth-century factory, the *compagnonnage*[3] of the ancien régime, or of the city in antiquity. The condition of youth cannot be the same in societies with completely different demographic regimes. From a demographic point of view, one might compare the twelfth century in Europe with a modern Third World country, where half the inhabitants are less than twenty years old, giving the society a dynamism and "style" quite different from those of our aging Western societies.

The contrast between epochs is thus significant, as is the inequality between social classes. Because of this inequality, the living conditions and cultural choices open to the "golden youth" (every era has such a group) concern only a minority, even if its presence in documents and the appeal of its example are significant. We shall be careful not to overlook slaves, peasants, workers, poor students, the unemployed, beggars, and hooligans.

Differences between the sexes: During youth, the cultural differences between boys and girls, already quite marked during infantile socialization, assume institutionalized forms. From the earliest times in life, education in its various forms, periods of freedom, even recreational activities, all prepare the sexes for diverging destinies. Yvonne Verdier has authoritatively shown how, in the countryside, in an era still quite close to our own, the training girls received in needlework, embroidery, or cooking was intended not so much to provide them with a truly practical education as to imbue them with an early notion of their necessary destiny as wives and mothers. Ideological models and behavioral norms have no other goal than to found, fix, and justify the difference and inequality of social and familial roles—as, for example, in regard to sexual morality. This is so true that one should never speak comprehensively of "young people" without stating in each case the precise effects of this differentiation.

Explicit classifications (ages in life, coming of age, and so on): Evidence suggests that these have only an indicatory value. They are not sufficient to define the framework of a social and cultural history of youth. There are several reasons for this: the absence of homogeneity in vocabulary, and the semantic slippage by which a word like "childe" can designate a young warrior in a medieval chanson de geste such as the *Enfances du Cid*, while the Roman or medieval notion of *juventus* greatly exceeds the age limits we would set on youth today. Conversely, when the terms remain unchanged in appearance, the semantic content is constantly being renewed. If we compare the old conceptual matrices with our own representations, expecting to recognize approximate correspondences between them (since the words *childhood, adolescence,* and *youth* are still in use), we have to agree that the words no longer have the same meanings. For example, whereas the old texts frequently employ the word *adolescence,* they accord it only a biological, juridical, or symbolic sense, with none of the emotional content that modern psychologists, educators, or doctors attribute to it when speaking of the "critical phase of adolescence." Put back in their original context, however, words, categories, and classes regain, for the historian, their full significance. How can we not pay attention to juridical pronouncements, for example, when the threshold for coming of age is simultaneously being lowered in all the modern democracies? This "rejuvenation" of the age of discretion is a patent index of important transformations, such as the worldwide increase in the level of school attendance and the liberalization of mores, allowing adolescents forms of behavior that enable them to be assimilated more rapidly into the ranks of adults. But here again, we must be cautious: it is very unlikely that the psychological life of young people—which is also linked to their perceptions of their own future and to the material conditions of their existence—develops at the same speed as the provisions of the law.

Effective models: If the boundaries of youth pose problems for historians, the same may be said of the models offered to young people at different periods. What is happening in our own time perfectly illustrates the ambivalence of such models. Whereas advertising extols youthful values (beauty, strength, speed, energy, freedom), everyday social life is marked more by a fear of young people, and of the disturbances for which they are held responsible by the defenders of public order and convention. At a more distant time, courtly literature extolled the youthfulness of brave knights, representatives of Love and Spring, while staid old men dreamed of plunging into the Fountain of Youth. But at the same time, clerics issued warnings against youth's lack of discernment, declaring that in an aging world inexorably hastening toward its end *(mundus senescit),* it was a good idea to flee as far and fast as possible from the transports and temptations of youth. Even in the case of Christ, the Gospels say nothing of his life between the age of twelve to the beginning of his public ministry at age thirty—creating the impression that he had no youth at all! Yet Christ appealed constantly to young people (young Francis of Assisi, among others, heard his call), charging them to leave their fathers and mothers for his sake, and to love him more than them (Luke 14:26; Matthew 10:33–37).

Young people, actors in the public sphere: Exaggerating slightly, one might say that young people are the first active individuals in history. Children for the most part have only a passive role. Here again, let us continue the dialogue between present and past. We have already indicated how the development of modern states radically modified the role of young people: as the territorial bases of communities widened, young people became a social group whose solidarity overstepped the boundaries of villages or districts. The social structures of reference corresponded to territorial aggregates far larger than in the past, altering both the image that young people had of themselves and the image that society had of them. First romanticism affirmed the natural link between youth and the nation; then in the nineteenth century, throughout Europe, bourgeois youth embraced the ideas of the Revolution; later on came various youth movements, both Catholic and Protestant, followed by the mobilization of young people under fascism and Nazism. More recently, we have witnessed the student revolt, from American campuses to the Parisian barricades of May 1968, in an era when media attention causes "current events" to resonate instantly all over the planet. All these phenomena show the growing power of a new perception of youth, a global perception—first national, then international—of youth's problems (the "generation gap"), its models (the stars young people "idolize"; popular music; English, the language of rock singers), and perhaps, we hope, its new bonds of solidarity.

In conclusion, we would like to say a word about the organization of this book, which alternates traditional historical exposition with iconographic documentation. Why is this? Because iconography (too often, the *terra incognita* of historians) must help readers understand the complexities we have just listed and assist in revealing others. For a history of youth, we therefore considered it important to show the wealth of suggestions contained in the available iconographic sources. In visual imagery, the view society has of young people blends with the image young people have of society and sometimes of themselves. In imagery, also, the explicit and implicit elements of representation combine, and for those trained to interpret visual images, this combination is never fortuitous but always significant. The presence or absence of young people in a painting or series of paintings, and the attitudes and roles pictorially allotted them, lend themselves to a multiplicity of possible readings. A comparison between social historians (most of our authors) and art historians (the minority) reveals diverging interpretations of the same illustrations. In a case where social historians tend to assume Caravaggio deliberately wanted to represent the conflict between young and old, art historians, more prudently, prove hesitant to accept as voluntary and explicit material that, they think, is only implicit and at best unconscious. Readers can decide for themselves whether these cross-disciplinary observations have proved fruitful.

Rather than a completed synthesis, then, the two volumes of this work provide perspective on a field of research and an avenue for reflection and debate. We hope that our readers, whether or not they are, by inclination or profession, historians, will find these contributions as stimulating as did the book's authors when writing them.

CHAPTER 2

IMAGES OF YOUNG PEOPLE IN THE GREEK CITY-STATE

Alain Schnapp

PAIDEIA AND THE CITY

For the Greeks, the city was the expression of a well-ordered social life. It was an institution so common and so profoundly linked to a particular cultural situation and form of community life that it is hard to define and characterize it without attempting a truly Aristotelian typology of social institutions. The backbone of life in society was paideia, or education, the distinction that gave young men access to a communal knowledge essential to the city's very existence. The city depended on a balance of institutions and customs that presupposed an art of living, a style of behavior, and a social ease all embodied in the idea of paideia. In this respect, Plato represented the culmination of a long process: one that originated in the distant past of the Archaic city, and anticipated a form of paideia that subsequently became dominant in the Hellenistic age. The aim of paideia was not simply to adapt the citizen to the city. It was also to help bring out potential human qualities present in all future citizens, qualities that had, however, to be discerned and developed through specific exercises. Paideia was identified with a comprehensive comportment, with psychological and moral qualities that went beyond training in certain military techniques:

> If you ask about the education in general of all who are educated, the answer is not difficult: those who are well educated become good men, and becoming such, they act nobly in other respects, as well as in winning

victories when they fight their enemies. Education [*paideia*] brings victory, although victory sometimes brings a loss of education; for many have grown more insolent because of victories in war, and through their insolence have been filled with ten thousand other vices.[1]

In the general acceptance Plato gives the word "paideia" in this passage, he means not simply the educational techniques but also the qualities that mold a young man into a fully functional citizen, capable of judgment that does not confuse cause and effects. If courage is a consequence of good education, it is not reduced to the simple exercise of military virtues. Better than a victorious soldier, the cultivated man must be a responsible citizen. Gymnastics and *syssitia* (meals taken in common), customs so characteristic of the Boeotians and of certain Ionian cities, were harmful "in the event of civil strife."[2] The aims of paideia were to establish solid bonds between young people, and to strengthen relationships between age groups; but it could also, on occasion, encourage factions that might ruin the city from within. It was thus necessary to define an educational program useful to the entire city, and not just to a few privileged groups capable of putting their own interests before those of the city as a whole. An ideal paideia had to avoid two pitfalls. There was the danger of factions deriving from the habit of restricted sociability, limited to those young men who met at exaggeratedly elitist activities or banquets such as those held at Miletus or in Boeotia. There was also the danger of a specialized training that prepared the young man for too particular a career, whether carpentry or war.[3] First and foremost, *paideia* was the art of living in the city: "The education from childhood in virtue, that makes one desire and love to become a perfect citizen who knows how to rule and be ruled with justice."[4]

As Morrow has emphasized in *Plato's Cretan City,* this concept of paideia was the culmination of a long evolution, to which each of the Greek cities contributed in creating specific institutions. Before analyzing the particular role of youthful behavior in the city, I would like to examine this lengthy, contrastive history of educational institutions.

HOMER AND AGE COHORTS

The study of age groups in the Homeric world was first tackled by H. Jeanmaire.[5] Following the work of M. I. Finley,[6] a majority of historians now reject the idea of Homeric chivalry so dear to Jeanmaire; but certain of the traits Jeanmaire revealed help explain the role of age cohorts in ancient Greece.

The *kouroi*[7] were a particular group of men who had specific, defined tasks in both war and peace. The word *kouroi* was understood to mean "sons of the Achaeans," and they were contradistinguished from the *gerontes*, the Fathers or Ancients, who with them made up the army. They formed a military group that seconded the king and commanders on diverse social occasions—sacrifices, banquets, assemblies—as well as in combat: "The Homeric *kouros* was not only . . . a warrior or a young warrior, a man called to bear arms. He was a noble warrior, destined by his birth and education to a career in arms; and this calling had been instilled in him by a training that also shaped him in accordance with the habits and refinements of a certain ideal."[8] Based on the earliest available texts, Jeanmaire's investigation reveals the existence, in precity Greece, of a group of young men trained to participate in military exercises and social pomp and ceremony, a group marked by the distinction of its members and the particular relationships between them. The young men were linked by *homêlikia*, or age parity, and this created the relationships, habits, and bonds of solidarity that united the group of the *kouroi*. There is no need to follow every point of Jeanmaire's demonstration, which makes Homeric commensality the basis of an economic system advantageous only to the warrior class.[9] I shall, however, emphasize that Homeric *comradeship (hetaireia)* was one of the social forms that guaranteed the society of warriors its cohesion and autonomy: the *hetairoi* were companions who found justification and equilibrium in rendering reciprocal services. According to Jeanmaire,[10] bonds forged between young men took the place of blood bonds; in any case, they show the existence of a particular sociability that allowed the *kouros* to maintain his rank and even exercise some influence. While we know little of the training and collective habits that united the *kouroi*, the existence of a group (albeit ill-defined) of young men linked by exercises and particular behavior indicates a basic structure of education before cities invented paideia.

CRETANS AND SPARTANS: FOUNDERS OF EDUCATIONAL DISCIPLINE

From earliest antiquity, historians, philosophers, and mythographers have recognized Crete and Sparta as the birthplaces of a particular type of educational institution that conditioned the Greek concept of paideia. The specific nature of Cretan and Spartan institutions, and the role attributed to the Dorians in establishing a military society that supposedly constituted the primitive form of the city, are already recurrent phenomena in ancient historiography.[11] But it was modern German historiography that made a decisive, almost hegemonic, contribution to the debate in the form of K. O. Müller's monumental work of 1844[12] and the decisive studies by E. Bethe.[13] For German scholars, the supremacy of the Dorians derived from the aristocratic quality of their institutions, which permitted the emergence of a stable, almost egalitarian military society. The *homoioi* or *kleioi* were trained in military exercises, with refined forms of competition that made them the very best among the Greeks. The entire organization of society helped to develop military values, and to affirm the physical qualities of the governing group. And this constant effort was supported by educational institutions whose excellence—barring a few reservations—the German scholars cannot help but admire. For Müller and his successors, comradeship *(hetaireia)* was the key to Dorian paideia: "All the *gerontes* were the young men's educators."[14] Without deigning to compromise the moral prohibitions of his time, Müller thus recognized—at least among the Spartans and the Cretans—the sexual nature of the bonds uniting the older men and the young. He observed that among the Cretans the *educational* homosexual relationship (between a young man and an older one) was institutionalized by a ritual that imitated marriage. He added that "institutions of this kind did not develop anywhere else, but that this psychological attitude was basically common to all Dorians."[15] For a strict Protestant like Müller[16]—the son of an army chaplain, to boot—recognizing the reality of pederasty was no easy matter. But being a good Prussian patriot, he managed to transcend his moral reservations through an admiration for Dorian military abilities.

Almost a century after Müller, E. Bethe's "Die dorische Knabenliebe, ihre Ethik und Idee" (The Love of Boys among the Dorians: Its Ethics and Its Concept) provided what was to become the classic definition of pederasty among northern Greeks.[17] Bethe takes up Müller's theories in general, but gives them an anthropological definition. For him, the sexual relationship between *erastês* (lover) and *eromenos* (beloved) was not an aberration of pedagogical institutions but the actual cornerstone of paideia, the very basis of Dorian power. For although homosexuality was a current practice in ancient Greece, the Dorians alone held it to be "the closest intimate relationship that can exist between two comrades of the same sex. From this emanated, in all their plenitude, the noblest impulses in striving for personal perfection, emulating others, and making the most absolute gift of oneself to the beloved, whatever the danger and even unto death, in the very springtime of life. Thus the true ideal of martial comradeship and lofty aspiration were realized in these pederastic couples."[18] These theories have dominated the study of Greek homosexuality until a recent date, being echoed in the work of W. Jaeger and H. I. Marrou.[19] For Jaeger, the equation of Dorianism, pederasty, and military companionship was obvious. Indeed, it was the basis of Dorian specificity: "After all, it is easy to understand how a passionate admiration for handsome bodies and well-balanced souls could have arisen in a race which, since time immemorial, has considered the combination of physical valor and mental harmony the greatest good man could aspire to . . . A very profound sentiment of honor prevented lovers linked by the male Eros from committing any vile deed."[20]

Although written in an entirely different context and in a perspective critical of German scholarship, H. I. Marrou's famous book has in some measure helped disseminate an image of Dorian education still largely dependant on Müller's model. Misconstruing Müller, Marrou saw the habits of the Ionians as "the effect of a more precocious development of conscience in Asiatic Greece, in which, in the classical age, pederasty was judged more severely than in the rest of the Hellenic world."[21] Where

Müller condemned Ionian lasciviousness, Marrou discerned a consciousness rebellious to the Dorian influence. He reversed the positions of German scholarship while still accepting its interpretive framework: "In my opinion Greek pederasty was in fact one of the most obvious and lasting survivals of the feudal Middle Ages. In essence, it was a comradeship of warriors."[22]

We owe to K. J. Dover[23] a decisive advance in the understanding of Greek homosexuality, and this is thanks to the crossed fire of his dual approach. Through a resolutely phenomenological analysis of Dorian homosexuality, Dover made a clean slate of the Dorian theory, and by resorting systematically to illustrative sources, he completely modified the interpretive framework. What was so profoundly original in Greek homosexuality was not so much its diffusion as its social recognition. The specific place of male eroticism in social life was not as linked to military institutions as German erudition had affirmed. The role that pederasty may have played in the education of young warriors cannot be dissociated from other juvenile activities: gymnastics, hunting, horseback riding. Masculine images, solicitations, and erotic experiences conditioned not only military training but the entire world of youth. What defined erotic values in ancient Greece was the equivalence of the concepts of homosexual and heterosexual love, the absence of boundaries between the two. The definition of desire, and the means to realize it, resulted from the same erotic impulse that could seize any male person (or rather, any adult citizen). Certainly the amorous relationship did not assume the same form whether directed toward a boy or a woman. The woman who responded to the male eros gave love in exchange for love: *anterân*. This response was all the more expected in that, for the Greeks, female erotic capacity was superior to that of males. In contrast, the reaction of the *eromenos* to the demands of the *erastês* had to be reserved: he could accept the solicitations of the *erastês*, but must not show any pleasure. In fact, the term *anterastês* acquired opposite meanings in heterosexual and homosexual vocabularies; in homosexual terminology, *anterastês* indicated the lover's eventual rival, not his partner. Eros was not the avowed goal of heterosexual love, which aimed at developing *philia* between the lovers. Heterosexual love was a

relationship of reciprocity, whereas homosexual love was one of sociability. This particular sociability imposed behavior, attitudes, and a style that,
whatever viewpoint we adopt, informed the pedagogical concepts of the
Greeks.

Thus the originality of Dorian institutions resided not in an overt
display of pedagogical homosexuality, but in the very particular body of
practices that, according to Ephorus, governed the paideia:

> The children must learn, not only their letters, but also the songs pre-
> scribed in the laws and certain forms of music. Now those who are still
> younger are taken to the public messes, the "Andreia"; and they sit
> together on the ground as they eat their food, clad in shabby garments,
> the same both winter and summer, and they also wait on the men as well
> as on themselves. And those who eat together at the same mess [*syssition*]
> join battle both with one another and with those from different messes.
> A boy-director [*paidonomos*] presides over each mess. But the older boys
> are taken to the "Troops" [*agelai*]; and the most conspicuous and influen-
> tial of the boys assemble the "Troops," each collecting as many boys as
> he possibly can; the leader of each "Troop" is generally the father of the
> assembler, and he has the authority to lead them forth to the hunt and to
> run races, and to punish anyone who is disobedient; and they are fed at
> public expense; and on certain appointed days "Troop" contends with
> "Troop," marching rhythmically into battle, to the tune of flute and lyre,
> as is their custom in actual war; and they actually bear marks of the blows
> received, some inflicted by the hand, others by iron weapons.[24]

This classic portrayal of Cretan education, which has attracted the
attention of numerous scholars,[25] reveals an educational system in which
age cohorts played a decisive role. The world of children formed a micro-
society subject to particular rules imposed by contact with the adult world.
It was a harsh education that emphasized collective training, the ability to
resist cold and fatigue, and competition. This competition became decisive
when the boys were recruited into the *agelē* through a procedure that
placed them under the patronage of the most prestigious among them. The
rules imposed on children were similar to those followed by members of
the *agelai*, but with this basic difference: the man responsible for the youths
was no longer the *paidonomos*, he was the father of the boy who had

recruited the members of the *agelê*. The youths then formed a group under the command of a leader. Their training was divided into three activities: hunting, races, and simulated combats—exercises that revealed both their personal abilities and their collective aptitudes, making them precitizens who could excel at the physical exercises proper to the *kleinoi*, whose importance Jeanmaire has shown.[26] These habits of Cretan adolescence led to a decisive stage, the Cretan initiation, which has so monopolized the attention of scholars:

> They have a peculiar custom in regard to love affairs, for they win the objects of their love, not by persuasion, but by abduction; the lover tells the friends of the boy three or four days beforehand that he is going to make the abduction; but for the friends to conceal the boy, or not to let him go forth by the appointed road, is indeed a most disgraceful thing, a confession, as it were, that the boy is unworthy to obtain such a lover; and when they meet, if the abductor is the boy's equal or superior in rank or other respects, the friends pursue him and lay hold of him, though only in a very gentle way, thus satisfying the custom; and after that they cheerfully turn the boy over to him to lead away; if, however, the abductor is unworthy, they take the boy away from him. And the pursuit does not end until the boy is taken to the "Andreium" of his abductor. They regard as a worthy object of love, not the boy who is exceptionally handsome, but the boy who is exceptionally manly and decorous. After giving the boy presents, the abductor takes him away to any place in the country he wishes; and those who were present at the abduction follow after them, and after feasting and hunting with them for two months (for it is not permitted to detain the boy for a longer time), they return to the city. The boy is released after receiving as presents a military habit, an ox, and a drinking-cup (these are the gifts required by law), and other things so numerous and costly that the friends, on account of the number of the expenses, make contributions thereto. Now the boy sacrifices the ox to Zeus and feasts those who have returned with him; and then he makes known the facts about his intimacy with his lover, whether, perchance, it has pleased him or not, the law allowing him this privilege in order that, if any force was applied to him at the time of the abduction, he might be able at this feast to avenge himself and be rid of the lover. It is disgraceful for those who are handsome in appearance or descendants of illustrious ancestors to fail to obtain lovers, the presumption being that

their character is responsible for such a fate. But the parastathentes (for thus they call those who have been abducted) receive honours; for in both the dances and the races they have the positions of highest honour, and are allowed to dress in better clothes than the rest, that is, in the habit given them by their lovers; and not then only, but even after they have grown to manhood, they wear a distinctive dress, which is intended to make known the fact that each wearer has become "kleinos," for they call the loved one "kleinos" and the lover "philetor." So much for their customs in regard to love affairs.[27]

This text is one of those that has caused rivers of ink to flow, for in the form it takes, it constitutes the most complete available account of the Cretan initiations. Since Bethe, of course, historians have mainly been interested in the homosexual aspect of these practices. But more recently A. Yoshida and B. Sergent have drawn attention to the series of gifts and the trifunctional interpretation they suggest.[28] Clearly this text casts particular light on Cretan educational institutions; but we should also note that the relationships described were connected with amorous customs. The *harpagê*, or kidnapping, characterized a select elite, the *kleinoi*, who thus acquired a particular social status. Compared with the collective exercises and training controlled by the city and financed by public funds, the kidnapping appears as a personal relationship between two of the elite, the *philêtor* and the *kleinos*, distinguished by the individual qualities of the partners. This represents a stylization of individuality as compared with the collectivity, but of an individuality that depended on collective recognition. The *erastês* and the *eromenos* were viewed by their peers, and their relationship was judged by an aristocratic world attentive to their rank. The bond uniting the two partners was by definition ostentatious: we see this ostentatiousness in the social distinction, and in the exchange of presents, and also in the mutual behavior: "then he makes known the facts about his intimacy with his lover"—the *eromenos* made known the details of his intercourse with the *erastês*. What separates this narrative from other evidence of the same kind is its exhibitionistic character. In the context of Greek education, the relationship of *erastês* to *eromenos* had in itself nothing strange about it. The Cretan custom was distinguished by its public

and aristocratic character. An *eromenos* gained not only prestigious gifts—
and even a flattering reputation—from his kidnapping but also the public
distinction granted him at festivals, gymnastic competitions, and diverse
civic meetings. The homosexual relationship and its accompanying activities, such as hunting and banquets, contrasted with the severe character of
daily life in the *agelai,* adding an aristocratic dimension to pedagogical
practices normally imbued with equality and fraternity. The fascination
aroused by this type of behavior doubtless derived largely from this
inherent contrast; between the rough, dull world of the *agelai* and the
luxury of hunts and banquets involving the *kleinoi* lay all the distance
separating daily life from dream.

In an article written in 1913, H. Jeanmaire drew attention to the
initiatory nature of the Spartan *krypteia.* Irrefutably, he demonstrated that
the system of age cohorts prevalent in Sparta derived its rationale from an
initiation, the specific nature of which had been illumined by ethnographic
discoveries. In *Couroi et Courètes,* he completed this analysis by giving a
global interpretation of the Spartan *agôgê:*

> The Spartan constitution was divided and hierarchized in sections corre-
> sponding to age cohorts. These cohorts corresponded to groups whose
> numerical importance steadily decreased and to which access was increas-
> ingly restricted. This constitution thus presented some characteristics of
> a society with multiple degrees of initiation. Its apparent form was the
> egalitarian regime of the *hominoi* and the communism of the *syssitia;* but
> the more complex reality was that the whole of its political life was
> dominated by an organization of which certain mechanisms probably
> escape us, and which seems to have had some occult characteristics.[29]

Jeanmaire's discovery gave Spartan society a new face: not simply the face
of a military society entrenched in the defense of its privileges, but also
the face of a city that had modeled the Archaic institution of age cohorts
into an educational system that seemed quite original to other Greeks. The
influence exerted by the Spartan model derives from the identification—so
unnatural for a Greek of the classical era—of paideia with civic institutions. All the cities had forms of juvenile initiation, but that did not mean
they transformed them into public institutions. The prestige and renown

of the Spartan paideia cannot be found elsewhere. As was the case with the Cretans, their institutions reveal a more complete, more sophisticated educational model than that of other Greek cities; the *krypteia* fascinates by its very excesses. In both the Spartan and the Cretan model, the education of young men partook of a form of pederasty. The Spartans did not have the Cretan *harpagê*, but Xenophon and Plutarch attest to the decisive role played by the *erastês* in the education of young Spartans.[30]

P. Cartledge[31] has to some extent done justice to Jeanmaire's intuitions. His conclusions remain very close to the latter's. Although he does not give an opinion as to the precise dates of the system attested to by Xenophon and Plutarch, Cartledge tends to see Sparta as a paroxysmal exaltation of the "men's club." Should we use the term "initiation" nevertheless? In a recent article of 1989, Dover criticized the indeterminate use of this expression in regard to the Greek city-state. However, I find it hard to deny that the Cretan customs had an initiatory dimension, apparent not only in the abduction of the young man, but also in the ritual and theatrical aspects of the kidnapping.

THE ATHENIAN EPHEBE

Cretans and Spartans, often mentioned in the same breath, were central to the pedagogical debate involving the classical city; but what of the Athenian traditions?

Ever since the Archaic period it seems that Athens, like the other Greek cities, had a special training for young men, in which nineteenth-century scholars thought they recognized the classical institution of the ephebate.[32] Because of the poverty of the epigraphic sources, this thesis has often been debated. Nonetheless, a study written thirty years ago by C. Pélékidis made short work of this hypercritical attitude: "In my opinion, the ephebate dates back to at least the first half of the fifth century B.C.: it followed on from more ancient institutions intended to control the education of boys and young men in the Greek world generally."[33] Certainly the ephebate we discover through Aristotle and various inscriptions was an institution of the fourth-century city. Its distinctive element was that it organized a collective training paid for by the state, and open to all citizens.[34] After spending the first year in the garrison at Piraeus, young men were given military equipment and took part in guarding fortresses. This rather modern concept of military service was the result of a historical evolution whose different stages we cannot reconstruct. But it was also a civic institution that retained some typical elements, such as the provisional seclusion and collective training that, in the Archaic period, marked the education of young people. Any attempt to explain the history of juvenile representations through the institutional history of cities, proposing a comparative analysis of institutions and educational theories—as Grasberger[35] once tried to—is doomed to failure. In his "Retour au chasseur noir," P. Vidal-Naquet tried to point out the pitfalls awaiting hasty historians who tend to confuse the *agronomoi* of the *Laws* with the Spartan *kryptoi*, the Athenian ephebes, the Cretan *kleinoi*, or the *logades* of Argos. For Xenophon, Plato, and their contemporaries, these varied groups of young men were, in their very diversity, examples that enabled them to describe civic institutions, that helped to explain the crisis of the city and to propose a future city. In this general reflection on the paideia, what mattered, as P. Roussel pointed out,[36] was the opposition between the "principle of seniority" and the "principle of youth." According to Aristotle, "Nature has given the distinction by making the group that is itself the same in race partly younger and partly older, of which two sets it is appropriate for one to be governed and for the other to govern."[37] Paideia occupied a central place in civic institutions because it did not simply dispense an education but also implied a social order that diametrically opposed the old and the young, forming a natural fulcrum for the city's equilibrium: "Action is for young men, well-considered decisions are for mature men, and dreams are for the old."[38]

YOUNG MEN AND THE HUNT

In Plato's view, the Persians represented a model of political power whose sudden rise was as unexpected as it was uneven. But, he felt, the decadence of the Persian empire was equalled only by its expansion, for a single, if decisive, reason: "Now I divine that Cyrus, though in other respects a good general and a friend to his city, failed completely to grasp what is a correct education."[39]

The aim of Plato's *Laws* was to endow the city with the least dreadful form of constitution. Accordingly, paideia was the principal means of guaranteeing the community a body of citizens capable of respecting the laws of the ideal city. For Sparta and Crete—which offered models of a paideia imbued with a civic sense—the ultimate goal of education was to prepare citizens for the war necessary to ensure the city's independence: "If you look at it this way, you are pretty sure to find that the lawgiver of the Cretans established all our customs, public and private, with a view to war."[40]

The citizens' psychological and physical aptitude for war was one of the legislators' main preoccupations. The educational system and collective training were supposed to guarantee the martial qualities of the entire city. This confusion between personal and collective qualities appears in the classification of blessings proposed by the Cretans: "Health leads the lesser goods; in the second place is beauty; third is strength, both in running and in all the other motions of the body; and fourth is wealth—not blind but sharp-sighted."[41]

While the Cretans emphasized running, the Spartans viewed hunting as a component of civic life: "Didn't we assert that the common meals and the gymnastics were devised by the legislator with a view to war? . . . Thirdly, I and any Lacedaimonian would say, he devised hunting."[42]

The city's preoccupations thus centered on its corps of young men. In matters ranging from training, aptitude for collective living, and nourishing diet, the city watched over the adolescent world as if guarding its own vital nucleus. It is therefore not surprising that an elite group of *neoi*, the *agronomoi*, was charged with inspecting the city's territory,[43] divided into twelve sections like the twelve tribes. But the young men were not supposed to focus on one part of the territory, for the city existed only in the mobility of its citizens; each month, for a year, the *agronomoi* went scouting in the territory of a different tribe, and then at the end of the year they began the inspection again, in reverse order, "so that all will become experienced and knowledgeable about the whole country."[44]

The young men's military service was a period of full apprenticeship, a preparation for collective living regulated by severe discipline—cold meals, a total absence of servants, and, above all, this incessant inspection of the territory: "It's likely that no learning they pursue is more important than that which gives all of them accurate knowledge of their own country. It's for this reason, as much as for the rest of the pleasure and benefit such activities bring to everyone, that a young man should go in for hunting with hounds and the rest of hunting."[45]

Thus the civic and military guard of *agronomoi,* which retained the frugal characteristics of the Lacedemonian *krypteia,*[46] was identified with surveillance of the territory, with knowledge of places and pathways obtained through reconnaissance and the pursuit of game. Hunting was an educational experience not simply because of its immediate usefulness, but because it conferred a familiarity with flora and fauna; in short, with the city's territory. The groups of young men who went roaming through the territory had to be disciplined and controlled, so that they did not behave like an army on a campaign—or like the unbridled Spartan *krypteia:*

> Your regime is that of an armed camp and not of men settled in cities. You keep your young in a flock, like a bunch of colts grazing in a herd. None of you takes his own youngster apart, drawing him, all wild and complaining, away from his fellow-grazers. None of you gives him a private groom and educates him by currying and soothing him, giving him all that is appropriate for child rearing. If you did, he would become not only a good soldier but someone capable of managing a city and towns.[47]

The rules of education had to be tempered through personal contact between master and pupil (between *erastês* and *eromenos*); military training was part of a more general education relating to civic *(polis)* and city *(asty)* matters. A synthesis of Spartan and Athenian education, the paideia of the *Laws* had to help form complete citizens. The model of the city-state divided into twelve parts, symmetrically patrolled—in both directions— by groups of young men, was the means of equilibrating the city's centripetal structure through a "centrifugal" circulation that integrated each

division into the larger ensemble. According to this concept, the hunters
were also *runners* in the Cretan manner. Their mobility and knowledge of
the territory were proof of a more complete citizenship that enabled them
to tolerate both the rigors of country life and the civil regulations of city
life. Hunting is a potent and logical factor in conceiving the relationship
between town and country, war and education, the military city as opposed
to the democratic city. The hunters were, of course, the young men who
roamed through the territory, but they were also the ones who led tamed
animals around the gymnasia, exhibited cynegetic trophies, and exchanged
gifts largely related to hunting.[48] These two aspects of hunting thus corresponded to the two faces of ideal city-state: the *polis*, in the broader sense
that included the *chora*, or territory; and the city, *asty*, with its urban
elements and rules of behavior.

HUNTING AS INITIATION

Among the exercises designed for young men, the legislators gave hunting
a particular role. Didn't Plato point out that Lycurgus imposed the *syssitia*,
gymnastics, and hunting on the Spartans? And didn't this mythical legislator invent an institution that practically embodied these three symbolic
characteristics of the Spartans' social life?

> He devised hunting . . . In the fourth place I at least would try to put the
> great attention that we pay to endurance of suffering, in the fistfights we
> hold with one another and in certain practices of theft we have, which
> always involve many blows. Then, too, there is a practice called the
> "secret service" [*krypteia*], which is amazingly full of the sort of toils that
> instill endurance; they go barefoot and sleep without blankets in winter,
> and they have to take care of themselves without any servants as they
> wander by night as well as by day through the whole territory.[49]

An admirable exercise, the *krypteia* did not elude Plato's criticism, as
we have seen. It was far better suited to the repressive system the Spartan
hippeis imposed on the serfs than to a balanced education combining
military training with civic instruction.[50] Unlike the *kryptoi*, the *agronomoi*
mentioned in the *Laws* did not roam through the territory like intruders,
always on the lookout for a theft or some act of aggression. Their training

was strict, but it was within the framework of a balanced education that linked physical and intellectual exercise. Gymnasts, dancers, mathematicians,[51] the *agronomoi* were also hunters. And the hunt in all its diversity appears as the conclusion of this ideal program: "At this point one should declare that the legal customs regarding the subjects that pertain to education have reached their end. But about hunting and all things of that sort one should think in the very same way."[52]

At this point in his analysis, hunting forms a kind of conclusion to the educational program. But in Plato's mind it was not limited to the mere capturing of animals; it embraced in an extraordinarily diverse manner all the activities of quest and capture:

> For hunting is a very widely extended activity even though it is now comprehended, for the most part, in a single name. There is much hunting of things in water, and much of winged things, and very much of beasts who move on their feet, which includes not only wild beasts, but also a hunting of human beings which is worth reflection. One sort occurs in warfare, but there is also a great deal of hunting—sometimes praiseworthy, sometimes blameable—that occurs through friendship. The assaults of robbers and of armies against armies are hunts.[53]

In a way, the polymorphous vision of hunting that emerges from this description is like a general theory of cynegetics. The pursuit of game parallels the capture of men both in the name of war and of eroticism: hunting is the metaphorical means for thinking out relationships among men. Diverse, then—because it symbolizes this exorbitant aggressiveness inherent in man's nature—hunting must be carefully classified and analyzed. In distinguishing between good and bad hunting, Plato defines the social values we must seek and those we should avoid. Everything that corresponds in hunting to the use of traps, ambushes, surprise attacks, and deceit must be rejected. Only hunting as pursuit, the athletic kind of hunting, is acceptable: "What alone remains and is best for everyone is the hunting of four-footed prey that employs horses, dogs, and the bodies of the hunters themselves. In this type the hunters use running, blows, and missiles thrown by their own hands to prevail over all their prey, and this is the type that should be practiced by whoever cultivates the courage that is divine."[54]

The kind of hunt thus prized by Plato was the kind that allowed the hunter to confront the animal directly, either by pursuit on foot, which exhausted it; by attacking with a weapon such as a spear or a stick; or by hurling some projectile, such as a javelin or a light lance. Respectful of the city's laws and possessions,[55] the hunter was esteemed more for his courage than for his knowledge; his personal qualities had to prove superior to his technical abilities. Similarly, in gymnastics, stand-up wrestling was supposed to prevail over the cunning tricks of fistfighting.[56] To anyone wanting to discipline his body through the most suitable exercises, Plato's "good" kind of hunting offered a model of collective integration, a social philosophy at the service of the city. Rejecting both moral permissiveness and animosity, the paideia of the *Laws* took after the *krypteia* in the emphasis placed on physical training, on life among men, in contact with nature. But as civic, egalitarian service, it did not make main virtues of pretense and cunning, which were so dear to the Spartans; the training of the *neoi* left as much room for war as for music.[57]

A collective educational service organized by the city under the control of magistrates and salaried teachers,[58] the paideia of the *Laws* had only distant connections with initiations of the Archaic period. Through its resolutely conservative nature, however, it reveals an educational philosophy that made youthful activities of central importance to the city.

For Plato, hunting was not a simple matter of pursuing game in open country without the aid of traps. The model he offered young men, in its great variety of hunting techniques, was intended to exalt their courage and their skill: the catalogue of prohibitions gives an exact measure of the symbolic nature of the proposed training. Hunting was a matter of style, and consequently of (good) education.

The Greeks of the classical and Archaic ages clearly invented practices designed to give young men a very precise idea of their role as future citizens. Even today, we know far too little to be able to reconstruct the precise framework of youthful institutions, which varied with each city. We can, however, be certain—without succumbing to the mirage of an

Archaic polis seen through the models of African or Melanesian initiations—that the social boundary separating boys from adulthood was ritualized and aestheticized. The "young men" *(neoi)* stood out as a particular
group, subject to precise conduct. Physical exercise, hunting, and military
training all played a decisive role in this formative period, indistinguish-
able, in Athens, from the ephebate. But the young men's role in city life
was not limited to this period of their lives. Once the ephebate had ended,
a young man enjoyed full civic status; he could start a family and take part
in the city's political life. But he was still a *neos* who attracted the attention
of his fellow citizens because he embodied the transitory state of maturity
and physical beauty that games in the stadium, competitions, even military
prowess, all revealed.

IMAGES OF YOUTH AND
PAINTINGS OF YOUTH

Youth is a state of grace, and figurative arts are a means of emphasizing
this particular stage in a citizen's life. Because of their anthropomorphic
character, sculpture and pictorial art provide unequaled source material for
studying youthful imagery. After all, Greek painting was *zoographic,* an art
of representing living beings—an art whose goal, from the *korai* and *kouroi*
of the Archaic period, had been to capture the unconquerable grace of the
handsome bodies of young men and women. As Xenophon wrote of a
visit he paid the painter Parrhasios: "Is not painting the representation of
visible objects? At least you represent substances, imitating them by means
of colour, whether they be concave or convex, dark or light, hard or soft,
rough or smooth, fresh or old . . . And when you would represent beautiful
figures, do you, since it is not easy to find one person with every part
perfect, select, out of many, the most beautiful parts of each?"[59]

Pictorial activity, expressed abstractly in the polarities that organized
painting's different values, could not be dissociated from the expression of
the *sômata,* from the painting of bodies. To seek out figurative beauty was
not simply a mimetic operation; it meant idealizing the subject. Since one
single man could not in himself constitute a model of beauty, painters
"selected out of many the most beautiful parts of each," thus representing

"figures beautiful in every part."[60] The painter's art consisted in using observation to transcend the individual peculiarities of human beings; by using the best in each subject, he attained an aesthetic quality that transcended detail by integrating it into the unity of a work. For, transcending aesthetic experience, his ultimate target was the identity of the soul.[61] As Socrates concluded, painting was basically concerned with depicting feelings manifest "both in the looks and gestures of men, whether they stand or move."[62]

Both Plato and Xenophon conceived pictorial art as, above all, a means of studying and reproducing human bodies. The anthropomorphism of painting was analogous to the anthropomorphism of worship. True painting was hardly possible unless it involved representation of the human body, just as worship could hardly be imagined without *agalma* (representation of the divine).

THE MYTHICAL FOUNDERS OF THE EDUCATION OF YOUNG PEOPLE

Almost half a century ago, L. Gernet drew attention to a custom of Archaic Greece according to which the education of young men of good families was entrusted to some illustrious person (for example, Autolycos, the maternal uncle of Ulysses). Gernet compared this widespread practice to the custom of fosterage observed by ethnologists in a number of Archaic societies. The most famous such example was the education of Achilles. Abandoned by his mother (the goddess Thetis), the young Achilles remained in the charge of Peleus, his father. Peleus entrusted the child's education to the centaur Chiron. For the Greeks, centaurs were ambiguous creatures, halfway between men and beasts. Mythology attributes behavior to them that is alternately praiseworthy and terrifying. Chiron and Pholos belonged in the category of good centaurs (there were also bad ones, like those that attacked the Lapithes at the wedding of Pirithoos and Hippodamia); masters of hunting and medicinal herbs, they trained young men in the practice of these arts. In both Archaic and classical vase painting, the theme of young Achilles being handed over to the centaur is a frequent motif, existing in two versions. In the first, Achilles is a very small child being carried in the arms of his father or of Hermes, the messenger god; in the second, he is a *pais,* a young boy setting off with his father to see the schoolmaster.

On one black-figure amphora in Boulogne-sur-Mer (fig. 1) Peleus, draped in a *himation* (long cloak) bears on his right arm an extremely small figure who faces him, hands held apart as if in conversation; in his left hand Peleus is clasping the hand of the centaur. Chiron is also dressed in a long cloak that covers his human torso, and on his shoulder he carries the branch of a tree, from which game is suspended. This image, the work of a painter of the late sixth century B.C., shows the principal components of the myth: the centaur is depicted as an intermediary figure between nature and culture—not only in his physical appearance, half man, half beast, but also in his mastery of a technique necessary to human beings, the hunt, which he practices with different weapons and methods. A hunter would normally suspend animals from his *lagôbolon* (a stick for killing hares), whereas the centaur carries a natural element, the branch of a tree—which is not, however, a weapon, since the centaur catches animals by running (a skill only heroes could acquire). Opposite him Peleus assents with outstretched hand—the *dexiôsis*—to the pact they are concluding. Achilles is seen as a child still almost in the cradle, but only his size reveals his age. Archaic art typically represented children, even very young infants, as sized-down adults. Achilles is draped in a cloak, and no particular sign identifies his features. This iconographic means of representing childhood is even more evident in a slightly older amphora (fig. 2) preserved in the Louvre. Here Achilles is naked, legs slightly bent, carried at arms' length by his father: his body, long and muscular, is scarcely that of a suckling child, but in its pictorial naïveté, it does tell us that the child is a small adult:

> Achilles, as a fair-haired child, staying at Philyra's
> home, amused himself with greatness, often wielding
> windswift javelins with shortened shafts,
> or killing savage lions he'd overpowered,
> or spearing boars and bringing back their pulsing
> carcasses to Cronus' Centaur son—

at first, when he was six; then ever afterward,
Artemis and brave Athena were impressed
as he bagged stags with neither nets nor hunting dogs
(he ran them down). Now I shall tell what has been told
before: the learned Chiron nurtured Jason
in a stony cave and then he taught Asclepius
the science of the use of soothing drugs;
he also gave a bride away—brightbreasted
Thetis, Nereus' daughter—and raised her mighty
son, tutoring his talents to complete precision.[63]

The centaur offered the young men entrusted to his care something
that no human master could provide: he transformed childhood and adolescence into a sylvan enchantment that wholly obliterated the distance
between nature and culture. Rather than teaching his pupils the complex
rules of hunting in the forest, he made them into runners, like Achilles,
who hunted on foot in the woods, rejecting traps and weapons. He con-
founded categories, and his knowledge was not transmitted by instruction;
he imparted his gifts to the children entrusted to him and transformed them
through a kind of structural modification of their personality. The story
of the centaur is a mythological version of initiation. And the painters'
work respects this magical connivance of the occult by representing not
the games played by infants and boys in the realm of the centaur, but the
precise moment when they were consigned to the enchanter: fragile creatures held in their father's arms, and who seem to be resisting this separation. Educating boys was men's business. Even if Achilles' mother Thetis
is present in some scenes (contrary to literary tradition), she is never the
one who hands her child to the magician. On a *stamnos* in the Louvre
(fig. 3) Peleus, dressed as a traveler, javelins in hand, accompanies a naked
child who is facing the centaur; the latter still has the branch with hunting
trophies on his shoulder and is extending his hand toward the child, as if
the *dexiôsis* should now be concluded between the centaur and his pupil
rather than with the father, who stands at a slight distance. In portraying
a child of about ten who is no longer a nursling, the painters add a
psychological dimension to the scene. On his own initiative the naked child

walks toward his master, claiming the fosterage that is part of his heroic status.

At the beginning of the *Cynegetics,* Xenophon draws up an impressive list of heroes who were Chiron's pupils: Castor and Pollux, Cephalos and Melanion, Theseus, Peleus, and many others. Missing from this list, however, is the most fabulous of heroes, that indefatigable hunter who, relying only on the strength of his arms and legs, managed to overcome that most ferocious animal, the lion. Herakles needed no apprenticeship, no cynegetic training; he was, simply by virtue of his magnificent body, the absolute hero, the solitary hunstman who, living on the fringe of humanity, subjugated monsters that threatened on all sides. Herakles thus appears as the least youthful of heroes; for how could one imagine an initiation for the man who conquered the Hydra of Lernos, or the lion of Nemeus? In Herakles, heroic exploit and initiation were one and the same. Even so, there is an amphora in Munich (fig. 4) on which the centaur, accompanied by a dog, is holding a hand out to Hermes, who is running in the opposite direction, his face turned back toward his interlocutor. Under one arm he holds a child, carefully swathed in his cloak; an inscription round the infant's head informs us this is Herakles. It is an enigmatic image, which clearly refers to the well-known theme of Achilles' being carried to the centaur's home. But in the Munich amphora there is no *dexiôsis,* and Hermes is fleeing as if Herakles risked some danger at the centaur's hands. Because he is more than just a simple hero, Herakles escapes from fosterage; in him there is too much strength, too much wildness—in short, too much magic for us to imagine him among the centaur's disciples. Herakles is by definition rebellious to any education. If he practices the disciplines of mind and body that make him a *kouros,* it's almost as if he does so through spontaneous intuition. Even when he excels in arts so essentially foreign to his nature as music, one should not expect him to be an attentive pupil—as Linos, the preeminent music teacher, learns to his cost. A cup in Munich (fig. 5) shows four young men throwing up their hands as if scandalized: armed with a stool, Herakles hurls himself at the master who is trying to escape, lyre in hand. If Herakles embodies youth, it is through his rebelliousness, his rejection of order, his refusal to recognize the strict discipline of archaic education. The revolt of student against master is symbolized by this beardless Herakles, a young man among other young men, who contests magisterial authority as imperturbably as he fights monsters. To emphasize the educational context of the scene, a closed writing tablet is included in the visual field. What does this youthful Herakles—a fellow student of attentive young men learning to write and play the lyre—have in common with Herakles the slayer of monsters? What bond links the ephebes, seen exercising in the palaestra, and Achilles, racing through the forests after his centaur?

An answer to this question may be found on a *hydria* in Berlin (fig. 6). On the shoulder of this vase, nude young men practice taming bulls, encouraged by men dressed as hunters, draped in their *himation*, javelins in hand. In the center of the scene a female dog is leaping, a bull's hoof in her mouth. Here the heroic theme of the bull tamer is crossed with the cynegetic implication of the two bearded men armed with javelins, and with the dismemberment of the prey suggested and symbolized by the dog. On the central part of the vase, Peleus is walking toward Chiron, followed by Thetis and a four-horsed chariot. It is hard to imagine a better way of emphasizing the connection between the mythological scene of fosterage and the education of young men.

THE ART OF BEING A YOUNG MAN

On a cup in Berlin (fig. 7), three teams of oxen are followed by a sower, and all the persons depicted are nude and beardless. Deer are shown at pasture around the outer edge of the bowl, and a laborer is threatening one of them with a javelin or stick while another young man bounds toward some undefined prey, the same kind of weapon in his hand. In the central medallion, a crouching ephebe raises his *lagôbolon*. In this particularly complex scene, hunting and productive activities are combined, on a scale almost unique in vase painting, showing the prey found in forests, animals of cultivated regions, and even chthonian animals like lizards. Bull tamers and huntsmen, these young men are also cultivators who squat on the ground, who have a relationship with the nourishing earth. From hunting to agriculture, they affirm the dominion of the city over the territory.

The strict education prescribed in the *Laws* recommended that the *neoi* practice hunting the hare in order to acquire "experience and knowledge of the territory." Whether he tracked the hare *lagóbolon* in hand, as on a lipped cup in Tarquinia (fig. 8), or flushed out the animal on horseback, as on a cup in Cambridge (fig. 9), the hare hunter was usually a beardless youth, naked or dressed in a short chiton. When shown pursuing (as in Plato's "big game hunting") the hart (fig. 10) or the wild boar (fig. 11), the hunter's youthfulness was always what the painters tried to express. They represented young beardless men with scarcely delineated muscles confronting the animal. At the end of the sixth century B.C., black-figure amphoras and *hydriae* often had a decorative band *(predella)* beneath the principal scene, depicting young men on horseback pursuing harts and boars. On the shoulder of a *hydria* in Wellesley (fig. 12), a combat among hoplites is shown. Below this, the main scene presents women at a fountain. One of them is filling her amphora. The others are waiting, visibly engaged in animated discussion. On the *predella* four horsemen are encircling a doe. In these slices of life, the universe of warriors (almost certainly heroes from the Trojan war) is juxtaposed with the feminine world, and with the exploits of horsemen brandishing boar spears. Before acquiring the glory of heroes, young men display the grace of youth. The naked young huntsman exhibits his prey—a hare—between two men in cloaks carrying lances, while an older hunter raises his hand in salute (fig. 13). On an amphora in Munich (fig. 14), the same painter has depicted young hunters bringing their prey to Dionysus: opposite the god, who holds a cantharus in his hand, a nude young man is pouring wine. Behind them, on either side, two other ephebes are carrying game—a fox and a hare— suspended from a stick. A fifth figure bears a goatskin full of wine. The ephebes are not the traditional protagonists in scenes of *symposion*, the collective, ritualized libations practiced by adults. All the young men shown facing the god are beardless, and they do not drink the wine but are pouring a libation; this was probably a sign of the reserve and knowledge young men had to acquire before using this dangerous substance. On the back of the amphora four horsemen, accompanied by a dog, are setting off at a gallop.

Reconnoitering the territory and engaging in physical exercise: according to Plato, that is how young men were supposed to spend their time. But youth was also a time of apprenticeship, emulation, and competition. In this context the relationship between *erastês* (the mature man) and *eromenos* constituted a fundamental dimension of the city's ethics. The capture of animals, and especially of young animals that they could try to tame, was a recurrent theme in this youthful and erotic iconography. The game was not intended to be eaten—at least not *only* to be eaten; what mattered was to display the animals that had been hunted, caught, or domesticated. On an amphora in Providence (fig. 15), two couples of *erastês* and *eromenoi* stand facing each other. On side A (left), a naked, bearded man is stretching his arms toward the head and genitals of a young man who is holding a hen and a cockerel. Between them is a young hart. On side B, the young man is holding two cockerels and the bearded man is offering him a dog on a lead. Cockerels and hens are animals with strong sexual connotations, and cockfights were often featured in vase painting. The presence of the dog and hart further clarifies the meaning of these scenes: hunting was one of the ways in which an accomplished young man could assert himself. But it required training and exercises that were a customary part of the relationship of a couple. The imagery of the vase painting thus provides direct testimony confirming the tradition of cynegetic initiations described, at least in regard to Crete, by Ephorus. If any doubts remain as to the nature of the bonds linking *erastês* and *eromenos,* we need only look at an amphora in London (fig. 16). On each side we find couples of *erastai* and *eromenoi* engaged in diverse sexual activities. The artist has provided multiple details, positions, and attitudes. Moreover, the age and status of each partner are clearly indicated. The *eromenoi* are beardless and their sexual organs are systematically reduced in size. In contrast, the *erastai* are bearded and exhibit imposing virile attributes. K. J. Dover has humorously drawn attention to these anatomical particularities, characteristic of black-figure paintings. Various scenes of touching, embracing, and actual coitus take place in an empty space uncluttered by accesories—but for the game on side B (right), a fox and a hare, suspended like trophies. On the other hand the partners, even when engaged in the most ardent activities, are festooned with gifts: wreaths, cockerels, and, as in the case of the first couple on side B, young live animals (another hart). Life is opposed to death, and the taming of wild animals, even when of short duration, is an element of distinction and ostentation. In the pederastic relationship, wasn't the ephebe, too, a quarry that the *erastês* tried to captivate, tame, and even capture?

A Boeotian *exaleiptron* (a kind of box mounted on feet) conserved in Berlin (fig. 17) displays on its various sides and faces a whole range of images that seem almost to form a model of male conduct in the archaic city. On the lid, in the center, is a hunting scene. A hunter is unleashing two large dogs, who rush toward a hare darting toward a net. The scene is surrounded by a frieze of animals: sirens, lions, and panthers. On the outside of the belly of the vase, three series of recorded events unfold, one after another. On one side (image C) is a sacrificial procession: a pig, followed by four men, moves toward the altar; underneath, a lion is devouring a bull. On another side (image D), five nude, bearded dancers move in line, led by an *aulêtês* (flute player); below them, two sirens face each other. On the third side (E), two couples of banqueters are lying on beds. At the two extreme ends of the scene, servants are pouring wine, one into a *skyphos,* the other into a phial; an *aulêtês* is playing the flute. In the image underneath, two sphinxes sit face to face. In addition to this complex program, the three feet of the vase are also decorated, each being adorned with a double motif. On the first, a decapitated Medusa appears with a Gorgon, above two wrestlers; on the second, another Gorgon is running, and two boxers stand facing each other; on the third, Perseus is fleeing, with a bag containing the Gorgon's head at his side, and another man is throwing the discus, watched by his trainer, who has a stick in his hand. The vase's iconography can be summarized as follows:

cover	hare hunt					
	procession of animals					
belly	Medusa and Gorgon	sacrificial procession	Gorgon	*komastài*	Perseus	banquet
	wrestlers	lion and bull	boxers	sirens	discus thrower	sphinxes
	foot		foot		foot	

An object with multiple faces, the *exaleiptron* links diverse themes that cannot be considered simultaneously. On the lid, hunting and mythical animals are shown. There is an obvious contrast between the quarry (the hare) and the mastiffs—themselves larger than the lions and panthers—and the hunter, who is minute. What counts is not the man but the animal hunt, and the bodies of the dogs and hare are treated far more accurately than the body of the hunter. In fact the entire decoration of the vase plays on the opposition between the theme portrayed and the fragmentation of the space. The hunt is connected to a unitary action represented in a single scene. The animal frieze consists of a series of separate figures: the beasts are presented in sequence, with no connection from one to another. The same is true of the belly of the vase: only one of the three sides can be contemplated at any one time, in a sequence linking the three images of the belly to the four images on the two feet flanking it. This complex composition contains contrasts. If most of the scenes are independent of each other (sacrifice, *komastai,* banquets, animals facing each other, wrestlers, boxers, discus throwers), the images of Perseus and the Gorgon must, on the contrary, complement each other to be intelligible; the viewer must pass from one face to another, either moving around the vase or turning the band of images to understand its development. To grasp the adventure of Perseus, whose entire story is based on the necessity of seeing without being seen (since whoever meets the Gorgon's gaze is immediately struck by lightning), the *exaleiptron*'s potential owner must turn it in his hands to connect the episodes. In so doing, he discovers that the sacrifice, the dance

1. Peleus entrusting
Achilles to the care of
Chiron, the centaur.
Black-figure amphora,
Boulogne-sur-Mer, 572,
Beck 11, circa 520 B.C.

2. Peleus entrusting Achilles to the centaur. There is nothing mythological
about this "educator of princes," but the hare dangling from a tree on the
left reminds us of his skill as a hunter. Black-figure amphora, Paris, Louvre
Museum, F21, *ARV2* 207, 140, circa 490 B.C. Photo: RMN.

3. The babe in arms is now a boy. Red-figure *stamnos*, Paris, Louvre G 186, *ARV2*, Beck 17, circa 500–475 B.C. Photo: RMN.

4A–B. The centaur holds out his hand to Hermes, who runs off carrying the newborn Herakles. Black-figure amphora, Munich, Staatl. Antikensammlungen 1615 A, *ABV* 486, 6, *CVA* Munich 9, All. 48, pl. 31, circa 500 B.C.

5. Herakles rebels against his music-master. Red-figure cup, Munich, Staatl. Antiken-sammlungen 2646, Beck 26, circa 480 B.C.

6. Taming bulls; hunting animals; cutting up meat. Black-figure *hydria*, Berlin, Staatl. Mussen zu Berlin, Preussischer Kulturbesitz F1900, *ABV* 385, 27, Beck 15, circa 510 B.C.

7. Agricultural scenes are depicted on the middle band, while aspects of the hunt are shown in the center and around the edge. Black-figure cup, Berlin, Antikenmuseum F1806, *Antike Kunst* suppl. 7, 1970, pl. 19, 2, circa 530 B.C. Photo: Jutta Tietz-Glagow.

8A–B. Hunting the hare on foot. Black-figure cup, Tarquinia 2, II, 26, pl. 40, 6, circa 540 B.C. Photo: Soprintendenza Archeologico Etruria Meridionale.

9. Flushing out the prey.
Black-figure cup,
Cambridge, circa 560 B.C.
Photo: Fitzwilliam
Museum, Cambridge
University, GR 46–1864,
CVA Cambridge 1, G. B. 6,
pl. 20, 1 and 6.

10A–B. Hunting a stag on horseback. Black-figure cup, Basle, Beazley *Para*. 102,
44; circa 540–530 B.C. Photo: D. Widmer.

11. Confronting a wild boar.
Black-figure cup, Heidelberg,
Archäologisches Institut, S13,
CVA Heidelberg 4, All. 31, pl. 156,
2, circa 550–525 B.C.

12. Top band, hoplites fighting; middle band, women at the foun-
tain; bottom band, hunting. Black-figure *hydria*, Wellesley College
Art Museum, 1961, 5. D. M. Buitron, *Attic Vase Painting in New
England Collections*, Cambridge, Mass., 1972, 16, p. 41, 3, circa 430
B.C. Photo: David Stansbury.

13. Returning from the hunt. The young man shows his trophy to a man of mature age and two older men. Black-figure amphora, Paris, Louvre F26, *ABV* 150, 5. D. von Bothmer, *The Amasis Painter and His World*, London, 1985, pp. 94–96, 11, circa 550 B.C. Photo: RMN.

14. Dionysus with hunters. Black-figure amphora, Munich, Staatl. Antikensammlungen 8763, Beazley *Para.* 65, D. von Bothmer, *The Amasis Painter and His World*, London, 1985, p. 79, 4; circa 550 B.C.

15A–B. The hunt, and lovers exchanging gifts: fowl, a stag, and a hunting dog. Black-figure amphora, Providence, Museum of Art, Rhode Island School of Design 13, 1479, *ABV* 314, 6, *CVA* Providence 1, USA 2, pl. 9, circa 550 B.C.

16A–B. Scenes of overt homosexuality, with trophies of the hunt featuring significantly. Black-figure amphora, London, British Museum W39, *ABV* 297, 16, Koch-Harnack
1983, fig. 53; 550–540 B.C.

W. 39.

17. A: On the lid, hunting the hare with a net, and a frieze of animals. B: Under the belly, a lion devouring a bull; a pair of sirens; a pair of sphinxes facing each other. C: On the belly, a sacrificial procession. On the feet, a decapitated Medusa with Gorgons *(above)*; wrestlers and boxers *(below)*. D: On the belly, a *komastes*. On the foot, Perseus fleeing *(above)*; a discus thrower *(below)*. E: On the belly, a banquet scene. Three-footed Boeotian *exaleiptron* with black figures. Berlin, Antikenmuseum F1727, *ABV* 29, 1, circa 570–560 B.C. Photos: Jutta Tietz-Glagow (A–C, E) and Isolde Luckert (D).

18. A sphinx is represented in the middle; then, in successive circles, cockerels and hens, athletic exercises, animals facing each other (panther-ram, lion-hart, panther-goat), and sirens. Black-figure cup. Berlin, Antikenmuseum der Staatl. Museen, 1805, *ABV* 223, 65, circa 530 B.C. Photo: BPK.

19. Runners in a pack. Black-figure cup, Paris, Louvre F64, *ABV* 53, Beck 169, circa 560 B.C. Photo: RMN.

20 A–B. Hunting or footrace?
Black-figure *skyphos*,
Glasgow Museums, Burrell
Collection, 19. 108, circa
525–500 B.C.

21. A: Athletic exercises. B: Achilles overpowering Troilus. C: Riders and chariot racing. Black-figure cup, Paris, Louvre 1684, *ABV* 64, 27, Beck 193, circa 560–550 B.C. Photo: RMN.

22. Athletes and a referee. Black-figure cup, Florence, Soprintendenza Archeologica per la Toscana 3893, *ABV* 64, 26n, Poliakoff 6, p. 24, circa 560–550 B.C.

23. A: Riders in the stadium; the column *(terma)* on the left marks the finishing line. B: Athena in majesty. Inscription reads: "The Prize of Athens." Black-figure amphora, New York, Metropolitan Museum of Art, Rodgers Fund 07.286.80, *ABV* 369, 114, Beck 216, circa 510–500 B.C.

24. A: Training in javelin and discus throwing. B: Preparation for a riding exercise. Red-figure cup, Berlin, Antikenmuseum, F 262, *ARV* 72n-15, *CVA* All. 21, Berlin 2, pl. 55, circa 520 B.C. Photo: Jutta Tietz-Glagow.

25A–B. Javelin and discus
throwers. Red-figure
amphora, Munich, Staatl.
Antikensammlungen 2344,
ARV2 182, 6, Jüthner 1968,
LVII, circa 480 B.C.

26A–C. Personal hygiene. Hegesias is pouring oil from an *aryballum* into the palm of his hand; Lykos is carefully folding his clothes. Against the black background we see an inscription: *"Leagros kalos"* (handsome Leagros). Red-figure krater in the form of a chalice. Berlin, Antikenmuseum der Staatl. museen, F 2180, *ARV2* 13, 1, Beck 145, circa 510 B.C. Photo: BPK.

27A–C. Inside, in the middle, a discus thrower and an *akontistes*. Outside, on the surrounding band, typical palaestra exercises. Red-figure cup, Munich, Staatl. Antikensammlungen 2637, *ARV2* 322, 28, circa 500–480 B.C.

28. A: A referee and two young men conversing at the palaestra. B: A referee and a discus thrower stand facing each other, while another athlete prepares the track with a pickax. Red-figure cup, Courtesy of Museum of Fine Arts, Boston, 28448, *ARV2* 882, Beck 143 and 150, circa 475–450 B.C.

29A–B. The house of learning, music, and poetry. On the unfolded scroll we see the words "Muse, on the banks of the Scamander / find me the subject of my song." Red-figure cup, Berlin, Antikenmuseum, F2285, *ARV2* 431, 48, Beck 53, 54, circa 480 B.C. Photos: Johannes Laurentius and BPK.

30. A: On the path to knowledge: a closed writing tablet. B: A procession of dutiful students? Red-figure cup, New York, Metropolitan Museum of Art, Rodgers Fund 17.230.10, *ARV2* 784, 25, Beck, 58, 59, 69, circa 475–450 B.C.

31. Hunting and the stadium. Red-figure cup, Kassel, Staatl. Kunstsammlungen Kassel AHG 58, *ARV2* 328, 122, circa 510–500 B.C.

32. Music and athleticism: symbols of the arts of mind and body. Red-figure cup, Malibu, Collection of the J. Paul Getty Museum, Beazley *Para*. 375, 51b, circa 480 B.C.

33A–B. Dutiful students and handsome young men reading about the Centaur's adventures (the chest of papyrus rolls contains the *Chironeia*, or teachings of Chiron). Red-figure *kyathos*, Berlin, Staatl. Museen zu Berlin, Preussischer Kulturbesitz F2322, *ARV2* 329, 134, Beck 75, circa 510–500 B.C.

34. A young girl reading to her companions. Red-figure *hydria*, London, British Museum E190, *ARV2* 611, 36, Beck 351, circa 475–450 B.C.

35. Apollo listening to Marsyas, while a Muse hands a writing tablet to a female companion. Red-figure krater, Heidelberg, Archologisches Museum H1, *ARV2* 1189, Beck 364, circa 420 B.C.

36. A young girl dancing to music of a flute. Red-figure *lekythos*, Syracuse, Museum of Archeology 20966, Beck 364, circa 425–400 B.C.

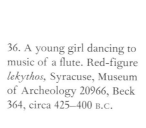

37. Chorus of young girls practicing a dance under the direction of a master. Red-figure astragal, British Museum E804, *ARV2* 765, 20, circa 450 B.C.

38A–B. The huntress Atalanta, armed with the sword and shield of a hoplite, confronts the Calydon monster. *Hydria* from Caere, Copenhagen, Nationalmuseet 13567, J. M. Hemelrijk, *Caeretan Hydriae*, Mayenz, 1984, pl. 9, 530–520 B.C.

39. Atalanta wrestling
with Peleus. Red-figure
amphora, Munich,
Staatl. Antikensamm-
lungen 1541, Beck 413,
circa 500 B.C.

40. This young girl in a "bikini," showing off on the track, can only be Atalanta, the preeminent female athlete. Red-figure cup, Paris, Louvre CA 2259, *ARV2* 797, 137, Beck 409, circa 450–440 B.C. Photo: RMN.

of *komastai,* and the banquet are related not only to the imaginary world of fabulous animals but also to physical exercises, to the training that men of the city undergo on every occasion that allows them to assert the singularity and power of the male world. Hunting, wrestling, boxing, discus throwing—these themes are not linked by chance; they illustrate masculine activities on countless vases, mixing different age groups and making young men spectators and protagonists in the grand game of society.

A cup in Berlin (fig. 18) demonstrates to what good account the artists managed to turn representations of athleticism in the late Archaic period. This cup is very close in composition to another by the same painter (fig. 7), illustrating young men's agricultural activities. In the second of these cups, a sphinx takes the place of the hunter armed with a *lagôbolon.* Around it, three concentric friezes unfurl: the first represents a succession of cockerels and hens; the second, athletic competitions; and the third, a series of animals. The animals are symetrically arranged: there are three pairs of animals facing each other—panther-ram, lion-hart, panther-goat— alternating with two other scenes, one depicting two panthers flanking a siren, and the other, two harts and a siren. Here again, the imagery is explicit based on a series of simple oppositions: wild animal/tame animal, wild animal/hunted animal, wild animal/mythical animal. Cocks and hens, as we saw, were among the amorous gifts exchanged by young men. As in the Berlin *exaleiptron,* therefore, the painter has surrounded the main composition with a series of emblematic relationships linking athletic competition with the animal world. Cockerels and hens have erotic implications, while the animals facing each other emphasize the agonal nature of the contest; the mythical animals are simultaneously spectators in the conflicts that occur in both animal and human worlds, and victors in the battle between strong and weak. In the middle circle, seven different types of athletic activity are shown: boxing and long-distance running, then the five canonical exercises of the pentathlon—sprinting, javelin, discus, long jump, and wrestling. Here again, but with greater detail than on the Berlin *exaleiptron,* the athletes provide perfect symbols of the highly stylized exercises of young men: moreover, they are all beardless. On the belly of the vase we see a young horseman carrying a javelin, accompanied by an athlete and another horseman.

The artists' goal is to emphasize the young men's athletic qualities, and the power of their running. On a cup now in the Louvre (fig. 19), ten ephebes are shown running, legs wide apart, arms moving in rhythm with their feet, while on the cup's other side horsemen of the same age ride in procession. Young men could practice racing in the stadium, as well as running after hares and foxes, using only their bare hands to hunt, without the help of weapons. Unlike the Berlin vase of fig. 17, a *skyphos* in Glasgow (fig. 20) boasts a hunter who is naked, running with all his might in pursuit of animals—a fox and a hare, the young man's customary quarry. In images of this kind, the themes of athleticism and hunting are united, as if the combination of these two activities emphasized how familiar ephebes were with both.

On another cup in the Louvre (fig. 21), three pairs of athletes face each other, surrounded by umpires holding sticks. In the center two men are wrestling; on either side of them, boxers confront each other; and on the other side of the cup, two horsemen ride before a chariot drawn at a lively pace. The bottom of the cup represents a hoplite attacking a young rider who is leading a second horse at a gallop. This is Achilles ambushing Troilus: a heroic theme in which the hoplite (Achilles) plays the role of *erastês* and Troilus, hair floating in the wind, that of the *eromenos*. Instead of confronting his adversary in single combat, the hoplite prepares an ambush: in this adventure the experienced warrior resorts to cunning against one who is clearly little more than a boy. But let us turn back to wrestling. Here victory depends on the hold, for the wrestler must throw his opponent to the ground. On a cup from the same period, now in Florence (fig. 22), the umpire is bending down to verify that at the crucial moment the athlete's shoulders touch the ground. Young men took part in running, boxing, and wrestling as often as they did hunting. The artists were attentive to realism in these scenes, observing details of personal grooming and portraying the young men's skill. Signs of the city are always present in this exaltation of the body, as certain types of vases make clear. On an amphora now in New York (fig. 23), the fact that the horse-race takes place in the stadium is symbolized by a post *(terma)* marking the finishing line. On the other side of this same vase, a victorious Athena appears, wearing helmet and buckler and bearing a lance, between two columns surmounted by cockerels. An inscription—"The Prize of Athens"—runs beside the first column. These special Panathenaic amphoras were vases ordered specially as prizes for the champions in the Panathenean games. They all had the same inscription and image of the goddess Athena on one side, and on the other some scene associated with the games: wrestling, boxing, and the like. In fact, production of this type of vase corresponded to the development of sporting events in the city. As H. J. Pleket has shown, despite the paucity of epigraphic sources for the history of sport in the sixth century B.C., we can infer from the diverse documents available that the cities' sporting institutions enjoyed undoubted momentum at the time.[64]

THE ART OF SOCIAL EXISTENCE

The painters of red-figure vases—who were often, at least initially (late sixth century B.C.), also black-figure painters—were faithful to the themes chosen by the pioneering artists of the first half of the sixth century. They did, however, introduce subtle differences that gradually modified the atmosphere and decor of youthful imagery. On a cup in Berlin dating from the second half of the sixth century B.C. (fig. 24a), young men are seen exercising to musical rhythms provided by two flautists. Opposite the first musician, a young javelin thrower is starting his run, and opposite the other, a discus thrower is raising his discus while a boxer appears to be bandaging his hands. The painter has paid more attention to the preparation for these diverse actitivities than to the actual exercises. On the other face of this vase, a young man is holding two horses by their halters, as if trying to bring the second horse, who is beginning to rear, closer to the first. Instead of the classical motif of the dashing rider, what we see here are preparations for some exercise in equitation or harnessing. Several complex positions are depicted on the neck of an amphora by the Kleophrades painter, a vase conserved in Munich (fig. 25). On side A, three young men are shown: two of them are javelin throwers *(akonistai)* and the third is a discus thrower, but instead of turning his discus sideways he is holding it face on, as if presenting it to the spectator. We also see pickaxes, used for turning the earth inside the stadium, and a sponge and an *aryballum* hang in the background. On the other side, we again find three athletes. The first is holding two pairs of javelins in one hand; the second is preparing to throw; the third is waiting, discus in hand. A discus and pickaxe are lying on the ground.

This new observational style is expressed on a krater in Berlin (fig. 26) by the painter Euphronios, with a skill that has never been equaled. On side A, six people are represented. To the left an athlete, hailed by the inscition *"Leagros kalos"* (handsome Leagros), is in the process of infibulating himself, a frequent practice among athletes and one often depicted by red-figure painters. Facing him is a small child, designated by the inscription "young boy." In the middle we find two young men; the first, called Antiphon, is preparing to throw his discus; the second, Hipparchos, stands facing him, holding the umpire's stick in one hand while pointing to Antiphon's genitals with the other. On the right an athlete by the name of Polyllos is taking off his cloak and handing it to a child who is holding an *aryballum*, one arm raised in greeting. Here the spectacle is not so much one of physical effort, of the perfect athletic gesture, as of the daily life of young men caught in the most ordinary activities. Precisely for that reason, it illustrates a certain style of life. Painting has now been transformed; it's almost as if we are bursting in on the characters and gaining intimate glimpses of their lives. No longer do we see heroes with great names; we see groups of young men who become notable because they are forming a society, an age cohort that has caught the attention of the painter and his public. On the reverse side of the vase, three young men and two boys appear. To the left, Hippomedon is shown in three-quarter view. A young boy—Tranion—is examining his left foot in order to remove a thorn or splinter. Who are these boys, servants, and attentive companions? Their size, which the painters have deliberately reduced, almost certainly indicates that they are slaves, necessary helpers to their masters. The central scene further emphasizes the painter's interest in a

specific moment, in representing time and place. The first athlete
(Hegesias) is catching oil from an *aryballum* in his palm, and his clothes
are placed on a stool. Opposite him Lykos seems to be carefully folding
his cloak before putting it down. A child seems about to help him. On the
krater by Euphronios and the amphora by the Kleophrades painter, we see
an iconography emerging that showed greater sensitivity to detail and the
bonds between young people, and correspondingly less interest in depicting athletic exploits. No doubt these painters, who were keenly aware of
their own talent, used an inherited Archaic theme to show how their own
aesthetic work involved a search for content, an effort to describe the
society of young men while seeking to attain a kind of psychological truth.
Between the spectator—the buyer of the vase—and the artist they were
trying to establish a kind of understanding, based on a common sensibility
and experience. Naturally, the painters had not given up portraying scenes
from the palaestra, but the representation was now more accurate, more
composed than the images on black-figure vases. In the central medallion
of a cup from Munich (fig. 27), a man throwing a discus and another
hurling a javelin are shown, both caught in the tension of the act. Above
them we see weights and an acclamatory inscription. On the vase's outer
edge, two groups of athletes, separated by columns, are engaged in classical exercises: discus throwing, javelin throwing, and wrestling, in the case
of the first group. Bags containing discuses, weights for jumping, a strigil,
and a sponge hang on the walls. The second group contains four figures:
the first is holding a javelin and preparing to apply some corrective device
before throwing it; the second is training with dumbbells; the third, a
bearded man, weight in hand, turns toward the fourth figure, a javelin
thrower. In the background, strigils, sponges, and discuses are seen hang-
ing. On a cup now in Boston (fig. 28) the artist has successfully blended
the two types of representation—athletic exercise, and social behavior at
the palaestra. In the center (not shown), two young men are conversing,
one draped in his *himation,* head covered; the other stands with his torso
uncovered, hands spread demonstratively in a conversational gesture. On
both faces of the cup, a column indicates that the scene is taking place at
the palaestra. On side A, an umpire is pointing his stick at a young man

who is bending down and preparing to spring forward, while another young man faces him, dumbbell in hand; a bag with a discus is shown in the background. On the cup's other side, the umpire is helping with preparations for the exercises. An athlete hands him the discus bag, while carrying javelins in his other hand; behind him, a second figure is holding a pickaxe. Athletics, even more than hunting, were a sign of social distinction, of an age of radiance and physical perfection. By engaging in athletic exercises, a young man was able both to assert himself and to attract attention. This attention was expressed through conviviality, games, and social contacts in and around the palaestra.

ARTS OF BODY AND MIND

As we have seen, paideia involved the education of both mind and body. While physical exercises, hunting, and eroticism were familiar themes for Archaic black-figure painters, scenes depicting young men's intellectual activity were extremely rare at this time. They seem almost exclusively connected to episodes concerning Achilles' fosterage, and to the adventures of Herakles. This was not at all the case with red-figure painters, especially those of the first half of the fifth century B.C. Contemporaneous with scenes of athletic conviviality, scenes representing moments in intellectual education—often depicted by the same painters—frequently appeared: writing, music, games. A cup by the painter Douris, now in Berlin (fig. 29), takes us into a kind of pedagogical universe. The space is furnished, and some of the figures are shown seated on stools or preciously wrought chairs. The walls are decorated with diverse suspended objects: cups, lyres, flute cases, writing tablets, squares (?). To the left we see a music lesson in which the master (bearded, larger figure) and student (smaller, beardless) are seated opposite each other, each playing the lyre. In the center the master seems to be giving his pupil an epic poem to study: he is unfurling a scroll, turned toward the spectator and inscribed with these lines:

> Muse, on the banks of the Scamander
> Find me the subject of my song.[65]

The verse refers to the river flowing toward Troy, often evoked by the classical epic poets. Facing the master is a beardless young man, standing as if about to read a lesson. Behind him another bearded figure, leaning on his cane (the *erastês?*) is following the scene attentively. The contents of the scene on the other side of the vase are identical. A master is playing the flute while a pupil stands opposite him; another master (beardless) sits facing a student while holding on his knees an open tablet on which he is about to write something with a stylus. Another older, bearded man, also holds a cane in his hand; though seated facing the other way, he is turning to contemplate the scene.

These scenes take us far from the fields, hills, and pathways where the ephebes were supposed to roam. We find ourselves back in the city, near gymnasiums and *agora*, where all the elements of city life are assembled. From the beginning of the sixth to the beginning of the fifth century B.C., we witness a kind of interiorization of the urban landscape on the part of the painters. The architectural context in which young people meet is, increasingly, defined by colonnades, furnishings, objects connected with athletics, writing, and music, all of which were for the most part absent from Archaic painting. The artists of the early fifth century lingered over detail, dwelling on the smallest particular that helped to make a scene realistic. Boys intent on learning to read and manipulate writing tablets and papyrus scrolls became frequent themes. On the bottom of a cup without handles, now in New York (fig. 30), a young man is walking, holding a closed writing tablet. On one of the sides, two very young boys approach a third, who is seated on a block of stone, stick in hand, as if he were the teacher. One of the new arrivals carries a scroll in one hand, and the other has a writing tablet. A similar scene is repeated on the other side of the vase. The red-figure painters gave a more intellectual and disciplined interpretation of paideia, though without losing their sense of humor or of erotic provocation. On a cup in a German collection (Schloss Fasanerie 134, *ARV2* 875, 17, *CVA* all. 16. 2. 67; 470–460 B.C.; not shown), a young man with his body carefully concealed in a cloak is trying to decipher an inscription composed of letters that have no meaning. The one part of his anatomy visible beneath the cloak is his rear end. J. Svenbro has made the brilliant suggestion that we have here a case of erotic wordplay that is also a play on images: the spectator who tries to read an incomprehensible inscription is the victim of the engraver, the stonecutter who has chiseled it in stone; he is "possessed." And this "possession" is a consequence of the young man's posture: he is an *eromenos* at the mercy of the unknown spectator observing the scene. As Svenbro has shown, the sexual parody of writing is a constant in Greek imagery. The person reading is more or less consciously the plaything of the person who writes. It is an image within an image involving the *eromenos,* who is learning to read and who is the victim of an *erastês* who is offering him up to public ridicule. After all, this is a rather more refined form of amusement than to write in giant letters that a faithless *eromenos* is a *katapygon,* an asshole. Reading and literary studies were among the aims of paideia, but at the same time they were part of the homosexual sociability of the ephebes. An epigram from the *Palatine Anthology* makes this abundantly clear:

> Fortunate little book, I am not jealous of you: in reading you a boy will touch you, holding you beneath his cheek, or will press you against his lips, or even unroll you on his tender thighs, oh most blessed of books! Often you will be put away inside his shirt; or placed on his chair, you will fearlessly dare to touch certain secret things. You will have many conversations alone with him; but I beg you, little book, speak to him sometimes about us.[66]

Young men were at the center of a web of desire, the desire of the *erastai,* which permeated images, allusions, memories, all laden with a symbolism that was more or less sexual. Painters drew inspiration from Archaic themes and created a new imagery in which intellectual activity was combined with athleticism and hunting. On a cup from Kassel (fig. 31) we see a young man whose left shoulder and lower limbs are draped in folds of cloth (his genitals are visible), holding a hare in both hands. A pickaxe is lying at his feet, and in the background we see a discus bag, an *aryballum,* and a strigil; all this indicates in the clearest manner possible that the capture and temporary taming of the live hare were a part of the ephebes' world. In linking the stadium with the hunt, this image perfectly illustrates the fifth-century painters' preference for gentility, allusion, and subtle seductiveness. The same kind of allusion is found on a cup from the Bareiss collection in Malibu (fig. 32). On one of the sides of the vase, two *eromenoi* are seated opposite some *erastes* who are courting them, leaning on canes. One of the young men has a hare on his knees. In the background we see lyres, sponges, and a bag. Between music, hunting, and athleticism, this young man is a prime example of a coveted *eromenos,* an object of desire for every citizen. His reserve is the measure of his distinction, but it in no way implies he is refusing the sexual relationship proposed to him.

Where did education begin, and where did seduction end? The line between the two seems never to have been very precise. On a *kyathos* in Berlin (fig. 33), a young man sits reading a papyrus between two *erastai* who are leaning on their sticks. There is nothing unusual about that, except that at the young man's feet a small chest containing papyrus has been placed. Inscribed on the chest is the word *Chironeia:* the teachings of Chiron. At this point, red-figure painters no longer needed to show Chiron welcoming Achilles.[67] All they had to do was draw a few anonymous ephebes busy reading, and the idea took root that they, too, were pupils of the centaur. No longer were they legendary heroes embarking on a period of fosterage; they were young men from ordinary life who, through the magic of words, suddenly became epic figures.

MASCULINE YOUTHFULNESS AND FEMININE YOUTHFULNESS

The city was to some extent a "men's club," a social system that magnified masculine values and relegated women, mothers, wives, and daughters to obscurity. Even in the Archaic period, however, a few female voices were raised, providing glimpses of a world quite different from the world of men. Studies by C. Calame[68] have amply shown how, coexisting with male culture, a distinctly female culture was making its presence known even at the dawn of the city-state. There is no lack of historical proof concerning the importance of female initiations in Greece. One of the best-known was the ritual of the *arkteia,* in Brauron. In this sanctuary of Artemis, situated a few miles from Athens, very young girls (less than ten years old), carefully selected, would meet to take part in festivals held in honor of the "bear": before marrying, they had to "act like a bear." This meant participating in rituals that involved wild animals, hunting practices, and animal disguises. Vases intended for religious use have been found in Brauron, giving us an idea of what took place during these ceremonies. These rituals have recently been described and illustrated by L. Bruit-Zaidman.[69] Therefore I shall simply recall that the division of sexual roles in the city-state did not preclude a specialized education for young girls that was a particular form of paideia.

There are numerous iconographic proofs of this. Admittedly, young girls did not take part in games held in the stadium (except in Sparta),[70] unless—as in the case of Atalanta—they were tomboys. But they did become poets, musicians, dancers, and occasionally even swimmers or gymnasts. On a *hydria* in the British Museum (fig. 34), a young woman sits reading a scroll in the center of a group of three women, one of whom is offering her a chest similar to the box that contained the teachings of Chiron in Fig. 33. The Muses were, of course, patronesses of writing. On a krater in Heidelberg (fig. 35), two couples are portrayed. To the right, Apollo is listening to Marsyas playing the lyre, and to the left, a Muse is handing a writing table to her partner. Dancing and music constitute the classical themes of female iconography in the fifth century. On a *lekythos* in Syracuse (fig. 36), a flute player is making a very young girl dance, with just a chlamys on her shoulders: the upper torso is drawn in frontal view, and her anatomy—breasts and thighs—is carefully detailed.

A favorite pastime of young men and girls was playing with *astragaloi* (knuckle bones). Not surprisingly, on an astragal now in the British Museum (fig. 37) we find a chorus of young girls, shown dancing to a rhythm beaten by the dancing master. For young men and women, dancing was a key element of savoir vivre:

> So, taking pity on this suffering that is natural to the human race, the gods have ordained the change of holidays as times of rest from labor. . .
> The other animals, the argument goes, lack perception of orders and disorders in motions (the orders which have received the names of "rhythm" and "harmony"); we, in contrast, have been given the afore-mentioned gods as fellow-dancers, and they have given us the pleasant

perception of rhythm and harmony. Using this they move us and lead us in choruses, joining us together with songs and dances; and that is why they bestowed the name "choruses"—from the "joy" which is natural to these activities . . . So the uneducated man will in our view be the one untrained in choral performances, and the educated ought to be set down as the one sufficiently trained in choral performances.[71]

Civility, however, implied that each sex kept to its place in city life. If the girls were to begin competing with the boys on their own ground, the social equilibrium might totter. The huntress Atalanta,[72] also an athlete, threatened the male world in its three spheres of excellence: hunting, wrestling, and running. On an Ionian amphora now in Copenhagen, we see her armed with a hoplite's shield, confronting the wild boar of Calydon (fig. 38). Female hunters always met with a dire fate in Greece, as in the case of Procris and also of the Bacchae, who pursued fawns and does when not tearing men apart. However, just as the Amazons contested masculine military superiority, right in the heart of Athens, so Atalanta challenged Peleus (himself a pupil of Chiron) in wrestling. On a black-figure amphora in Munich (fig. 39), Peleus and Atalanta are engaged in a hold. At their feet is an opponent who has doubtless just been vanquished; a clothed man, who must be the umpire, and a young man stand on either side of the central scene. Red-figure painters crossed another threshold of iconographic provocation in depicting an Atalanta ready for a footrace (fig. 40), amid all the insignia of male athleticism: stadium finishing post, sponge, and strigils. Here again we find a type of stylization that led painters to treat Archaic themes in the figurative vocabulary of the fifth century B.C. That a tomboy, a wild woman of ancient tradition, should assume the severe appearance of an athlete, exposing her body—equipped with underpants, brassiere, and skullcap—on the cinders of the stadium: this was clear evidence of the artists' efforts to transfer images from the past into the context of the fifth-century city. C. Bérard has recently drawn attention to a series of red-figure images of young women at their toilette in a gymnastic context, suggested by aryballoi, sponges, and strigils.[73] He points out that female gymnastics were portrayed as a passive activity. We see young women washing themselves or preparing for an exercise; never in the tension of an actual effort. This was not because they could not train, but because their exercises were not worthy of being depicted.

Between the Archaic and the classical age, the representation of young men and women in ancient Greece moved from periphery to center, from woods and hillsides to the tracks of stadiums. Was this the result of an interiorization that eliminated the countryside to show that city life was civilized—and wasn't civility paideia?

CHAPTER 3

ROMAN YOUTH

Augusto Fraschetti

ROMULUS AND REMUS:
TWO YOUNG MEN AND A MYTH

According to Roman legend, Rome was founded
by two young men who, even though they were twins, had very different
destinies. Their hapless mother, Rhea Silva, had long been imprisoned by
the treacherous Amulius, their uncle: after avenging her, and restoring the
throne of Alba to their grandfather Numitor, Romulus and Remus apparently
decided to found their own city, together with a group of young male
comrades. According to Livy, Romulus and Remus "were suddenly seized
by an urge to found a new settlement on the spot where they had been left
to drown as infants and . . . subsequently brought up": that is, on the banks
of the Tiber. But according to the Greek Dionysius of Halicarnassus, the
idea came from Numitor, an old man of great prudence: having reestablished
order in Alba after the fall of the tyrant Amulius, Numitor "presently
thought of providing an independent role for the youths by founding
another city. At the same time, the inhabitants being much increased in
number, he thought it good policy to get rid of some part of them,
particularly of those who had once been his enemies, lest he might have
cause to suspect any of his subjects." And Plutarch, for his part, added that
Romulus's and Remus's decision to found their own city had perhaps
become necessary, since "such a body of slaves and fugitives collected
about them," and "the inhabitants of Alba did not think fugitives worthy
of being received and incorporated as citizens."[1]

While it was common in the ancient world to ascribe illustrious origins
not only to the founders of a city but also to its first inhabitants, the case

of Rome stands out on more than one account. Apart from a few Alban
families of Trojan origin who had migrated to the new city with the
evident goal of ennobling their descendants, the majority of future citizens
who joined the two founding heroes were apparently "slaves and fugitives"
with whom the citizens of Alba did not wish to be confused; at best, they
were previously seditious citizens whom King Numitor thought wise to
remove from his realm "lest he might have cause to suspect" them.
Scarcely had our two heroes arrived at the site of Rome than, dismayed
at the already dubious origins of their acolytes, they hastened to create "a
sanctuary of refuge for all fugitives, which they called the temple of the
god Asylaeus, where they received and protected all, delivering none back,
neither the servant to his master, the debtor to his creditor, nor the murderer into the hands of the magistrate, saying it was a privileged place,
and they could so maintain it by an order of the holy oracle; insomuch
that the city grew presently very populous."[2] Despite this justification from
the Delphic oracle (the right to asylum was not recognized in Roman
sanctuaries of the historic period), and despite the presence of a "god
Asylaeus" (a divinity mentioned only by Plutarch), the picture could not
be more alarming: Rome's first citizens, supporters of the splendid twins,
were not only slaves, rebels, and former conspirators, they were also
fugitives, insolvent debtors, and murderers recognized as such by magistrates of other cities. With the influx of such persons, drawn by the right
to asylum, the Roman civic body was rapidly consolidated; the subsequent
abduction of the Sabine women (Romulus's idea) permitted the town to
be populated swiftly, and thus to survive.

Despite various narrators' efforts to "normalize" these legendary
events, the oddness of the social elements mentioned in this founding myth
corresponded to the status of Romulus and Remus, the aspiring founders.
To put it simply, the twins were not only young, like their companions;
they were also young men whose infancy and adolescence had been so
singular as to warrant further mention here. Their lives began under the
auspices of savage nature: after being abandoned on the Tiber, the two
newborn babies were suckled by a she-wolf and subsequently raised by

shepherds. Furthermore, the Alban family from which they descended on their mother's side, the Silvii (from whom Amulius had tried to wrest them), by its very name (*silva* meant forest) belonged in a world "on the side of Nature."³ This was the world of the god Faunus, the legendary king of the Aborigenes and the mythical ancestor, through Latinus, of the Alban Silvii. In the historical period Faunus still presided over nondomestic areas, especially the woods and countryside, and in general over all territories deemed antithetical to the composed, orderly world of the city. Thus Romulus and Remus, sons of a "Silvia"—and conceived in a wood, according to another tradition—could not help but be drawn to the sylvan world. In fact, while growing up among the shepherds, they sought out even wilder spaces: they grew restless "staying in the sheep pens and near the herds," preferring to "go hunting, and roaming through the mountains." This youthful passion for the hunt was obviously not without precedent: we immediately think of the Athenian ephebes and their nocturnal hunts, carried out with snares, on the borders of ancient Greece; of the Spartan *krypteia*, hunting helots; and of the young Cretans, whom their lovers took to the countryside to spend two months alternately hunting and resting (see Pierre Vidal-Naquet's famous study, *The Black Hunter: Forms of Thought and Forms of Society in the Greek World*). In Rome of the historic period, young men also displayed a passion for *venationes*. These were hunts in the true sense of the term, considered to be formative physical exercises like fencing or horseback riding—or like the wild-beast hunting that went on in the circuses, part of the "spectacles for young people" I shall discuss later, which the young men not only watched as spectators but also took part in as huntsmen in the arena. And even in the Celtic world (or rather, in a Celtic world that rapidly became Romanized), hunting remained important. In 21 A.D., when Sacrovir incited the young noblemen of Gaul to revolt against the Romans, the equipment he gave them was typical: "His army was forty thousand strong; one-fifth were equipped like Roman soldiers, the rest with hunters' spears, knives, and other such arms." These young men were students, who had come to Autun to receive a liberal arts education—an intellectual training that should have facilitated their integration into Roman civilization; nevertheless, as this episode shows, they had not relinquished their hunting equipment.[4]

Romulus and Remus were not alone when they hunted and went roaming through Faunus's realm: a band of young men had formed around them. Together they fought with other shepherds over rights to pasture, and attacked or ensnared those who tried to steal cattle from them. Significantly, Remus proved more gifted than his brother in ventures of this kind: one day, after celebrating a sacrifice and setting the victim's flesh to roast, the two brothers were practicing a few sports—boxing, archery, and hurling large stones (exercises typical of future Roman youth)—while waiting for the meat to cook, when a companion came to warn them that thieves were trying to steal some of their cattle. Not waiting even to dress (exercises were performed in the nude, a topic I shall return to), the twins dashed off in different directions, each taking half the young men with him, and ran after the thieves. But it was Remus who recovered the stolen cattle, and it was also Remus who ran back to the camp before his brother, snatched the half-cooked meat from the coals, burst out laughing, and proclaimed himself and his band sole victors in the affair.[5] The Romans connected this episode with one of their festivals, the Lupercalia, and even saw it as the origin of this holiday. But since the Lupercalia will be discussed later in connection with initiation rituals, I shall for now simply summarize the behavior ascribed to these bands of young men and their legendary leaders.

The young followers of Romulus and Remus were conspicuous for their taste for hunting and brawls, their division into rival bands, their races, and their "nudity." Above all, however—as appears in the behavior of the "victor," Remus—they evinced a certain disdain for the ritual conviviality that later obtained among citizens of historical Rome, and that determined the character and pace of every sacrifice. In snatching the half-cooked meat from the spit and declaring he would eat it alone with his friends, Remus was excluding his brother, Romulus, and his companions from a feast that should have been shared by all. Moreover, in eating meat that was still "half-raw," Remus committed a "barbaric" deed which would have shocked the future citizens of Rome; Romans of the historic period not only waited until the meat was fully cooked, but also until it had been cut up and distributed among the magistrates and priests who had performed the sacrifice.[6]

The first phase of the twins' life ended, rather brutally, with the foundation of Rome. After receiving their grandfather Numitor's authorization and surrounding themselves with slaves and rebels, Romulus and Remus—as if suddenly transformed into skilled augurs—decided to consult the "signs" that permitted communication with the gods, to ascertain which of the two should be the founder: as they were twins, no criterion of seniority could intervene. Romulus settled on the Palatine and Remus on the Aventine. In retrospect this topographical separation seems not to have been accidental, for the future founder chose the hill destined to receive the temple of Jupiter Optimus Maximus (Jupiter the Best and the Greatest), while his brother chose a hill that long remained outside the holy enclave of the city—until the reign of Claudius, in fact. The gods (prominent among them Jupiter Optimus Maximus, supreme guarantor of omens) favored Romulus: they made twelve vultures appear above the Palatine, whereas Remus, on the Aventine, received only six. In contrast to the episode of stolen cattle, when Remus got the better of his brother, the victor of the omens was Romulus. Obviously this was a determining factor in the choice of founder; yet it appears even more significant when we consider that the legality of future Latino-Sabine kings, and subsequently of magistrates in the republic, was based on their skill in taking and interpreting omens. But scarcely had Romulus finished tracing the perimeter of the future city with a plough than his brother, dressed in armor, leaped across the furrow and made a mocking gesture. So then Romulus killed him.[7]

Even the Ancients had questions about the value and the "function" of this murder—when they were not simply trying to deny it ever happened (as still occurs) and place the blame on someone else. Toward the end of the republic and especially at the beginning of the imperial age, Romulus's murdering his brother came to be seen as a sort of premonitory sign of the future civil wars that would tear Rome apart, so that even its founding myth was marked with an indelible sign of blood: if the city is seen as a family, then the murdering of one brother by the other is an excellent prefiguration of the internecine horrors of a civil war. But the murder of Remus was also interpreted as the legendary *aition* at the origin of the prohibition, manifest in the historic period, against crossing the walls of the city armed. Other explanations have, of course, been offered; leaving them aside I shall simply analyze the episode of Remus' death through the categories, evidently correlated, of difference and exclusion. Scarcely had he outlined the sacred enclosure than Romulus, the founder whom the gods chose through their auspices, gave up living in the woods and forests and entered into his new life as a city dweller. Clearly, this new phase in his existence could not include his wild and youthful "double": this twin who refused to yield to superior omens, who respected neither the boundary that Romulus had traced nor the new "lifestyle" it implied and who, with a simple leap, tried to recreate within this perimeter the lifestyle of the preceding phase, with its brawls and incursions into other people's territory. The sad fate of Remus thus became an emblem of exclusion, by which illicit practices and attitudes were banned from the city—so illicit, indeed, that they constrained a brother, with a deliberately exemplary deed, to kill his own twin.[8]

FESTIVITIES AND INITIATION RITES

The brotherhood of the Luperci was, in its archaism, one of the strangest in Rome. It was thought to have originated in the period when our illustrious twins were living in the wild. Every year, on February 15, the day of the festival of Lupercalia, the Luperci ran "naked" around the Palatine hill, a strip of goatskin wrapped tightly round their waist and another strip held in one hand. During this tumultuous, unbridled race, the Luperci used the second strip of goatskin to give lashes to people in the crowd that lined their path; as the Greek Plutarch, torn between stupefaction and irony, observed, people held out the backs or the palms of their hands "like in school." Those stepping forward to receive these blows were usually women who were either sterile or had just become pregnant: to be touched by a Lupercus guaranteed easy conception or felicitous childbirth. The strips of goatskin came from a sacrifice performed before the race in a grotto known as the Lupercal, situated at the foot of the Palatine; the very same cave, according to tradition, in which the she-wolf (Lupa) had suckled Romulus and Remus. This is how Plutarch described the prerace ritual: "There are goats killed, then, two young noblemen's sons being brought, some are to stain their foreheads with the bloody knife, others presently to wipe it off with wool dipped in milk; then the young boys must laugh."[9]

The Lupercalia have variously been interpreted as a purification ritual, a fertility rite, or even as a celebration of the dead. While we may readily exclude this last hypothesis, I must observe that, in Rome, the categories of purification and fertility were not mutually exclusive; on the contrary, they were closely intertwined. Furthermore, and more generally, it is hardly possible to reduce a festival and the system of elements that articulate it to the convenient denominator of one sole "valence."[10] More pertinently, on the other hand, the ceremonies that took place at the Lupercal grotto have been analyzed, revealing traces of an ancient rite of initiation involving young Romans, especially young noblemen. In this context I propose taking a further look at the places and various stages of the festival, and at the strange behavior of the Luperci who were indisputably its protagonists.

First of all, the places: originally the Lupercal was a grotto in the middle of a wood, with springs gushing from rocky outcrops on the Palatine. At a later date, the wood disappeared beneath various buildings, but at the time of Augustus the grotto and one spring were still to be found at the foot of the Palatine, on the way leading to the Circus Maximus. Situated at the foot of the Palatine, the grotto was thus on the perimeter of Romulus's city. This topographical marginality was in some way emphasized by the grotto's environment: clearly, it was part of "nature" and must have been perceived as such, for when Augustus ordered its restoration he did not alter this fundamental characteristic. As for traditions concerning the foundation of the sanctuary and the god who was honored there, they also originated long before the city developed, in a space quite antithetical to it. The god was Pan Liceus, or Faunus, to give his Latin homologue: the very same god who presided over wilderness regions, such as those where Romulus and Remus had formerly roamed.[11] Apart from a few passages from Plutarch already quoted, we know little of the rites that took place in the grotto before the Luperci began their run. The two young boys who were touched with the bloody knife and then wiped with woollen cloth certainly represented the two bands of Luperci, the Fabiani and the Quintilii; but the bloody knife, the cloth soaked in milk, and the concluding laughter are elements that could well belong in an initiation rite. As for the relationship between the Luperci and the legendary twins, two further elements are particularly interesting: first, the fact that the Lupercal was identified as the grotto of the she-wolf that suckled the twins and that the Luperci were named after it; and second, that the Romans themselves interpreted the two boys' laughter as a kind of annual repetition of Remus's laughter in the episode of the stolen cattle—not to mention that of Romulus, who in turn burst out laughing when he saw that Remus and his friends had already devoured the half-cooked meat.[12]

Just as the twins of myth, in the juvenile phase of their existence, were strangers to the world of the city, in the same way the Luperci limited themselves to racing wildly round the Palatine, the "city of Romulus," without actually entering it. Just as Romulus and Remus had rushed off "nude" in quest of the stolen cattle, the Luperci, too, were "naked." Without going into too much detail, I should point out that the Latin word *nudi* (and the Greek word *gymnoi*, used by Plutarch) do not necessarily imply a total absence of clothing, but the absence of the toga, the loose garment typically worn by city dwellers; citizens were obliged to wear it as proof of their status, and it was thus strictly forbidden to foreigners and exiles.[13] But not only were the Luperci "nude," there was also the matter of the actual race. Georges Dumézil has admirably pointed to the general, fundamental contrast existing in Rome between the "mystique of *celeritas* [swiftness] and the morality of *gravitas* [solemnity]." Indeed, the Romans actually thought running was unworthy of a citizen and deemed it an activity for slaves; as a character in Plautus said, "It is more appropriate for freemen to walk through the streets, taking short steps: I consider running and hurrying to be typical of a slave."[14]

On the day of the Lupercalia, therefore, and under the auspices of the god Faunus, the Luperci revived a mode of living antithetical to that of the city dweller, a style that imitated the life of the original Luperci, Romulus and Remus. It was thus perfectly consistent with their status for the Luperci not to enter the old Palatine city—they simply ran round it; in the same way, the Athenian ephebes could be termed peripoloi (etymologically, "those who go round" the city). As in the case of the Athenian ephebes, the Roman Luperci's marginal status was not purely topographical,[15] but reflected their annual run on behalf of Faunus and unbridled nature. According to Varro, the great antiquarian who had actually been present at the race, the Luperci formed human herds—human herds of *"creppi"* (goats), according to another commentator. This "goatlike" quality derived from the initiation ritual that took place in the grotto and from the two strips of goatskin, one worn round the waist and the other brandished in one hand. Blows from this strip were supposed to encourage fertility in women: in Ovid's *Fasti*, in one of the *aitia* on which the festival was based, this act was seen as a substitute for penetration by the actual he-goat, a remedy bestowed by Juno on Roman women afflicted with sterility. Thus, once every year, and under the sign of the lascivious Faunus, the Luperci had to compensate for fruitless conjugal unions through the miming of a promiscuous but effective sexuality. Such behavior was well suited to their fraternity, for, as Cicero tells us, it had been instituted in the forests, before humanity gave itself laws, and long before the Roman laws concerning marriage.[16]

A celebrated episode of an entirely different order from that involving the Luperci provides information about youth and its initiation rituals during the monarchic period. In the time of King Tullius Hostilis, during the war against Alba Longa, three young Roman brothers (the well-known Horatii) met three young Alban brothers (the Curiatii) in single combat. To avoid enormous losses in both camps, it had been agreed that the outcome of the battle would be decided by these six champions.

I shall not deal here with the choice or the actual fighting of this duel (they were typical), but only with the results: after two of the Horatii had been killed, the sole survivor succeeded in killing the three Curiatii, one of whom was to marry his own sister. Returning triumphantly to Rome amid popular rejoicing, he found his sister in tears, weeping for the death of her fiancé, and in an excess of rage he killed her. Such a deed was punishable by death. Intending to save the young hero, however, King Tullius Hostilius created a tribunal composed of two judges, the *duumviri perduellionis,* charged with judging cases of "high treason." He also encouraged the murderer to appeal to the people, who absolved the young man but required his father to perform expiatory sacrifices. Then "a piece of timber was slung across the roadway and the young Horatius was made to pass beneath it with covered head, as under the 'yoke' of submission." Livy adds that "the timber is still to be seen—replaced from time to time at the State's expense—and is known as the Sister's Beam *(tigillum sororium).*"[17]

A function of this legendary tale, so rich and complex, is to explain the birth of fundamental Roman institutions, such as the right to appeal to the people. However, I shall dwell mainly on the last part, in which the father makes his son pass beneath the beam, "with covered head." At the time of Livy and the Emperor Augustus, this ancient monument was still in existence, situated in the Carinae, on the outskirts of the archaic city. In the eighth century B.C. the city comprised only the Palatine and the Velia (which had been added to the original compound when the community installed on the Palatine began to spread toward the Forum and the Esquiline). Next to the *tigillum sororium* were two altars: one dedicated to Janus Curiatius and the other to Juno Sororia. In Rome, Janus was the god who presided over beginings and passages; in the present case, as his name indicates, he presided over entry into the curiae, or courts. According to tradition, Romulus had instituted the division of citizens into curiae, and curiae committees had been organized on this basis. As for the adjective describing Juno, the verb *sororiare* indicated the first appearance of breasts in young girls, and Juno Sororia was the goddess who protected this growth. The choice of these two divinities and the connotations of their names (entry into the curiae for men, puberty for girls) corresponds to the different civic duties assigned the two sexes: the men took care of war and politics, and the women took care of birth, the physical reproduction that guaranteed the survival of the city.[18]

There has been much discussion as to the meaning of Horatius's being made to pass beneath the beam. Evidently, the act was not simply expiatory; or rather, it was expiatory only to the extent that expiatory values are almost always present in initiation rituals. Besides, Horatius's father had performed other expiatory sacrifices to purify his son after the murder of his daughter. On the other hand, in making the young man walk beneath the beam with his head covered, he performed a far more essential and significant act: after the people had absolved the young man, he reintroduced his son physically and symbolically into the heart of the political community—the community of citizens organized into curiae—from which the young Horatius had been implicitly excluded by his deed and by the accusation of "high treason."

Yet the association of Juno Sororia with the *tigillum* suggests a further dimension. The *aition* behind the origin of this beam was of course linked with the legend of Horatius and the murder of his sister (to such an extent that the adjective *sororia* came to connote this episode). But the fact that Juno Sororia presided over female puberty, and Janus Curiatius over the entry of young men into the curiae implies that walking under the *tigillum* (beyond the specific instance of the legend) was probably connected with rites of passage involving young people from the time when Rome consisted of the Palatine and the Velia. Given the marginal position of the *tigillum* in relation to the Velia, these rites must have been rites of introduction to the city. For boys—future members of the curiae—they took place under the auspices of Janus, and for girls, under the auspices of Juno, who protected their nascent sexuality.[19]

BEING "YOUNG" IN ROME

From the young Luperci and their annual run around the Palatine we have moved on to rites concerning young people of both sexes, involving a community that was not only territorially more extensive (Palatine and Velia) but also more structured politically and socially. For boys, the community was above all structured by the curiae. There citizens met for banquets, at which it was imperative to respect the codes of conviviality among "equals," the same codes that the youthful Remus had so visibly disdained. According to Roman tradition, the wise king Servius Tullius was responsible for creating all the institutions of republican Rome. When he instituted the census (as a basis for a new political institution founded on the *comitiae centuriati*), he apparently showed particular concern for young people:

> And wishing also, as Lucius Piso writes in the first book of his *Annals*, to know the number of the inhabitants of the city, and of all who were born and died and arrived at the age of manhood, he prescribed the piece of money which their relations were to pay for each—into the treasury of Ilythia (called by the Romans Juno Lucina) for those who were born, into that of Venus of the Grove (called by them Libitina) for those who died, and into the treasury of Juventas for those who were arriving at manhood *(hyper ton eis andras archomenon syntelein)*.[20]

Dionysius of Halicarnassus, who provides these particulars, had no difficulty in translating the name of the Roman goddess Juventas (Youth) as Neotes in Greek. He may, however, have encountered problems in defining the age and treasury relevant to her: why was it necessary to pay money into the treasury of Juventas, not for those embarking on "youth" (a category the Greeks knew well, since it was the age of the ephebes), but for those reaching "manhood" *(andras)?* The explanation of this anomaly (which is only an apparent anomaly) was probably to be found in the taxonomy of age cohorts in Rome. According to Varro, *pueritia* (boyhood) lasted until fifteen years of age; *adulescentia* (adolescence) from fifteen to thirty; and *juventus* (youth) from thirty to forty-five. By the time Isidor of Seville was writing, in the seventh century A.D., some slippage had occurred: *infantia* (childhood) lasted until a child was seven; *pueritia*, until he was fourteen; *adulescentia*, until he was twenty-eight; and *juventus* until he was fifty. The disparity between these definitions of age cohorts and the biological cycles of human life is immediately apparent, with adolescence lasting until the age of twenty-eight, and *juventus* until fifty.[21]

To explain such "oddities," the military and political institutions of ancient Rome have been evoked. It has been emphasized that the Servian reform of the army (another of the numerous reforms attributed to Servius Tullius) allowed for the *juniores* to become *seniores* at forty-five (the end of *juventus,* according to Varro), and that fifty (the end of *juventus,* according to Isidor of Seville) was the minimum age set by Romulus for becoming leader of a curia. But it is hard to believe that the age limits supposedly established by Romulus in regard to the curiae could have influenced definitions of age cohorts at a far later date; moreover, it would seem that the army's separation of *juniores* from *seniores* at the age of forty-five was the consequence, not the cause, of a specific social organization. For my part, I shall take a different path. To clarify this excessive prolongation of *adulescentia* and *juventus,* we must turn to a typically Roman institution, that of the *patria potestas,* or paternal power. It is no accident that Rome has been termed a "city of fathers." Not only did a father have the right of life and death over his children; the *potestas* also gave him the right to determine each phase in the lives of his progeny until he himself died, whereupon they in turn became "family fathers," reproducing those same mechanisms of power to which they had been subject.[22] The existence of an institution like the *patria potestas* provides the best explanation both of the "social" extension of adolescence and youth (a paroxysmal extension, beyond biological limits) and of the violent generational conflicts that resulted from them (especially between fathers and sons). These conflicts were seen not only in the plays of Plautus and Terence, but also taking place in the tribunals; it was as if adolescence and youth were artificially prolonged to the sole end of emphasizing the subordinate position of sons in regard to their omnipotent fathers.[23]

So far as women were concerned, it should be stressed that, unlike men, they were classified not by age but by their social or physical condition. They were classified physically as *virgines* (virgins) before marriage, socially as *uxores* (wives) after marriage, and then as *matronae* (matrons) if they had children; only with the term *anus* (old woman) did classification by age reappear. In its way, this social categorization confirms all the social

elements in the age classification of males. Since women were initially—
and for quite a long period—destined to remain subject to the power of a
father, brother, or husband, without ever reaching full emancipation, it
would be socially irrelevant to indicate their age; what mattered fundamentally were their relationships with the family, either the one they was
born into or the one they entered by marriage.[24]

If we keep rigorously to the age limits established by Varro and Isidor
of Seville, the *juvenes* in question would be men aged thirty to forty-five,
or twenty-eight to fifty. In the upper classes, they would be men entitled
to become consuls; that is, capable of occupying the most elevated magistracy to which a citizen could aspire. In the lower classes—taking into
account the average duration of life in the ancient world—they would be
adults already in their declining years. If we applied these same definitions
to women, we would find ourselves dealing with *matronae:* women endowed with progeny, who were seldom *univirae*—that is, married for ever
to one and the same husband.[25]

We must thus examine the characteristics of an age cohort whose limits
do not correspond strictly to those given by Varro and Isidor. The actual
Romans are of some help here, for in everyday speech they often used the
words *juvenis* and *adulescens*—even *adulescentulus*—indiscriminately, in
speaking of the same person. With an equal lack of discrimination, they
might also designate someone as a *juvenis* or *puer* (boy), a failing for which
the punctilious Virgil reproached his commentator Servius. Youth may be
said to begin at the moment of some formal act: for a boy, the first time
he was allowed to put on his *toga virilis,* his manly toga. For a young
Roman of the upper classes, it came to an end when he became eligible
for the magistracy, thus entering into the adult world and assuming (par-
tial) autonomy. In the lower classes, the problem is made more complex
by the existence of the family and social framework already mentioned;
by the omnipotence of the father, from which it was impossible to escape;
and by the social rule that, for the essential moments of public life (for
example, public assemblies) fixed the transition from junior to senior at
forty-five years of age.

THE *TOGA VIRILIS*, THE FORUM, AND THE CAPITOL

In a list of festivals celebrated every year at Cumae (in Campania) in honor of Augustus and various members of his family, we find this note in regard to October 18: "On this day Caesar [Augustus] put on his manly toga. Supplications addressed to Hope and Youth." The fact that this day had to be celebrated annually, just like the other major dates in Augustus Caesar's life (for example: his birthday; the anniversary of the day when he first became a consul; the day he was appointed *Pontifex maximus,* or head of the Roman religion; the anniversaries of his victories in battle) clearly indicates the value the Romans accorded this ritual: a true "rite of passage" in which the *toga praetexta* was abandoned in favor of the virile toga. We know very little about the rites of passage young men experienced in the Lupercal grotto under the sign of Faunus, near the *tigillum sororium* and under the double protection of Janus Curiatius and Juno Sororia. On the other hand, we are relatively familiar with the ceremony of this change in clothing, through which the young Roman acceded fully to his status as a free citizen—though still, of course, subject to the *patria potestas.*[26]

For boys, the ceremony generally took place between fifteen and sixteen years of age, at the boy's home, and obviously the boy's father—the omniscient paterfamilias—presided. As a good omen *(ominis causa),* the young Roman went to sleep the night before wearing a special tunic *(tunica recta),* as did virgins on the night before their wedding. The next morning, he removed the "signs of boyhood" *(insigniae pueritiae).* His *bulla,* an ornament worn round the neck to repel evil spells, was then dedicated to the household Lares (divinities who protected the territory of the house, and thus the family residing there). He would then take off his "pretext toga," decorated with a purple band, and put on the manly toga, the white "free" toga, that quintessential garment of the Roman citizen (this, we recall, the young Luperci removed only once each year, on the day they ran "naked" round the Palatine). This private stage of the ceremony was followed by a public one: the boy was accompanied to the Forum, even to the Capitol, by friends and parents. Depending on the family's social rank, wealth, and noble alliances, these processions could be magnificent affairs. Occasionally they were of a sumptuous ostentation comparable to that of triumphs—processions accompanying the victorious general from outside the sacred compound to the temple of Jupiter Optimus Maximus, where he would place a laurel wreath on the knees of the statue of the seated god. This procession accompanying the young man to the Forum, the public square where justice was administered and where adults met to discuss politics, was a true initiation into public affairs. Apart from the "apprenticeship" that followed (and which could be undergone in the Forum or in the army), the *deductio in forum* was the essential moment in a young Roman's introduction to the life of the community. Even in the Augustan age, as a particular honor to Augustus's two adopted sons, Gaius and Lucius Caesar, the Senate decided to admit them to its sessions beginning on that very day.[27]

Commenting on some verses from Virgil's celebrated *Fourth Eclogue* (the one in which the poet speaks of the birth of a *puer* who would inaugurate a new world), Servius remarks: "Truly, it is justly said that Jupiter takes care of growing boys, for when they have put on the manly toga, they go to the Capitol." Thus, according to Virgil's commentator, the final stage in the procession accompanying the young citizen was neither the Forum nor the temple of the Capitoline Triad (Jupiter, Juno, Minerva), the city's most renowned temple for protective divinities. In the opinion of Servius, the cortege's final destination was directly related to the god who protected growth, Jupiter. In this context I must note that on this same Capitol there existed another cult, also connected with youth, and far older than the cult of the Capitoline Triad. This was the cult of Juventas, Youth, the divinity associated at Cumae with hope, in public prayers marking the anniversary of the day when Augustus put on his toga. After Rome was devastated in a fire set by the Gauls, Livy records the good Furius Camillus delivering a speech to his fellow citizens, enjoining them—successfully—not to abandon their city: "Here is the Capitol, where in the days of old, the human head was found and men were told that on that spot would be the world's head and the seat of empire; here, when the Capitol was to be cleared of other shrines for the sake of Jupiter's temple, the two deities Juventas and Terminus refused, to the great joy of the men of those days, to be moved." The episode Camillus was referring to took place in the time of Tarquin the Proud: the king apparently wanted to free the Capitol from all its preexisting sanctuaries and dedicate it entirely to the Capitoline Triad and a new temple. That a cult to Juventas survived on the Capitol is proved, beyond any element of legend, in the historical era by the presence of an altar dedicated to this divinity in the temple of Jupiter Optimus Maximus, in the room of Minerva: above it was a painting by Nicomachus, representing the Rape of Proserpine.[28] The persistence of this cult is all the more significant in that Juventas had another temple in the town, one that was hers alone: the decision to build it had been made in 207 B.C. by Marcus Livius Salinator, at the time of the battle of Metaurus, and it was consecrated sixteen years later, in 191 B.C., by Gaius Licinius Lucullus. This was the era of the second Punic War, and given the duration of the conflict and the enormous losses it involved, this appeal to Juventas is highly understandable: not only was she the goddess of the young men fighting in the army but she was also the goddess of Roman youth in general, responsible for their growth and preservation. Moreover, when the conflict had begun in 218 B.C., Juventas had received a lectisternium—a religious ceremony in which food was offered to effigies of gods placed on couches—at the prompting of the sybilline books.[29]

The boys' pilgrimages to the Capitol, after the adoption of the manly toga, may thus be interpreted as a double act of homage involving Jupiter and also Juventas, who had, significantly, refused to abandon the Capitol and was still honored at an altar inside the temple of the Capitoline Triad. If Juventas was the protective divinity of young people, the goddess to whom they prayed on the anniversary of the day when Augustus put on his manly toga, Jupiter Optimus Maximus was the supreme guarantor of their "new life," of their new status as citizens, full members in the tribunals and *centuriae* that structured Roman popular assemblies. Just as the old division into curiae fell into disuse during the historic period, so

Janus Curiatius fell into oblivion, as did the ceremonies and ritual practices that used to take place by the *tigillum sororium*. Janus Curiatius's role was thenceforth entrusted to Jupiter, who presided with Juventas as young people were introduced into the city of adults, entering the civic and institutional framework through which Roman life was organized.

Augustus adopted the virile toga on October 18; his successor Tiberius, on April 24; Virgil on October 15, in Cremona; and the son of Cassius, Caesar's murderer, on the Ides of March in 44 B.C. In this last case, the choice of date may not have been dictated purely by tactical considerations (certain conspirators close to Cassius had joined in the procession accompanying his son), but may have resulted from the father's ideological intentions: perhaps he wanted his son's adoption of the "free" toga to coincide with the day of the dictator's assassination, thus with the restoration of traditional republican freedoms.[30] I have listed the few dates we are certain of to demonstrate that in the late republican period and in the first days of the Empire, there was no set day for the ceremony of putting on the toga. Nonetheless Ovid, a contemporary of Augustus and Tiberius, seemed to think otherwise, for he gave March 17 as the date of this ceremony. This was the day of the Liberalia—festivities in honor of the god Liber, identified by Ovid and many others as the Roman equivalent to Bacchus:

> It remains for me to discover why the gown of liberty is given to boys, fair Bacchus [*candide Bacche*], on thy day, whether it be because thou seemest ever to be a boy and a youth [*puer . . . juvenisque*], and thy age is midway between the two; or it may be that, because thou art a father, fathers commend to thy care and divine keeping the pledges that they love; or it may be that, because thou art Liber, the gown of liberty is assumed and a freer life is entered upon under thine auspices. Or was it because, in the days when the ancients tilled the fields more diligently, and a senator labored on his ancestral land, when a consul exchanged the bent plough for the rods and axes of office, and it was no crime to have horny hands, the country folk used to come to the city for the games (but that was an honor paid to the gods, not a concession to popular tastes, the discoverer of the grape held on his own day those games which now

he shares with the torch-bearing goddess); and the day therefore seemed not unsuitable for conferring the gown, in order that a crowd might gather round the novice?[31]

The last of the "explanations" given by Ovid is typical of his *Fasti*, referring back to an uncorrupted past: "When the ancients cultivated their fields more diligently," and so on. A certain preference has been shown for this explanation, leading to the assumption that the custom of making March 17 (day of the Liberalia) the day of the toga ceremony was certainly extremely old, but that it was subsequently gradually abandoned.[32] But this hypothesis is not only undemonstrable, it is also contradicted by Ovid's use of the present: "It remains for me to discover why the gown of liberty is given to boys . . . on thy day." More interesting, on the other hand, is the connection Ovid establishes, through a coherent system of representations, between the name of the god Liber, his description as "father" *(Liber pater)*, and one of the definitions of the virile toga *(toga libera)*. These connections, operative in Ovid's time, suggest that during the Augustan and Tiberian age, and also in the late phase of the Republic, many people chose the day of the Liberalia to perform this ceremony— especially since a sacrifice was made to Liber on his feast day, on the Capitol. However, the choice of day could vary and was always a prerogative of the child's father, as is shown by the different dates I quoted in regard to Augustus, Tiberius, and the son of Cassius.[33]

The case of girls was far simpler. Once the archaic rituals that had taken place under the sign of Juno Sororia fell into disuse, there was only one sole rite of passage, in the historic period, for *puellae* and *virgines* after reaching puberty, and that was marriage. After dedicating their dolls to the family Lares, as the boys had done with their *bulla*, and having also worn the *tunica recta* as a good omen on the night before the wedding, the virgins went into the marriage ceremony with a special hairstyle, and covered with a red veil, the *flammeum;* they also wore a woollen belt fastened round their waist, which the husband later untied in the marriage bed. Thus, immediately after puberty, the girls were destined to become *uxores* and *matronae* (wives and mothers); the rite that introduced them to youth corresponded to their social function of reproducing the civic body. The ambiguity of this function, especially in the upper classes, is evident: though clearly subaltern, the woman's role was not devoid of power, since the reproduction of males depended on the *uxores*, as did the establishment of kinship so essential in the political struggles of husbands and fathers, flanked by their relations.[34]

THE MILITARY

Once clad in the virile toga, the young Roman could begin his *tirocinium*, a kind of apprenticeship in adult life. At a later time this apprenticeship could take place in the Forum (training in oratory and politics); but originally it must have involved an education that was primarily military. This military training was all the more necessary when even Cicero viewed courage, arrogance, and ferocity (all qualities connoted by the Latin word *ferocitas*) as the characteristic traits of *juvenes*. The Roman army obeyed an iron discipline, which also determined the development of military tactics: the outcome of a battle depended less on the prowess or acts of courage of the individual combatants than on the striking power of the mass of foot soldiers regularly disposed in their units. In a system of combat that set *disciplina* against *ferocitas*, young men's reckless daring and temerity could be seen as elements of potential danger, not to mention insubordination.[35]

There is a military episode that must, from this point of view, be seen as most significant. The incident involved a clash between the dictator Lucius Papirius Cursor and Quintus Fabius Maximus Rullianus, his *magister equitum* ("master of the horse"), a man whose powers were far inferior to his but who was nonetheless his colleague. During the second war against the Samnites (whose mountainous territory, the Samnium, stretched between Latium and Campania), Lucius Papirius Cursor decided to return to Rome to take new auspices: in his view, a requisite for waging war. Before leaving he warned his colleague not to engage in combat under any pretext. But Quintus Fabius was not only an *adulescens*, he was also *ferox* (spirited): observing that the enemy lines were thin, he launched an offensive and won a memorable victory, inflicting 20,000 losses on the enemy. Back in Rome, where he learned the news, the dictator declared that, despite the victory, such behavior constituted a grave breach of discipline and an affront to the auspices (for which he had gone to Rome). On returning to Samnium he summoned Quintus Fabius to appear before his tribunal. Despite protests from the army, he intended to condemn him, but Fabius Quintus fled to Rome, where he appealed to the tribunes of the plebs and to the people. The matter was extremely serious, for nothing—neither his youthful status nor the victory he had won—seemed able to excuse the "master of the horse": only the pardon of Lucius Papirius Cursor could save his life, while at the same time preserving respect for military discipline.[36]

In the course of this episode, recounted at length by Livy, the figure of the accused's father appears, energetically employed in the defense of his son and successfully rallying to his cause "the majesty of the Senate, the favor of the people, the support of the tribunes of the plebs, and the memory of the absent army." Livy then evokes the strictness of the "fathers of old," who had very different attitudes toward undisciplined or seditious sons. He recalls the firmness of the consul Lucius Giunius Brutus, one of the "founding fathers" of the Republic who, discovering that his sons had plotted against the new state, watched impassively as they were executed; above all, he recalls the severity of Titus Manlius Torquatus, a true hero of military discipline.

Before becoming a model of paternal virtue, the young Titus Manlius had covered himself with glory. In 361 B.C., during one of the Gallic wars, an enemy had come to challenge one of the young Romans to single combat, to see which of the two races would prove the more valiant. Whereas the "best of the young Romans" remained conspicuously silent on seeing the size and strength of the challenger, Titus Manlius sought out the dictator Titus Quintius: "Commander, without an order from you [*injussus tuo*], I could not fight outside the ranks [*extra ordinem*], even if I were sure of victory; but if you permit me, I would like to show this savage beast, who is boldly swaggering before the enemy standards, that I come from a family that defeated the Gauls at the foot of the Tarpeian rock." Young

Manlius's proud reference was to Manlius Capitolinus, who, in 390 B.C., had defended the Capitol against the Gallic invaders, and I shall return to the young hero's pride in defending the honor of both his fatherland and his family. But for now, I stress only his respect for military discipline: scarcely had he received the authorization to accept the challenge "and to fight outside the ranks" than Manlius rushed against the Gaul and killed him. The only spoils he took were the Gaul's necklet *(torques)*, which he put round his own neck, thus earning the nickname of Torquatus, "the man with the twisted necklet."[37]

Twenty years later, the valiant Titus Manlius Torquatus had become a consul and was fighting a very difficult war against the Latins, who until then had been allies of Rome. Faced with the prospect of a hard campaign, the two consuls explicitly forbade "anyone to fight outside the ranks." But one day while out on reconnaissance, the son of Titus Manlius—a young man with a "ferocious" temperament, serving in the cavalry—was challenged to single combat by Geminus Mecius, a nobleman from Tusculum who was also young, and serving in the enemy cavalry. Obviously young Manlius wanted to repeat his father's exploit, and he did indeed emerge victorious from the duel: laden with the victim's spoils, he returned to the camp and went straight to the *praetorium*, his father's tent. But on hearing of the duel and its favorable outcome, the inflexible Titus Manlius Torquatus did not hesitate to condemn his son to death for violating the explicit order of the consuls and the discipline required of the army. He knew the example he was setting was a painful one, but he deemed it salutary for the future of Roman youth *("triste exemplum sed in posterum salubre iuventuti")*.[38]

Only in exceptional situations, therefore, and with the express permission of a superior officer, could a young Roman soldier fight "outside the ranks," showing a personal valor that had more to do with *ferocitas* or cunning than with military discipline. As in the case of the hapless younger Manlius, the young men so enamored of dueling were often cavalrymen from the nobility, serving in a branch of the army in which the single combats dear to the aristocracy of the Archaic period were still prevalent. It was certainly no accident that during the sixth and fifth centuries B.C.,

in Rome and throughout Italy, this method of combat was supplanted by
the "revolutionary" development of an infantry. This great innovation in
military tactics, based on the massive unity of foot soldiers, also brought
about deep political changes, since it implied greater "equality" among
citizens.

Valerius Maximus, a contemporary of Tiberius who wrote nine
books of *Memorable Deeds and Sayings,* recounts that twice a year young
men of the equestrian order staged grandiose spectacles. The first took
place on the Ides of February—the same day as the above-mentioned
Lupercalia—and the second on the Ides of July, with the "procession of
riders" *(transvectio equitum)* mounted on white horses and with olive
branches tied round their foreheads. According to tradition, the procession
of July 15 commemorated the Roman defeat of the Latins at Lake Regillus
in 496 B.C. The cavalry had played a decisive role in that victory, thanks
to the support of the Dioscuri, Castor and Pollux. Not only had the twin
gods participated in the battle dressed as Roman cavalrymen, but legend
had it that they had then rushed off to Rome to announce the victory.
Another tradition held, more simply, that the ceremony had been instituted
by the censor Quintus Fabius Maximus Rullianus, in 304 B.C. However we
interpret these diverging accounts, it is no surprise to find the Dioscuri
associated with the origins of this procession. Castor and Pollux were
excellent examples of what the Greeks termed *kouroi* (young men), objects
in Latium of a very ancient cult whose temple was situated in the Roman
Forum. Nor, in the other tradition, is it surprising to find a figure like
Quintus Fabius Maximus Rullianus, that same "master of the horse" and
ferox adulescens who won a victory over the Samnites by disobeying the
dictator's orders.[39]

The Lupercalia and the *transvectio equitum* both involved young men
of the equestrian order, either running around the Palatine or riding
through the city; they also paired two complementary and antithetical
moments involving young men of the second of the Roman orders. These
connections were not simply a product of the erudition of Valerius
Maximus. In reality this duplication was widespread, at least in the first

two centuries of the imperial age, as is shown by a series of funerary bas-reliefs collected and classified by Paul Veyne. On all these reliefs (for example, on the funerary stele of Tiberius Claudius Liberalis now in the Vatican Museum), the young man who has died is shown on one face as a Lupercus, with his goatskin belt, and on the other as a horseman, wearing a wreath. Evidently these were young men of the equestrian order who died prematurely, and the only salient public events to record in their short lives were the Lupercalia and the *transvectio equitum* in which they had taken part. Paul Veyne was quick to connect this iconography with the Augustan reform that limited membership in the Luperci to the equestrian order, the other societies being open only to the senatorial nobility. The cultivated and prudent Augustus had well understood the difference between these twice-yearly rituals in which youths were permitted to "cut loose" and the other sacerdotal rites, which in contrast required composure and *gravitas*.[40]

YOUNG AND OLD

To grasp the full ambiguity in the relationship between young and old in Rome, we must turn back to Romulus. After he had founded the city—and excluded his own savage "double," Remus, from its walls—Romulus nonetheless maintained his privileged bonds with young men, as if nothing could efface the memory of hunting and roaming over hill and dale. Having created a Senate composed exclusively of elders as an organ to assist him in government, Romulus thus felt the need to create a personal guard, composed exclusively of young men, who would constantly surround him in both war and peace: these were the *celeres* (swift ones), whose very name contrasts with the *gravitas* of the elders. I am not about to examine the well-known connections between these *celeres* and the origins of Roman knighthood; nor shall I discuss the "tyrannical" interpretation of Romulus's decision (an interpretation that had already been proposed in antiquity), connecting the *celeres* with the bodyguards of Greek tyrants. I shall, however, stress that these proud young men accompanied Romulus in all his ventures, from the rape of the Sabines to his numerous wars, without ever leaving him. The final phase of the founder's earthly life has been characterized as tyrannical, a perception doubtless furthered by the constant presence of the *celeres;* Romulus became openly opposed to the elders, neglecting their opinions and advice. But when Romulus mysteriously vanished, the whole of Roman youth, not just the *celeres,* stood speechless and amazed: either he had ascended miraculously into heaven during a thunderstorm, as the *patres* of the Senate maintained; or else he had been assassinated at the behest of these same elders, his body cut into pieces and scattered so that nobody would ever find it.[41]

Romulus was therefore in conflict with the *patres,* whom he had nonetheless constituted into a senatorial body; all the young men, however, were on his side, including the sons of the senators. Be it in terms of legend or of representation, the episode reveals the difficulty of father-son relationships, which were anything but idyllic. In examining the ambiguous nature of these relationships, we see that not only was this ambiguity to some extent inherent in the Roman nobiliary system, but it was also designed to guarantee the system's survival. With this in mind, let us take a further look at the Manlii, whose conduct has been analyzed by Maurizio Bettini. Before obtaining permission to fight the Gaul in 361 B.C. and acquiring the cognomen Torquatus, Titus Manlius had spent his youth in the country. In effect he had been banished by his father, Lucius Manlius Imperiosus, who became dictator in 363 B.C. It was by no means rare in Roman society for young men to be "exiled" to the country, to spare them the "dangers" of the city. But Titus Manlius had been sent away for different reasons: he was not very eloquent, and thus seemed ill-suited for the political career normally expected in his family. When his father Imperiosus retired from the dictatorship, a tribune of the plebs decided to bring him to trial for excessive harshness: not only for his harsh treatment of citizens when he was dictator, but also for his severity toward his own son, who had had to go and work on the land like a slave. The night before the trial, however, Titus Manlius returned to Rome, went to the house of the tribune of the plebs, and asked to see him privately. The tribune was delighted, thinking that the son was bringing new evidence against his father. Instead, Titus Manlius took out a knife and threatened to kill the tribune unless he swore to "dismiss the case against his father before the assembly of the plebs." Though perhaps not a gifted orator, young Titus Manlius was not lacking in courage or filial affection, and by this exceptionally dutiful gesture he saved his father Imperiosus, to the unanimous acclaim of his fellow citizens.[42]

To accept abuses of paternal power and then to defend at all costs the father who had inflicted them, even to prevent his behavior from being judged by a tribunal—at first sight this might seem masochistic, or at least paradoxical. Yet the aim of such devotion was quite clear: it was to preserve the Roman family system, with its basic principle of *patria potestas*—a father's unlimited power over his children. The respect shown by the sons naturally implies that when it was their turn to be fathers, they too would exercise this power, thus perpetuating the system. As we have seen, Manlius Torquatus proved to be an even harsher father when, as consul, he condemned his own son for accepting a challenge without leave from his commandant. The central figure in three generations of Manlii, Torquatus showed exemplary devotion both to his father *(pietas erga parentem)* and to his country *(pietas erga patriam);* these two forms of devotion were inseparable, and central to the same code of honor. For if the *patria potestas* had necesarily to be renewed by succeeding generations, it was inconceivable for a son even to think of interrupting the process, since this would compromise his future prerogatives as a father. Then again, since the customs and laws of the city gave fathers this power, it was equally unthinkable for a father not to avail himself of these customs and laws when necessary against his own son, in a society that, at least in fancy, tenaciously placed love of country before love of family, thus producing these famous "examples." On learning that Titus Manlius watched unflinchingly as his own son was executed, Livy's readers were probably reminded of Lucius Gaius Brutus, the imperturbable magistrate who had watched while his sons were put to death for conspiring against the young republic. It was yet another patriotic reason for the citizens to keep quiet about their personal disagreements, especially those that might have led to a civil war. On the day of Augustus's funeral, those present were divided between two opinions. For some, it was the duty of sons to take vengeance on their fathers' political enemies, and the *pietas erga parentem* justified the civil war launched by Octavius—the future Augustus—to avenge the assassination of Caesar, his adoptive father. But others more prudently considered that a "private hatred" (even when inspired by the death of an adoptive father killed by conspirators) could never in any case take precedence over the public good.[43]

If the sons, subject to the power of harsh and inflexible fathers, had many reasons to fear them, the fathers also had reason to be afraid of their sons. The comedies of Plautus often depict young rogues who dream openly of their father's death. Addicted to the pleasures of city life among prostitutes and pimps, all of whom must be paid, these young men contract huge debts. Only their inheritance—if they can obtain it, and quickly—can solve their problems. The same situation, in an even more brutal form, recurs in the Catiline conspiracy: when the time came to assign duties to the conspirators, the sons of senatorial families involved in the plot each received the specific task of killing their own father. These conflicts in relationships between fathers and sons have been studied in all their complexity by Yann Thomas, who takes as his model a famous example: the trial of Macedon.

The event took place in the reign of Vespasian. Macedon was found guilty of parricide: he had killed his father to obtain his inheritance and pay his debts. Since his crime was thought to be the most horrible a man could commit, the penalty had to be equally dreadful ("the penalty of the sack"). For whatever resentment he had harbored against his father, the murderer had, above all, tried to bypass the patrimonial aspects of the *patria potestas*. This power entrusted management of the family patrimony entirely to the paterfamilias, leaving the son only a *peculium* (the same word, *peculium*, also designated the property of slaves). To avoid an increase in such crimes, of which examples had already occurred, the Senate passed a *senatus consultum*, or formal resolution, prohibiting and invalidating any loan that expressly required repayment "after the death of the father" *(post mortem patris)*.[44]

Clearly, Macedon was far from demonstrating the filial *pietas* shown by Titus Manlius Torquatus. We could easily attribute this difference in mentality to the "decadence" of Roman society in the imperial period, to the change in moral values and the code of honor. But an obvious objection would arise: while such changes did indeed occur over the course of centuries, the *patria potestas* for its part remained almost immutable. The system still required the absolute submission of sons to fathers, against which young men were already seen grumbling on Roman stages in the comedies of Plautus at the end of the third century and the beginning of the second century B.C., and which motivated the open rebellion of well-born young men in the Catiline conspiracy. In Rome, the ambiguous relationship between young and old was based entirely on this discipline: it was a relationship structured by traditions and laws but rich in potential conflict in a state where traditions and laws seemed always to favor the fathers.[45]

YOUNG MEN'S ORGANIZATIONS

In the time of Augustus, not only was there a *princeps* as the head of state, a prince superior in rank and authority to all other *principes civitatis* (princes of the state, or "principal citizens," as senators were called), but there were also "princes of youth" *(principes juventutis)*, who happened to be the emperor's two sons. As Augustus wrote in his *Testament* with evident pride: "And then all the Roman knights called them both princes of youth and gave them presents of shields and silver lances." The boys in question were Gaius Caesar and Lucius Caesar, Augustus's two adopted sons, born to his daughter Julia and her husband Agrippa who, before his death, had shared the "supreme powers" with Augustus. Gaius and Lucius received the honor of their title when they adopted the virile toga (in 5 and 2 B.C., respectively). Obviously, the circumstances that obliged the entire equestrian order to call the two boys princes of youth were rich in significance: Augustus was the *princeps* of the senators, and their sons (not yet in the Senate) and all the other Roman knights now had their princes too: the two sons of the *princeps*. There had also been princes of youth in the republican era: for example, the 300 young men whom Mucius Scaevola led against the Etruscan king Lars Porsena. And Cicero sometimes used the term when referring to Lucius Domitius Aenobarbus, Curio, and Brutus. But in the Augustinian era, just as the other principal citizens gave way to a single *princeps,* the previous princes of youth did not carry the same weight as the sons of Augustus. In their case the term was an official title, which therefore appeared in inscriptions and on coins; it also heralded what should have been the following stage, for they were supposed to become *principes* of Rome and the empire when Augustus died. But both boys died young, Gaius Caesar in 4 A.D. and his brother, Lucius, in 2 A.D. Lamenting this premature loss, the inhabitants of Pisa spoke of Gaius as one who was "already designated a *princeps,* as just and virtuous as his father." Thereafter the title of prince of youth was still conferred on "heirs to the throne"—rather like the title of caesar, which also anticipated future accession to the position of "Augustus."[46]

During this same imperial period, there were in Rome some young men's associations that had all the characteristics of real societies. As Silvio Panciera has shown, their structure corresponded to the fourteen districts and numerous *vici* into which the city was divided. While this topographical division of Roman *juvenes* obviously matched the specific dimensions of Rome, we nonetheless find similar associations in the ancient urban centers of Latium and Etruria. These organizations of young men thus existed throughout Italy and, with but a few exceptions, in all the western provinces of the empire, especially in the second and third centuries A.D. According to Mikhail Rostovsev, Augustus instituted these associations, which were apparently modeled after the Greek ephebate and *neoi,* with military preparation as their objective (a view previously expressed by Theodor Mommsen in his work on border zones). More recent studies, however, have easily contradicted this theory: not only is there no proof of Augustus's having taken this initiative, but there are several indications that similar associations of young men existed in the republican era, at least in Campania. Moreover, important regional differences have been noted, contradicting the hypothesis of a single model; and although the military activities of these associations are well documented, they seem to have been limited to serious crises.[47]

Setting aside the complex problems connected with the Oscan *vereiia*

and its subsequent, debatable continuation in the *juventus* of Pompei, the
survival, in the imperial age, of certain public offices associated with youth
in the old cities of Latium and Etruria indicates that these urban centers
had specific forms of young men's associations, of which no trace is found
in Rome in the republican period. An inscription in Lanuvium, probably
dating from the time of Augustus or Tiberius, tells us that Marcus Valerius,
a great benefactor to his town, was not only an aedile and a dictator but
also a *praef(ectus) juventutis,* "prefect of youth." It is legitimate to wonder
if this prefecture of youth should be put on a level with the dictatorship
and aedileship; if it should be considered, with those offices, as a magis-
tratracy characteristic of Lanuvium before the town was integrated into
the Roman state, and that survived the integration, as did the two other
offices. One might ask similar questions about the "praetors of youth"
known to have existed at Nepi, and possibly at Sutri, in Etruria, where the
Latin word *praetor* is a translation of the ancient office of *ʒilath.* This
question of magistratracies linked to the world of youth leads us back to
the old debate about institutional "borrowings" between Rome and Italy.
Did Rome directly and forcibly introduce her own institutions into the
cities she had conquered or brought into her sphere of influence? Or
should we imagine a far more complex process, with Rome and the Italian
towns reciprocally exchanging influences and institutions? The case in
point would seem to militate in favor of the second hypothesis: the magistratracies connected with the youth of Latium or Etruria could not have
resulted from Roman influence, since they did not exist in Rome at the
time.[48]

The possibility of autonomous developments in the Italian towns—
that is, developments not due to some model imposed by Rome—may also
be inferred from the "young men's spectacle" *(lusus juvenum).* This spectacle was organized every year by young men's associations in different
urban centers in Italy or in the western provinces; the young men played
an active role, taking part in various competitions designed to show them
to good advantage. Some scholars have tried to make this spectacle correspond to the Juvenalia in Rome, initiated by Nero in 59 A.D. to celebrate

the first shaving of his beard; but these festivals almost certainly came after the spectacles in other Italian towns, and therefore could not have been the model for them. As for Rome and spectacles showcasing young men, the only one we know of, before the Juvenalia of Nero's time, was the *lusus Troiae,* an ancient parade that took a sinuous route through the city, featuring very young riders from the noblest families.[49]

Whatever their origin, the spread of young men's organizations through Italy and the western provinces beginning in the first century A.D. must necessarily have taken into account social realities proper to each region or city, of which we know little. Some of those realities also helped to determine the actual nature of the associations. The organizations were not, as Mikhail Rostovsev previously maintained, totally aristocratic in the choice of their members; the recent work of M. Jaczynowska has shown that they were also open to rich freedmen and to the emerging class of urban "bourgeoisie." This did not, however, prevent senators or knights from being at the head of these organizations, which, like all Roman associations, were formed around the cult of a divinity. The gods most frequently chosen were Hercules—who was not only a youthful god but also the author of heroic deeds; Mars and Diana, linked with war and hunting respectively; and Nemesis, associated with hunting as practiced in the amphitheater.[50]

The organizations of young men could also play an active role in municipal politics. This is shown by a series of electoral "posters" found in Pompei, where the local *juventus* disseminated propaganda on behalf of various candidates for the supreme magistracy (in this case, the duumvirate) or for the aedileship. As one might expect, the candidates the young men supported were not only honest and worthy but also young themselves, and the electoral propaganda clearly appealed to generational solidarity. While the wealth of these electoral documents from Pompei is quite exceptional, young men's associations must also have been very active in elections held in other towns, whether in Italy or the provinces. That these organizations were firm features of urban life in the Romanized west during the first centuries A.D. is absolutely certain. Their objective was twofold: to introduce young men, especially those of the minor aristocracy and "bourgeoisie," to the political life of the city (a political life that was for more energetic and pugnacious than is generally thought), and, at the same time, to exert some control over an age cohort that occasionally seemed "dangerous," by channeling its energy into the appropriate offices.[51]

CHAPTER 4

THE WORLDS OF
JEWISH YOUTH IN
EUROPE, 1300–1800

Elliott Horowitz

In speaking of the lives of Jewish young people in Europe over the course of five centuries, we cannot speak of their world but only of their worlds. This is true not only because, as one historian has remarked, eighteenth-century Europe was "an utterly different place" from the preindustrial Europe of even two centuries earlier,[1] and certainly from the era before the Black Death, but also because of immanent differences in the lives of the various groups who together constituted the young in Jewish society. The lives of boys and young men, devoted in large part during their childhood and adolescent years to the study of religious texts, often (and in some cases even after their marriage) away from home, were decidedly different from the lives of young women, which, while almost always including some education, were centered more closely on the domestic hearth and led at an earlier age to the marriage canopy. And the lives of the young among the wealthier classes engaged in trade or banking, who would marry earlier than the artisans and the poor, and who would often be fed, clothed, and educated at their parents' expense until (and sometimes after) the time of their marriage, were markedly different from the lives of those young people, male and female, who in early adolescence would be sent to live in the homes of others as domestic servants or apprentices.

To a lesser extent than differences of gender and class, cultural differences between various Jewries persisted over time as well, so that the Mediterranean Jewish societies of late medieval Spain and early modern

Italy, for example, offered in some ways different worlds and modes of experience to the young man than did the "northern" Ashkenazic Jewries of the German-speaking lands and eastern Europe. And, needless to say, beyond these differences were the considerable differences in age between those who, in various Jewish societies, might be included within the category of the young—that is, those who were no longer considered children, but were not quite yet full adults. Within this category we might include, at one end of our period, the thirty-year-old German Jew whose student tuition was still being paid by his mother, and at its other end, the ten-year-old Jewish orphan in England whose aunt and grandmother, after caring for him for eight years, turned him out of their home on the grounds that he was by then old enough to support himself.[2] In the female sphere we might include the not inconsiderable number of ten- or eleven-year-old Jewish brides in medieval Spain or eighteenth-century Poland whose childhood also effectively terminated at that age, side by side, for example, with Jewish maidservants in their late twenties in seventeenth- or eighteenth-century Italy still hoping, with the aid of a dowry grant from an employer and perhaps his pious confraternity, to marry and start their own family.

On occasion, then, individuals who were separated by rivers, mountains, and centuries may be seen, depending on the circumstances of their lives, to have inhabited similar worlds of Jewish youth, whereas in other instances young Jewish people living at the same time and even under the same roof may have belonged nonetheless, due to distinctions rooted less in age than in gender, social structure, and mentality, to radically different worlds. And yet the subtle and not always predictable dynamics of domestic life, especially in larger households, could sometimes cause these different worlds of youth to mingle and even to merge, as in the continuing phenomenon of wealthy and educated young Jewish men performing ostensibly false (but legally problematic) acts of betrothal on the Jewish maidservants whom they encountered in the homes of their parents, teachers, or neighbors. Such "irresponsible" acts on the part of otherwise upstanding young men and the social panic that they invariably engendered would seem to reflect, rather paradoxically, both the proximity of the various worlds inhabited by Jewish youth and yet their irremediable distance from each other.

Technically any lad of thirteen (the age of bar mitzvah, and thus of legal majority) could bind himself in such a union, but the Lithuanian communities of the early seventeenth century, for example, decided that any act of marriage performed by a young man under the age of eighteen without the permission of his father or relatives would be considered null and void. Similarly, early in the sixteenth century the German-born rabbi of Padua, Rabbi Judah Minz, had sought to alter the local Italian custom of permitting thirteen-year-old youths to perform ritual slaughter (quite necessary for the provision of meat in small communities when fathers were away on business), decreeing that thenceforth only those eighteen and over would be permitted to do so.[3] These are only two small indications of how the age of responsible adulthood in Jewish society was, in many respects, contingent rather than given, determined more by concerns of the moment than by ancient traditions. And the age could fall below thirteen (or twelve for females) just as it could rise, as we shall see, considerably above it. For the purposes of our treatment in the present chapter, the age of thirty shall be regarded as the termination of youth, and the age of ten as its onset, not because there was to be found a consistent view in Jewish society over five centuries that regarded these two decades as a single "age" in the "ages of man," but because these were the years of life in which one might be considered in practice no longer a mere child but not yet fully an adult.

> Why urge reproach upon a lad of ten?
> Soon enough he will grow and find his chastisement.

So wrote the renowened Hispano-Jewish poet and philosopher Judah Halevi (d. 1141) in one of the few medieval Jewish compositions devoted to the ages of man. "Speak to him rather, tenderly, in a graceful tone," continued the quatrain, "A delight shall he be to his parents and family."[4] Yet this somewhat relaxed approach to the upbringing of youth is not the only one to be encountered among medieval Jews, even within the His-pano-Jewish tradition itself. This may be seen, for example, in the com-ments of Rabbi Israel al-Nakawa of Toledo (d. 1391) on the noted verse in Proverbs (22:6): "Train a lad according to his way; Even in old age he will not swerve from it." According to al-Nakawa's interpretation, the verse was to be read as a warning. "*If* you train a lad according to his way—what is the way of youth? Neither to study nor to pray, but to sit idly and pursue pleasure—if you allow him to follow this contemptible path . . . even in old age he will not swerve from it."[5] This line of interpretation, moreover, whether or not it actually began with al-Nakawa, proved highly influential over the period to be discussed here, later finding expression in the works of such geographically and culturally diverse authors as Rabbi Joseph Hahn Nordlingen of Frankfurt (d. 1637) in the seventeenth century, and Rabbi Elijah ha-Kohen of Smyrna early in the eighteenth.[6]

Halevi's poem managed to travel widely as well, both through the liturgical tradition (having been accepted in the Sephardic rite for use on Yom Kippur) and through the popular commentary on the rabbinic tractate *Pirkei Avot* (Chapters of the Fathers) written by Rabbi Samuel Uceda of sixteenth-century Safed.[7] In that work was to be found the classical Jewish division of ages according to their character, beginning with 5, 10, and 13, and concluding with 100,[8] and Uceda chose in his commentary to quote, together with some of the interpretations of the passage that he there anthologized, the above-mentioned poem of Halevi's, which was then attributed, however, to the latter's younger contemporary Abraham ibn Ezra (d. 1167). Although, as scholars have noted, the poem, in which the ages of life are divided exclusively by decades, is not really based on the rabbinic passage in *Pirkei Avot*,[9] it does provide a window on the percep-tion in medieval Jewish culture of the transition from childhood to adult-hood.

The age of twenty, identified by the rabbis with pursuit, though it is not made clear precisely of what,[10] is associated in Halevi's poem with the image of a strutting youth highly suspectible to female charm:

Swift as a hart . . .
Disdainful of discipline . . .
A graceful doe his entrapment and ruin.

Thirty, however, the age of strength for the rabbis, is depicted by the medieval poet, not without ambivalence, as the point by which the young buck has become thoroughly domesticated:

At thirty, into the hands of woman he falls
He rises, and finds himself inside a net
Pressed from all sides by arrows . . .
The hearts' desires of his wife and children.[11]

Although at least one medieval Jewish philosopher saw the period of youth as spanning the two decades from twenty to forty,[12] evidence from the five centuries here to be surveyed suggests that the age of ten was frequently perceived as the end of childhood and the age of thirty associated, for better or worse, with the full responsibility of adulthood. Toward the beginning of our period, we find one of the leading rabbis in Spain, Rabbi Asher b. Yehiel of Toledo (d. 1327), willing to consider a ten-year-old as possessing majority for the purpose of effecting business transactions.[13] And, at the opposite end of our age spectrum, we encounter the proposal on the part of some prominent Spanish and Provençal Jews, during the second "Maimonidean" controversy of the early fourteenth century, that scientific and philosophical studies ("Greek or Chaldean books") be permitted only to those thirty and above, on account of their potentially corrosive impact on traditional beliefs and values.[14]

Thirty seems to have been chosen by these anti-Maimonideans not only because it was the age by which one could be presumed to have already acquired a firm foundation in Jewish learning but also because it was perceived as the age, as Halevi had noted in his poem, by which the undisciplined passions of youth gave way to domestic stability. Thirty, seen by the rabbis as the age at which one attained full strength, was also seen, relatedly, as the age at which physical decline began to set in, following a long tradition in Western thought, of which both St. Augustine and

St. Bernard of Siena were representatives.[15] The way in which thirty could be associated with both stability and decline may be seen, at the end of the sixteenth century, in the sumptuary regulations ("pragmatica") of Padua's Jewish community. These prohibited women below the age of thirty, whether married or not, from stepping out of their home or store "to sit or stand outside for any extended period of time, on weekdays as well as Sabbaths and holidays."[16] Such public exposure on the part of Jewish women over thirty may have been regarded as both less likely and less provocative. Relatedly, Ludovico Ariosto, early in the sixteenth century, had referred in his *Satires* to thirty as "that age when furor, quick to desire and quick to repent, has ceased." These were composed by Ariosto in Ferrara between 1517 and 1525, and it is noteworthy, therefore, that the local Jewish pious confraternity, Hevrat Gemilut Hasadim, decided, in 1517, to grant special status to its members over thirty and to reserve for them certain responsibilities that it would not entrust to its more youthful members.[17]

Ariosto had recommended delaying marriage until the age of thirty, and even in Jewish society, despite the traditional ideal of early marriage for both sexes, one finds the age of thirty sometimes associated with marriage, especially in the case of men. Thus, in midseventeenth-century Venice, the council of the "Italiani" community decided that members would be permitted to vote during their father's lifetime only if they were either thirty years old or married.[18] A century later, Rabbi Aryeh Leib Epstein, who left Lithuania in 1745 to serve as rabbi in Königsberg, commented critically on the custom among the more westernized Jewish men of Prussia to postpone marriage until the age of thirty.[19] In eighteenth-century Poland, however, Jews were marrying much earlier, which prompted some of those interested in halting their demographic growth (for example, the bishop of Kiev in 1760) to propose that they should be permitted to marry only at the age of thirty in the case of men, and twenty-five in the case of women.[20]

Periodic rumors of the imminence of such decrees would sometimes lower the age of marriage among Jews in eastern Europe, according to some testimonies, to six or seven, but the marriage of girls at the age of eleven or twelve was not rare during the eighteenth century, even under normal conditions.[21] The marriage (and not merely betrothal) of girls as early as the age of ten seems to have been quite commonplace among the Jews of late medieval Spain.[22] As a parallel phenomenon, however, it was not unusual, especially in later centuries, for Jewish parents of limited means to send their young daughters into domestic service at an equally young age, sometimes with the express purpose of thereby gaining for them a dowry. In late sixteenth-century Kraków, for example, it appears to have been customary for poor Jewish girls to go into domestic service as early as the age of ten. Parents unwilling to send their daughters into service would forfeit their right to receive welfare payments from the Jewish community, and the girls themselves would later be ineligible to apply for communal aid for their dowries.[23] Leaving home to engage in domestic service was, as we shall see, a common, if not sufficiently recognized, stage of life, especially in early modern times, for Jewish girls and young women, and doing so at the age of ten would undoubtedly mark that age as the end of childhood no less than would the act of entering beneath the marriage canopy.

There were other ways, as well, in which the age of ten came to represent in many Jewish communities, for members of both sexes, a decisive break between childhood and adulthood, especially in early modern times. Thus when the northern Italian Jewish community of Cremona decided, in 1575, on a series of penitential "health regulations" in anticipation of the impending plague that had already struck nearby towns, among the steps taken was the ban on all games of chance for members of the community over the age of ten. Similarly, in Verona, the sumptuary regulations that the community imposed upon itself in 1613 included banning the wearing of masks in the ghetto at night, but permitting them, however, to those who were younger than ten years of age.[24] Although the community of Mantua had previously exempted boys under thirteen and girls under twelve from most limitations imposed by its sumptuary regulations, from 1635 the age of ten was established as the cutoff point for members of both sexes.[25] Late in the eighteenth century the Bikkur Holim confraternity of that same community, which took upon itself the care of the sick among the local Jewish population, stipulated that it would dispense its members (by lot) to stay at the bedside only of those of the infirm who were ten years of age or older. Those between the ages of ten and thirteen would have two members of the confraternity staying the night with them, whereas those over the age of thirteen would be entitled, like other adults in the community, to have four members attending them through the night. It is noteworthy that in this instance the period between ages ten and thirteen is seen as constituting a kind of intermediate stage in life.[26]

A different perspective on the age of ten as constituting a turning point comes from the interesting testimony of a Jewish teacher from Pressburg (Bratislava) in Slovakia, late in the eighteenth century. The teacher, while noting that it was widely acknowledged that parents were obligated to educate their sons until the age of thirteen, laments the fact that it was common for youths in his region to leave school three years earlier. "When he reaches the age of ten he removes the yoke (of education) from his neck, and he can be found outside or in the city's streets, prancing about and causing damage . . . with one sin bringing on another."[27] Requiring education until the age of thirteen was, however, a relatively late development in Jewish society, as can be seen from the fact that the community of Frankfurt in the early 1660s still made education compulsory for boys only until the age of twelve.[28] True, there is evidence in earlier centuries of parents' providing in their wills for the education of sons until the age of thirteen,[29] but one senses a clear difference between rich and poor in this matter.

Moreover, it would appear that the communal efforts, beginning in the sixteenth and seventeenth centuries, to impose on the poor such educational habits of the rich as education until a relatively advanced age were related to concerns not only with the provision of knowledge but also with the establishment of social control. The same Kraków statutes of 1595 that encouraged the daughters of the poor to be sent into service at the age of ten provided their sons with financial aid for education until the age of thirteen, after which parents would be required to send them out of town.

A major concern of the community's educational policy was discipline. Each teacher had to see to it that his students did not run about in the streets ("for our generation is very licentious"); there was also a truant officer whose responsibility it was "to beat and whip those youths" who were found not to be in school, and "to drive them away from the market and from all the streets."[30] The poor of the predominantly Ashkenazic community of Padua were informed in 1624 that they were required to send their sons to study with the community's schoolmaster until they reached the age of thirteen. Any parent who failed to do so would no longer be eligible to receive charity funds. There, too, a truant officer was hired four years later, in 1628, to ensure that the youths came to study. The officer in question, Judah Bianchi, was also—evidently not by mere coincidence—one of the two salaried butchers of the community.[31]

A year later, in a move that could hardly have been unrelated, the neighboring (and also heavily Ashkenazic) community of Verona authorized the committee of four that had been appointed to maintain order in the synagogue "to take particular care that the youths shall not wander to and fro . . . and they may patrol the synagogue with a rod and whip in their hands with which to beat those youths who do not obey them, and no one may interfere."[32] The twin educational policies of using economic pressure to keep the sons of the poor in school and of using truant officers to keep the local youth off the streets may also be found in Verona later in the seventeenth century and early in the eighteenth. There, however, the age of compulsory education was raised over the years from thirteen to sixteen, so that "they would be raised on the knees of their teacher during the prime of their youth," and anyone hiring a servant or apprentice under the age of sixteen was to be severely punished. The stress on social control is evident in the warning to teachers not to leave students unattended even for a moment, "for it is not study in itself that is paramount as much as the practice of diligence in pursuit." Yet although the 1688 educational statutes of Verona authorized the truant officer to use a whip if necessary to drive even older students into school, by 1714 he was explicitly instructed to avoid the use of force.[33]

In other Jewish communities as well, the age of compulsory education was on the rise during the seventeenth and eighteenth centuries. In Pisa it was set at fifteen as early as 1638, and during the first decade of the eighteenth century, the children of the poor in Mantua were required to send their children to school until that age as well, and members of the community were prohibited from hiring any pupils under the age of fourteen. By the 1740s the community forbade the employment of youths under the age of eighteen, and in 1767 it went a step further, stipulating that pupils receiving support from the community were not permitted to leave its school before that age. In the same year, the statutes of Ferrara's Talmud Torah confraternity also required those youths receiving financial aid to continue their studies until the age of eighteen. The statutes provided for two beadles whose duties included patrolling the streets twice a day (morning and afternoon) in search of errant students, but they did not even hint at the use of physical force. Similarly, in the Mantua statutes of 1767 teachers were warned not to hit their students "in a hostile or cruel way," and the two beadles appointed were allowed no harsher measures than the denial of breakfast to students guilty of laziness or bad behavior.[34]

Further to the east, eighteenth-century evidence for the extension of education until the age of eighteen may be found in the criticism, on the part of the Lithuanian kabbalist Rabbi Alexander Susskind (d. 1793) of Grodno, of those who removed their sons from Torah study at the ages of sixteen and seventeen in order for them to engage in commerce.[35] An intermediate stage in the move toward age eighteen may be discerned in the community of Metz, where in 1689 full-time schooling was made obligatory for youths until the age of fourteen, and at least one hour per day of (religious) study was required between the ages of fourteen and eighteen.[36] We have seen, then, on a number of levels, a tendency between the sixteenth and eighteenth centuries to postpone until the age of eighteen various rights of adulthood (to perform ritual slaughter, to betroth a woman, to leave school) that had previously been associated with the age of thirteen, and this tendency may reflect a growing recognition of adolescence as an intermediate (and problematic) stage in life.

Such a sense of eighteen as a turning point may be seen in the decision, for example, on the part of the founding members of the Zerizim confraternity in Asti, in 1619, to limit membership to youths *under* the age of eighteen, and, on the other hand, of the council of Verona's Jewish community five years later to permit only those *over* eighteen to stand guard over the synagogue.[37] Nevertheless, it is clear that eighteen was not yet the age at which one was fully accepted into the community. In the same 1624 Verona statutes that stipulated eighteen as the minimum age for standing guard, twenty is given as the age below which one would not normally serve as precentor *(hazzan)* in the synagogue on Sabbaths or holidays. It was feared that those under that age might err in their recitation of the prayers and thereby cause much laughter and levity in the synagogue—presumably on the part of other young men.[38]

Some two decades earlier, when the Mantuan physician and polymath Abram Portaleone drew up his last will and testament, he too gave expression to the widespread sense that the age of twenty marked a significant turning point in the achievement of maturity. In his 1605 will, Portaleone requested that his three sons remain together after his death until the youngest of them had reached the age of twenty. He seems to have been referring not only to financial matters but also to joint residence, for it was not rare for even married brothers to share the same household.[39]

In many Italian communities, however, it was not age but rather marriage that was seen as the prerequisite for achieving full acceptance as a responsible adult. Thus, in late 1591, Verona's Jewish community council decided that thenceforth no individual who was not married or had not been married previously could be chosen for any communal position. Less than four years later, apparently by no mere coincidence, a nearly identical proposal concerning the unmarried was passed by the community council of the Jews in neighboring Padua.[40] Indeed, as Baron noted in 1942, in Jewish society "unmarried men generally lived under a cloud of suspicion and were victims of widespread ostracism."[41]

This distrust could take different forms in different places at different times, but it was generally linked to the perception that bachelors were helplessly enslaved to a continuous battery of unchaste thoughts, which could easily lead to unchaste actions. As early as talmudic times, the view had been expressed (*Kiddushin* 29b) that one who had not married by the age of twenty would spend the rest of his days either in (sexual) sin or in its contemplation, and this had led a number of later authorities (such as Rabbi Asher of Toldeo) to suggest that after the age of twenty a man could be forced by the local Jewish authorities to take a wife. Although Rabbi Moses Isserles, in sixteenth-century Poland, testified that in his day no such coercion was used,[42] one does encounter various ways in which, in early modern times, bachelors over twenty were stigmatized. Thus the French traveler Misson, after visiting Italy, reported that the Jews there, "and particularly those of Rome, as some of themselves assured me, do scrupulously observe the Law that enjoins them to marry at twenty years of age at the farthest, under pain of ignominy, and being treated as a person living in sin." Although in practice many Italian Jewish men *did* marry well after the age of twenty, the testimony given to Misson that bachelors over that age were regarded as if they were living in sin would appear to be no exaggeration. A mideighteenth-century ordinance of the Jewish community of Jerusalem, it may be noted, denied bachelors between the ages of twenty and sixty not merely the privilege of holding public office, but the very right of residence in the holy city.[43]

The ordinance pointed to a certain widespread paradox in the status of young men in Jewish society. On the one hand, one achieved increasing status and respectability as one moved from adolescence into adulthood, but on the other, reaching a certain age while still a bachelor could undermine one's status and invite suspicion. The ideal of early marriage as a means of avoiding sexual sin, especially for men, was mentioned by many moralists in early modern times, but it was generally observed by relatively few beyond the very wealthy and the very pious. Regarding the latter, we have the testimony of Rabbi Abraham ha-Levi Berukhim about his fellow pietists in sixteenth-century Palestine: "There are some who see that their sons and daughters are married at the age of thirteen and fourteen, in contrast to those who wait until they reach the age of twenty-five or older out of financial considerations, by which time they have already committed a number of sins for which capital punishment is deserved." And regarding the former, we have the account of the rabbi Joseph Hahn, who lived in Germany at the start of the seventeenth century. He wrote that the wealthy members of his community tended to marry off their sons at the age of fourteen or fifteen.[44] Jacob Katz has written persuasively of Ashkenazic Jewry in general during the sixteenth to eighteenth centuries, stating that although parents who arranged an early marriage for their children might have been considered praiseworthy, "it would be a mistake to suppose that such early marriages were the rule among society as a whole."[45]

In sixteenth-century Italy, even a kabbalist such as Rabbi Abraham of San Angelo was able to express the opinion that his son, at the age of sixteen, was still too young for marriage, even though he was already engaged.[46] Ariel Toaff has recently suggested that among Italian Jewry between the midfifteenth and midsixteenth centuries, twenty-four to twenty-five was the average age for marriage among men and twenty to twenty-one for women, with the wealthy classes marrying much earlier than the poorer ones. At the beginning of the seventeenth century, some of the (male) pious confraternities in that community set marriage *or* the age of twenty-five as a prerequisite for membership or the holding of office, suggesting that, among young men, bachelorhood would commonly terminate at the age of twenty-five.[47]

Not only in Verona and Padua, as we have seen, but also in such diverse places as Carpentras in the midseventeenth century and Russia in the eighteenth, bachelors were often denied full membership in the Jewish community.[48] It was also not uncommon for Jewish pious confraternities in central Europe to deny membership to those who were not yet married, or to relegate the unmarried to an inferior status, denying them, for example (as in the case of a Moravian burial society in 1655) the right to vote.[49] In some cases, a year of marriage was required for admission to a confraternity, and two years of marriage or more were sometimes required for certain positions of communal responsibility, particularly for holding the more advanced rabbinical titles, such as Morenu.[50] In the eighteenth century, that title was denied to Moses Mendelssohn by Rabbi Jonathan Eibeschutz explicitly on the grounds that he was not yet married.[51]

There were other expressions, in the ritual sphere, of the stigmatization of bachelors. According to one widespread custom since medieval times, an unmarried *kohen* (priest) could not perform the priestly blessing in the synagogue, a custom explained in the highly influential, late thirteenth-century mystical work, the *Zohar*, on the grounds that God's holiness could not dwell in the body of an unmarried man, who was essentially removed from the domain of sanctity.[52] It may have been under the influence of this custom that the Jews of Tenes in North Africa decided, in the late fourteenth or early fifteenth century, to debar all bachelors from being called to the Torah in the synagogue, fearing that an unmarried male would be unable, even for a few minutes, to curb his sinful thoughts.[53] The *Zohar* had regarded masturbation as a sin so severe that no penance for it was possible, and it is noteworthy that kabbalistic moralists from the sixteenth century on, when railing against onanistic practices, commonly referred to them as "the sins of youth."[54] Some, such as R. Meir Poppers (d. 1662) of Jerusalem, sought to limit kabbalistic study to those who were both married and over twenty.[55] At the end of the seventeenth century, the community council of Verona decided that, regardless of age, no one unmarried would be permitted to elevate the Torah scroll at the synagogue service.[56]

By that point even the *podestà* (mayor) of Verona was complaining of what it considered the scandalous behavior of some of the young Jewish men in the community. A broadside of 1682 described a state of affairs in which, in the ghetto, there were "diverse Hebrews, particularly young ones, who led a relaxed and scandalous life, giving rise to talk and commotion, with disturbance of the peace of that Place" *(diversi Hebrei, particolarmente della gioventù, che menano vita rilasciata, e scandalosa, con delatione d'Armi, causando sussuri, e commottioni, con perturbatione della quite di quel Luogo)*.[57] It is not surprising that, during the same period, the Jewish community, as mentioned above, raised the age of compulsory education from thirteen to sixteen with the express purpose of keeping the young men away from the streets and marketplaces.

In the pre-ghetto period as well, the exposure of the young to the streets and marketplaces had been a matter of communal concern. As early as 1555, Verona's community council had decided that no unmarried male would be permitted to promenade on Sabbaths and (Jewish) holidays, whether during the day or night hours, in the city's central marketplace, at the risk of a fine. Shortly afterward, however, the prohibition was emended to permit those who had reached the age of thirteen to promenade there (only) after the midday meal on Sabbaths and holidays, but in groups no larger than two.[58] The document is an important one, for it touches on a number of issues that, over time, were central to the lives of youth in Jewish society—the (perceived) danger of exposure to the streets and markeplaces, with which, paradoxically, the young appear sometimes to have had an almost ritualized connection; the special status that marriage could confer and the suspicion shown toward the unmarried; and the matter of those Sabbath and holiday leisure activities especially cultivated by the young.

In early fourteenth-century Spain, Rabbi Asher of Toledo had explained the rabbinic view that a teacher of Scripture was permitted to accept a fee on the grounds that he served also as a guard for his students, that "they shall not wander in the streets and alleyways and cause damage and become educated in evil ways." Three centuries later, Rabbi Azariah Figo of Venice (d. 1647) saw the rabbinic adage recommending that sons be "set between the knees of rabbinical scholars" (Berakhot 28b) as stressing the importance of diligence in study so that the children, by sharing continually the company of their teachers, would not "wander to and fro in the streets and thoroughfares" where they would "notice every woman passing by . . . married and unmarried, good and bad, and they would actually be led to follow their hearts and eyes."[59] At around the same time Rabbi Isaac of Posen, in his popular moralistic work *Lev Tov* (1620), advised that children should be kept in the *heder* all day and not be permitted to run in the streets, "for this makes them insolent, and causes them to forget what they have learned."[60]

Such roaming of the streets seems to have been especially prevalent among the Jewish youth on Sabbaths and holidays, and to have aroused, over the centuries, no small measure of criticism and discomfort on the part of their elders. Rabbi Pinhas ha-Levi of Barcelona explained in the introduction to his *Sefer ha-Hinnukh,* a work on the 613 commandments written in late thirteenth-century Spain, that he had composed the book in the hope that "perhaps, as a result, the young men will become more interested in them, giving them attention on Sabbaths and holidays, and desist from raving wildly in the city streets."[61] Early in the sixteenth century, in a move reminiscent of the Veronese statute cited earlier, one of the communities of Spanish exiles residing in Manissa (Turkey) issued a decree prohibiting those "youths and young men" who were in the habit of "going for a stroll each Sabbath outside the town to certain places where serious and evil sins are committed" from continuing to do so. The effectiveness of the decree, it may be noted, lasted only until the Sabbath before Purim (Shabbat Zakhor). On that occasion, we learn from a responsum of Rabbi Joseph Karo, a group of "base fellows" went out promenading nonetheless, claiming that the prohibition extended only to the one specific place mentioned (evidently a brothel), "and they were followed by many of the youths and young men, and by some worthless and reckless men (cf. Judges 9:4)," all of whom went promenading and broke the agreement.[62] The prohibition was not totally ignored, but only conveniently interpreted as narrowly as possible, so that the young men went walking *among* questionable establishments, but not *into* them. The carnivalistic Purim spirit may have spurred those "base fellows" on to joyfully claiming what (they believed) was rightfully theirs, just as festivity and justice had often intermingled, sometimes dangerously, in medieval celebrations of that holiday.[63]

In some of the eighteenth-century Ashkenazic communities, the particular concern was with the Sabbath and holiday promenading of young men *and* women, which would sometimes take them outside "the street of the Jews," leading, in the opinion of the authorities, not only to desecration of the Sabbath, but also to "much lasciviousness." Such promenading was explicitly prohibited by communal statute in Eisenstadt during the first half of the eighteenth century (with specific references to servants and maidservants) and in Alsace in the later half of the century. In 1806 similar efforts were made in London to fight strolling with study. The committee of the Ashkenazi Talmud Torah (an educational association) was disturbed by "many irregularities" that it believed were resulting from the Sabbath promenading of the boys enrolled in its school. It decided, therefore, to keep them in school for part of the day with "religious and moral lessons."[64]

In addition to promenading, ball games and the imbibing of strong liquor emerge as popular forms of Sabbath amusement among Jewish young men. When, in 1559, Rabbi Moses Provenzali of Mantua penned a responsum on the permissibility of playing ball on the Sabbath, he referred to it as a characteristic activity of the youths. Similarly, when nearly two decades later the community of Padua took steps to prohibit ball games (apparently tennis, as in the case of Provenzali's responsum) on the Sabbath, or at any time in the synagogue courtyard, it was anticipated that the transgressors would be among the young men. The decree stated that a householder would be obliged to dismiss his servant or apprentice *(man-hig)* when he was pronounced as such, "and he shall not permit him to return to his house until he renounces his evil path and pays the penalty; and similarly a father toward his son."[65] Rabbi Joseph Hahn, in early seventeenth-century Frankfurt, criticized those young men whose practice it was to "sanctify the day" on Saturday morning with hard liquor, getting so drunk after the morning synagogue service that they would forget to recite the "additional prayer" *(musai)* for Sabbaths.[66] Later in the seventeenth century, one particular Sabbath, the Sabbath after Purim, was recognized in Worms as "belonging" to the students and young men of the community. After a festive procession to the synagogue, they took over the proceedings there, mocking their elders and engaging in other forms of ritual reversal, all of which culminated in heavy drinking on the following day.[67]

The day that was most widely recognized, however, as a festival of youth (and especially students) was that of Lag ba-Omer, the spring day on which the seven-week period of mourning observed between the holidays of Passover and Shavuot was temporarily suspended. Its observance as a festival of yeshiva students is attested to first in fifteenth-century Mainz and then in sixteenth-century Piedmont, where it was customary on that day for the rabbis to hold banquets for their students. Relatedly, in 1619 a youth confraternity known as Havurat Zerizim was founded in the Piedmontese community of Asti on Lag ba-Omer, and its annual confraternal celebration took place on that day as well. The element of role reversal in the day's observance is perhaps most noticeable later in the seventeenth century in the community of Worms, where Lag ba-Omer was one of the two days in the year on which the teacher was required by custom to distribute at his own expense not only cakes but also hard liquor to his students as he emerged from the synagogue in the morning. The other day on which he was required to do so was the fifteenth of Ab, which in many communities and yeshivas was the last day of studies before the summer vacation.[68]

Another festive and sometimes disruptive feature of the culture of youth in both Italy and the Ashkenazic communities north of the Alps during the seventeenth century was the recognized right of youths, under certain circumstances, to demand a portion of a bridegroom's dowry. In Padua this took the form of a version of the Italian *mattinata*, known elsewhere as charivari. A communal statute of 1627 stipulated that every widower marrying a widow would be required to pay a fee equivalent to one-half percent of his dowry, which would be divided half and half between the yeshiva (for purchase of candles) and the young men of his neighborhood. If the widower did not deposit these funds with the elders of the community before his wedding, as was required, it was decreed that "anyone who desires may rattle and perform a *mattinata* as is the custom of Padua," but if he did, none would be permitted "to clamor with any sort of noisy instrument," at risk of a substantial fine.[69] Significantly, the community council saw reason to add that not only would fathers be responsible for their sons, but also masters for their servants, suggesting that members of the latter category not only participated in the noisemaking but were also entitled, together with the other neighborhood youths, to a share of the dowry.

This, in fact, was a matter of controversy later in the seventeenth century in some of the German-Jewish communities. Traditionally, we learn from a document of 1698, it had been customary for any bridegroom passing through Bamberg and the communities in its vicinity to distribute among those local youths engaged in religious study a gift from his dowry. Recently, however, other youths, including servants, who were described as "lacking in knowledge and wisdom," had also begun making allegedly rude and excessive demands of the visiting bridegrooms. It was decided, therefore, that in communities with at least six householders and a resident teacher, the bridegroom's gift would be divided equally between those local youths engaged in study and those (including servants) who worked for their living. In a community, however, that housed an advanced talmudic academy, only those youths who had acquired a fair degree of talmudic learning would be entitled to divide between themselves a percentage of the visiting bridegroom's dowry.[70] No explicit mention is made of the consequences for the bridegroom of nonpayment, but one suspects that traditions of "rough music" developed among Jewish youth north of the Alps as well. The document does point rather explicitly, however, to the tensions that could develop between young men of the working class and those whose intellectual abilities (or parents' wealth) allowed them to continue their studies, with the former expressing a rather bold unwillingness to honor some of the traditional privileges of the latter.

The dowry had become a matter of concern among young Jewish men in early modern Europe for quite another reason: the widespread custom of shortchanging on the part of the father-in-law, after promising his daughter's future husband a sum appreciably higher than he was actually able to afford. Early in the sixteenth century, Rabbi Joseph Arli, who had frequently earned his living as a tutor in the homes of the wealthy, attempted, in a letter to his future son-in-law, to convince him to accept a dowry of 150 scudi rather than the 250 he had promised, basing his request in part on his need to educate his son as well as marry off his daughter.[71] Rabbi Isaac da Lattes, who succeeded Arli as tutor in the Rieti household in Siena, married his daughter in the late 1560s to Rabbi Mordecai of Foligno, and also was unable to pay out the entire sum he had promised as dowry. Rabbi Mordecai demonstrated his displeasure by failing to address Lattes as "my father-in-law" in the letters they exchanged and by not signing off as "your son-in-law," omissions that were rather pointedly acknowledged by Lattes.[72]

At the end of the sixteenth century, the Polish rabbi Mordecai Jaffe, who had spent considerable time in Prague and Venice, wrote of an incident in which "the (wedding) canopy was erected but the groom refused to go through with the ceremony since he had not received the full sum of the dowry." An argument ensued, at the conclusion of which "it was offered to another that he accept the dowry and step beneath the canopy immediately, and he agreed." His younger contemporary Rabbi Isaiah Horowitz (d. 1630), who had served in the rabbinate in Frankfurt and Prague, was also aware of "those who are in the habit of deceiving the groom in any way they can in the matter of the dowry and of forcing him to marry even without receiving the entire sum promised him." He added rather dryly, "It is not clear to me how they justify this practice."[73]

The few extant autobiographies we have from this period frequently make mention of this questionable yet common practice. Asher Levy, who grew up in Metz and left home at the age of fourteen to study in Prague, recounts how he became engaged in 1620, at the age of twenty-one, with plans to be married slightly more than two years later. The engagement lasted, however, nearly three years, and even during that period his future father-in-law did not manage to raise the promised sum, paying him only 60 percent of it.[74] This was precisely the percentage that Rabbi Joseph Arli had sought to convince his son-in-law to accept nearly a century earlier in northern Italy.

From the autobiography of the Venetian rabbi Leon Modena (d. 1648), who married off two daughters in the early decades of the seventeenth century, we learn of some of the difficulties involved. The first daughter, Diana, was engaged at the age of thirteen, at which point Leon pledged her a dowry of 450 ducats in cash and another 200 in clothing, relying, as he later wrote, "on heaven's mercy," for the sum was no less than thrice his annual salary. The engagement, not surprisingly, lasted more than two years (a period of time then common), and as the date of the marriage approached, the bride's family, as her father later recalled, was "in a great dither trying to come up with what was needed for her dowry." Finally, he wrote, "after much trouble and grief, we collected what I had pledged to give her." Despite these tribulations, Leon promised an even larger dowry to his next daughter, Esther, who was engaged at the age of fifteen and whose wedding date was twice postponed on account of the difficulties entailed in raising the necessary funds. When the wedding did take place, in September of 1620, Leon felt that it had been "through God's kindness," for he had somehow managed to give her even a bit more than the total of 800 ducats he had originally promised.

He had managed to do this, although this went unmentioned in his autobiography, with the aid of two grants (the latter of which was approved on the very day of Esther's wedding) from the Hasi Betulot confraternity of Venice (founded in 1576) devoted to the dowering of brides. This somewhat irregular favor of a second grant was apparently related to Leon's earlier having served the confraternity as its scribe. So was the fact, apparently, that Esther managed to receive dotal aid from the confraternity despite being, even at the time of her marriage, under the age of eighteen—the minimum age set by its founders for applicants for aid from its coffers.[75] This was evidently related to the relatively late age of marriage of most Italian Jewish girls at the time, which was linked, as was the extended period of engagement then also customary,[76] to the difficulties involved in putting together an honorable dowry—of which confraternal aid was rarely more than a small fraction. Just after midcentury, however, the confraternity for the dowering of brides established by the Levantine Jewish community of Venice in 1652 set fifteen as the minimum age for applicants, and this policy continued through at least 1689.[77]

Fifteen was also the age established among some of the communities of eastern Europe earlier in the seventeenth century. In 1623 the Lithuanian Council decided to begin allocating dotal aid to prospective brides among the poor over fifteen years of age, but five years later it introduced an interesting policy change that distinguished between applicants from within the communities and those from the outlying areas. Both groups were eligible for grants of twenty-five gold florins each, but young women from outlying areas were required, before applying for aid from one of the communities, to submit written proof that they had served as a maid-servant in the home of a local householder for at least three years since the age of twelve. During their years of domestic service, these girls were to receive a fixed fee of ten florins per annum, which would be paid by their employers directly to the community's overseers. Thus, when they eventually applied for communal aid toward their dowries, they would be receiving funds that they themselves had actually earned. A young woman from the outlying areas who applied for dotal aid and had not spent the requisite period in domestic service would, according to the Lithuanian statute of 1628, be assigned to the home of the community's leading taxpayer, provided he could offer suitable quarters.[78]

Although Baron has asserted somewhat apologetically that "there is no evidence . . . that these illiberal norms were ever adhered to," the case of seventeenth-century Poznan would seem to suggest otherwise. There, as in Lithuania, the community council began early in the 1620s to discuss the matter of dotal aid to daughters of the poor, and in 1628 (the same year as the above-mentioned statute) reference is first made to a communal body known as the *memmunim 'al ha-betulot,* or trustees of the virgins. Members of the community would apparently "rent" young women from these trustees for fixed periods of time, paying them a set fee that was presumably recycled back as dowry aid upon their marriage. This system is still alluded to in documents of the Poznan community in 1685. In 1726 the Ashkenazic community of Hamburg-Altona passed legislation whereby needy young women could obtain dotal aid by first working three years in domestic service, as in the Lithuanian statute of a century earlier. If their work was found satisfactory, they would receive a sum of twenty marks from the community.[79]

Connections between dotal aid for young women and domestic service could also take different forms. In Venice the aforementioned confraternity of the Levantine Jews decided in 1664 that each year one or two maidservants who had served in the home of a member would be eligible for aid, provided they had served for six years and were found to be both poor and worthy *("povere e benemerite")*. By 1689 the requirement for eligibility was increased to eight consecutive years of domestic service, which reflects both the early age at which daughters of the poorer classes would enter into service and the relatively late age at which they would marry. It was also not rare in the seventeenth and eighteenth centuries for householders to assure a maidservant's dowry in their will, or, as in the community of Metz, to actually take upon themselves, in rather paternalistic fashion, the expenditure of the wedding celebration itself.[80]

Jewish servants, both male and female, who were generally both young and unmarried, were an integral if sometimes neglected component in many a Jewish household, and their presence must be taken into consideration in any evaluation of the dynamics of household life. In early seventeenth-century Frankfurt, Rabbi Joseph Hahn Nordlingen devoted two consecutive sections at the end of his influential work on Jewish law and custom, *Yosif Ometz*, to the two ostensibly related topics of raising children and "dealing with the members of one's household."[81] The latter section dealt primarily with a specific sector of the household—that of domestic servants, to whom a paternalistic attitude was shown, especially in matters of religious observance. The master was exhorted to educate his (Jewish) male and female servants in the details of the dietary laws and those of the Sabbath, and to command the maidservants, in particular, to recite their daily prayers and the grace after meals, "for in all these matters they are unjustifiably very lenient." But even greater attention was devoted to another area of considerable laxity—nocturnal visits by men to the maidservants' quarters. Rabbi Joseph required the householder to take every precaution at night, so that while he slept upstairs with his wife, "no man [should] remain below with the maidservants, whether they are virgin or widowed, for . . . we have seen many obstacles resulting from this."[82]

To some of these obstacles we shall return, but Rabbi Joseph also sheds interesting light on the social profile of some of those young men who, in his day, entered into service in the homes of others. Not all were youths who, at the age of thirteen or fourteen terminated their religious studies abruptly, whether on account of limited funds or limited abilities, and began a period of apprenticeship or domestic service. In some cases, we learn, a package deal was struck, so that a householder accepting a yeshiva student into his home for meals, whether on weekdays or Sabbaths,[83] could also arrange with him that he would regularly perform certain household duties in return.[84] As opposed to members of this rather scholarly class of servants, however, not many of those who served as simple apprentices in their youth left any sort of written record of their experiences. One who did, albeit at the very end of the period under discussion, was the Anglo-Jewish pugilist Daniel Mendoza, born in London in 1764, who, according to his own account, was "of the middling class of society" and was sent "at a very early age to a Jewish school." Before he celebrated his bar mitzvah, however, he was already serving the first of several apprentice-ships that involved living in the homes of others. "As our family was very large, my father was accustomed to place his children in different situations and employments very early in life. Accordingly before I had attained the age of thirteen I went to live with a glass-cutter." By the time he was sixteen he was already in his third residence in service, this time with a tea dealer (before that he was with a greengrocer, and he would later be with a tobacconist) in the defense of whose honor he first attracted attention as a boxer. And Mendoza's experience, it must be stressed, was not that of the poor but of the (lower) middle class.[85]

Just as there were many sorts of young men among the Jews of early modern Europe who found themselves living for a time, and providing services, in the homes of others, so too could a variety of circumstances propel young women, and even girls, into periods of domestic service. In addition to the schemes already mentioned linking dotal aid with such service, the loss of one or more parents could also initiate such a stage in the female life cycle. An example of this may be glimpsed in the story of Sarah Eisik-Katz of late sixteenth-century Padua. When she and her sister were left without parents after the death of their father, Jacob, during the plague of 1575, the community arranged to place Sarah in the home of one of the local householders, who let her go, however, some three years later. In February of 1578 she was placed in the home of one of the community's more prominent members, who committed himself to keep-ing Sarah for a period of four years, provided she earned her keep by working in his house and received no additional salary beyond room and board. After slightly more than four years, her second employer informed the Paduan community council that he would keep Sarah no longer, but that he had arranged with Rabbi Samuel Judah Katzenellenbogen, chief rabbi of Venice, to take her in as a maidservant for a period of two years (renewable for another two) at a salary of five ducats per year, with which she would provide her own clothing.[86] Her sister, who had been serving in the home of another Paduan householder, had been informed by the latter in May of 1579 that he would keep her no longer, and that he was passing her on to his brother-in-law in Venice, who promised to employ her as a maidservant for three years. It may well be that when Rabbi Katzenellen-bogen turned to the Jewish community of Padua in January 1586 with a request for dowry aid on behalf of an unnamed virgin,[87] it was for one of the two Eisik-Katz sisters, whom difficult circumstances had forced to leave their native town and to work as maidservants in the teeming Ghetto of the city of lagoons.

Their precise ages are not known to us, but we do know that rather than making a long-term career of it, household servants in early modern Europe tended to be in service for only a specific period in their life, and they were overwhelmingly young. In early fifteenth-century Florence, according to the famous *catasto* of 1427, 41.5 percent of the known male servants and 34 percent of the known female servants were between eight and seventeen years old.[88] Although such statistical figures are hard to come by for a Jewish society, we know, for example, according to censuses conducted in the three Italian Piedmont communities of Carmagnola, Alessandria, and Casale in 1734 (225 households in all), that the average age of the thirty-three maidservants living in the homes of others was twenty-three, and of the twenty-six manservants, male clerks, and appren-tices living under such circumstances, twenty-five. Rather strikingly, an overwhelming 88 percent of both groups fell between the ages of thirteen and thirty. It is evident, then, that no discussion of young people in early modern Jewish society can afford to ignore this class of individuals.[89]

Carlo Cipolla has found that in the cities of Europe during the fifteenth to seventeenth centuries, domestic servants represented about 10 percent of the total population. The percentage of families possessing at least one servant was, moreover, often quite high, as in the case of Florence, whose 1551 census indicates that only 54 percent had no servants at all.[90] Jewish statistics are hard to come by before the eighteenth century, and even then they are quite spotty, but a picture does nevertheless emerge. We do know that in late fifteenth-century Nuremberg, 24 percent of the Jewish men were in some sort of service (either as domestics or teachers) in the homes of others, and that fourteen of fifteen households had at least one such person resident.[91] In the Piedmontese community of Alessandria the percentage of servants (including clerks and apprentices) living in the homes of others remained fairly constant at 7 percent between 1734 and 1761, and the percentage of Jewish households with at least one servant ranged between 20 and 30. In Trieste in 1769, servants made up about 10 percent of the total Jewish population, and at least one, whether male or female, was to be found in nearly a quarter of the Jewish households. In some instances, as in the small Piedmontese community of Ivrea whose ten households were headed, in 1791, primarily by merchants and bankers, 70 percent had live-in maidservants or clerks, who consisted of 14 percent of the local Jewish population.[92] Among Polish Jewry the figures were evidently lower. In the region of Lublin, according to the census of 1764, some 7 percent of the Jewish families, whether rural or urban, had Jewish maidservants living with them. In the relatively small community of Opatow, the percentage of Jewish households with servants of either sex was, during the 1760s, not much higher than 8.[93]

No discussion, moreover, of the lives of servants, who were generally not only young but also unmarried, can ignore the sexual element that often shaped their relations with their masters, with each other, and with other members of the community. In the Polish community of Opatow, rather full documentation has survived of two cases involving sexual exploitation of female domestic servants by men other than their employers in the two decades detween 1759 and 1778.[94] Exploitation by employers was far more common and, except in cases resulting in pregnancy, generally went unremarked. In Casale, one of the three Piedmontese communities mentioned above, a householder named Yedidiah Luzzatto, who happened also to have been a member of a local Jewish pious confraternity, was accused by his maidservant, Rachel Foa, of having been the father of her child as a consequence of having seduced her on several occasions during the spring and early summer of 1715, including the first night of Passover! Luzzato, for his part, denied the claim of paternity, asserting "with arrogance and contempt" before the investigating rabbinical court "that he had always had intercourse with her unnaturally, with mere contact between their organs." Rachel's father, Joshua Isaac Foa, it might be added, was a fellow member with Luzzatto in Casale's Ner Mitzvah confraternity. Although this may have played a role in the latter's decision to hire her, it seems not to have prevented his taking advantage of her particular vulnerability once she had come under his roof.[95] And under a single roof, there was often enough more than one potential suitor. In Alessandria more than 10 percent of the Jewish households in 1734 had both male and female staff living there simultaneously, and two decades later 14 percent of the households maintained such an arrangement.[96] This, of course, could lead to complications, such as the sort that occurred in the home of Rabbi Jacob Saraval of Mantua in 1778, when a servant of his seduced a young maidservant who had come from Modena to work there,[97] expecting, no doubt, to find herself in a wholesome and God-fearing environment.

Liaisons of this sort between male and female servants living under a single roof, described sometimes in fairly graphic terms, had been, since the sixteenth century, a favorite topic in Jewish imaginative writing in Italy, whether in dramatic comedies such as those of Leone Sommo de Portaleone of Mantua (circa 1550) or in the highly literary letters sometimes composed by Jewish youths (such as those of the noted Rieti family of Siena) as classroom exercises.[98] The link between maidservants and sexuality had earlier been pursued by the celebrated poet Immanuel of Rome (d. circa 1330), who in one of the more lighthearted sections of his *Cantos*, or *Mahberot*, presented an imaginary exchange of poetic banter between himself and a contemporary, in which he responded in verse to the latter's brief but seemingly endless questions. When asked, "Will you lend me so and so your maidservant?" Immanuel had himself replied, with a biblically derived double entendre (paraphrasing Genesis 23:11): "I give her to you in the presence of my people, bury your dead."[99] This section of his work was somewhat playfully entitled "She'elot u-Teshuvot" (Responsa), the name then (and now) commonly used to designate the learned collections of rabbinical replies to queries in matters of Jewish law. In the "real" rabbinical responsa of his time and of following generations, however, allusions to the sometimes commonplace sexual intimacy between young Jewish maidservants and their (Jewish) employers are often encountered as well.

In those, for example, of Rabbi Solomon ibn Adret of Barcelona (d. circa 1310), the leading rabbinical authority of his time for Spanish and Provençal Jewry, a number of questions related to this theme are discussed. One deals with the case of a man who brought a young woman into his home, "according to her consent and that of her parents, in order to serve him and work for him." The employer, however, had been married for ten years without his wife's giving birth or even becoming pregnant. Shortly after the new maidservant moved into his home she became pregnant by him, after which he took her as his (second) wife. The matter came to Rabbi Solomon's attention only because of the question of the legality of the marriage, in light of the well-known enactment against polygamy attributed to the eleventh-century sage Rabbi Gershom of Mainz. In another instance, which occurred in Toledo, complicated questions regarding paternity arose when the master of a Jewish household declined at first to recognize as his own the son born to his Jewish maidservant, refusing even to attend the circumcision ceremony, but he later relented and provided the child both with material support and paternal affection.[100] If the householder had not died, however, leaving a substantial estate to which his son by another woman claimed exclusive right, the story would not have surfaced in ibn Adret's responsa, for such liaisons were far from unusual among Spanish Jewry at that time.

Just how far from uncommon they were is further underscored in a letter written to Rabbi Asher of Toledo (d. 1327). The correspondent mentioned in one of his queries to the rabbi, almost in passing, that "in this land it is customary for them [male employers] to be intimate with the maidens who work in their homes."[101] The same correspondent asked whether, in a case in which rumors had spread that a householder was maintaining intimate relations with his maidservant, her parents were entitled to file a complaint that she be removed, to preserve the family's honor. Rabbi Asher's response was that "not only was the girl's family entitled to protest, but the Jewish courts *required* him to discharge her," for it was well known, he maintained, that such servant girls are too embarrassed to visit the ritual bath (intended primarily for married women) and their masters were thus guilty of the sin of having sex with the menstrually impure.[102] More noteworthy, however, than the fact that Rabbi Asher saw the technical infringement of the laws of menstrual impurity as constituting the major problem in the intimate relations that frequently developed between young Jewish maidservants and their masters, is his very deft use of the past tense in referring to the intervention of Jewish courts in such instances. Rabbi Asher understood that in fourteenth-century Spain, rabbinical authorities could object in theory to such liaisons, but generally had to be reconciled to them in practice.

Later in the fourteenth century, Rabbi Nissim Gerondi (d. circa 1375) dealt with a somewhat different case (apparently in his own community of Barcelona)—that of sexual relations between a young maidservant and the son of her rather eminent employer. Here, too, the question arose only on account of a technical problem. After the girl became pregnant, the young man provided her with separate quarters where he would visit her "as a man entering the home of his concubine." Some months after giving birth, however, she consented to marry another. Rabbi Nissim was asked whether the young woman was required to wait three months before marrying, as would be the case for a married woman, in order to ascertain that she was not already pregnant from the father of her first child. His ruling, which would appear to have been influenced by the conventionality of such concubinage, was that theirs was to be regarded as a licit rather than promiscuous relationship, and the young woman would consequently have to wait the customary three months before entering beneath the marital canopy.[103] Had no one asked for her hand, however, her liaison with her employer's son would hardly have merited discussion. It may be noted that some generations later Samuel Abrabanel (b. 1473), son of the noted Don Isaac and scion of the outstanding Iberian Jewish family of his age, fathered a "natural child" by a Jewish "concubine," who had probably been a maidservant in the family household.[104]

Among the Jews of Renaissance Italy, to which Samuel eventually made his way after the Spanish expulsion, one encounters examples as well, sometimes rather striking, of more than merely sexual relations between members of the servant class and their masters—of both genders. The difficulties of male servants in achieving the financial independence necessary for marriage, and especially of maidservants in acquiring the funds necessary for a proper dowry, undoubtedly contributed to this situation, as did, most probably, the frustrations endemic to the arranged marriages customary among members of the more established classes who employed them. One may also cite in this connection the sexual permissiveness seen since Burckhardt to have been especially characteristic of Renaissance culture, and which some historians, notably Roth, have seen as influencing Jewish society in Italy as well.[105]

An instructive if not necessarily typical case was reported in the early 1540s. A young man serving as a banking apprentice, managing a loan bank while living in his employer's home, seduced one of his employer's engaged daughters, and, after she became pregnant, fled to Rome. There he was hired in a similar capacity by another Jewish banker, and also continued his sexual adventures, this time with the married daughter-in-law of his employer. Her husband, however, was quite slow in recognizing that there had been any wrongdoing between the two, even when his mother reported finding them in bed together in their home at night! Only after repeated reports from several sources who had seen the rather shameless couple together (especially during the hours of evening prayer, when the male members of the household were in the synagogue), and after his wife gave birth to a second child (of whose paternity he was not certain), did the hapless husband turn for rabbinical advice to Rabbi Isaac de Lattes, from whom we learn the story.[106]

At around the same time, we learn from Rabbi Isaac's esteemed colleague to the north, Rabbi Meir Katzenellenbogen of Padua (d. 1565), of another question of bastardy, apparently in Venice, resulting from a then more common type situation—the allegedly ongoing relationship between a certain Moses Ovadiah (later a member of a pious confraternity there) and his maidservant Mira. The latter, after bearing her employer a daughter, was eventually formally betrothed according to Jewish law to one of his other employees. After the betrothal, her fiancé was sent by Ovadiah on a two-month business trip, during which time Mira was returned to domestic "service." The two were seen (perhaps by the other servants) at least once in bed together during this period, and precisely nine months later (only eight months after her fiancé's return—and seven months after their actual marriage) Mira bore a son who, though given the auspicious name Shem Tov (Good Name) at birth, was later called by some a *mamzer* (bastard). Rabbi Meir managed to find reasons for considering the boy nonetheless legitimate, making the argument that his mother's intimate and well-publicized relationship with her employer before her betrothal did not brand her as the sort of loose woman who would do the same thing after being betrothed to another. Relations of this sort, it would appear, were evidently fairly widespread; in another case mentioned by Rabbi Meir, that of a man who married his "concubine" off to another (perhaps by providing her dowry), the man later, after her divorce, finding himself and his wife still childless, sought to take her back on a somewhat more legitimate basis.[107]

Relations of an intimate nature between masters and servants could take different forms in Jewish cultures, and also elicit different sorts of reactions. In the more puritanical Ashkenazic cultures of northern Europe, openly sexual relations between employers and their servants were undoubtedly less common than among the aforementioned Mediterranean communities, but in many households the frequent contacts across the conventional barriers of both class and gender created an atmosphere that was hardly bereft of sexual tension. Toward the end of the period in question, the philosopher Solomon Maimon (b. circa 1753), in his autobiography, poignantly recounted his sexual awakening as an early adolescent boy growing up in Poland, an experience that would appear to have been not unusual among the middle classes of traditional Ashkenazic society:

> A poor but very pretty girl of about my own age was taken into our house as a servant. She charmed me uncommonly. Desires began to stir in me, which I had never previously known. But in accordance with the strict rabbinical morality, I was obliged to guard against casting an atten-

tive eye on the girl, and still more against speaking with her, only now
and then was I able to throw a stolen glance.

It happened once, however, that the women of the house were going
to bathe . . . By chance my instinct drove me without reflection towards
the place where they bathed, and there I suddenly perceived this beautiful
girl, as she stepped out of the steam-bath and plunged into the river
flowing by. At this sight I fell into a sort of rapture. . . From that time I
became restless, was sometimes beside myself; and this state continued
till my marriage.[108]

Such stolen glances and rapturous moments, and the restlessness they
could ignite in young men, would sometimes lead, in other households, to
half-serious acts of betrothal, which often had rather serious consequences.
Rabbi Jacob Reischer, one of the leading rabbinical authorities of German-speaking Jewry earlier in the eighteenth century, discussed a case of
a not very unusual sort in which a young man of a wealthy family
betrothed, before the required two witnesses, a young Jewish woman who
worked as a servant in his home. Afterward he regretted his rash act,
which, not surprisingly, elicited the protest of both his father and other
members of his family. The maidservant, however, refused to accept from
him a bill of divorce, and this ostensibly prevented him, on account of the
abovementioned medieval enactment prohibiting polygamy, from marrying the woman whom he (and his family) felt would be more appropriate
to his station. Rabbi Reischer's response is perhaps no less revealing of
social realities than the case itself. He held the maidservant responsible for
allowing herself to be betrothed outside the normal channels of arranged
marriage, and perceived the danger of her betrothal's being regarded as
fully binding: for then "all the maidservants . . . shall cast their eyes upon
the wealthy [male] members of the household, and give themselves over
to loose behavior with them so that they might be led into betrothal."
Evidently Reischer did not find these maidservants as weak and helpless
as some modern historians have portrayed them.[109]

Some three centuries earlier, a rather bizarre but widely discussed event
had occurred among Ashkenazic Jewry that similarly underscored the
unpredictable consequences of "innocent" young men coming into contact

with "clever" maidservants. One evening in 1414, as four teenage Talmud
students sat before their teacher, Rabbi Zalman, in Mainz, the rabbi interrupted their study session to repay a debt to his maidservant. In an apparently spontaneous gesture, one of the four, the sixteen-year-old Nathan
Epstein, took the coins that remained on his teacher's table and with them,
in the presence of his classmates as witnesses, betrothed the maidservant
Rachel, who was about twenty-four years his senior! Nathan, who belonged to a wealthy and influential family of Frankfurt Jews, was already
engaged (but not formally betrothed) to a girl from Mainz, and was to be
married the following week. He later explained that he had been in a state
of excitement that day after receiving a letter from his father, "and on
account of his joy and longing for his future bride, his mind was fastened
upon the matter of betrothal, and his mouth led him astray to fool with
this particular woman."[110]

One wonders, however, if Nathan's apparently impetuous act was not
intended to forestall his arranged marriage and whether, like many young
men of good families, he found in the rough charms of maidservants
somewhat greater appeal than in the more genteel graces of the young
women of his class. Rachel, who had fallen on unexpectedly good fortune,
was less willing afterward than young Nathan to regard the matter as a
joke, which posed some difficulties for those rabbinical authorities inclined
to permit him the possibly bigamous act of marrying his original fiancée
without divorcing his teacher's maidservant. In the end, to ensure that she,
too, would recieve a dispensation from the rabbis to marry another, Rachel
arrived as an uninvited guest at Nathan's wedding in Frankfurt, preventing
the ceremony from taking place until she was given such permission.
Whether she ever found a husband is not known, but she too, and not only
on account of her age, belies the stereotype of the helpless maidservant
wielding no power over her own fate.[111]

An incident recounted during the same period in a responsum of Rabbi
Israel Isserlein (d. 1460), a leading Ashkenazic rabbinical authority, also
sheds considerable light on the world of the servants, both male and
female, in the Jewish households of his day. In his account, too, "dangerous
liaisons" appear, but between the servants themselves. A married woman

who was responsible for raising her employer's young children slept, according to their arrangement, in his home, where she shared a room with the children and with an older girl employed in the household. The latter reported that another member of the staff, an unmarried male servant, had been making suspicious nocturnal visits to the room. When confronted by the master of the household, the male servant eventually admitted to having had sexual relations with the married woman, and he even, following the spirit of the medieval Ashkenazic pietists, asked for advice concerning penitence. The woman herself was more equivocal in her reply to her employer's interrogations, suggesting that there had been sexual intimacies between herself and the manservant, but not actual intercourse. These details were all of importance, because the woman in question was not only married, but married to a *kohen* (a member of the priestly tribe), and there was serious question as to whether she could return to her husband.[112] Had the manservant more prudently chosen the married woman's younger roommate for his nocturnal dalliances, the matter most likely would not have come to rabbinical attention.

It would appear that with time, a kind of double standard emerged with regard to Jewish maidservants. This is evident in the early eighteenth-century (1730) statute of the Jewish community of Eisenstadt, prohibiting its members from keeping married maidservants in their homes except as wet nurses. Anyone doing so would pay a rather steep fine of twenty reichstaler. That the community was suspicious, and not completely tolerant, of the sexual activities of male and unmarried female servants is evident from the statute of the same year requiring householders to keep close watch on them, and to dismiss immediately any servant who had sinned.[113] The double standard that obtained vis-à-vis married and unmarried maidservants, rendering the latter fair prey for their masters and others, may be seen also in the reply of Rabbi Yair Bachrach, late in the seventeenth century, to a query on the part of a wealthy, childless man who had employed in his home a young woman who was not only attractive but also, according to his testimony, learned, and familiar with both crafts and languages. The employer, whose wife was terminally ill, had asked whether he might betroth his maidservant (without marriage) before his wife's death in order to "reserve" her for later, since she was desirable to many. Among the arguments offered by Rabbi Bachrach against such a move was that it was "the custom of the youths of Israel" to take certain freedoms with virgins that they would abstain from in the case of married women, and that after her betrothal the maidservant might continue to be the object of such freedoms—which might lead to actual adultery.[114]

The widespread suspicion in Ashkenazic society concerning the life-styles of domestic servants and apprentices, who were often grouped together under the joint rubric of *meshartim*, is evident earlier, in the community of Poznan. Its leaders decided in 1629 that since most of the young men engaged there in service or apprenticeship "deviated from the ways of God," none would be permitted to marry in Poznan unless he was first investigated by the community and then approved by two-thirds of its members. One such young man, whose widowed mother resided in the community, was ordered, just after Yom Kippur of 1632, to leave town on barely ten days' notice, although he was not explicitly charged with any particular wrongdoing.[115] However, his expulsion is reminiscent of a decision that had been taken by the community of Prague some two decades earlier, threatening with forced exile those young men *(bahurim)* or servants *(meshartim)* who were in the habit of "engaging in shameful and immoral acts with virgins, or unmarried women who were no longer virgins."[116] One suspects that many of the young women, virgins or not, with whom these young men were engaging in such shameful and immoral acts were themselves domestic servants living in the homes of others.

Another reflection of the contemporary perception of those young Jewish men who found their way into apprenticeship or service rather than the yeshiva is provided by the statutes of Kraków's Talmud Torah society in the late 1630s. Although the society was traditionally concerned with the promotion of Torah study among the young, it also chose to call attention to the impious behavior of those older youths from poorer families who, having completed their compulsory studies, "have no guide, but follow the crooked path of their greed and evil intentions, stealing or begging to fill their bellies, and giving no thought to the performance of such basic commandments as prayer and the donning of phylacteries [*tefillin*]." The Kraków society took it upon itself to require these wayward youths to attend synagogue twice daily, and wear their phylacteries, "and to assign them to householders as domestic servants, or to craftsmen as apprentices," providing financial incentives to those craftsmen who would otherwise not take them on.[117] It was apparently believed that by living and working in the homes of respectable householders, these youths would be returned to the proper path.

That this was not always the case, however, even in traditional Ashkenazic society, may be seen from the very revealing autobiographical account composed by an anonymous writer (b. 1668) late in the seventeenth century. Our autobiographer reports that after having been sent by his widowed father at the age of nine to study in Prague, he was taken in by a householder there "who gave me meals in his house and kept me for about six months for a small sum." In return, despite his own youth, he served as companion and tutor to the householder's small son, taking him to school daily and going over his lessons with him. "At that time," he later wrote, "I was very humble and ready to be a slave to everybody, and to do anything I was ordered."[118]

Some five years later, after having wandered between several communities and having acquired (by his own admission) a rather uneven education, our author was in Prague again, this time as a tutor (at the age of fifteen) in the house of a wealthy man who had two small boys. He then moved to yet another position, where he received lessons himself from the master of the household in return for helping the latter's son review his studies. This "situation" lasted two years, which the author later saw as having been the happiest in his life. His further comments about those same years, however, reveal how Jewish young men of his class, which included those engaged in domestic service as well as those whose work in the homes of others was of a somewhat more cerebral nature, could, even when living with the most upstanding families, take part simultaneously in a rather coarse youth culture whose values were at variance with those of the established culture at whose margins they lived.

Unfortunately no one looked after me, and I fell into bad company. They constantly talked to me about women, and led me in their evil ways. We were a misguided set of young men, of different ages, wasting our time with useless things and fooling with girls, as was their habit. I finally came to think that this is the whole aim of life, since during the entire time we never spoke of anything but of following the inclinations of the heart. The greater part of my days I spent with my young friends who lived an immoral life. Among them were some who were over twenty-three years old, and had more talmudic knowledge and better manners than I. Therefore, with the consent of my father, I joined them and followed in their footsteps . . . thinking in my simplicity that the purpose of good manners was to find favor in the eyes of women, and that this is human happiness in one's youth.[119]

CHAPTER 5

COURTLY CHIVALRY

Christiane Marchello-Nizia

Not every young man in the Middle Ages was necessarily a brave warrior like Roland or a courtly lover like Lancelot or Tristan. But he would have heard the names, and possibly the stories, of these epic, courtly heroes whose adventures pervaded the entire Middle Ages. For even in churches their stories were represented, in the stained glass windows and on the capitals of columns. And they were always portrayed as young men, or at least men who possessed the qualities of youth.

Accordingly, when we wonder what kind of lives young people led in medieval times, we find the only young people we actually hear about in this period are men, and generally noblemen. And when we try to perceive what values governed their behavior, it is literature, and especially texts written in the vernacular, that provides this information.

It is clear that between the eleventh and the sixteenth centuries, two concepts connected with love and valor essentially dominated European literature: chivalry, and courtliness. By studying these themes, we can at least partly comprehend the system of values, even imaginary, that guided the lives of these young men, so far from us in time, and in many respects so profoundly foreign to us.

TWO FOUNDING MYTHS
OF WESTERN CULTURE

Chivalry and courtliness are two ideas eminently—perhaps even originally—linked to the emergence and formation of a body of literature

written in the vernacular, to its aesthetic development through specific
forms of writing, and therefore, more generally, to the elaboration of
written vernacular languages. These two notions are found in the very
beginnings of European literature.

In fact these are two founding myths, connected to symbolic figures
still highly significant in Western postindustrial societies: the figures of
Emperor Charlemagne and King Arthur, of Roland and Gawain, and, in
particular, the figures of Tristan and Yseult, of Lancelot and Guinevere.
As Gottfried of Strasbourg wrote of Tristan and Yseult:

> And although they are long dead
> Their sweet name lives on
> And their death will endure
> For ever to the profit of well-bred people . . .
> With this their death lives on.
> We read their life, we read their death
> And to us it is as sweet as bread.
>
>> (Prologue to the *Tristan* of Gottfried,
>> lines 222–233, Penguin edition)

> *Al eine und sin si lange tot,*
> *Ir süeȝer name der lebet iedoch*
> *Und sol ir tot der werlde noch*
> *Ze guote lange und iemer leben . . .*
> *Hie mite so lebet ir beider tot.*
> *Wir lesen ir leben, wir lesen ir tot*
> *Und ist uns daȝ süeȝe alse brot.*
>
>> (Prologue to *Tristan*, ed. G. Weber, lines 222–236)

Naturally, much was written in the Middle Ages about both chivalry
and courtliness. These texts had to do with definitions, evaluations, casu-
istry, and so on—even if they initially appeared as fictions, romances,
poems, or epics. But these are not moral notions, although the themes of
both reflect great effort, even ascesis: judgment, evaluation, comment,
glorification, or rejection were all provided by the group, society, or
community a person wished to belong to—a collectivity that also sang,

read, financed, and produced the literary works in question. What would we know about courtliness and courtly love, were it not for literature—for poetry and, above all, fiction?

And what is true of courtly romances is perhaps even more true of the epic chansons de geste. In regard to the accolade, or dubbing ceremony—a fundamental institution of chivalry—Jean Flori writes: "The chansons de geste . . . are . . . our best sources of information."[1] And Michel Zink confirms this: "Not only is the chanson de geste one of the oldest forms of our literature. The Middle Ages never stopped making it the privileged mode of existence, in both military ventures and the struggles of Christianity"[2]—two of chivalry's fundamental missions, as we know. Moreover, a striking number of French terms originated in the field of chivalry, defining or describing that domain before subsequently acquiring broader meanings. These terms first appear in the earliest French chanson de geste, *La Chanson de Roland*, in its oldest version, the Oxford manuscript of around 1100. In this text we find the first appearance of the terms *chevalier* (knight), *chevalerie* (chivalry), and *courtois* (courtly); also the words *aduber* (to dub or equip with arms; to invest) *adub* (investiture, dubbing), and *adubé* (dubbed, equipped as a knight); *baceler* (bachelor, aspiring young knight), *barnage* (power, wealth), *debonaire* (debonaire, good), *fier* (proud), *fierté* (pride), *gent* (noble), *hardi* (valiant), and *hardement* (boldly); *loial* (loyal), *prod* (valiant), and lastly, *proece* (bravery, valor, prowess) and *prodome* (valiant man).

In fact, as soon as these concepts entered the domain of writing, language found or invented for them a speech that was theirs alone, a metalanguage, a rhetoric, even a poetics. Language equipped them with a whole array of technical terms. A good many of these have come down to us, and their requisites are still at the basis of our social morality, our attitudes, our modes of being and loving. It is impossible to deny this historical depth, for much of our moral and social behavior is still expressed—quite naturally and sometimes necessarily—through these terms, even through these concepts.

CHIVALRY, A PROFANE ETHIC

Chivalry is a concept that requires definition, and one that has given rise to many important studies. We are now fairly familiar with the characteristics of this institution, and we know the chronological and geographical stages of its development in medieval Europe, from the eleventh to the fifteenth century. As historians and literary analysts have shown, what best helps us understand this social and cultural phenomenon, so specifically medieval, is an analysis of the terms used in connection with this notion, the contexts in which such terms appear, and the accompanying words and phrases. While charters, notices, and other documents in Latin are valuable sources, they remain rather scanty, whereas fictional texts in the vernacular are often more explicit about this institution, which was fundamentally, though not exclusively, linked with the aristocracy. Indeed, even if "any nobleman could call himself a *miles* [knight, cavalryman]," the two terms are not exactly synonymous. As D. Barthélemy has justly written, "Nobility is a matter of birth and parentage; chivalry is a military and judiciary activity . . . the *miles,* or 'knight,' is the active member, with a full stake in feudal society. In the eleventh century, almost every reference to the moment when a man became a knight [*iam miles, miles factus:* 'now a knight,' 'made a knight'] is compared to the moment when he became a seigneur, or lord, thus also a vassal. It is the moment when he came of age."[3] Nobleman and knight, then: they were not the same thing. The terms are complementary rather than synonymous, the second specifying the qualities, real or imaginary, needed for the nobleman best to fulfill his function as a warrior.

The word for chivalry—*chevalerie*—is in itself emblematic of a vast and complex semantic field. Accompanying it we find not only *chevalier* (knight), but also *chevalereus* (chivalrous). Linked to these notions, and defining them, a whole group of adjectives appears: *preu, bacheler, juene, hardi, noble, fier, vaillant,* as Theo Venckeleer has shown;[4] also *large, fort,* and the terms connected with investiture, *adouber* and *adoubement.* French is not the only language involved: we should also take note of the Latin *miles* and *militia,* the English word *knight,* and the German *ritter* and *ritterschefte,* among others.

An attempt was actually made in the Middle Ages to define what was meant by *chevalier* and *chevalerie.* But this came mainly in the thirteenth century, at a time when the institution had become fixed and generalized, and was thus at risk of—and perhaps in the process of—losing some of its meaning and importance. This was precisely the time to resemanticize the term. And, indubitably, the courtly romances offer the best "ideal" definitions; consider, for example, the definition that the Lady of the Lake gives Lancelot to complete his education, just when he has to take leave of her:

> Knights were not created lightly, nor with regard to their noble origins or to their birth, more illustrious than that of the common man, for all humanity is descended from the same parents. When envy and covetousness increased in the world and might began to vanquish right, men were at that time still equal in lineage and nobility. But when the weak could no longer accept or endure the vexations inflicted by the mighty, they established for their own protection guarantors and defenders to ensure peace and justice and to put an end to the wrongs and outrages to which they were subject.
>
> To guarantee this protection, men were selected who, in the general opinion, had the most qualities: those who were tall, strong, handsome, agile, loyal, valiant, bold—those who were rich in moral and physical resources. But the order of knighthood was not conferred upon them lightly and as a meaningless title; they had to assume a heavy burden of duties. Do you know which? When the order first began, anyone who wanted to become a knight and obtained the privilege by legitimate election had to be courteous without baseness, good without felony, compassionate toward the needy, generous and ever ready to help the wretched, to kill thieves and murderers, to give equitable judgments without either love or hatred, without weakness of heart to profit what was wrong and damage what was right, and without hatred so as not to harm right by making wrong triumph. A knight must not, for fear of death, carry out any deed stained by the suspicion of shame, but must fear shame even more than death. Chivalry has the essential mission of

protecting the Holy Church, for the Church cannot take up arms in vengeance nor return evil for evil.

Chevaliers ne fu mie fais a gas ne establis, et non pas por che qu'il fuissent au commenchement plus gentil homme ne plus haut de lignage li un de l'autre, car d'un peire et d'une meire deschendirent toute gent, mais quant envie et covoitise commencha a croistre el monde et forche commencha a vaintre droiture, a chele eure estoient encore pareil, et un et autre, de lignage et de gentilleche. Et quant li foible ne porent plus souffrir ne endurer encontre les fors, si establirent desor aus garans at desfendeors por garantir les foibles et les paisibles et tenir selonc droiture et por les fors bouter ariere des tors qu'il faisoit et des outrages.

A cheste garantie porter furent establi chil qui plus valoient a l'esgart del commun des gens. Che furent li grant et li fors et li bel et li legier et li loial et li preu et li hardi, chil qui des bontés del cuer et del cors estoient plain. Mais la chevalerie ne lor fu pas donee a gas ne por noient, anchois lor en fu mis desor les cols moult grans fais. Et savés queus? Au commenchement, quant li ordre de chevalerie commencha, fu devisé a chelui qui voloit estre chevaliers et qui le don en avoit par droite election qu'il fust cortois sans vilonie, deboinare sans felonie, piteus envers les souffratex et larges et appareillés de secoure les besoigneus, pres et aparelliés de confondre les robeors et les ochians, drois jugieres sans amour et sans haine, et sans amour d'aidier au tort pour le droit grever, et sans haine de nuire au droit por traire le tort avant. Chevaliers ne doit por paor de mort nule chose faire c'on l'en puisse honte connoistre ne aperchevoir, ains doit plus douter honteuse cose que mort a souffrir. Chevaliers fu establis outreement por Sainte Eglize garandir, car ele ne se doit revanchier par armes ne rendre mal encontre mal.

(*Lancelot, roman en prose du XIIIe siècle*, ed. A. Micha, vol. 7, pp. 249–250)

As I have said, it was around 1100 that the word *chevalier* first appeared in French. But it had long been preceded by the Latin word *miles,* which meant cavalryman in medieval Latin. The eleventh century was the century of the rise of the *miles,* as Georges Duby and Léopold Génicot have shown.[5] This was a phenomenon that varied according to the region, of course, but the process was undeniable,[6] and documents attest to this, be they charters or chronicles of the crusades.

In French, however, the words *chevalier* and *chevalerie* first appeared in a literary rather than historical work: the *Chanson de Roland.* It is important to note that the lexical field of chivalry did not simply encompass the Francs, the *pairs* (peers) of Charlemagne's entourage. This text offers fifty-one instances of the term *chevalier*, three of *chevalerie*, and one of *chevalerus*—used to designate a pagan, Malpramis. But *chevalerie* is used here only to denote the acts or qualities of a knight. As for *chevalier*, it serves both to indicate the valiant Christians and their enemies, so long as the enemies are equally valiant. The first use of the term in the *Roland* involves Blancandrin, an intimate of the Saracen king Marsilie:

> Blancandrin was among the wisest of the pagans;
> Through his valor he was a good *knight*.

> *Blancandrins fut des plus saives paiens;*
> *De vasselage fut aseʒ chevaler.*
>   (*La Chanson de Roland*, ed. G. Moignet, lines 24–25)[7]

The noun *chevalier* is one of the most frequently employed terms both in the chansons de geste and in most of the medieval romances. It is most instructive to examine its uses. In the plural, and especially when preceded by a demonstrative or a possessive, it designates men fighting in the service of a particular lord or sovereign. In the singular, it is used to designate the hero or heroes, and then it is very often accompanied by extremely revealing adjectives. Indeed, as Denise McClelland has observed in regard to the *Lais* of Marie de France,[8] the word *chevalier*—like the word *amour* (love)—strikes us by "the extraordinary wealth of its adjectival associations." It has no less than eleven in the *Lais,* including *bel* (handsome), *bon* (good), *gent* (noble), *large* (generous), *leal* (loyal), *povre* (poor), *de grant pris* (of great worth), *pruʒ* (gallant), *vaillant* (valiant). In the *Chanson de Roland* we find it further accompanied by *gentil* (noble), *de bon aire* (good), *franc* (frank), and *hardi* (daring); or else it is connected to *vassal* and *vasselage,* which indicate the valorous qualities needed in a combatant:

> Count Roland returns to the battlefield;
> Brandishing Durendal, he strikes valiantly . . .
> The pagans flee before Roland.
> The archbishop says: "You are working wonders!
> A *knight* must possess such valor

When he bears arms and rides a good horse;
He must be strong and proud in battle,
Otherwise he isn't worth four deniers,
But should be a monk in some monastery."

Li quens Rollant el champ est repairet.
Tient Durendal, cume vassal il fiert . . .
Devant Rollant si s'enfuient paiens.
Dist l'arcevesque: "Aseȝ le faites ben!
Itel valor deit aveir chevaler
Ki armes porte e en bon cheval set:
En bataille deit estre forȝ e fiers,
U altrement ne vaut .iiii. deners,
Einȝ deit monie estre en un de ceȝ mustiers.

(Ibid., lines 1869–1881)

These are the same adjectives that Benoît de Sainte-Maure would use during the years 1173 to 1185 in his *Chronique des ducs de Normandie* (Chronicle of the Dukes of Normandy), enlarging on the attributes of the kings of England as seen by his predecessors Wace and Jean de Marmoutier. As Jean Flori has shown, chivalry assumed a very elaborate form in the kingdom of the Plantagenets during the third quarter of the twelfth century,[9] and the vocabulary records this advance.

However, it was in romances written in the last third of the twelfth century that the term *chevalier* achieved its greatest success. The five major romances of Chrétien de Troyes contain almost nine hundred instances of the word, either singular or plural, designating either anonymous characters or the principal heroes, such as Gawain, by whom "chivalry is made illustrious" *(de lui est . . . chevalerie anluminee)*. There are scores of fictional works whose title includes the word; many of these titles were given at a later date, but some were nonetheless chosen by the author. Here again, Chrétien de Troyes was probably a pioneer:

Chrétien begins his book
About the *Knight of the Cart.*

Del Chevalier de la Charrete
Comance Crestïens son livre.   (*Lancelot*, pp. 24–25)

There is also a *Chevalier au lyon,* (Knight of the Lion), a *Chevalier au papegaut,* a *Chevalier au cygne* (Knight of the Swan)—the ancestor of Godefroy de Bouillon, who conquered Jerusalem!—the *Chevalier aux deux épées* (Knight of Two Swords) and, in English literature, *The Green Knight.* Later on, in Italy (though written in French) came the *Chevalier errant* of Thomas de Saluces.

The noun *chevalerie* first denotes, as we have seen, the qualities of a knight, or else a deed worthy of a knight; in the oldest texts, the knight is first and foremost a good warrior. This is the meaning of the word intended in the titles of such chansons de geste as *La chevalerie Ogier* and *La Chevalerie Vivien.* But in the second half of the twelfth century, it frequently designates knights in general: the social category and, more specifically perhaps, the professional and ethical group they form, a group fundamentally different from *clercs* (clerics) and *paysans* (peasants)[10]—those who prayed or did productive labor with their hands. This is also the meaning intended in the expression *ordre de chevalerie,* order of knighthood, which had a long and lasting success. The expression appears in Chrétien de Troyes's *Conte du Graal* (see below), it was used by the author of the *Quête du Saint-Graal,* and it reappeared at the end of the thirteenth century in the title of a didactic work by Ramon Llull, *Libro d'Orde de Caballeria.* It acquired a fresh meaning during the Hundred Years War, when the expression served to denote a kind of fraternity uniting the partisans of a faction or an idea. I shall return to this point.

Although the word *chevalerie* was not used very frequently during the twelfth century, it occurs with great regularity in Arthurian romances of the thirteenth century. The term is used almost fifty times in the *Quête du Saint-Graal,* for example: in a third of these instances it designates traditional chivalrous qualities, and it is then often paired with *bonté* (valor). But in the majority of instances it designates the social and ethical group, the order of knighthood, whose power and qualities are explicitly linked with the existence of the Round Table: *"La Table reonde . . . ou la chevalerie a puis esté si fort par la douçor et par la fraternité qui est entr'ax"* ("The Round Table, where knighthood has been so strong on account of the sweetness and fraternity existing between them," *Quête,* ed. A. Pauphilet, p. 156).

The expression *ordre de chevalerie* appears ten times in the *Quête,* often qualified by the word *haut* (high, lofty), or accompanied by the verb *entrer en* (to enter into): *"Einsi garniȝ de toutes bontés et de toutes vertuȝ terriennes entras tu ou [en le] haut ordre de chevalerie"* ("Thus endowed with every goodness and earthly virtue, you entered the high order of chivalry," *Quête,* p. 125). These words are addressed to Lancelot by the hermit who, in the middle of the romance, reveals to him the meaning of his life and experiences up to that point. And in this romance the expressions *chevalerie terrienne* and *chevalerie céleste* (earthly chivalry, celestial chivalry) appear in opposition for the first time, there being ten or so instances of these two syntagmas. This opposition suggests that in the first half of the thirteenth century, chivalry had become an institution that could arouse mistrust, and in trying to redefine the concept in its purity, the anonymous author of the *Quête* reveals its potential discredit. But even in the twelfth century—as can be seen in the *Couronnement de Louis*—some reticence was manifest, even on the part of heroes and authors who were not very susceptible to Christian delicacy. In short, we should emphasize that the vast majority of instances of the word *chevalerie* occurring in the *Quête* concern Lancelot and Galahad, personifications of these two newly-defined types of chivalry. But if the *Quête du Saint-Graal* marks a significant limit, and perhaps a hesitation, in society in regard to its institutions, it remains an isolated case. The subsequent romances—for example, *La Mort du roi Arthur,* in which the term *chevalier* occurs repeatedly (almost five hundred times) and which follows the *Quête* in the Lancelot-Graal cycle—no longer contain this opposition.

In the thirteenth-century verse romances, on the other hand, *chevalier* remains a frequent term. But from this point on, the function of the word in courtly romances seems to be to define the group, the category, of men that ladies and young women are permitted to meet socially and to love; thus, it defines the social category a character must belong to in order to become a hero of romance. In Jean Renart's romance *Guillaume de Dole,* a further syntagma appears, which subsequently met with great success: the *chevalier errant,* or knight errant.[11]

The situation changes entirely with the *Roman de la Rose* of Guillaume de Lorris, the first part of which was written around 1230: here there are only six instances of the word, usually in its most general sense. The social background of the first-person narrator-hero is never made clear: he is to tell of an adventure he once had in a dream, and the only personal information he provides is his age at the time of the dream—twenty. He thus places himself in the category of *jeunes gens,* young men:

> *In my twentieth year*
> *At the time when Love collects his toll*
> *From young men . . .*
>
> *Ou vintieme an de mon aage*
> *Ou point qu'Amors prent le paage*
> *Des jeunes gens . . .*
>
> (*Roman de la Rose,* ed. Poirion, lines 21–23)

With these words a new concept—at least, a new literary concept—of young men appeared, a concept linked first and foremost to their age.

Closely connected with *chevalier* and *chevalerie* we find an important verb that, in the customary medieval vulgate, marks the young man's rite of passage into knighthood: the verb *adouber,* to dub. Its appearance, the evolution of its uses, the constructions and contexts it occurs in, and thus its meanings—all reveal something of what chivalry became during the eleventh and twelfth centuries. "A rite of nobility, of seigneury, of feudality,"[12] dubbing marked a young man's accession to a certain number of rights and empowered him "to act as an adult"; it was originally a secular ceremony.

The verb, whose etymology is debatable, not to say uncertain, appears in French in the *Chanson de Roland.* However, it appears only in the reflexive form ("*s'adubent,*" they equip themselves, or "*adubent lor cors,*" equip their bodies, which amounts to the same thing) or in the past participle, *adobez* ("*Adobez sunt a lei de chevaliers,*" they were equiped as knights; "*Li adubez en sunt li plus pesant,*" those that are armed are the heaviest). In this ancient European epic, the verb is still connected purely with the trappings—arms and armor—of the warrior-knight. According to J. Flori, in this early period "the fact of being dubbed a knight involved

no change in the social condition . . . of the one being knighted."[13] This
was probably the reality reflected in the famous scene in the Bayeux
Tapestry, in which William is placing a helmet on Harold's head. This is
not the first picture of a dubbing ceremony, or investiture, in the sense it
acquired during the next century,[14] but a simple matter of handing a piece
of armor to a young prince who is leaving to fight a battle.

Only quite rarely, in the oldest chansons de geste, does the verb *adober*
stop being reflexive and become transitive. It then denotes the first time
that arms are given to someone who has not previously fought, or who
has never had occasion to bear arms: in effect, he receives the "tools" of
his new trade. Thus, in the *Couronnement de Louis,* Guillaume recruits a
porter whose warlike remarks he has heard, and whose good sense he has
experienced firsthand; he immediately asks his nephew Bertrand to provide
him with the equipment needed for fighting:

> He calls Bertrand: "Listen, my lord nephew:
> Did you ever hear a porter speak so well?
> Give him the equipment of a knight."
> Bertrand replies: "Willingly, dear sir."
> He looked at him, at both his hands and feet,
> And finding him handsome, elegant, and svelt,
> He *equipped him as a knight,*
> With a strong hauberk and a steel helmet,
> A good sword and a sharp spear,
> A horse, a squire and his mount,
> A palfrey, mule, and packhorse;
> And much money for his service.

> *Bertran apele: "Entendez, sire niés:*
> *Oïstes mais si bien parler portier?*
> *Adobez le a lei de chevalier."*
> *Respont Bertrans: "Bels sire, volentiers."*
> *Il le regarde et as mains et as piez,*
> *Molt le vit bel et gent et alignié,*
> *Si l'adoba a lei de chevalier*
> *De fort halberc et de helme d'acier,*
> *De bone espee et de trenchant espié,*
> *Et de cheval, de roncin, d'escuier,*

De palefrei, de mulet, de somier;
De son servise li dona bon loier.

(*Couronnement de Louis*, lines 1644–1655)

There is no ceremony here, as we see; but the porter in question had nonetheless been described as *corteis*, courtly, which shows that the confidence Guillaume has in him is justified and the arms will not be put to ill use. That is, however, all: it is simply a matter of his assuming his functions as a professional warrior.

On the other hand, in the chansons de geste composed at the end of the twelfth century, *adober* is used increasingly to mean this first investiture with armor; according to Flori, the verb is used in this sense at least 60 percent of the time. Furthermore, the assumption of knightly functions seems to become increasingly solemn: it is now a matter of arming a knight, of making a young man into a knight, the expression *faire chevalier* being sometimes equivalent to *aduber*. From then on, when indicating the fact of being equipped with—or equipping someone else with—the weapons and armor needed for combat, the verbs *(s')apareillier* and *fervestir* (with its adjective *fervesti*) are preferred: "to prepare oneself," "to put on armor." And at the turn of the century, between 1180 and 1200, the first evidence of the Christianization of this ritual appears, in literary works like Chrétien de Troyes's *Conte du Graal* and those of Hélinand de Froidmont. The Church then began developing rituals and providing texts to mark the ceremony and its meaning.

This lexical and institutional evolution appears clearly in *Aliscans*, a very fine chanson de geste from the Guillaume d'Orange cycle, which was composed at the very end of the twelfth century, thus relatively late. The narrative is punctuated by the exploits of an extremely awkward but valorous young giant, Renoart, who is initially employed as a cook, but whom Guillaume subsequently recruits as a combatant. He turns out to be the son of a Saracen king and the brother of Guibourc, a noble pagan woman whom Guillaume has converted and married. This extraordinary character is knighted, *adoubé*, twice in the story; but the two occasions are quite different. The weapon that best characterizes Renoart is the *tinel*, a kind of bludgeon with which he works wonders. When Guibourc meets him, she questions him and realizes that he is her brother; she then proposes giving him the equipment suited to his function as a warrior:

> "A man unprotected, unarmed, cannot last for long . . .
> But now out of affection I would like to ask you
> To allow me *to equip* your body."
>
> "*Hom nuʒ sans armes puet mout petit durer . . .*
> *Mes or vos voill par amors commander*
> *Que tu me sofres ton cors a* adouber." (*Aliscans,* lines 4718–4722)

She makes him put on a hauberk, fastens the lining for him, buckles on his sword. The results are not particularly successful: Renoart goes along with all this, but then reverts to his bludgeon! There is thus nothing ceremonious about Renoart's first investiture with the "tools" of the warrior.

In contrast, Renoart's second *adoubement,* which takes place at the very end of the narrative, is of quite a different nature. The young man is now twenty-five, and his noble origins have been recognized; he has proved himself in every way necessary. Guillaume means to baptize him, then make him a knight:

> Guillaume said: "Renoart, hear me!
> It is now fitting to *make you a knight.*"
>
> *Et dist Guillelmes: "Renoart, or oïeʒ!*
> *Des ore mes vos convient* adouber." (Ibid., lines 7918–7919)

As in the preceding episode, arms and pieces of armor are given to the young man, and this time he also receives a *destrier,* or war horse. Above all, Guillaume immediately invites him to test himself at the quintain, a kind of jousting exercise. We should also notice that from now on Guillaume calls him *ber* (baron):

> "Baron Renoart," he said, "Now show your worth!
> I ask you, out of friendship for me, joust
> At the quintain."

> *"Ber Renoart, dist il, or esprove{!*
> *Par moie amor vos pri que vos joste{*
> *En la quintaine."*   (Ibid., lines 7970–7972)

Seizing his shield *"a loi de chevalier,"* as a knight would do, and drawing his sword *"courtoisement,"* in a courtly fashion, Renoart passes the test, thus earning the title of knight.

> The Franks exclaimed: "There's a good knight!
> Roland and Oliver were no better!"
>
> *François escrient: "Ci a bon chevalier!*
> *Onc tiex ne furent Rollant ne Olivier."*
>   (Ibid., lines 7992–7993)

The transitive use of *adouber* shows the importance from now on attached not only to the person who is dubbed a knight, but also to the person who knights him, the agent whose deed signals a social promotion: in this case, Guillaume. In the romances, however, it is King Arthur, head of the Round Table, who becomes the quintessential "dubber"; all the young heroes dream of receiving the emblems of knighthood from Arthur—equipment no longer seen simply as tools of the warrior's trade. At the same time, a ritual becomes established, marked by the essential gestures. As Jean-Claude Schmitt has written, "Among the actions of a warrior, the first is dubbing. It is the emblem and the condition of knighthood, since it validates the warrior's entry into the chivalrous order."[15]

In works written by Chrétien de Troyes between 1170 and 1180, dubbing always appears as a ceremony of entry, of accession to a specific status now termed for the first time an "order." Thus, in the *Conte du Graal,* young Perceval becomes a knight in rather a haphazard manner: all he knows is that King Arthur makes people knights by giving them equipment. And indeed one of these magnificent beings, whom he has met and admired in the forest on his mother's estate, actually reveals himself to be a knight, answering Perceval's question in this way:

"Who equipped you thus? . . ."
"Just five days ago,
King Arthur gave me this equipment
When he *dubbed me knight.*"

*"Qui vos atorna donc ensi? . . .
—N'a mie ancor cinc jors antiers
Que tot cest hernois me dona
Li rois Artus qui m'*adoba.*"*

(*Conte du Graal,* ed. Poirion, lines 285–290)

For the uninitiated Perceval, knighthood is certainly a matter of clothing and appearance; and when Arthur agrees to give him the arms of the
Red Knight, the young man thinks he is by this very fact armed as a knight.
He has to wait until Gornemant has educated him, however, before he is
worthy of a true dubbing, conferred essentially by the bestowal of spurs
and a sword:

Noble Gornemant bent down
to put on his right spur . . .
He took the sword to buckle it on,
then kissed him, saying
that with the sword he had given him
the highest order created and commanded by God:
the order of knighthood,
which must be devoid of baseness.

*Et li prodom s'est abessiez,
Se li chauça l'esperon destre . . .
Et li prodom l'espee a prise,
Se li ceint e si le beisa,
Et dit que donee li a
La plus haute ordre avoec l'espee
Que Dex a fete et comandee,
C'est l'ordre de chevalerie,
Qui doit estre sanz vilenie.*   (Ibid., 1624–1638)

In the last lines of this unfinished romance, Gawain has become lord
of a kingdom that has been inactive for some time and that he is restoring
to life. He begins by dubbing 500 young men, thus forging new links with

history and the normal evolution of society. He makes them bathe and then keep vigil in the church until dawn; then he attaches their right spur, buckles on their sword, and gives them each a shield. In Gottfried of Strasbourg's version of the *Tristan* romance, the same ritual is followed when King Mark, who has just learned that Tristan is his sister's son, makes the young man a knight: Mark buckles on his nephew's belt and sword and attaches his spurs, gives him some advice, and hands him a shield. Tristan then immediately dubs his companions, equipping them with sword, spurs, and shield:

> Then Mark took charge of his nephew, buckling on his sword and attaching his spurs. "My nephew," he said, "my nephew Tristan, now that your sword has been consecrated and you have become a knight, think of the glory of knighthood and give thought to yourself, to who you are. Let your birth and nobility be ever present in your mind: be modest and sincere, be truthful and courteous; be ever kind toward the poor and ever proud toward the mighty; cultivate a good appearance; treat all women with honor and with love. Be generous with your possessions, and unfailingly loyal! For believe me, on my honor: gold and sable never sat better on lance and shield than loyalty and generosity." Then he handed him the shield. He kissed him and said: "My nephew, now go forth, and may almighty God grant you joy in your chivalry! Be ever courteous, ever gay!" Then Tristan in turn invested his companions, exactly as his uncle had done, with sword, spurs, and shield.

> *Mark nam do Tristanden*
> *Sinen neven ʒe handen,*
> *Swert unde sporn strict er im an.*
> *"Sich, sprach er, neve Tristan,*
> *Sit dir nu swert gesegenet ist*
> *Und sit du ritter worden bist,*
> *Nu bedenke ritterlichen pris*
> *Und ouch dich selben, wer du sis;*
> *Din geburt und din edelkeit*
> *Si dinen ougen vür geleit:*
> *Wis diemüte und wis unbetrogen,*
> *Wis warhaft und wis wolgeʒogen;*
> *Den armen den wis iemer guot*

Den richen iemer hochgemuot;

Ziere unde werde dinen lip,

Ere unde minne elliu wip;

Wis milte unde getriuwe

Und iemer dar an niuwe!

Wan uf min ere nim ich daʒ,

Daʒ golt noch ʒobel gestuont nie baʒ

Dem sper unde dem schilte

Dan triuwe unde milte. "

Hie mite bot erm den schilt dar.

Er kustin und sprach: "Neve, nu var

Und gebe dir got durche sine craft

Heil ʒe diner ritterschaft!

Wis iemer höfsch, wis iemer vro!"

Tristan verrihte aber do

Sine gesellen an der stete,

Rehte als in sin oeheim tete,

An swerte, an sporn, an schilte.

(Tristan, ed. Weber, lines 5019–5049)

On the other hand, this same episode of Tristan's investiture is treated quite differently in the two older versions of the story. One of these, composed between 1170 and 1190 by Eilhart von Oberg, was based on a text that probably also served as the model for Beroul; the other was written in Norse by Friar Robert for the king of Norway in 1226, based on the romance by Thomas. Eilhart gives no precise description of the ceremony, apart from remarking on its solemnity. As for Friar Robert, he seems to consider the event a simple conferral of arms: Tristan asks the king to "procure him armor," and the king has some very fine armor made ready for him; his spurs are fastened on, Mark hands him a sword and gives him a "strong blow on the neck" (*Tristan et Yseut, les premières versions européennes* [Paris: 1995], p. 811).

Perhaps these differences reveal a trace of the successive stages the institution passed through as it developed. As Flori has in fact shown,[16] this conferral of arms was originally an act with a professional function, intended only for young men of the highest nobility, designed to introduce them into the class of noblemen and warrior chiefs as future successors of the lords currently in power. This ceremony usually took place when the young men were between the ages of thirteen and twenty-two, after the youths in question had been trained by some allied or related lord. As is apparent from fictional texts and from historical records, the maternal uncle often assumed responsibility for instructing a young man in the profession of arms, by making him a squire. Guillaume, who would later be known as "Le Maréchal" (William Marshall) and "the best knight in the world," followed an exemplary course of instruction and was knighted at the age of twenty.[17] This initiation seems at first to have involved only princes and great lords; not until later was it extended to the lower strata of the aristocracy.

In the next century, around 1230, the *Quête du Saint-Graal* almost begins with the investiture of young Galahad—a figure very close to that of Perceval. Galahad is being dubbed by another knight reputed to be the best in the world, Lancelot:

> Lancelot remained in the abbey and spent the night in the chapel beside the young man who was keeping vigil. Next day, at the first hour of morning, he *made him a knight*. He fastened one of his spurs, and Bohort fastened the other. He girded on his sword and handed him his shield, telling him he hoped God would make him a worthy knight, for he had certainly endowed him with beauty.
>
> *Cele nuit demora laienz Lancelot et fist toute la nuit veillier le vaslet au mostier, et a l'endemain a hore de prime le* fist chevalier, *et li chauça l'un de ses esperons et Boorz l'autre. Aprés li ceint Lancelot l'espee et li dona la colée, et li dist que Diex le feist preudome, car a biauté n'avoit il pas failli.*
>
> (*Quête, du Saint-Graal*, ed. A. Pauphilet, p. 3)

This passage is instructive in several respects. Written almost fifty years after the romance by Chrétien, it presents the same episodes, and specifies the two characteristics a knight must necessarily possess: beauty and valor (*prodomie*). Most notably, however, it expresses the definitive forms this solemn investment ceremony would assume in the collective memory and for future history. Thenceforth, and certainly after the last quarter of the twelfth century, a point of perfect balance was attained in the representation of this ritual.

Clearly, study of the term and concept of dubbing reveals a double evolution. As a rite of passage involving the nobility, *adoubement* began as a simple conferral of professional tools, before it became an initiation ceremony gradually invested with Christian ritual (how could the Church have passed up such an opportunity?); originally a matter for princes, in the twelfth century it began to involve all seigneurs and also the Church. And literature—in the early stages, epic literature—must certainly have been a privileged vector in the spread of this institution, as in the constitution of its forms and ritual in the medieval imagination.

In addition to the two terms *chevalier*, which marked the social status of the "noble warrior," and *adouber*, which indicated his rite of passage into that state, there were several words used to designate young men—young noblemen, of course; nothing, or exceedingly little, is said about the others.[18] Among those words is a term which, in an extremely specific way, says much about the social condition of young men: that word is *bacheler* (bachelor).

In the chansons de geste, beginning with the *Chanson de Roland*, the word *bacheler* has the very precise meaning of a young knight whose activity is to fight in the service of a lord. What characterizes the term in more than 80 percent of its uses is that it designates a young man, as Flori has again shown.[19] Thus, in the collective expressions dear to Old French (the young, the old, the big, the small, and so on, when describing a group), *bacheler* is often set against *chenu* (old, white-haired) or *vieil*, to which it is semantically opposed. At the beginning of the *Chanson de Roland*, for example, when Charlemagne is resting in an orchard, surrounded by his knights and peers:

> The emperor is in a large orchard,
> With him are Roland and Oliver . . .
> The knights are seated on white carpets;

For entertainment, the wisest and the old
Are playing at draughts and chess,
And the wild *young ones* are fencing.

Li empereres est en un grant verger,
Ensembl'od lui Rollant e Oliver . . .
Sur palies blancs siedent cil cevaler,
As tables juent pur els esbaneier
E as eschecs li plus saive e li veill,
E escremissent cil bacheler *leger.*

(*Chanson de Roland*, lines 103–113)

These "young ones" seen practicing for combat are the young knights the emperor calls "his children," as Baligant makes clear when describing the army of the enemy:

The one who sounds the horn is very brave;
His companion answers with a bugle,
And both ride in the vanguard
With fifteen thousand Franks,
Young men whom Charles calls his children.

Cil est mult proʒ ki sunet l'olifant,
D'un graisle cler racatet ses cumpaignʒ
E si cevalcent el premer chef devant,
Ensembl'od els .XV. milie de Francs,
De bachelers *que Carles cleimet enfanʒ.*

(Ibid., lines 3193–3197)

As has been shown,[20] in most of the cases in which age can be stated precisely, this term refers to young men aged fifteen to thirty; the word *enfant* often denotes the youngest, and *juene* the older ones.

Bacheler had yet another connotation in the Middle Ages: accompanied by the adjective *povre* (poor), it refers to young men who are not yet settled, who have no resources, who are not yet in possession of a fief, and who are not employed in anyone's service. These are the *povres bachelers* recruited by Guillaume in *Le Charroi de Nîmes* to go and conquer a country:

Guillaume stood up on a table;
And in his clear voice began to shout:
"Hear me, barons of France . . .
I want to say this to the *poor young knights,*
And squires dressed in rags:
If they come with me to conquer Spain
Helping me to free the country
And impose God's law there,
I shall give them so much money and shining silver,
So many castles and territories, dungeons and fortresses,
And Spanish warhorses, they shall be well equipped."
When they heard this, they became joyous and happy,
And began to call out loudly:
"Lord Guillaume, in God's name, make haste:
Those without horses will follow you on foot!"

Seur une table est Guillelmes montez;
A sa voix clere commença a crier:
"Entendez moi, de France le barné . . .
Ce vueill ge dire as povres bachelers,
As escuiers qui ont dras depanez,
S'o moi s'en vienent Espaigne conquester
Et le païs m'aident a aquiter
Et la loi Deu essaucier et monter,
Tant lor dorrai deniers et argent cler,
Chasteaus et marches, donjons et fermetez,
Destriers d'Espaigne, si seront adoubé."
Quant cil l'oïrent, si sont joiant et lié;
A haute voiz commencent a huchier:
"Sire Guillelmes, por Deu, ne vos targiez.
Qui n'a cheval o vos ira a pié."
(*Le Charroi de Nîmes,* ed. J.-L. Perrier, lines 635–637 and 649–660)

In this example the word *bacheler,* according to the collective formulas already mentioned, forms a contrasting pair with *barné* (baron), which denotes a knight, often of high rank, in any case well equipped and of stable social status. There is a further example in Chrétien de Troyes:

For the barons and *bachelors*
Were very eager for this expedition.

Car molt i voloient aler
li baron et li bacheler.   (*Yvain*, ed. M. Roques, lines 675–676)

Through his exploits as a warrior, the *bacheler* could obtain the necessary equipment, together with the social rank of an enfeoffed knight. But sometimes a lord the knights have fought for would forget to pay the price. As young Bertrand explains to his uncle at the beginning of *Le Charroi de Nîmes*, the Emperor Louis has not seen fit to reward them:

"Our emperor has given fiefs to his barons:
Land to this one, a castle to that one, cities
Or a town to someone else, as he sees fit;
You and I, uncle, have been forgotten.
It doesn't matter in my case, I'm just a *young man*,
But it matters for you, my lord, who have proven
Such a knight, and endured so much hardship,
Staying awake at night and going all day without food."

"Nostre empereres a ses barons fievez:
Cel done terre, cel chastel, cel citez,
Cel done vile selonc ce que il set;
Moi et vos, oncle, somes oublié.
De moi ne chaut, qui sui un bacheler,
Mes de vos, sire, qui tant par estes ber
Et tant vos estes traveilliez et penez
De nuit veillier et de jorz jeüner."   (*Charroi de Nîmes*, lines 36–43)

To Guillaume's subsequent reproaches, Louis makes this answer:

One of these days one of my peers will die;
Then I shall give you all his land,
And his wife too, if you want her.

Un de ces jorz morra un de mes pers;
Tote la terre vos en vorrai doner,
Et la moillier, se prendre la volez.   (Ibid., lines 76–78)

This must have been a common practice, at least in the early feudal period, when fiefs could perhaps still be considered as not necessarily hereditary. Guillaume replies:

> "God!" said Guillaume, "What a long wait
> *For a young man of my age,*
> Who has nothing to give and nothing for himself.
> I must provide food for my horse;
> And yet I don't even know where to find grain.
> Do you think, king, that none of this bothers me?

> *Deus! dit Guillelmes, com ci a longue atente*
> A bacheler qui est de ma jovente!
> *N'a que doner ne a son hues que prendre.*
> *Mon auferrant m'estuet livrer provende;*
> *Encor ne sai ou le grain en doi prendre.*
> *Cuide tu, rois, que je ne me demente?*   (Ibid., lines 88–93)

The words *"bacheler . . . de ma jovente"* should probably be interpreted ironically here: Guillaume, a knight in the prime of life, finds himself as materially impoverished as a young knight just starting on his career.

Jean Flori has certainly given an accurate summary of the meanings of the term *bacheler:* "He is not always a knight, nor always a warrior; nor is he always a nobleman, a servant, a vassal, a man of no property, nor even a bachelor in the modern sense. But he is always a young man, or at least a man who possesses the virtues of youth." We can, however, take the definition a step further. It is a term that never has pejorative connotations: the *bacheler* is "promotable," a future lord, who must therefore possess the appropriate virtues, and display them. The word refers to a young man who is in a transitional state, be it socially (an unmarried "bachelor") or professionally (an unfeoffed bachelor); his status is ephemeral, unlike that of the seigneur or the chevalier, whose situations are permanent.

The function of these young men described as *bachelers* is also clear: it is their help that makes any victory possible, that keeps the established powers in their place. "The victory of good over evil is only possible thanks to the young," says Flori. We should now examine the implications of this remark, and see how power could make these young men risk their lives supporting lords they hope eventually to replace—lords whom some of them are destined to succeed.

The literary exaltation of a caste of young aristocrats who constitute a body of warriors reflects a specific aesthetic. This literature of chivalry, represented by the chanson de geste, is a "literature of violence and excess, savored in intensity,"[21] as Jean-Charles Payen has pertinently observed, discerning therein, in a highly evocative article, what he felicitously terms a "poetics of joyful genocide."[22]

This "destructive, murderous joy" is an attribute of young men: it is a trait that distinguishes them utterly from the older combatants or from the men who rule. When Roland incites Charlemagne to reject Marsilie's offers of peace and to pursue the war unceasingly—

> "Never again trust Marsilie! . . .
> Make war as you have undertaken to do,
> Lead your assembled army to Saragossa,
> And lay siege to it for the rest of your life, if need be."
>
> *"Ja mar crerez Marsilie . . .*
> *Faites la guer cum vos l'avez enprise,*
> *En Sarraguce menez vostre ost banie,*
> *Metez le sege a tute vostre vie."*
> (*Chanson de Roland*, lines 196,, 210–213)

—his words are countered by the advice of Ganelon:

> "Do not trust this brawling rogue . . .
> Let us leave the fools alone, and listen to the wise men!"
>
> *"Ja mar crerez bricun . . .*
> *Laissun les fols, as sages nus tenuns!"*   (Ibid., lines 220, 229)

Both Ganelon and Duke Naimes advise Charlemagne to agree to negotiate, and this is doubtless the intention of the emperor himself, who is thrown into perplexity by Roland's speech. The last lines of the *Chanson de Roland*

provide a perfect example of this contrast between Roland's love of
fighting and the emperor's desire for peace; when a divine messenger
enjoins him to return to war, Charlemagne responds with tears and regrets:

> Saint Gabriel comes to tell him on behalf of God:
> "Charles, summon the armies of your empire!
> With force and arms you will go to the land of Elbira,
> And aid King Vivian at Imfa,
> The city that the pagans have besieged:
> The Christians are calling, asking for your aid."
> The emperor would prefer not to set forth again:
> "God," says the king, "How full of pain my life is!"
> He weeps, and pulls at his white beard.
> Here ends the story that Turoldus relates.

> *Seint Gabriel de part Dieu li vint dire:*
> *"Carles, sumun les oz de tun emperie!*
> *Par force iras en la tere de Bire,*
> *Reis Vivïen si succuras en Imphe,*
> *A la citet que paien unt asise:*
> *Li crestïen te recleiment e crient."*
> *Li emperere n'i volsist aler mie:*
> *"Deus, dist li reis, si penuse est ma vie!"*
> *Pluret des oilz, sa barbe blanche tiret.*
> *Ci falt la geste que Turoldus declinet.*   (Ibid., lines 3993–4002)

In the chansons de geste, this festival of violence and death is enhanced
by an aesthetic of color and light: the color of red blood glistening on the
green grass, the sight of armor flashing in the sunlight:

> The battle is wondrous and quick,
> The French strike with vigor and with rage,
> They cut through fists, ribs, backbones
> And clothes, to the living flesh.
> *On the green grass the bright blood is flowing.*

> *La bataille est merveilluse a hastive,*
> *Franceis i ferent par vigur e par ire,*
> *Trenchent ces poinz, cez costez, cez eschines,*

Ceʒ vestemenʒ entresque as chars vives.
Sur l'erbe verte li cler sans *s'en afilet.*   (Ibid., lines 1653–1658)

When the emperor goes looking for his nephew,

On the field *he finds the flowers of many plants*
Red with the blood of our barons! . . .
On the green grass he sees his nephew lying.

Quant l'empereres vait querre sun nevold,
De tantes herbes el pré truvat les flors
Ki sunt vermeilz del sanc *de noʒ barons!* . . .
Sur l'erbe verte veit gesir sun nevuld.   (Ibid., lines 2870–2876)

"Hey, Durendal! How *handsome, clear and white you are!*
Glimmering and flashing in the sun!

"E! Durendal, cum es bele e clere a blanche!
Cuntre soleill si luises e reflambes!   (Ibid., lines 2316–2317)

The day was clear, *the sunlight was beautiful;*
All their equipment *shone.*
A thousand bugles sounded, to make it even finer.

Clers fut li jurʒ e bels fut le soleilz;
N'unt garnement que tut ne reflambeit.
Sunt mil grailles por ço que plus bel seit.   (Ibid., lines 1002–1004)

Death as the culmination of a young man's life: it was not so hard to make the idea seem acceptable or even desirable—so long as it was grandiose and beautiful.

THE TWILIGHT OF CHIVALRY

One of the final products of the chivalrous, courtly civilization of the eleventh, twelfth, and thirteenth centuries was among the more interesting. In the fifteenth century, a strange figure appears in literature: the character of the "knight errant" who, a century later, will provide the model for Don Quixote. A notable example is Jacques de Lalaing, a valiant knight who, in the middle of the Hundred Years War, went from tournament to tournament for the sake of glory and what proved to be an outdated ethic: he died when struck by a cannonball.

Social politics tried to put the values of chivalry to a new use. Between 1348 and 1469, in little more than a century—and, it should be emphasized, at the time of the Hundred Years War—at least fifteen orders of knighthood appeared, created not only by the warring sovereigns but also by lords of varying degrees of grandeur. These included the Order of the Garter, created by Edward III of England; the Order of the Star, created in 1352 by his opponent, Jean le Bon; the Order of the Golden Fleece, created in 1429 by Philippe le Bon, Duke of Burgundy; and the Order of Saint Michael, created in 1469 by Louis XI. Following the same model, though sometimes less successful, were the Order of the Annunciade of Amédée of Savoy; the Order of the Porcupine of Louis d'Orléans; the Order of the Green Shield of the White Lady of Boucicaut; the Order of the Crescent of King René of Anjou, and so on. What was the point of these institutions, which appear to have been totally anachronistic at the time? Their purpose was clear: it was to restore ties of interdependance, to reinforce loyalties and attachments that occasionally wavered. Such institutions almost always appeared during or before some projected war or crusade. And the expression "order of knighthood" thereafter acquired a somewhat different meaning. The important element was no longer the knight's entry into a category both social and professional—that is, into a group of nobles likely to inherit responsibilities, and into the official warrior corps; what mattered was that he belonged to one particular clan rather than another.

COURTLINESS: A SOCIAL ETHIC

Unlike knighthood and everything connected with it, courtliness was also—and perhaps mainly—women's business. Although courtly romances are often titled after male heroes, it is impossible to imagine one without a heroine. A few titles reflect this through metonymy: the *Roman de la Rose ou de Guillaume de Dole* by Jean Renart, for example, and the *Roman de la Violette ou de Girart de Nevers* by Gerbert de Montreuil, the rose and the violet being birthmarks found on the breast and thigh, respectively, of the young herrines. Even so, however, priority is given to the actions and feelings of the young men.

The terms *courtois(e)* (courtly, courteous) and *courtoisie* (courtliness) could actually apply to both men and women. Admittedly, though, the behavior that justified the use of this adjective was not the same for both sexes; rather, it was symmetrical and complementary. The courtliness of Lancelot is balanced by that of Guinevere, but the ways in which their courtliness is expressed and functions are not the same.

The adjective *courtois* first appears, once again, in the *Chanson de Roland*. In two of its three occurrences, it is linked with *preux* and applied to Oliver, according to the usual celebrated formulas:

> His nephew Roland will be there, I believe,
> And Oliver, *the valiant and courteous.*
>
> *Iert i sis niés, li quens Rollant, ço crei,*
> *E Oliver, li proz e li curteis.*
>
> (*Chanson de Roland*, lines 575–576)

(Charlemagne himself uses this formula in line 3755.) Roland, given his excessive behavior, cannot be described as courtly. As for the adverb *courtoisement*, in this text, as in many others, it describes the speech and elaborate mode of expression of which only certain characters are capable: *"Curteisement a l'emperere ad dit . . ."* (courteously he said to the emperor . . .).

Lancelot and his two cousins, Bohort and Hestor, are described as courtly by King Arthur himself, the central figure in the court that standardized these virtues:

> And the king said to those who were with him: "By God, these three men have qualities for which truly everyone should praise them; there is more *courtliness* and nobility of heart in them than in anyone else, and they are so endowed with knightly prowess that their equals do not exist in the whole world."
>
> *Et li rois dit a ceus qui o lui sont: "Par Dieu, voirement a il moult en ces trois homes por quoi touȝ li mondes les doit loer; qu'il i a cortoisie et debonereté plus*

*qu'en nule autre gent, et de chevalerie sont il si bien garni qu'il n'a en tout le monde leur pareu*ʒ.*"*   (*La Mort du roi Arthur*, ed. J. Frappier, par. 147)

There is an explicit connection here between the *courtoisie* that prompted the three men to welcome King Arthur most respectfully even though he is now their opponent, their nobility of birth and heart *(debonereté)*, and their valor as warriors *(chevalerie)*. While we are intermittently reminded that a *vilain* (peasant) can be innately courtly, it is nonetheless better to be well born and a knight. This is, however, one of the topoi accompanying courtly love: through its formative nature it can reveal latent potential and radically alter a man, changing a boor into a refined person. This theme had already been expressed by the first of the troubadours, Guillaume IX of Aquitaine, in describing the lady he loved:

> Through the joy she gives she can cure a sick man,
> And through her anger can make a healthy man die;
> She can make the wisest man foolish
> And alter the beauty of the most handsome;
> She can make the courtliest man boorish
> And *make all the boors courtly.*

> *Per son joy pot malautʒ sanar,*
> *E per sa ira sas morir*
> *E savis hom enfoleʒir*
> *E belhs hom sa beutat mudar*
> *E.l plus cortes vilanejar*
> *E totz vilas encortezir.*

> (Guillaume IX, *Molt jauʒens, mi prenc en amor,*
> ed. Jeanroy, lines 33–36)

Numerous poets throughout Europe would later take up this formula to describe the power of a perfect, refined love.

Here again the epithets accompanying the word *cortois* are instructive. Men are described as *vaillant, leal, sage, bien parlant, preuʒ* (valiant, loyal, wise, well-spoken, worthy). Women—for as I said, courtliness was also women's business—are described as *franche, bele, senée, acesmée* (frank, beautiful, sensible, elegant). As Moshe Lazar has shown, Provençal *corteʒia*, like northern *courtoisie*, subsumes the virtues that are attached to it.[23] Clearly, these terms denote not only innate qualities, but also acquired virtues, such as elegance or eloquence. The narrator-hero of the *Roman de la Poire* (Romance of the Pear) wrote, in the midthirteenth century:

> I am entirely hers, and with good reason;
> I here proclaim myself her liege man,
> *And shall thereby be with courtliness enfeoffed.*
>
> *Suens si sui ge, bien est reisons;*
> *g'en devieig ci ses liges hons,*
> *s'en tendré cortoisie en fié.*
>
> (*Roman de la Poire*, ed. C. Marchello-Nizia, lines 13–15)

The lover becomes the vassal of the lady he loves, and this voluntary dependence allows him to attain to the values of courtliness.

Courtliness was certainly a social ideal, and therefore a reality; but above all it was a literary invention—indeed, a poetic one. The lyrical poetry of southern France, the poetry of the troubadours, "invented" what later became a topos in the north. Not only did the verbs *amar* and *cantar* (to love and to sing) rhyme, they were practically the same thing. One was the source of the other, and the expression of love actually *became* love. The perfect lover was the best poet:

> It is no wonder that I sing
> better than any other singer,
> for my heart draws me more strongly toward love
> and I submit better to its commands.
> Heart and body, knowledge and mind,
> strength and power have I devoted to it.
>
> *Non es meravilha s'eu chan*
> *Melhs de nul autre chantador,*
> *Que plus me tra. l cors vas amor*
> *E melhs sui faih\z a so coman.*
> *Cor e cors e saber e sen*
> *A fors'e poder i ai mis.*
>
> (Bernart de Ventadorn, beginning of *Canso* I, ed. R. Nelli)

At least in its origins among the troubadours, this love was not usually reciprocal. In any case reciprocity was not assured, and consequently this was a deeply narcissistic form of love. A trace of this "intransitive" concept of love, a love directed entirely toward itself, may perhaps be found in an odd characteristic inherited by the romance literature of the north: in the early forms of courtly romance, there was no amorous dialogue. The reciprocal avowal of mutual love, which is one of the first stages of the amorous narrative, was a secondary invention. Thus, in the *Eneas*, the first French and even the first European romance marked by concepts of courtly love, there is no amorous dialogue, either between Dido and Aeneas in the first part or, what is even stranger, between Aeneas and Lavinia—even though the medieval author has added a very long episode (the love between these two young people) completely foreign to Virgil's *Aeneid:* through all this wholly medieval ending, Lavinia and Aeneas exchange not a word. Introspective confessions, in the form of soliloquies or interior monologues, fill the entire space: Lavinia's first soliloquy takes up 250 lines. And while the *Tristan* of Beroul probably contained no episode of confession, we may suppose that the inventor of the amorous dialogue was Thomas, in his version of the *Tristan*.[24] Here we find the famous scene where Yseult, having imbibed the love potion, confesses she is suffering from a certain malady, *lamer*. She leaves it to Tristan to guess the meaning of the two syllables she has just pronounced: is it seasickness? sadness brought on by the sea air? the pain of love? [Trans. note: This plays on *mer*, "sea" and *amer*, "to love".] The first amorous dialogue in European literature is thus triggered by this enigma, by this ambiguous signifier.

In northern France after 1150, and in other European countries a few decades later, romance was the genre that exalted courtliness, making it into a literary aesthetic and an ethical system. And not only for young people: in *La Mort du roi Arthur*, Guinevere is more than fifty, and Lancelot must be about the same age.

The first romances habitually described as "courtly" made their appearance in the circle of several grand "courts." Foremost among these were the courts of Henry Plantagenet II, of his wife, Eleanor of Aquitaine, and of Marie de Champagne, the daughter of Eleanor's first marriage to Louis VII, king of France. Reto Bezzola has advanced the theory that courtliness and the literary forms it spawned (lyrical poetry, romance) and found expression through actually accompanied the emergence of an authentic form of monarchy, first in England, then in Sicily and the seigneurial courts patterned on the same model.[25] In the same way, it has been thought that epic literature helped make chivalry a social concept that characterized the feudal age of the eleventh and twelfth centuries.

A distinction must immediately be made between the actual medieval meaning of the words *courtois* and *courtoisie,* and the modern expression "courtly love" introduced in 1883 by the medievalist Gaston Paris.

Like their Old Provençal counterparts *cortes* and *cortezia,* the terms *cortoisie* and *cortois* were equivalent to the Latin words *facetus* and *facetia* or the German word *hübsch.* In a general way they designated certain noble and chivalrous qualities, frequently allied: generosity, loyalty in personal obligations, elegance of heart and manners, constant politeness; in short, the ability to behave well in society toward anyone at all. Originally, a courtly or courteous person was one who knew and respected the social norms of a specific place, the *cort* (court), and of a specific milieu, the flower of the court. Scholars are still debating the origins of this idea, so important to the development of a certain ideal of civilized social behavior and individual constraint. The thesis of Edmond Faral, who argued in favor of an essentially clerical concept of courtliness,[26] has been made more complex by the addition of Reto Bezzola's theory: Bezzola has definitively shown the fundamental role played by the great courts of Europe in introducing and developing courtly ethics. These were the royal courts of England and France, the imperial courts in Germany, and the seigneurial courts, such as that of Marie de Champagne. More recently C. S. Jaeger has reconsidered the question, and he too has adopted the theory of clerical origins. At the same time, however, Jaeger argues clearly that Germany played an essential role in defining the concept of *courtoisie.* The ancient idea of *urbanitas* was, he thinks, taken up and developed by clerics of the German courts, especially the curial bishops, before passing into northern France. Here it had an immediate influence on romance literature, before returning to Germany through the adaptations of twelfth-century French romances.[27]

In themselves, however, these terms would never have defined anything more than a kind of aesthetic or ethical varnish that attenuated knightly brutality. What rapidly constituted the essence of courtliness, then and in the following centuries, was the link associating it with a certain form of love.

In certain contexts, *courtois* and *courtoisie* actually take on a more restricted sense, describing a certain art of loving, an aesthetics of passion and disciplined desire expressed through a small number of characters of romance, the models of which are Tristan and Lancelot. Gawain is certainly courtly, but incapable of courtly love. This particular art of loving was known in medieval France and Languedoc as *fin(e) amor(s)*, or perfect love; also as *bon'amors* (good love) and *vera(e) amors* (true love). The expression *cortez'amors* is only employed once, by the troubadour Peire d'Alvergne. The most common expression was that used by Yseult in the *Tristan* of Thomas. When the two lovers have to separate, she gives him her ring of green jasper as a sign of recognition between them: she will do whatever he asks, if his message is accompanied by the ring. "*Je vos pramet par fine amor*," she adds: "I promise, because I love you with a perfect love" (line 2722).

Whereas worldy *courtoisie* was doubtless invented in the north, either in France or Germany, the concept of courtly love originated in the south, in the lyrical poetry of the early twelfth-century troubadours. Although the romances later elaborated certain aspects—in particular, desire and the satisfaction of desire were no longer counteropposed—the essential characteristics stayed the same.

The second half of the twelfth century, north of the Loire and especially around Angers, witnessed an extraordinary development in romance literature. Above all, the behavior and characteristics that defined courtly love—its ethics, in effect—are reemphasized in these romances. Love goes hand in hand with *courtoisie*, *prouesse* (prowess), *largece* (largesse, generosity), and *oneur* (honor), as demonstrated in this perfect formula from the beginning of a famous romance by Chrétien de Troyes:

> For those who loved formerly
> deserved to be known as courteous,
> brave, generous, and honorable.
>
> *Car cil qui soloient amer*
> *Se feisoient cortois clamer*
> *Et preu et large et enorable.*   (*Yvain*, lines 21–23)

A further characteristic of courtly love appears in *Le Chevalier à la charrette* by the same author: the lover's absolute submission to the will of the lady he loved.

> He who loves knows how to obey.
> Quickly and willingly he does
> What pleases his beloved,
> If he loves with all his heart.
>
> *Molt est qui aimme obeïssanz,*
> *Et molt fet tost et volentiers,*
> *La ou il est amis antiers,*
> *Ce qu'a s'amie doie plaire.*
>   (*Le Chevalier à la charrette*, ed. Poirion, lines 3798–3801)

Lancelot obeys Guinevere unhesitatingly when she orders him not to defeat his opponent, Meleagant. And this attitude of "service" implies that he is owed something in return: the beloved lady owes her knight help and goodwill. This implicit obligation is what justifies the severe opinion expressed by Baudemagu, a "noble and courtly king," when he realizes that Guinevere is not disposed to offer a kind welcome to Lancelot:

> "Don't say that, Madam," said the king,
> Who was very generous and courtly;
> "Where did this terrible mood come from?
> Certainly you are too disdainful
> To a man who has served you so well
> And who therefore often had
> To risk his life for you."

"Avoi! Dame," ce dit li rois,
Qui molt estoit frans et cortois,
"Ou avez vos or cest cuer pris?
Certes vos avez trop mespris
D'ome qui tant vos a servie
Qu'an ceste oirre a sovant sur sa vie
Por vos mise an mortel peril."   (Ibid., lines 3947–3953)

Clearly, an exact parallel exists here between the amorous relationship and the canonical feudal relationship. In the *Tristan* of Thomas, this is stated explicitly: the knight in love is the "liege man" as well as the lady's lover. As we have seen, this is the condition by which courtliness is achieved, but it entails reciprocal duties:

Kaherdin is alone with Yseult:
"Lady," he says, "Now listen
To what I shall say, and ponder it.
Tristan, your lover, promises you
Love, faithful service, and greetings,
You, his lady and his lover
On whom depend his death and his life.
He is your liege man and your friend . . .
He tells you he will not survive
Without your help,
And that is why he sends me;
He summons you, by the trust
And loyalty you owe him, Yseult,
To come and join him,
And may nothing in the world prevent you."

Kaherdin est suz a Ysolt:
"Dame, fait il, or entendez,
ço que dirrai, si retenez.
Tristan vus mande cum druz
Amisté, servise e saluz
Cum a dame, cum a s'amie
En qui main est sa mort e sa vie.
Liges hum vus est a amis . . .

> *Mande vos qu'il ne vivrad mie*
> *Se il nen a la vostre aïe,*
> *E pur ço vus mande par mei,*
> *Si vus sumunt par cele fei*
> *E sur icels lealteʒ*
> *Que vus, Ysolt, a li deveʒ,*
> *Pur ren del munde nel lasseʒ*
> *Que vus a lui ore ne vengeʒ."*
>
> (Thomas, *Tristan et Yseut*, ed. C. Marchello-Nizia,
> lines 2860–2888)

There is, however, a further characteristic connecting *courtliness* to the chivalrous ideal. One of the fundamental elements of courtly love is its link with knightly prowess and warlike courage. The connection between the knight's valor and love is first made apparent in Geoffrey of Monmouth's *Historia regum Britanniae:*

> Courtly ladies . . . did not deign to receive love from someone unless he had proved himself at least three times in combat. Therefore the ladies behaved chastely, and out of love for them the knights behaved more nobly.
>
> Facetae *etiam mulieres . . . nullius amorem habere dignabantur, nisi tertio* in militia *probatus esset, Efficiebantur ergo castae quaeque mulieres et* milites *pro amore illarum nobiliores.*
>
> (Geoffrey of Monmouth, *Historia regum Britanniae*, ed. N. Wright)

Reto Bezzola has shown that this necessary connection between love and knightly prowess was a trait particular to courtly love in northern France: fighting well, rather than simply singing well, was proof that one loved, and it was also the condition for being loved. Tristan is certainly a talented harpist, but he is first and foremost a formidable warrior, capable of vanquishing the Morholt.

In his *Traité de l'amour courtois,* André Le Chapelain also establishes a precise connection between courtly love and knightly valor: "Ordinarily, it is male valor in particular that arouses the love of women and maintains the will to love."[28] When the hermit in *La Quête du Saint-Graal* exhorts him to confess and repent, Lancelot replies:

"Sir," said Lancelot, "It is true, I live in a state of mortal sin because of a woman I have loved all my life, Queen Guinevere, wife of King Arthur. Nonetheless, it is she who has given me the abundance of gold and silver and the sumptuous presents I have sometimes given to poor knights. It is to her that I owe my splendor and the elevated rank I occupy. *It is out of love for her that I have accomplished the exceptional deeds of which everyone speaks.* It is she who made me pass from poverty to riches, and from misfortune to a life of every earthly pleasure."

"Sire, fet Lancelot, il est einsi que je sui morȥ de pechié d'une moie dame que je ai amee toute ma vie, et ce est la reine Guenievre, la fame le rois Artus. Ce est cele qui a plenté m'a doné l'or et l'argent et les riches dons que je ai aucune foiȥ doneȥ as povres chevaliers. Ce est cele qui m'a mis ou grant boban et en la grant hautece ou je sui. Ce est cele por qui amor j'ai faites les granz proeces dont toz li mondes parole. Ce est cele qui m'a fet venir de porvreté en richece et de mesaise a toutes les terriannes beneurteȥ."

(Quête du Saint-Graal, p. 66)

It can therefore be said that the *Tristan* of Beroul is not a courtly romance. In fact in Beroul, love appears not as an incitement to valor, but as an obstacle. After three years have elapsed and the love potion loses its effect, Tristan begins to return to his senses, recovering some perception of chivalrous and social values:

> Straightaway he began to repent:
> "Ah! God, I have so much hardship! . . .
> *I have forgotten chivalry,*
> And the life of a knight at court . . .
> I should be at court with a king,
> A hundred squires in attendance,
> Learning to take up arms
> And preparing to enter my service.
> I ought to go to another land
> And fight battles to earn rewards."

> *A lui seus senpres se repent:*
> *"Ha! Dex, fait il, tant ai traval! . . .*
> Oublïé ai chevalerie,
> *A seure cort et baronie . . .*
> *Or deüse estre a cort a roi,*

Et cent danzeaus avoques moi,
Qui servisent por armes prendre
Et a moi lor servise rendre.
Aler deüse en autre terre
Soudoier et soudees querre."

(Beroul, *Tristan,* ed. Poirion, lines 2160–2178)

In the twelfth- and thirteenth-century romances, there is a basic concept that subsumes the different aspects of courtliness, without, however, being reduced to them: the concept of adventure. This term marks the passage from chivalry to courtliness, from South to North, from poetry to romance, for this was the idea that immediately determined the structure of the courtly romance, organizing its narrative and punctuating the stages of courtly perfection. From being a knight, the hero becomes a lover, and thus courtly to perfection; but adventure is the criterion, the testing ground of this ascesis. Here again, this is one of those key terms in medieval literature that have survived and are still used to blaze narrative trails, marking the rhythm of biographies and personal itineraries.

In the Middle Ages the word *adventure* had no precise content, except in the sense of an ordeal; it was a general term that always and only had one "programmatic" meaning. An adventure simply implied that it would be necessary to prove oneself in some way: but under what circumstances? facing what difficulties? through what kind of behavior? All this remains unknown. The ability to resolve these questions—that is, to recognize and identify the ordeal destined to reveal the hero, then to respond adequately—is the real sense and meaning of *aventure,* rather than the situation it subsequently denotes in the narrative thread.

This word, which appeared in French at the end of the eleventh century, is not in fact used in the chansons de geste: it is unknown in the *Chanson de Roland* and occurs only once in *Le Charroi de Nîmes,* where it means "the future" (line 808, *"De l'aventure vet tot en Damedé":* What must come of it is in the hands of God).

Adventure becomes an essential notion of medieval literature—and, more broadly, of European literature—in the courtly romance. It is defined more by its effect than by its content: as I have said, an adventure serves partly to test the courage and prowess of the knight. But, as Erich Köhler has shown in his masterly analysis of the concept of *aventure*,[29] its most important function is to overcome, and thereby efface, the contradiction between the exaltation of the victorious warrior and the integrity of the community he belongs to. For the victorious knight who has proved himself the best of all knights is actually a potential danger to the community, whose leader he might wish to become. Chivalry and courtliness are both designed, each in a specific way, to ward off this danger by focusing the young conqueror's potential energy on some secondary target: not the person of the king or leader, but glory, or the safeguarding of the institution, or religion, or else the queen's love—which is another way of "acting out" the rivalry with the king.

Adventure is probably best defined in the romances of Chrétien de Troyes; for example, in *Yvain ou le Chevalier au lion,* the introductory narrative by Calogrenant in some degree prefigures all subsequent developments:

> "I am," he said, "A knight
> looking for what he cannot find:
> I have searched at length, without success."
> "And what is it you would like to find?"
> "Some *adventure,* to test
> my prowess and my courage."
>
> *"Je sui, ce voiz, uns chevaliers*
> *qui quier ce que trover ne puis:*
> *assez ai quis, et rien ne truis.*
> *—Et que voldroies trover?*
> *—Avanture, por esprover*
> *ma proesce et mon hardement."*   (*Yvain,* lines 356–361)

But in the course of a century, an evolution takes shape. The *Quête du Saint-Graal* indicates an important stage, even if it did not exert a definitive influence on narrative schemas that are valid even today. This romance constitutes part of the great Lancelot-Graal cycle, the first true novel written in French prose. The *Quête* comes immediately after the *Lancelot en prose,* and its author was therefore quite familiar with courtly concepts.

What is important is his position in regard to them, and this is revealed through careful study of some significant terms. First of all, in this romance in which Lancelot (particularly in his amorous relationship with Guinevere), Gawain, and Mordred (also in love with Guinevere) all figure prominently, the adjective *cortois* appears only once, whereas in *Lancelot* and the *Mort du roi Arthur* it is used often, as we have seen. The adverb *cortois* appears twice, but only to describe greetings addressed to someone. The term *aventure* has some importance in the *Quête* and occurs fairly often—but it does not have quite the same meaning as in the works previously mentioned. In fact, *aventure* here refers either to purely knightly tests (in which the hero must display his physical strength, skill, and courage), or else to moral tests with eschatological significance, such as dreams. The common element in these different types of adventure is that they denote and describe an elite. What ultimately appears from this study of the two notions of chivalry and courtliness is that in both cases, it is a matter of defining what might be called criteria of selection, and applying them to poetic works, epics, or romances.

The Albigensian Crusade that took place in southern France in the thirteenth century devastated the social substratum that had spawned and fostered the courtly poetry of Languedoc. Later on, in the north, the general condemnation of remarks attributed to the Averroists also affected courtly love. But courtly themes continued to be used in poetry during the following centuries, even if the courtly ethic was thenceforth reduced to the laws of an entirely formal social etiquette.

One of the best examples of the final products of the courtly romance is probably *Jehan de Saintré*, written by Antoine de la Sale in 1456. Its success is indicated by the ten manuscripts and four editions that have come down to us. The first third of the text (inspired partly, it is thought, by the actual adventures of the author's companions) is a veritable manual for the "true and loyal lover," or the "perfect lover." Noticing the abilities of young Jehan, then aged thirteen, the Lady of the Lovely Cousins—a young widow who holds a privileged position at court—undertakes to educate him before making him her lover; their liaison, so carefully prepared, will subsequently last for sixteen years. The Lady begins by convincing Jehan that a loyal, constant love directed at a worthy lady is a sure means for a young man to acquire the most enviable virtues and social position: were not Lancelot, Gawain, and Tristan proof of this?

> "What inspired the great undertakings and knightly deeds of Gawain, Lancelot, Tristan, the courtly Guron, and all the other valiant knights of the Round Table? Or those of Pontus and many other valiant knights and squires of that kingdom, and countless others, that I would willingly enumerate if I had the time, if not the service of love, by which they acquired, and kept themselves in, the grace of the ladies they loved? I know of some who, for having been truly in love and served their ladies most faithfully, came to such high honor that we will hear of it for ever. . .
>
> My lord, you must choose a lady who is of high and noble lineage, who is wise, and who has the means to help you and satisfy your needs; and you must serve and faithfully love her, despite whatever pain you may suffer from it, so that she well knows the perfect love you honorably bear her."

> *"D'ou sont venues les grans emprises et les chevalereux faiz de Lancelot, de Gauvain, de Tristan, de Guron le courtois, et des autres preux de la Table Ronde? Aussi de Pontus et de tant d'autres tant vaillans chevaliers et escuiers de ce royaume, et autres sans nombre, que je bien nommeroye se je avoie temps, sinon par le service d'amours acquerir et eulz entretenir en la grace de leurs desirees dames? Dont j'en cognois aucuns qui, pour estre vrays amoreus et de bein loialment servir leurs dames, sont venus en si hault honneur que a tousjours en sera nouvelles . . .*
>
> *Sire, devez vous choisir dame qui soit de hault et noble sang, saige et qui ait de quoy vous aidier et mectre sus a vos besoings, et celle tant servir et loialment aimer, pour quelque peine que en aiez a souffrir, qu'elle cognoisse bien la parfaite amour que sans déshonneur lui portez."*
>
> (*Jehan de Saintré*, ed. C. Knudson and J. Misrahi, pp. 9 and 16)

The qualities of the perfect lover are listed in some detail:

> To obtain, by loving her, the much desired favor of the lady, he will endeavor to be gentle, humble, courtly, and gracious . . .
>
> *Pour acquerir par l'amant la tres desiree grace de sa dame, se efforcera d'estre doulz, humble, courtois et gracieux . . .* (Ibid., p. 17)

The true and faithful lover will strive only to serve his lady and his love honorably and generously, to keep himself and all his men well dressed and with good horses, depending on his condition.

Le vray et loial amoreux ne contendra que a toute largesse honorablement servir sa dame et amours, pour soy tenir bien abilié, bien monté, et toutes ses gens, selon son estat.   (Ibid., p. 22)

The wise, true, and faithful lover is, and must be, orderly and measured in all his words and deeds.

Le saige, vray et loial amoreux est et doit estre en tous ses faiz et ditz ordonné et mesuré.   (Ibid., p. 33)

The true and faithful lover is a gentleman, healthy and clean in mind and body, who strives day and night in the amorous quest, seeking the favor of his beautiful lady . . . , thus nature, right, and reason wish her to love, esteem, and honor him all the more, so much so that she will rejoice at his wealth, his honor and his whole advancement . . . And he . . . shall use his own wealth to make sure she is never in need.

Le vray et loial amoreux qui est gentil homme, sain et net de sens et de corps et qui jour et nuyt tent a l'amoreuse queste et grace de sa tresbelle dame . . . , si veullent nature, droit et raison que elle l'en doit trop mieulz amer, priser et honorer, et tellement que de son bien, de son honneur et de tout son avancement elle en sera joyeuse . . . Et lui . . . de ses biens a son besoing ne lui fauldra jamais.   (Ibid., p. 29)

But we are now in the fifteenth century, and the text ends with the failure of this love, so "courteously" delineated. During one of Saintré's absences, while he is far away proving his valor and his honor, the Lady takes up with a rich abbott, who is extremely seductive and cheerfully sybaritic. The abbott subsequently challenges Saintré to a wrestling match in which the courtly lover, reduced to a state of near nudity, twice gains the upper hand before exacting a rather bitter revenge on the abbott and his lady.

POWER AND YOUNG PEOPLE

At the end of this double, elementary analysis of the nature and function of the terms *chevalerie* and *courtoisie,* a question arises: how did these two concepts—purely medieval creations that seemed to concern only a limited group of people, the young ones—manage to interest the entire society of that time, and to arouse such lasting enthusiasm that they permeated and shaped an entire field of European art and literature?

For young men, it was obviously highly gratifying to identify with the heroes of a chanson de geste or a courtly romance. Georges Duby, in particular, has drawn attention to the compensatory nature of this litera- ture for a class of young men who were denied actual power. The aesthet- ics of this literature, the joyous violence of martial exploits and the joy of loving and seducing—all this was clearly directed at a specific public.

But if we venture beyond these initial appearances and analyze this literature more deeply, examining its themes and narrative schemas, some- thing quite different emerges: it becomes clear that its appeal was not limited to the category of *juvenes* but was felt far beyond, in the dominant class of those who had power and fortune. By examining the passages in which the functions of young men and their lords are expressed in these narratives, we can perceive their complementary aspects—and also the possible interest and charm these texts held for those who were not, after all, their heroes.

What is immediately clear in the chansons de geste is that the destiny of young men—meaning, on a symbolic level, their essential function—is to die, in an exemplary and if possible aesthetic manner, for the benefit of the institution and to ensure the survival of the group. The *Chanson de Roland* is entirely centered on the episode of Roncevaux, where Roland and Oliver die fighting. Three chansons of the Guillaume d'Orange cycle, composed in the twelfth century—*La Chanson de Guillaume, Aliscans,* and *La Chevalierie de Vivien*—narrate the same episode: the defeat of the Christians at Aliscans, during which the young count Vivien dies in agony, thus enabling his companion to go and warn Guillaume. Harried on all sides by the pagans, pierced by countless blows, tortured by thirst in the hot May sunshine, Vivien is portrayed in all three chansons as a very young warrior (Guillaume calls him "child" in the *Aliscans*) who is being sac- rificed and knows it, and who fights on until the very end. And just as the hero's death takes in *La Chanson de Roland* up several strophes, the *Aliscans* and *La Chanson de Guillaume*[30] relate every stage in the young knight's martyrdom:

> Vivien, on foot, wanders through the battlefield;
> His helmet is falling down on the nose-piece,
> And his intestines drag between his feet;
> He holds them in with his left hand,
> And in his right he holds a blade of steel:
> It is entirely red from tip to hilt,
> And his scabbard is full of liver and blood;
> He walks leaning on the point of his sword.
> He is in his death agony,
> And can stand only by leaning on his sword.
> Loudly he calls to all-powerful Jesus,
> Begging him to send Guillaume the noble warrior,
> Or Louis, the powerful warrior king.

> *Vivien eire a pé par mi le champ,*
> *Chet lui sun healme sur le nasel devant,*
> *E entre ses pez ses boals traïnant;*
> *Al braz senestre les vait cuntretenant.*
> *En sa main destre porte d'ascer un brant,*
> *Tut fu vermeil des le holz en avant,*
> *L'escalberc plein e de feie e de sanc;*
> *Devers la mure s'en vait apuiant.*
> *La sue mort le vait mult destreignant,*
> *E il se sustent cuntreval de sun brant.*
> *Forment reclaime Jhesu le tut poant,*
> *Qu'il li tramette Willame le bon franc,*
> *U Lowis, le fort rei cunbatant.*

> (*La Chanson de Guillaume*, ed. D. MacMillan,
> strophe 71, lines 884–896)

The schema we find here is one that structures a number of epic narratives. It is the schema of the disaster overcome, and it always begins with the sacrifice of a young man—one of the best of the young men. In avenging his death, the group regains its cohesion, recovers its monopoly on victory, and renews its power. In sacrificing his own life, the hero allows the community to regenerate: this, it seems, is the essential function of young men in epic literature. The figures of these heroes have even been compared to Christ.[31]

But the chansons de geste were not the only texts to describe these sacrifices that were knowingly, even enthusiastically, entered into by young men. There is no dearth of romances in which a young knight risks his life to save the kingdom from a deadly peril. Although he seems at first to represent something entirely different, Tristan is one of these emblematic figures of sacrificed youth. His first exploit, we recall, was the fight with the Morholt, an Irish lord who regularly exacted from Mark's kingdom a tribute of the handsomest and noblest young people, thus depriving Cornwall of its future defenders. By his victory, Tristan preserves the country's future. But in so doing he receives his first poisoned wound, a wound that Yseult initially cures. Nevertheless he ultimately dies of another poisoned wound from which Yseult, who arrives too late, cannot save him: the initial condemnation was only deferred. As for Lancelot, his first appearance in the world of medieval romance shows him saving the queen, who has been kidnapped by Meleagant; thus, in Chrétien de Troyes's *Le Chevalier de la charrette*, Lancelot restores Arthur's damaged honor and the integrity of his kingdom.

In those who hold power, provoke these sacrifices, and reap the benefits thereof—or even in the warriors who emerge victorious from combats that decide the fate of an entire community—a guilty conscience sometimes appears, rising to the surface of the discourse. Thus in *Le Charroi de Nîmes*, probably composed in the first half of the twelfth century, Guillaume (the future William of Orange) reminds King Louis of the battles he has won for him, all the deaths that these entailed, and, consequently, all the potential guilt felt by the victor. Admittedly, it is not often that we find such sentiments expressed, this sense of waste and sin, in connection with the chivalrous life:

> I have valiantly served you in arms,
> And have often supported you in battle,
> Thus *killing many noble young men;*
> The *sin* of this has pierced my heart.

Whoever they were, God made them.

May God save their souls, and forgive me!

Mes par mes armes t'ai servi comme ber;

Si t'ai forni maint fort estor champel,

Dont ge ai morz maint gentil bacheler

Dont le pechié m'en est el cors entré.

Qui que il fussent, si les ot Deus formé.

Deus penst des ames, si le me pardonez!

(Charroi de Nimes, lines 67–72)

Later in his tirade, Guillaume again raises this point:

"God," said Guillaume, "Who were born to a noble virgin,

Why have I killed so many fine young men,

And why *have I made so many mothers grieve,*

The sin of which I feel in my breast?"

"Deus, dit Guillelmes, qu'issis de virge gente,

Por c'ai ocis tante bele jovente,

Ne por qu'ai fet tante mere dolante,

Dont li pechié me sont remés el ventre?"   (Ibid., lines 272–275)

Rare indeed are the texts that evince this sense of guilt. Thus, at the beginning of *La Mort du roi Arthur,* when the few survivors of the quest for the Holy Grail meet at court, the king summons Gawain:

King Arthur had heard it said that Sir Gawain had killed many men, and invited him into his presence: "Gawain, I ask you on the oath you gave me when I made you a knight, to answer the question I shall put to you." "Sire," answered Gawain, "You ask me in such a way that I cannot but answer, even if I cover myself with shame, the worst shame that ever befell a knight from your court." "Well," said the king, I want to know *how many knights you think you killed with your own hand in this quest.*" Sir Gawain thought for a moment, and the king began again: "Upon my head, I want to know, because some say that you have killed so many it's cause for amazement." "Sire," said Gawain, *you wish to know my great misfortune;* I shall tell you, because I can see I have to. I tell you truthfully that I have slain eighteen with my own hand, not because I was a better knight than anyone else, but because *more misfortune befell me* than any of my companions. You should know that it was not the result of my chivalrous prowess, but of my sins; *there, you have made me speak of my shame."*

Le rois avoit oï consonner que messires Gauvains an avoit ocis pluseurs, si le fist venir par devant lui et li dist: "Gauvain, je vos requier seur le serement que vos me feïstes quant je vos fis chevalier que vos me diez ce que je vos demanderai.—Sire, fet messire Gauvains, vos m'avez tant conjuré que ge ne leroie en nule maniere que ge nel vos deïsse, neïs se c'estoit ma honte, la greigneur qui onques a chevalier de vostre cort avenist.—Or vos demant ge, fet li rois, quanz chevaliers vos cuidiez avoir ocis de vostre mein en ceste queste." *Et messire Gauvain pense un petit et li rois li dit autrefoiz: "Par mon chief, ge le vueill savoir, por ce que aucun vont disant que vos en avez tant ocis que c'est merveille.—Sire, fet messires Gauvains,* vos voulez estre certeins de ma grant mescheance; *et ge le vos dirai, car ge voi bien qu'a fere le couvient. Je vos di por voir que g'en ai ocis par ma main dis et uit, non pas pour ce que ge fusse mieudres chevaliers que nus autres, mes* la mescheance se torna plus vers moi *que vers nul de mes compaignons. Et si sachiez bien que ce n'a pas esté par ma chevalerie, mes par mon pechié;* si m'avez fet dire ma honte."

(*La Mort du roi Arthur*, par. 3)

As literary texts show and even explicitly say on occasion, being exposed to death was one of a young man's functions. Young men became knights precisely to fulfill this role as best they could, and numerous were the dubbing ceremonies that preceded the departure for a battle.

Given this interpretive perspective, there is an odd characteristic of epic narratives and medieval romances, French ones in particular, whose significance thus becomes clear: the abundance of nephews in these texts. Reto Bezzola was the first to point out the existence of this peculiarity, which nonetheless remained a puzzle to him.[32] But the explanation becomes clear if one takes the analysis beyond a simple head count. If we examine the fate of the hero-nephews of this literature, for example Roland, Vivien, Gawain, Mordred, and Tristan himself, we find that they are always sons of the king's sister. It sometimes transpires that the nephew is actually the result of an incestuous love between brother and sister. Such is the case of Roland and Mordred. All these brilliant nephews die through some deed of their uncle's, and some are even killed by his hand. This is what happens to Mordred, who mortally wounds his father-uncle, Arthur, and is killed by him, and to Tristan, who is killed by Mark in certain thirteenth-century prose versions. And doesn't Roland die for his uncle, his incestuous father according to the *Karlamagnussaga?*

Nephews or sons? In either case a young man, a possible heir, and a very brilliant one at that, is destined to die, and does die, on account of or by the hand of his royal uncle-father. Obviously this was a form of literature that must have been gratifying for the *juvenes.* But in some more hidden way it must have been equally if not more gratifying for the *seniores,* since it showed them surviving the deaths of their possible heirs and rivals. Roland, Gawain, Tristan, Mordred, Vivien: all splendid stories, but stories in which it is the young ones who die.[33]

Viewed from this same perspective, there is another basic theme of medieval literature that remains enigmatic but acquires a most surprising significance, very different from the one normally attributed to it, and that is the quest for the Holy Grail. For Perceval, or Perlesvaus, or to a lesser degree Gawain, the object of the quest is not so much the sacred and mysterious vessel containing the blood shed by Christ on the cross, nor is it the vessel that contains nourishment for an old and impotent king, the *roi méhaignié* (wounded king). Rather, it is the question that must be asked in order to heal the king and save his kingdom from destruction. Faced with the answer posed by the Grail, the hero must find the right question. This question is: What is the purpose of the Grail, and whom does it serve?[34]

The young man must in fact be capable of wondering not about the object of his quest, but about the ultimate purpose of this object. And the answer is clear: Its purpose is the salvation of the sovereign. The hero should be capable of formulating the question himself, for as soon as he utters its terms, he shows he has absorbed the very law to which he must submit. No longer does this law come to him from the outside; once it becomes part of his speech, he has internalized and accepted it. As a young man, he is at the service of his sovereign, an avuncular and probably paternal figure, and must agree to devote all his strength, and possibly his life, to ensuring the older man's survival and prosperity.

This, however, was not the only relationship of dependency uniting those in power—the seigneurs—with the young *bachelers*. A fundamental difference between the seigneur or king and the young man is their totally different behavior in economic matters. The king is distinguished by his financial caution, which contrasts to a sometimes ridiculous degree with the generosity, or *largece*, required of the knight. This want of equilibrium serves as a departure point for several narratives: often, the king has forgotten to reward some knight, for example Lanval in the *Lai de Lanval* by Marie de France, or the future Guillaume d'Orange in *Le Charroi de Nîmes*, both twelfth-century texts. Guillaume consequently finds himself unable to meet the demands of his social function: namely, to provide himself with arms and horses so as to fight effectively, and also with clothes, so as to be elegant; and to pay the salaries of the fighting men and squires who must accompany him. A knight must have money to maintain his rank; but money is controlled by the seigneur. If the seigneur fails in his duty, the knight is forced to look elsewhere for this indispensible wealth. Two solutions present themselves: there is the epic solution (to go and conquer, taking what he needs and perhaps becoming a lord himself in the process) and there is the courtly solution.

We might rightly think that the invention of the courtly relationship would permit, among other things, the young man's economic dependence on the lord to become less evident. The lady, who is married and of high social rank, thus has the possibility of helping the young knight she loves and who loves her. From Lancelot in the twelfth century to Jehan de Saintré in the fifteenth,[35] this is an essential function of the adored lady: she is a source of both social and financial support. A further proof of this is that the lady sometimes appears as a fairy, as in the case of the twelfth-century *Lai de Lanval* or the fourteenth-century *Roman de Mélusine*,[36] for in the Middle Ages this was the archetypal way of representing women as dispensing inexhaustible supplies of goods and unlimited powers.

But the courtly relationship has another, more obvious function. Not only consent but also loyalty must be obtained from this young man who must give everything, generously offering his life, his love, his possessions—often dearly paid for—and his social virtues too. The invention of courtly love would seem to fulfill this function. In a certain way, the lady is the knight's implicit reward for the faithfulness he shows the husband and seigneur: Arthur and Mark have no better champions than Lancelot and Tristan. In my opinion this is how we should interpret a rather atypical text, the *Lai de Graelent*, which relates a brutal custom: every year at Pentecost Arthur assembles his barons and, after a banquet, has the queen undress, makes her get up on a bench, and asks if anyone there knows of a more beautiful woman.[37] The seduction exerted by the queen is simply one of the attributes of royal power; she is nothing more than the mediator in a relationship of power between men.

Though exceptional, this scene should not in fact be interpreted purely in its singularity. Crudely and clearly, it states what a number of courtly texts simply suggest: that courtly love is perhaps, first and foremost, a matter of love between men. Indeed, if we examine the elements that typify the love we call courtly, some of them prove quite astonishing, and remain inexplicable unless they are integrated into a comprehensive interpretation that accounts for them.

It has long been observed that courtly love almost always involves a young knight and a married woman, the wife of his lord. But this relationship, presented as fundamentally binary, is in fact triangular, uniting not only the knight and the lady, but also the knight and the lady's husband. The texts express as much; we need only read them carefully. Thus Tristan, despite having lived for a while in Ireland and spent considerable time with Yseult, falls in love with her only after drinking the love potion—in other words, after she has been betrothed to King Mark, Tristan's lord and uncle. The prose versions of these romances, which date from the thirteenth century, are quite explicit: extremely handsome, Lancelot and Tristan exert a seductive charm over the powerful men they meet, and are themselves attracted to them.[38]

When Lancelot arrives at court, Arthur is utterly charmed by the young man's beauty and prowess. This is how the *Lancelot en prose* describes their first meeting: superbly dressed and elegant, Lancelot sits at the feet of the royal couple, on the thick green grass. The king's reaction is described first: "The king looks at him with great pleasure; if he found him handsome when he arrived, this was nothing compared to the beauty he discerned in him now." (*"Et li rois l'esgarde moult volentiers; s'il li avoit samblei biax en son venir, noiens estoit envers la biauté qu'il avoit ore."* *Lancelot,* vol. 7, p. 274.) Lancelot has, moreover, seduced the superb lord Galeholt, an extraordinary character in romance—"the most appealing and complex in the *Lancelot en prose,"* according to J. Frappier. Galeholt is the half-giant Lord of the Distant Isles who dreams of conquering 150 kings, and gives up his victory over Arthur out of love for Lancelot.[39] Later on, believing Lancelot to be dead, he allows himself to die. His epitaph is explicit: "Here lies Galeholt, son of the Giantess, Lord of the Distant Isles, who died for love of Lancelot." (*"Ci gist Galehout, li fiz a la Jaiande, li sire des Lointaignes Isles, qui por l'amour de Lancelot morut."* Ibid., vol. 2, p. 212.) And when he dies, Lancelot has himself buried not with Guinevere, but next to Galeholt:

> And that night they opened the tomb of Galeholt, who had more riches than any other man. Next morning they had Lancelot's body placed inside; afterward they had these words engraved: Here lies the body of Galeholt, Lord of the Distant Isles, and with him rests Lancelot of the Lake, the best knight who ever entered the kingdom of England, except for Galahad his son.

> *Et la nuit firent ouvrir la tombe Galeholt qui tant estoit riche com nule plus. L'endemain firent metre enz le cors Lancelot; aprés firent metre desus letres qui disoient: Ci gist li cors Galeholt, le seignor des Lointaignes Illes, et avec lui repose Lancelos del Lac qui fu li mieudres chevaliers qui onques entrast el roiaume de Logres, fors seulement Galaad son fill.*

> (*La Mort du roi Arthur,* pp. 262–263)

In this society of men, the courtly couple could never be an autonymous entity, even if, necessarily, it was represented as such: the knight and lady were actively involved in the masculine relationships of power and seduction.

To be loved, the lady had to be married, and a queen: she thus had the glamorous appeal of gold, of her husband's power and fortune, and she had the beauty of power. In fact she served as a reflection, a double, of the love the young man bore the lord, and of the charm he exerted over him. For the young man himself shared in feminine beauty and seduction, just as the lady shared in seignorial power.

A characteristic that reveals this function of courtly love and that has proved intriguing to scholars is the invariably sterile nature of these unions. The love between the knight and the queen, or the lady, does not have procreation as its goal: quite the reverse, in fact, for that would disturb the order of succession. The lady's essential role in seducing the young man is to put him in her husband's service; and the result of the unemployed young knight's seduction of the married lady is a metonymy of the seductive power he actually exerts over her husband, the king. The lady is an obligatory third party here; she veils—and thus authorizes—a relationship of seduction, pleasure,[40] and vassalage linked to the structure of medieval society, allowing an oblique representation of this relationship to be made. As we have seen, courtliness and chivalry go hand in hand.

A FLOWER OF EVIL:
YOUNG MEN IN
MEDIEVAL ITALY

Elisabeth Crouzet-Pavan

Was there such a thing as youth in medieval times? Apart from a few sermons or moral treatises composed, along the lines of L. B. Alberti's *Libri della Famiglia,* to instruct fathers of children and to establish rules of behavior, medieval uses of the term are relatively rare. Rare, too, are general references to an age group defined as young, identified with no hesitation or uncertainty of terms. We are not even sure if the word youth exactly mirrors the reality of "young men" found in all other written sources, be they narrative, normative, or documentary. The treatises provide neither precise information nor details as to the chronology of this age, and initially confuse it with a period of obligatory scolding. *"Jeunesse doibt estre naturellement ordonnée":* Youth must naturally be controlled, wrote Guillaume Budé in 1547.[1] Before him, Alberti had multiplied the same recommendation: "restrain," "moderate," "govern."[2] The aphorism appears constant, and the legitimacy of educational books was based on a repetition of this message. In the absence of further information, it does at least offer an image—always a negative one, even if the breadth of the condemnation varies. "Dissipation," we read, "license"; or, when the description calms down a little, "absence of moderation." Youth is a time of desires and their excesses; as such, it seems to follow directly after childhood. This tender age, when the body is still weak and the first elements of knowledge are acquired, is succeeded by an age of fragility and weakness in the mind and soul. Through lack of restraint and control, youth indulges in wrongdoing. To ensure the very survival of the community—a concern that runs through all the sermons of San Bernardino of Siena, for example—youth must be restrained. Physical development must thus be followed by spiritual development.

Through the intermediaries of Gregory of Tours and Isidor of Seville, antiquity has transmitted to us a rigorous computation of the various age cohorts.[3] The period of *infantia* (infancy) ended at age seven, when *pueritia* (boyhood) began. The same seven-year term delimited *adolescentia* (adolescence), between ages fourteen and twenty-one. And then youth began, with no theoretical milestone to mark its end. The vocabulary may be termed as uncertain as these limits probably were. With varying degrees of richness and accuracy, medieval Italian named and distinguished these different stages of growth. A *puer* (boy) was known by an abundance of terms; the word *putto* in northern Italy was confused in Florence with *fanciullo*.[4] The word *garzone* was used as a synonym, without necessarily connoting a socioeconomic condition of dependency.[5] It was harder for the language to define the next age, for which *garzone* again was used, and also *giovanetto*.[6] Then the period of *giovani* (young men) began, and with this single term texts of the period unhesitatingly identify an entire group of men.

To reconstruct a definition of *giovani* through biological or sociological norms nonetheless seems risky. If someone became a *giovane* at around twenty-three or twenty-four, he stopped being one after thirty, having by then been an adult for some time. Among the *giovani,* social and matrimonial conditions varied, as did the extent of their integration into the economical and political life of the city. In consequence, what typified the *giovani* in the eyes of their contemporaries was their common adherence to a set of sociocultural values. There was no ambiguity about belonging to this group: the *giovani* were revealed by their deeds. The record of a fifteenth-century criminal trial in Venice removes all doubt in the matter when, recognizing habitual practices in these excesses, it refers to a *mos iuvenum* (nature of youth) when condemning them.[7] Because they describe not so much an uncertain age cohort as a type of behavior that people generally disapproved of, the sources convey an image as negative as those one might find offered by the various moral institutions. They appear even more pessimistic, especially the normative ones, when deploring—in cases where the miscreants were already *uomini fatti* (adult men)—both the impossiblity of correcting them and the failure of repressive measures.

That each society nurtures a particular image of its "young" or "old" seems highly evident.[8] More worthy of interest, perhaps, is the somber image of young people reflected in various texts from the late Middle Ages in Italy, linking these *giovani* not so much to a function or to roles, as to behavior that was largely reprehensible.

Taking this image, as established in the final decades of the fifteenth century, as our point of departure, I propose commenting first on the dynamics of its function.

"O RIBALD, O UNBRIDLED YOUTH"

San Bernardino of Siena preached in the town where he was born, exhorting the fathers to protect his "beautiful Siena."[9] In his fight against the scourge of sodomy, he developed a singularly broad definition of youth: "And if I had sons, this is what I would do with them. As soon as they were three, I would send them all out of Italy, and not allow them to return until they were forty."[10] Ignoring the traditional divisions of the growing period, the preacher thus declared forty to be the end of the dangerous age. Constrained by his struggle against evil, he lumps together children, adolescents, and young men, without drawing a distinction between those whose faults are excused and whose punishment is mitigated by childhood, those for whom youth represents almost an aggravating circumstance.

In fact, in documentary sources the *aetas legitima* (lawful age) makes a seemingly clear distinction between the world of minors and that of others. Fathers of families recognized its importance when they made wills: in choosing their executors, they asked that sons who were still minors be integrated into the circle of close relatives on reaching "lawful age." Similarly, a close reading of wills indicates that the execution of the various clauses was subject to this same juridical norm. But a study of acts of emancipation reveals that the community did not use this procedure as a ritual stage sanctioning maturity. Whatever preoccupations explain this act within the family (economic or functional concerns,[11] relationships

within the family group, and so on), the extremely variable age of emancipation did not correspond to the legal coming of age under Roman law.[12]

Similarly, criminal judicial practice varied according to whether sensi-
bilities needed to be repressed or to evolve. Thus passive sodomites were
absolved until 1424 in Venice, so long as they were minors, and the Council
of Ten ordered their names to be stricken from the records of trials and
condemnations.[13] But after 1424 the penalties were made more severe:
thenceforth, the *patiens* (passive partner) was judged responsible after the
age of ten.[14] This development is to some extent explained by the increased
discretionary powers *(arbitrium)* granted judges during the fourteenth and
fifteenth centuries. In cases of sexual crimes against female victims, judges
tended increasingly to show equal severity in punishing those who attacked
young boys or little girls. Before 1360 the term *puella* was applied only to
girls under twelve. After that date, criminal archives contain cases of the
word being used for victims age fourteen. The age of innocence was thus
being extended in the case of victims; for the perpetrators, conversely, it
was tending to shrink. Only the real youth of the culprit justified an
occasional moderation of the punishment *(considerate etate sua):* then the
penalty was reduced or else applied in a different manner. Some trials thus
witnessed a departure from the publicity that was normally part of the
penal mechanism: the crime was not publicly proclaimed, and the whip
was administered not in the public square or street, but in the torture
chamber. The *pueri* (boys) whom justice seemed thus partly inclined to
spare no longer corresponded exactly to the group of *pueri* recognized in
all other spheres. They were much younger.

What conclusion should we draw from this? The age of full responsibility and the age of majority did not coincide. Above all, the age of
majority did not signify an attainment of maturity. San Bernardino set the
threshold of maturity at age forty, with the end of disorderly behavior,
weaknesses, and temptations. Did this figure mark a real departure, or was
it merely symbolic?

In the mass of notarized acts that have been preserved, it is easy to
pick out the wills of *giovani,* members of the urban bourgeoisie or urban
aristocracies. A first signal is the declension of identity. In these cases the

testator does not always mention his filiation. When he does subscribe to this practice, the *quondam* following his name clearly shows his status as the head of a family. The *giovane* is a "son of." And this obligatory enrollment in the group of parents constitutes a first similarity between the world of *juvenes* and that of women, who are "daughters of," "wives of," or "widows of." The entire tenor of the will derives from this initial observation. Executors of wills were chosen from among the nearest blood relatives—father, mother, brothers, uncles—and the legacies were divided between them. The pious clauses, which are rather less prolix, corresponded to general devotional practices, being clustered round the choice of burial in "our tomb." Above all, there is an absence of long and minute dispositions providing for the transmission and destiny, through several generations, of the most precious part of the patrimony: real estate. It makes no difference whether or not a wife is mentioned. All these wills are characterized by the weight of paternal power *(patria potestas)* and the absence of economic independence.

In this search for significant criteria concerning the group of *giovani*, the wills thus give evidence of a determining factor. The "young man" was defined by his incomplete socioeconomic integration. And only a change in his position within the family could enable him to change his status.

Marriage did not in fact constitute a line of demarcation, nor was it relevant whether or not a marriage proved fruitful. The average age of marriage has been calculated from data given in the survey register *(catasto)* of 1427. Given as twenty-nine for Florentines,[15] it did not divide the homogenous world of *giovani*. This is born out by the well-known description of the joust *(armeggeria)* given by Bartolomeo Benci and his companions for Marietta Strozzi, one night during the carnival of 1464 in Florence.[16] The procession formed at the first hour of night, in the Piazza de' Perutti, in front of the homes of the Benci family. Besides Benci, "lord and captain of this company," it included eight young horsemen, all magnificently attired. Each of them was surrounded by thirty footmen carrying lighted torches. But Benci's own retinue was even more imposing. Eight "young men" surrounded him on foot. One hundred fifty more "young men" on horseback, all dressed in his colors and bearing torches, escorted him. And Benci rode beside a Triumph of Love made up of allegories and symbols whose meanings could be understood by all. The spectacle of the riders' skill was offered to Marietta, who watched from her window. The Triumph was burned, in the hope that the young woman's heart would also catch fire at the sight. In front of the dwellings of "each of the ladies of the eight companions," the equestrian feats were repeated. Lances were broken, and golden ones at that. At dawn, the troup organized a serenade beneath Marietta's windows. The night ended at Benci's house, where a magnificent banquet had been prepared and the host received the entire company in great splendor.

Bartolomeo's declaration of love to Marietta did not lead to matrimony. Unions were the result of economic and symbolic interests among the families. In this case the amorous ritual was enacted in a different sphere. Several of the eight horsemen were already married.

The Signoria had had two bans *(bandi)* published, to keep everyone at a safe distance from the lances and horses, and to ensure that, for the entire night, nothing would disturb the success of the festivities. Two of Bartolomeo's brothers and two members of the Strozzi family guaranteed the orderliness and restraint of this amorous homage, which was formalized to an extreme degree. But, ritualized or not, courtly or violent, and regardless of whether they respected the explicit family and social codes, the activities of the *giovani* always brought together bachelors and married men. In an entry in his *Diaries* dated February 26, 1499, Sanudo describes an affair that created a great uproar in Venice at the time. A brawl broke out on the evening of February 25, before the door of a well-known courtesan. Among those nobles compromised in the affair—Morosini, Priuli, Venier, Vendramin—several were married.[17]

There was another threshold that the *giovani* crossed to an even greater degree, and this was their integration into the political life of the city. By means of a procedure known as the Balla d'Oro, the Grand Council of Venice lowered the voting age to eighteen for favored adolescent noblemen. On Santa Barbara's day, the names of young men who had given proof of their age and lawful aristocratic birth[18] were put into a hat. Those victorious in the drawing[19] were allowed to sit in the Grand Council as soon as they were twenty. The others—unless fortune favored them at the next Barbarella[20]—waited until they were twenty-five before taking their seats in the assembly, seats to which they were entitled by birth. After that point, they could be elected to office. And for a great number of them, the first election took place before they were thirty.[21] The liminal period that began with registration for the Balla d'Oro, and that varied in length according to the individual and his career, ended with a ceremony proving that the newly elected man was in fact old enough to fill his office.[22]

The race for public offices and their attendant income began early, since it was such a strong factor in the political, economic, and social importance of an aristocrat and his family.[23] Even in Florence, though less systematically, young men were allowed a little space. The families' interest in seeing their sons assume some office triumphed over the negative portrayals of the *giovani* as a group. Thus, during the Medici period, various expedients softened the institutionalized gerontocracy of the Florentine republic.[24]

But in both cities, the law still continued to restrict access to the more important offices by means of strict age limits: thirty, thirty-five, forty, or even forty-five.[25] Once the barrier to rapid and prestigious careers was removed, the *cursus honorum* (race for honors) really became worthy of its name. Following a slight redistribution in the hierarchy of magistracies, certain responsibilities signaled the beginning of a career during the fourteenth and fifteenth centuries in Venice. But more often than not, mistrust continued to dog these newcomers, who remained *giovani* for several more years. The Doge Mocenigo tried to forewarn the governing elite against the "young" Francesco Foscari.[26] And the chronicles of fifteenth-century Venice, rich in accounts of turmoil and violent acts committed within the bounds of the ducal palace by *nobiles juvenes,* some of whom were already members of the Grand Council,[27] prove that group solidarities prevailed over the apparent lines of political majority.

No doubt this ritualization (a new phenomenon in the fifteenth century) of the young men's entry into political life in Venice was due in part to a redefinition of patrician status and its political ideology. No doubt these first years of the *cursus* can also be interpreted as the formalizing of a veritable rite of passage intended gradually to integrate young men: to make them finally accept, share, and defend the norms and values of the oligarchy in power.[28] But this interpretation, which favors only the evolution of the patrician regime, its nature and objectives, must be weighed against another fact. To ensure its very survival and reproduction, the patriciate tended gradually to absorb its *juvenes*, the better to discipline them. The assumption that youth was wild and tumultuous thus gave legitimacy to the material and symbolic organization of this entry into political life. While the sons, or their fathers, recognized the importance of the Balla d'Oro—a solemn occasion made even more so by the presence of the Doge—this break was only partly accepted by the group of young men, who remained united in spite of everything. Not until the elective mandates accumulated did integration become a reality. Until then, turbulent and impulsive, young men could band together and even try to influence the councils. In their fear of all associations, meetings, plots, and conspiracies, the assemblies were also afraid that the young men might turn the elections to their own advantage. The ritualized intermediary passage thus lasted for some years.

These intermediary years, whose duration varied with each city, thus aimed at appeasing the ambition and impetuosity of the *giovani*. The case of Baschiera Tosinghi, a young Florentine from the second half of the thirteenth century, is an example of the consequences of excluding young men from power—perhaps rather an extreme example since, deprived of his father, he had no family support. The elders of his house took all the honors and profits for themselves, and made no attempt to advance him in the commune.[29] His warlike, factious passions seem to have been a direct result of this fact.

But in fifteenth-century Florence or Venice, despite more or less decided attempts on the part of the regime to integrate the *giovani*, chronicles and political treatises nonetheless continued to defend the ideals of republics of *geronti*, old men. And the Venetian Domenico Morosini reached the same conclusions as San Bernardino of Siena when he proposed excluding all men under age forty from deliberations of the councils.[30]

The definitions seem more certain when we consider the economic position of the *giovani*. The workplace created divisions based on age and status. So long as the father was alive, the world of business put the son in a dependant position. Was youth therefore coterminous with the period of economic dependency, at least for those who had the possibility of escaping from it one day? In bourgeois and aristocratic households, the death of the father would thus constitute a decisive break. It was not, however, enough to guarantee exit from the group of *giovani:* indispensable requirements of age and maturity also accompanied this passage, permitting true economic establishment.

This theme is present in both Boccaccio and Sercambi. If the father dies too soon, the sons live even more intemperately, indulging in all the excesses of youth. Lacking guidance and restraint, they follow only their whims and youthful desires. Through his description of a still seignorial splendor—dogs, horses, falcons, jousts, courtly gatherings, generous gifts—Boccaccio shows how a patrimony could be dissipated.[31] More succinctly, Sercambi evokes a similar picture of feverish spending and enjoyment.[32] Youth is identified with the wanton, unregulated consumption of every type of food and pleasure. And group solidarity is further strengthened by habits of sumptuous hospitality and generosity among young people, by the followers who collect around anyone offering banquets, hunting parties, and cavalcades.

As soon as a family disposed of a little extra money, there was always the threat of its being wasted by the *juvenes*. In a story by Boccaccio's contemporary, Sacchetti, a wealthy farmer from around Lucca sends his son to study law in Bologna. With books and daily expenses, the household soon loses a great deal of money. According to his second wife, the father is bleeding himself for "a dead body." Through her recriminations, Sacchetti explores two fertile themes: that of the jealous and unloving stepmother, and that of the young student, eager for pleasure and spending.[33] Fed and enriched by a vast contemporary literature, this picture of prodigal youth would seem to represent nothing other than the metamorphosis of a theme beyond history.

Some lives were devoid of this behavior so generally ascribed to a "golden youth." For example, the beginnings of the commercial career of Andrea Barbarigo in early fifteenth-century Venice reveal a young man's determined efforts to restore the position of his family, which his father, at his death, had left seriously undermined. But the first steps were difficult; restoring the patrimony was a lengthy business. Accordingly, the Barbarigo relatives who had settled in Crete lent him a helping hand, as did the Capello family, which eventually provided him with a wife.[34] An established position had to be paid for with years of waiting and dependence. In a different context, the first pages of Luca Landucci's *Diario* recount the principal dates in his personal and familial history and describe how long an apprenticeship could be, even for someone finally in a position to open his own shop.[35] Although family ties helped foster and organize business all through life, economic emancipation really constituted the most decisive stage.

In most cases the death of the father led to this emancipation. But all literary treatments of the subject, whether light or serious, present quite a different picture of this event. The father's death is eagerly anticipated, since it supposedly facilitates access to life's pleasures. Once it occurs, the sons' dissipation increases and patrimonies disappear. The literary image thus ignores the reality of this break, which saddled the inheritor with new values and responsibilities. Prodigal behavior was only one of the numerous scandalous signs of the enslavement of the *giovani* to their passions.

Even when married and admitted to sessions of one of the city councils, even when entrusted with minor responsibilities in family affairs, the son was still considered to be a *juvenis*. Thus the various socioeconomic definitions only succeed in providing an incomplete definition of what was less an age group—youth—than a group of men, the *giovani*. Between adolescence and a late-developing age of reason, all such men could behave like *juvenes*, regardless of their status. Not all, however, did. Few men who were well into their thirties mingled with these turbulent groups. Even so, they were still subject to the widespread suspicion that they might indulge in these excesses. The definition of *juvenes*—a definition more normative than biological—had been grafted on to the classical division of the ages in life. Consequently, in sources of the time, it is hard to dissociate these *giovani* from the images attached to them.

At this point we begin to notice a parallel. Like women, the *juvenes* were objects of fear. Both, though in different ways, formed obstacles to peace and salvation in a Christian society. Scholars have already pointed out the new place granted female listeners in manuals on preaching after the beginning of the thirteenth century.[36] And in the sermons that San Bernardino delivered on the Piazza del Campo in Siena—except when he was addressing Siena and his "fellow citizens"—women, far more than other members of the community, were cited, called on, and summoned to return the next day. All practical advice—buy meat the previous evening, cook it in the morning—was addressed to them, so that they could be present when the sermon began; likewise, the benevolent exhortations to listen, learn, and remember, and to make the sign of the cross afterward to show their commitment. This was thus a privileged dialogue that preachers were trying to institute.[37] But besides women, another category of beings was particularly admonished: the *giovani*.

Frequently, in fact, a sermon was directed toward these two categories and the need to reform their behavior. "O giovano, o donna," San Bernardino would intone, censuring both of them. United by the same luxurious and debauched tastes in clothing and ornaments, women and young men were the prey of indecent, shameful fashions. Together they took part in the entertainments, balls, and festivities that accompanied weddings. Only the worst could be expected of such moral fragility and lack of restraint. And even if the sermon was not composed around a central theme, such as clothes and fashionable ornaments, in its parenthetical clauses, in the *exempla* set forth, women and young men found themselves being condemned for the same weaknesses, the same lack of discipline in words, amusements, and behavior. Indeed, the same two of "obstinate sinners" crop up again in the sermons of Savonarola.[38] The empty-headed woman would spend the whole week waiting for Sunday and its dances to arrive; the young man would complain of being shut up in his shop every day. The woman wore clothes like a prostitute and spent the whole day having fun with the *juvenes*. The young man spent money, played games, adorned himself, yielded to all his desires.[39] The vices to be avoided and the corrections to be made thus bore a strange similarity.

Of all the objectives that sumptuary laws sought to attain, the need to moderate women's fashions seemed the most urgent. Through the abundant body of legislation preserved in each city, we may observe a continual struggle against increasing luxury—a struggle never abandoned despite its limited results. So it was in Venice, where the first laws were passed against the vast expenditures on clothes, jewels, and banquets necessitated by weddings. In the first decades of the fourteenth century, the texts particularly attacked these excesses, which compromised patrimonies and actually ruined certain families. On this front, war was continually waged, with the councils trying unsuccessfully to restrict the growth of dowries, to limit the magnificence of gifts to the bride, and to regulate the splendor of the wedding breakfasts. During these same years, when the first regulatory basis of the commune was established, certain limits were voted in, supposedly applicable to all women. As everywhere else, these limits curtailed the length of trains in wedding dresses, the richness of pearl necklaces or belts, and prohibited cloth embroidered with threads of gold or silver. Even here, the efforts were fruitless. As the splendor grew—as sleeves, for example, became fuller and richer and were lined with ever more precious cloth—the prohibitions became proportionately more numerous.

Against these "superfluous" and "disorderly" expenses, against these "futile" and "dangerous" splendors, public order and God's order waged a common war. The priests repeated their accusations against women who dressed up and wore makeup. "Useless" and "superfluous" ornaments and jewels were signs of vanity and pride and served the devil's work. The order of creation was disturbed by these deceitful practices. Women who were gaudily dressed were an even greater inducement to sin. San Bernardino of Siena encouraged women thus bedizened to be treated as prostitutes. And in 1480 in Venice, after the aid of the patriarch had been sought, the full apparatus of the Church, through confessors and parish priests, was brought to bear: Venetian women had to give up the immodest hairstyles that concealed the faces given them by God.[40] The peace of the city was defined as the practice of God's order. In the ruminations of the Council, fear of God's wrath was the determining factor—far more than fear that the city's wealth would be wasted in so much useless expenditure. These customs, "abominable to God and to the world," could cause "the Creator's indignation" to strike Venice.[41] "Whereas the tribulations of the time" were "already numerous, the infinite graces of our Lord God"[42] had to be preserved, together with "the reverence and honor in which he has always held Venice."[43]

The dynamics of preaching and legislation appear to have run parallel. Women remained the central target of restrictions and condemnations. But as the fifteenth century progressed, the *giovani,* guilty of the same excesses, were vituperated in their turn. Even in the early fourteenth century, regulations took note of luxurious male clothes. Any man past the age of ten was not supposed to wear velvet or silks woven with gold or silver.[44] A general concern with decency and dignity dictated these norms. In the second half of the fifteenth century, women and *juvenes* together introduced "fresh abominations," "deplorable habits," "errors," and "disorders." In these public acts, the ostentatious habits of young men were attacked first, through the banquets organized by festive societies. As in the case of wedding breakfasts, these feasts—where pheasants and peacocks, pasta, and dishes of all kinds were served on platforms set up in the streets or on canals—were roundly condemned.[45] Three wise officers still elected intermittently during the final decades of the fifteenth century, were charged with keeping a watchful eye on the ostentation and ornaments of women: *"sopra le pompe et ornamenti de le done."*[46] Admittedly, the parenthetical clauses of these texts did specify that the forbidden ornaments were forbidden to everyone. And when a vote was taken to suspend such limits temporarily, during festivities or solemn receptions for ambassadors, it applied to both women and young men: "And all the women invited to this festival may wear their necklaces, their pearls, and all the jewels and ornaments they wish. And all the young men who attend this festival may, for this day only, wear . . ."[47] In addition, the first decrees formalizing public ceremonies in Venice during these decades also regulated the dress of these two categories of persons.

Women and young men seem to have represented two equal threats, two weaknesses likely to destroy the temporal order and the fabric of society. The war on sodomy waged by religious and public authorities partly explains this fresh focus of attention on youth. The sermons of San Bernardino were unleashed against the accursed sodomites. And even when the preacher composed his sermon around more traditional themes, there is no doubt that this fear of sodomy implicitly fed his condemnation of indecent masculine fashions.[48] In the second half of the fifteenth century, the Venetian Senate gave a new, decisive reason for refusing to allow excessively costly gifts to be given the bride: "Because of these superfluous expenditures, weddings are now being abandoned,"[49] "and many young men refuse to marry."[50] These sumptuary laws still contain an echo of contemporary decrees that censured sodomy more explicitly, deploring the uselessness of a sexuality "exercised against the propagation of the human species."[51]

A gradual reversal of perspective thus seems to have occurred in the course of the fifteenth century. While women were still a preferential audience for the major sermons, and still had to be advised, guided, and reprimanded, their possible danger to society paled in significance when compared with these new threats. Attempts were still made to temper their frivolity and moderate their chatter, but society's fear now had a different object. "Do you understand me, women? In the teeth of all these sodomites I mean to take the side of women, and I say that woman, in her flesh, is cleaner and more precious than man."[52] Women's natural lasciviousness was less threatening to the general salvation than the scourge of sodomy. Indeed, women were even requisitioned to combat this contagion.[53] The temporal powers showed even less hesitation in dealing with this hierarchy of perils:[54] better that there be prostitutes, if they could curtail the "vice."[55]

Though extraordinarily extensive, the phenomenon of sodomy in fifteenth-century Italian cities—and the repression it gave rise to—are not enough to account for the violently negative image attached to the *juvenes*. Of all the scourges associated with them, sodomy was certainly the most dangerous, since it jeopardized the city's very future. But the young men's daily disorderliness was just as harmful to the balance and order of society. In the criminal archives of the fifteenth century, since crime was not separated from the image of its repression, intolerance was growing in regard to the *mos juvenum*.

In recent years, the history of disorders caused by groups united by ties of age and specific collective behavior has benefited from a new sensibility on the part of historiographers in regard to the study of crime and justice. Among the youthful felonies, gang rapes have attracted particular attention, and the example of Dijon is especially well known. In Dijon, sexual violence affirmed itself as a permanent dimension of urban life. Bands of young men regularly engaged in this type of aggression (once or twice a month, on average), and the statistical curve of these collective assaults is seemingly unaffected by seasons or holidays. One out of two young city dwellers took part in them. As an expression of rejection of the social and matrimonial order, collective rape may also be seen as a rite of admission into the youthful gangs, with their clear socioprofessional ties.[56]

To restrain these violent impulses, the collectivity attempts to socialize youth. The urban community promotes or controls brotherhoods of young men, which lend formality and structure to the solidarity caused by age. The young men's organizations then mainly make sure that the custom of matrimony is respected. Historical analysis concentrates on the forms this socialization assumes; also on the diverse rituals instigated by these associations, and on the degeneration, crises, or condemnations occurring in them.[57]

Criminal archives attest to many anomic or criminal practices through which gangs of young men were bonded together.[58] In Venice, these practices were typically nocturnal. Unlike the numerous daytime rapes committed inside the home or city, gang rape appears on the list of violent acts perpetrated at night. The ludic elements inherent in it, the insults and blows accompanying it subscribed to the general rules dramatizing violent group behavior. Like all other forms of nocturnal aggression, gang rape gave proof, inside a group, of a social ability based essentially on criteria of virility.

Violence against the police was also deemed proof of virile prowess. When a group of armed young men was approached by police intent on searching or aresting them, their code of honor required them to offer forceful resistance. But usually such a fight was more deliberate, provoked by an exchange of insults or a massive uproar on the part of the youth.[59] On one occasion, for no reason except that they had deliberately chosen such an adversary—the verdict notes—five or six ruffians attacked the police forces of the Council of Ten. The fight lasted for some time. Four young men, ordered to lay down their weapons, crossed swords with a guard and then waited for him outside when he took refuge in a house. They threatened him and finally wounded him.[60]

These same gangs committed other acts of violence seemingly less charged with provocation and significance. Even when relatively concise, the judicial acts always distinguish between different types of aggression and indicate those not motivated by theft. Without cause, *"sine nulla causa,"* some passersby are attacked; the verdict reconstructs the mockery and humiliations, the threats that mount in intensity until the encounter reaches its more or less dramatic conclusion.[61] At best, the victim finds himself being dunked in the canal. At worst, blood is shed. In another case, two young aristocrats spend the night wandering through the town. "Out of malice" they attack a passerby. The wound is almost fatal, and the guilty pair do not show up in court.[62]

Neighborhood loyalties and socioprofessional ties formed the substratum of solidarity in these gangs. But above all, these bonds were sealed by youth, with social homogeneity proving very strong in all instances. While their masters were in sessions of the councils, slaves and servants waited outside, playing at cards and dice, shouting and fighting in the courtyard of the ducal palace—unless, of course, they invaded the Piazza San Marco and went thieving in the shops.[63] Sanudo's *Diaries* mention the heavy fine imposed on some young patricians who had been loitering on the piers at night, smashing gondolas at their moorings. The wedding of Jacobo Dolfin was the cause of several scandalous scenes. Two Pisani brothers started the violence, and hit a guest, who promptly left the house.[64] Disturbances and insulting graffiti beset the entire community. Insults were yelled for the edification of the neighborhood, while horns and obscene drawings singled out the victim for public derision.[65]

Not only young people took part in such excesses. Some ruckuses seemed to have had more to do with neighborhood conflicts, or with professional tensions involving victim or perpetrators.[66] Nonetheless these disturbances and disorders reveal the existence of provisional associations, spontaneously formed, of young men united by age, their bonds consolidated by work or friendship. Their members evince a sociability that had its own forms, rules, and rituals, and which trial accounts saw as evidence of possible conflict. Nobles and members of corporations were not implicated together in the trials. But whatever their condition in life, the *juvenes* appeared in court for the same reasons: acts of vandalism and violence, causing disorder and general uproar. Above all—and this fact restores some dynamics to a history of violent practices that could otherwise seem invariable—in the fifteenth century, increasingly repressive measures were taken against the disorders and their instigators.

During the second half of the thirteenth century and the first decades of the fourteenth, the communes issued the first regulatory texts establishing a basis for controlling behavior. Then the first general plan was introduced; designed to bring peace to the city, it targeted certain practices and protected certain places and times. Whether institutional or qualitative, all the studies devoted to crime and justice show distinct modifications in Italian cities during the fifteenth century.[67] Repressive measures changed. Control was strengthened, legitimized by new definitions of order and disorder—or at least by a new awareness of these two realities. The dynamics of censure, with nuances and modulations proper to each urban milieu, proved to be extraordinary in the history of the fifteenth century. The framework tightened, and surveillance weighed more heavily on urban life. This reinforcement of the structures of control resulted as much from the creation of new institutions as from the reimposition of the old normative plan, accompanied by stricter guarantees concerning the application of penalties.

This evolution in repression may be followed and measured in concrete terms. By superimposing the structures of the police force, by enlarging and multiplying the areas and time subject to more intense surveillance, public authority redefined its own concept of order and imposed new spatial and temporal codes. After absorbing certain phenomena such as gambling and prostitution the better to control them, the towns tended to pass from an age of tolerance to an age of condemnation. The example of Venice shows that by the late fifteenth century, the process that brought about the decline of certain structures, such as the municipal brothel, had largely begun. Attention focused on young people and their disorderliness, and the concept—unknown in previous sources—of an identifiable and ever dangerous *mos juvenum* had a place in this new system of representations, and helped to define it. Leaving aside, for the moment, the meaning of their juvenile customs, whether deviant or criminal, youths now faced sharply increased condemnation.

To the detriment of all other biological or socioeconomic criteria, only moral criteria—or, more exactly, the absence of moral criteria—seem capable of grasping and defining the group of *giovani* in fifteenth-century texts. "Ribald, unrestrained . . .": literary sources and public acts reflect the same image. Youth was a time of turbulence and violence. The richest young men spent and gave away money, accumulating clothes, horses, women, luxuries, and pleasures. Even the poorest entered into the festivities, either as members of the large retinues the rich dragged after them, or else as participants in their own violent games, which they organized at night in the streets. All violated the rules laid down by Christianity and society. All were driven by the same impatience, the same negativity, the same redoubtable desires. And all were objects of suspicion and fear. The one true definition of youth seems thus to reside in these negative images, which became stronger in the fifteenth century. Confronted with these *giovani*, an entire society seemed afraid of parricide.

In contrast to the apparent immobility of certain literary themes, this dark and dangerous dynamic image of young men took shape during the late Middle Ages. For want of better remedies, the community resorted to repression—unless, following the example of the Grand Council in

Venice, it sought to integrate some *giovani*, hoping they would cease to behave like young men.

It is time now to examine the absence of a social function for this group, the *giovani*.

"TO THE GREAT SHAME OF CHIVALRY"[68]

In his chronicles, Agnolo di Tura del Grasso dwells at length on the festivities that, lasting for days, accompanied the dubbing ceremony of Francesco, son of Sozo di Bandinello Bandinelli, in Siena.[69] The family, which had produced a whole line of "doctors and knights," was ancient, wealthy, and powerful. And the author of the chronicles devotes great care to extracting facts and names from copies of ancient documents, fragile and eroded by time, revealing a preoccupation more ideological than archeological. Agnolo di Tura meant to bring about a resurgence of Sienese nobility and genteel society. Rather than restoring vanished splendor and wealth, he was trying to revive an honorable ideal in life, a system of values and their social substructure.

A week before Francesco's investiture, the *curia* or ceremonial court, began. Grand banquets marked the first few days. The joust *(armeggeria)* began on the Sunday of Saint Thomas. And for four days on end the armed games continued, with each of the city's *terzi* (three districts) providing the elite of its horsemen. The meals brought together both the notables of each district and their *juvenes,* who came to test their skill and courage. Day by day, district by district, Agnolo di Tura compiled the most complete lists possible. And in the process, he emphasized the union of different urban wards, more usually divided during games and holidays by symbolic rivalries and violent confrontations.

The glamor of the court certainly attracted nobles from all over Italy,[70] including those great lords to whom the new knight denied the honor of buckling on his sword. But the chivalrous, festive ritual was primarily of value to the city. The town benefited from having so large a group of young people communing honorably through these martial and theatrical activities, and from the participation of the urban community, represented by the elite of its three wards. In the chronicler's narrative, a complex ritual was grafted on to the actual investiture, a ritual as festive as it was warlike. Through it, an entire society, including its *giovani,* celebrated a new knight's entry into the world of warriors. The splendor and the extraordinary generosity evidenced by the quantity of guests, and by the wealth of dishes served, place this early fourteenth-century Sienese father in a lordly tradition of largesse that was necessary and approved. Similarly, the glorified scene narrated by di Tura relates this chronicler to a style of literature bent on discerning and identifying the gestures, lifestyle, and ethics of the aristocracy.

After viewing this tableau from the golden age of chivalry, several remarks are appropriate before turning to the obvious ambiguity of the scene within the communal society of the early fourteenth century. In the final decades of the thirteenth century and in the first decades of the fourteenth, narrative sources indicate numerous investitures. In Italy the emperor or the communes could confer the dignity of knighthood; the historical dynamics and typology of the forms and occasions of this ritual have been studied.[71] Here I shall simply focus on the profound effects these ceremonies had on families and society. Outside the field of battle, urban festivities and family rituals intertwined, bringing collective and individual investitures to the forefront of the urban scene.

Baudouin II of Courtenay, emperor of Constantinople, was received in Modena in 1270: "And many nobles of Modena were knighted by the emperor."[72] Weddings and courts also entailed their share of dubbing ceremonies.[73] Two courts were held in Parma in the year 1282. The first opened on Assumption Day. The games lasted for one month, and two sons from the Rubeo family were made knights.[74] A new court opened in the following months. In the case of Azzo, son of the marquis of Este, the rituals of dubbing and marriage were combined.[75] The alliance celebrated between the houses of Ferrara and Milan involved the same pairing of ritual forms. Accompanied by a large suite of knights and young men who had come from all the cities of Lombardy, Galeazzo met Azzo in Modena. Knighted with others in his escort by the marquis of Este, he then married Beatrice, the marquis's sister.[76] In Parma, young men "of the grandest and noblest families"[77] performed equestrian feats to celebrate the new couple's entry into the city. The commune bore the costs and paid for the clothes worn by members of its warrior elite, who provided this spectacle of their skills. For a full month, in Verona, Cangrande celebrated the capture of Padua. At the height of the festivities, Della Scala dubbed thirty-eight Lombard knights, showering them with gifts.[78]

The power of a city, like the strength of a family, was measured in part by the number of men able to bear arms.[79] If any function ever appeared capable of channeling and engaging the young men's energies, it was certainly the military function.[80] When the men of Siena left to do battle against the Florentines, the only people left in the town were women, old men, and the clergy—all of whom marched in procession bearing relics from the cathedral. Singing litanies and psalms, uttering numerous orisons, they visited one church after another.[81] When the city was directly threatened, they protected the children by hiding them in the surrounding countryside, and trusted to the courage of their *giovani*.[82] Even if the men who bore arms were not all young, the *giovani* symbolized a city's martial vigor. In 1327, when a papal legate arrived in Bologna, the whole population came out to meet him, olive branches in hand. But the welcoming ceremony was planned around a system of signs of peace, honor, and allegiance that was even more expressive. The city's war chariot led the procession, draped in a great standard and drawn by garlanded oxen. A brigade of young men, armed and on horseback, rode on either side. Preceding the entire community, these symbols and instruments of military might were intended to honor the papal envoy and celebrate peace.[83] From an analysis of these scenes, it would seem that war between communes continued to depend on the young, mounted warrior.

Similarly, in the late fourteenth century, the chronicles are punctuated by instances and scenes of dubbing ceremonies. Whether the emperor was arming the sons of Francesco Castracane in Pisa[84] or the commune was creating new knights for the opening of a grand peace ceremony,[85] the investitures appear unchanging. In 1385, Siena was reformed: suddenly the city was pronounced safe and at peace. And as a sign of rejoicing, many new knights were given arms.[86]

Equestrian spectacles and military celebrations also appear unchanging. In thirteenth-century accounts, civic festivities, courts, and dubbing ceremonies were accompanied by all the figures and expressions of the joust *(hastiludere, bagordare)*.[87] More than direct confrontations between knights, these events showcased skill in riding and tilting. Each commune organized similar war games to celebrate major local festivals and extraordinary events. In Perugia, for example, the games took place every year on All Saints Day, and on March 1 for the feast of the local patron saint, Saint Ercolano. But these same *ludi* also figured in the pageants given by Perugia to celebrate the visit of some important person, or to solemnize the advent of a new pope.[88] In Siena, when the Council of Nine decreed eight days of continual entertainment, jousts took place amid balls and masquerades.[89]

The innumerable events mentioned in thirteenth-century sources were not followed by a massive silence on the part of later sources. A century after the celebrations decreed by the Nine in Siena, a similar series of balls, banquets, jousts, and pageants was recorded.[90] Compagni mentions the races and games organized in honor of the king of Sicily or for Charles de Valois's entry into Florence in 1301.[91] Between 1382 and 1401, the text of an anonymous Florentine gives numerous descriptions of similar "games" occurring more or less spontaneously, or else carefully regulated by the commune. When Arezzo was taken, scarcely had the church bells stopped ringing when brigades of young men dressed in their family colors invaded the square, riding back and forth and breaking lances. Further "jousting" occurred in the city in 1386; also in 1387, 1390, 1392, 1399.[92] Even Venice was no exception. For the carnival in 1322, the city organized a joust that took place on the Piazza San Marco.[93] After 1415, tournaments and jousts approved by a favorable vote of eight members of the Council of Ten took place several times on the main city square.[94]

If we consider only the repetition of these ceremonies as mentioned in narrative sources or public acts, their chronology becomes monotonous. A story by Franco Sacchetti reintroduces a dynamic into this seemingly static history. In his tale, an old and gouty Florentine becomes almost incredibly rich through charging exorbitant interest on loans and is then elevated to the dignity of knighthood. Sacchetti uses this plot to draw pessimistic and indignant conclusions about the decadence of chivalry. He lists all the stages in the degradation of the order, which in his view had become an order of social unworthiness. Knights were being drawn from among bakers, wool combers, usurers, debauchees, and professional gamblers. The old order had ended up in stables and pigsties.[95] Beyond its aphoristic reflections on contemporary decadence, the story is of value as a study of social reality and the way it is portrayed.

Chivalry still existed, but it no longer defined or ritualized the military function of the nobility. Even the Ciompi created their own knights. Investiture had previously consecrated and made manifest a man's aristocratic status.[96] Now, however, war was evolving: the nobility was redefining itself and its self-awareness, primarily in terms of blood and ancestry. Ousted from its social and functional role, chivalry was becoming corrupt. No longer did it serve to reinforce the outlines of the aristocracy, and no longer did it mark a threshold for young men. Sacchetti's Florentine was old and gouty. Old, too, in all probability was the lord from Cortona who came to sign fresh pacts with Siena and was knighted with his two sons by the commune.[97]

Knighthood still existed, therefore, but it no longer coincided with a social class, nor, above all, did it signify a system of values and a way of living. Even the ritual that conferred it was transformed. Although its importance for the definition, cohesion, and reproduction of a social group had gradually been undermined, its prestige still lasted for a time. Then even the prestige disappeared. "What ugly, stinking chivalry this is,"[98] Sacchetti observed.

The investiture of Francesco, son of Sozo di Bandinello Bandinelli, thus took place during the period of transition. While his family still thought it important to perpetuate a long line of knights, warfare and sociopolitical organization had already changed. And all these radical changes had the effect of stripping the ancient gestures, ceremonies, and values of their meaning.

In his description of the battle of Campaldino, Compagni recounts the clash of two community militias. Before the fight, new knights were dubbed on both sides. But the footsoldiers of Arezzo, armed with knives, got beneath the horses and eviscerated them. As for the Florentine infantry, which won by virtue of its numbers, it massacred the fleeing victims without mercy. All the old values were upturned. Many brave fighters behaved vilely; many soldiers of no great renown proved valiant. Count Guido left the field of battle without having used his sword, whereas the newly-rich Cerchi behaved according to the norms of chivalry.[99] On the battlefield, as in the city, the rising classes were taking precedence over the old aristocracy. Most notably, a number of ordinary Florentines stood firm at Campaldino.[100] The fighting was thus quite unlike all the models of martial behavior codified by Rolandino.[101] Compagni does, of course, admiringly point out that chivalrous virtues survived in a few people. But it was now the infantry *(pedites)* that decided the outcome of a battle. Rolandino, on the other hand, scarcely mentions the infantry *(fanti);* his narrative dwells only on the figures of the knights *(milites)* and their respect for courtly and chivalrous ethics.

In half a century, war and the description of war had both been transformed. On the battlefields of the Trevisian March, knights maneuver, the enemy is provoked in accordance with the rules, and the prisoners are kept *curialiter* (courteously). In describing martial behavior, Rolandino stresses the archetypal themes of courtly violence.[102] His narrative adheres to the norms of literature. Despite their hatred, and despite the fact that the adversaries are, in Rolandino's presentation, violently opposed, all the protagonists subscribe to the same behavior and share the same rules. A fierce struggle rips the great families of the March, but the enemies still belong to the same brotherhood. At Campaldino, on the other hand, the battle is depicted as butchery.

With corresponding symmetry, during the decades that marked the passage from feudal war to war between communes, a whole way of life, complete with all the values, practices, and identifying signs of the ancient nobility, was being hounded and condemned. Among the criteria that soon served to distinguish the families of Florentine magnates, knighthood held a central place. And violence was among the more obvious traits—thenceforth forbidden—that typified this nobility. If we try to define the families that were subject to harsh judiciary rules and gradually deprived of political rights, according to the Ordinances of Florence, we see that the presence of a *miles* (knight) among the ancestors and the reputation of violence formed the bases on which lists of magnates were compiled.[103]

Though not monopolized by *juvenes* of the ancient aristocratic houses, violence was nonetheless a contributing factor in the solidarity of this group, a factor that helped delimit its social and symbolic role. A vendetta was no doubt handed down, within a lineage, together with all the other material and symbolic possessions. A state of war existed indefinitely between families until such time as the vengeance was completed—unless the author of the offense managed to obtain peace.[104] If, on the other hand, the offended party, and then his heirs, assumed the task of repairing the outrage, the help of blood relatives was requisitioned, and sometimes the help of friends and neighbors.[105] The process of vengeance thus went beyond the simple world of the family *giovani*, to include the larger spheres of *consorti* and, occasionally, friends. But the young men still played a decisive role in the exercise and defense of honor.

In the *Storie pistoresi*, an argument between *giovani* was the cause of the fierce struggle that divided Pistoia into Blacks and Whites.[106] Wine had been flowing freely, and a torrent of insults also poured forth, over a gambling incident. This led to the first act of violence. Vanni di Guafredi, a cut on his hand, was then wounded in the face. Precise retaliations were inflicted on the aggressor, who was nonetheless trying to make peace. He was cut on the hand he had used to cut Vanni. He was wounded on the face, just as he had wounded Vanni. On each side, the *giovani*, vigorous and proud, thought only of wounds and murders. Gathered together, and accompanied by their escorts, they planned and executed further violent deeds.

From a corpus that abounds with such accounts, we may extract several significant episodes related by Compagni. The struggle between the Cerchi and the Donati was punctuated by insults, provocations, wounds, and murders in which the *giovani* played a major part. A young nobleman named Guido Cavalcanti, who was courtly and bold, had several times tried to provoke Corso, his enemy. Corso was afraid of Guido, and tried to have him assassinated during a pilgrimage to Santiago de Compostela. Back in Florence, Guido surrounded himself with a band of young men determined to help him. One day, while riding with some of these friends, members of the Cerchi family, he charged at Corso's horse, lance in hand. However, he hurled it only after he had ridden past Corso's mount. This preliminary tilt thus amounted to a provocation—one sufficient to trigger an actual combat. The maneuver with the horses is reminiscent of the exercises and figures in the war games.[107] The insult led to a direct confrontation, although neither party incurred a death on that particular day. However, their hatred continued to grow. Another incident involved two young Donati who, followed by their companions, decided to settle accounts with Betto Brunelleschi. They inflicted several head wounds on him before leaving him for dead.[108]

In a society in which hatred accounted for rifts and factions in the same way that friendship bonded the partisan groups, the young aristocrats and their followers, quick to take offense and draw their weapons, assumed a central role in city life. The martial virtues they displayed on the battlefield were put into operation in daily political and social life, to defend and serve the honor and the interests of the clans. The pacification of civic life that the communes attempted to bring about in the second half of the thirteenth century was aimed precisely at this violence, at the mainspring of enmity, vengeance, and honor. It is clear that this repressive effort was very slow to take effect. One has only to read the chronicles or criminal archives to see how these confrontations between private citizens persisted in the city. The sheer number of sermons that San Bernardino of Siena devoted to the factional strife that was destroying cities offers further proof of its persistence. And in his struggle to bring peace to the sociopolitical life of cities, the preacher appealed to women—just as he did in his fight against sodomy—to moderate the wildness of their husbands and sons.

Nevertheless, the scale of these confrontations was gradually changing. Among men of equal status, honor and the defense of honor were everybody's concern. But the legislation of the communes marked the difference between what was tolerated and what was intolerable, and in the last centuries of the Middle Ages, that boundary shifted, continually restricting the field of admissible violence. An increasingly clear moral condemnation struck at the extremely violent lifestyle of the old aristocratic families. And legislation, like all contemporary reflections on vendettas, illustrated this evolution very well. Between the end of the thirteenth century and the beginning of the fourteenth, the authorities, without actually prohibiting vendettas, did at least limit their scope. Only death or serious wounding justified vengeance.[109] The circle of blood relatives authorized to exact revenge was reduced to the first four degrees of kinship, and vengeance against relatives of the offending person was forbidden. As for vendettas against vendettas, they were outlawed. Perceptions of vengeance, therefore, were changing. And more generally, a whole way of life, with its extreme manifestations of violence, was now subject to new condemnation.

An episode in Venice perfectly illustrates the evolution taking place. On September 25, 1349, a nobleman named Stefano Manolesso was arraigned by the Lesser Council and charged with killing a child while riding his horse on the Piazza San Marco.[110] A month later, the same council acquitted him. Horseback riding through the streets of Venice had been subject to regulations since the late thirteenth century and seems anachronistic in midfourteenth century. However, the scene casts light on two significant phenomena. During the decades in which it reorganized the flow of traffic and tangibly modified the urban landscape, the commune of Venice set limits on horseback riding in a city singularly ill-suited to such exercise.[111] The central public spaces of San Marco, the Mercerie, and the Rialto were particularly protected. But the aristocracy continued to exhibit a strong attachment to, and taste for, this prestigious animal. Manolesso belonged to one of those relatively recent houses that, together with the old aristocratic families of *judices* and *sapientes,* comprised the new dominant class. Admitted into this ruling circle, he copied—almost aped—the values and general behavior of the older clans. But the pretentious habit of riding on the Piazza San Marco to display equestrian skill (obviously lacking, in this case) was already becoming archaic. The great families were choosing other instruments of ostentation. While the horse, in its beauty and value, retained all its importance in Terra Ferma and during regimental exercises outside Venice, inside the city the very rich now preferred traveling in vessels rowed by private oarsmen. Postmortem inventories of wealthy Venetians describe the decorative *felʒe* that partly covered gondolas with the family's coat of arms, revealing that the emblems of wealth and nobility had been transformed.

An entire culture was thus disappearing, or at most surviving only in a modified form. And although the *juvenes* were not the sole trustees of this culture, they were nonetheless the main protagonists of its literature, its crucial rituals of investiture, and its violent habits—as a few examples show.

The chronicle of Rolandino contains a detailed description of the court held in Treviso in 1214; because of the brutal outcome of the festival and its grievous consequences, this court is traditionally known as the war of the Castle of Love.[112] The court was held at Treviso, but a number of men arrived from Venice and Padua, accompanied by several women. For the games, a castle had been erected in which ladies, young women, and their female servants took up their posts. Unaided by any men, they undertook to defend the besieged castle, which was fortified by and arrayed in costly goods: a profusion of furs and expensive fabrics. For helmets, the ladies wore crowns of gold decorated with pearls and every kind of precious stone. The attack began. It was conducted with volleys of fruit and flowers, apples, pears, dates, roses, lilies, and violets, with phials of perfume and a whole series of aromas and spices, in an orgy of colors and scents.[113]

But the game degenerated. The troop of young Venetians tried, as did the Paduans, to enter the castle. The Venetians began yelling insults. The Paduans answered by tearing apart the Venetians' standard, with its image of San Marco. This insult was so serious that the games were suspended. The war of the tower of the Bebbe, which broke out the following year between Venice on the one hand and Padua and Treviso on the other apparently originated in this episode. An allegory of courtly love and its rules, the siege of the castle thus reached a final conclusion on the battlefield. Apparently the young men's ardor in acting out, for the love of women, the illusion of war led to an armed struggle between three communes.

The purpose of these games and courts was more than simply to entertain youths: they reinforced the group's self-awareness through gestures and conduct that were perfectly appropriate to the themes and values of courtly culture. At the time, the year was organized around a full calendar of *solacii* (diversions), with Pentecost evidently the significant date. Thus the festivity described by Rolandino, held in 1208 in Padua beginning *in festo Pentecostes,* lasted for some days, to everybody's pleasure; the songs and tales of love and war comprised a blend of literature and collective behavior perfect for a chronicler.[114]

Similarly, the jousts and warlike games were a cross between military exercises and the stylization of those exercises, between theater and life. The participants fought while ladies and potentates looked on. Honor and dishonor rewarded the varying degrees of skill and bravery, and the prizes given to the victors were more than symbolic.[115] As further proof of how important and deeply rooted these encounters were, if a game as courtly as the Castle of Love could turn sour, jousts could also bring their share of troubles. According to the anonymous writer from Siena, Charles of Anjou lost Sicily because he had insulted one of his barons during a tournament in Messina. The offended party cleansed himself of the outrage by rebelling against his king.[116]

Even if the various *societates juvenum* that evidently existed in Italian cities of the thirteenth and early fourteenth centuries were not all identical, their links with a chivalrous, courtly culture are nonetheless clear. It is known that an armed society known as the Tabula Rotonda (Round Table) existed in Pisa in the years 1238 and 1239. While this city played an important part in creating and disseminating literature and chivalrous ideas in Tuscany during the first half of the thirteenth century, the Arthurian patronage adopted by this company proves a clear determination on the part of the aristocratic elite to adapt its behavior to chivalrous paradigms.[117] Thenceforth the society had precise political and military goals; it defended the city when tumult and danger threatened. But this provision of military aid only acquires its true significance when placed in the context of the bitter factional struggles. Although our sources permit neither true conclusions nor generalizations, these societies or brigades played a precise military and political role in the cities during the diverse epochs in which they were formed. They did so either by carefully maintaining the provisional sociopolitical equilibrium or, to the contrary, by attempting to change the existing order to their own advantage.

Thus, institutionalized by the very existence of the brigade, the major function assumed by the *giovani* in defense of the clans reappears, in the bloody vicissitudes of struggles between factions. On every battlefield, gestures and behavior were ritualized by the same ideals of valor, the same norms of a moral code infinitely refined by literary texts.

Inside the brigades, in accordance with a clear tradition of chivalrous customs—as seen, for example, in the account of the Este wedding—the links uniting courts and investitures were once again intermingled. The culture we are able to observe was both practical and symbolic. No doubt the Florentine company of 1283 was careful to maintain the city[118] in the peaceful state that benefited merchants, artisans, and particularly Guelfs.[119] The colors worn by all its members, and the position of the clan that founded the company and paid its expenses,[120] show clearly that this society was the society of one party. But its first, explicit goal was pageantry. It met under the authority of a lord known as Love, and held court for two consecutive months. The city was then filled with riders and musicians, dances, and banquets, while songs were sung by a troup of poets who had come specially for the occasion.

Some time previously, in his native city, Saint Francis of Assisi had "wretchedly wasted his youth" in such amusements.[121] He had been chosen leader of a society of young people whose purpose was to organize banquets and games. One of the most memorable feasts was one he gave on the evening of his election. On leaving the sumptuously prepared table, the entire brigade went singing through the city. Francis followed carrying a stick, the symbol of his function. In the transcript of the saint's life proposed by his various biographers, these pleasures often take the names of excess and debauchery. With his knowledge of Provençal lyric poetry and his taste for sumptuary extravagance, for luxurious clothes and food, Francis was simply reproducing the values and way of life of his class and his companions. There was in fact a determining factor swaying the votes of the young men in the society: the extreme prodigality of their future leader, and his habitually extravagant expenditures, which guaranteed pleasures for all.

Once again the theme of generosity appears, a quality always active in the hierarchy of chivalrous values. Like all brigade leaders, Francis drew his strength from this generosity. The very munificence that his hagiographers condemn was considered his most important quality by the young men of Assisi. Through such lavish acts—often excessive, in regard to the resources of his family[122]—the leader of a society could give proof and justification of his distinction.[123] No doubt the *brigata spendereccia* (lavish brigade) of Siena provides the best example of wealth distributed to the sole end of causing and obtaining pleasure. But all the other societies followed the same precepts, showing that their members adhered to a style of living idealized in the narratives and poems they listened to and sang.

Just as the chivalrous order did not decline overnight, neither did courtly culture suddenly decay. Under the seignory of the duke of Calabria, and during the government of the duke of Athens, knighthood again flourished in Florence. But the civic dimension gradually acquired increased importance in this dignity. Thus both the order and the dubbing ceremony lost their original character. From the end of the twelfth century, the "joyous" March of Treviso had been, for more than a hundred years, one of the most active centers for the dissemination of Languedocian culture in Italy. Around the feudal courts of the Este, da Romano, and da Camino families, a whole poetic and aristocratic culture had developed and spread. Certain ancient themes were still exploited by, for example, Francesco di Vannozzo; but the lyrical poetry of the court poets was thenceforth intended to celebrate the seigneurs. When the chivalrous model was still used, it served only to exalt the della Scala or da Carrara clans, and it contributed to the various great lords' struggle to obtain power and glory.[124] To give an example from the north, in 1340 a great court was held for eight days in Mantua.[125] Tournaments, jousts, dances, songs, and music were included in the seemingly traditional program of this aristocratic wedding. But the generous remunerations of clowns and musicians were paid by the prince—the central figure around whom a new civilization of the court was to develop.

The transformations and recomposition of the ethics of the old way of living had obvious consequences for both the role of the *giovani* and the image that society had of them. As knighthood was transformed into a civic dignity, the duty of loyalty bound the knight more to the commune than to the complex amalgam of close kin, friends, and relatives represented by the old brotherhood. Chivalrous war and its valiant deeds proved pitifully inadequate on battlefields where the outcome was determined by communal militias. Sacchetti's ironic observations on the state of knighthood were not simply part of a banal list of remarks on the decadence of mores and customs. With the same daring and intrepidness he showed in war, the knight was supposed to defend his family, earn the love of women, and distribute wealth. What had been valor became failure, sin, folly. What do the fifteenth-century sources condemn, if not this formidable prodigality on the part of young men, this excessive desire for pleasure, that disturbed the social order and eroded patrimonies? What do they condemn if not this aggressiveness, once needed in both war and city life? The ancient idea of valor had been transformed into intolerable acts of violence. And although cities still organized military games, even the forms of these ludic activities changed and were challenged by the evolution of society and of political regimes.

The mutations that became distinctive in the second half of the thirteenth century, and that proved decisive in the history of Italian cities, thus mark a clear turning point in the history of the *giovani*. By the very nature of the sources, this analysis has concentrated on a social elite, on its functions and values. Therefore it is all the more interesting to observe how the condemnation of values gradually came to encompass all the *giovani*, all seemingly guilty of the same aberrations.

THIS YOUNG AGE

Scholars have noted the extreme care with which Martin da Canal describes all manifestations of chivalry in his *Estoires*.[126] The Venetian chronicler is close to Rolandino in this respect, even though the aims and interpretations of the two authors are different.[127] For da Canal, festivities and jousting were part of the Venetian splendor that all the chronicles celebrated and idealized.

To celebrate Ranieri Zeno's election as doge, a joust was organized on the Piazza San Marco. Lorenzo Tiepolo, himself a doge's son and future doge, made the arrangements. A second figure emerges from the narrative: that of Marco Ziani, also a doge's son and armed, like his whole company of knights, with every sort of weapon. While the ladies watched, many gentlemen jousted and broke lances. Against a backdrop of fine blows delivered by foreign and Venetian knights, da Canal presents scenes of Venetian gentility. Marco Ziani, son of Pietro, heir to the prodigious Ziani fortune, belonged to the old aristocracy of the first commune. Lorenzo was a member of a more recent lineage that had sprung up when Jacopo began his dazzling political career. In da Canal's description, all differences disappeared; the entire Venetian nobility proved equally valiant. On the Piazza San Marco, as in operations by land or by sea, the *"chevetains venisiens"* (Venetian chieftains) behaved *"con vont li faucons prenant les oisaus"* (falcons at a bird hunt).[128]

Another joust was held in the city in 1272, when pacts were concluded with the Friuli. Once again ropes were stretched across the Piazza San Marco. And to honor the six squires of Friul, the Venetian aristocracy again took to its mounts. For three full days the young men charged at each other, in the presence of the doge, before ladies and young ladies. The flower of the local aristocracy displayed its military virtues. The nobility of the city on the lagoon continued to sanction war games and their rules late in the thirteenth century.

Although less frequently, no doubt, than in other cities, jousts and tournaments were still held during the fourteenth and fifteenth centuries. Sometimes organized by noble, rich *giovani*, they drew crowds and were occasions for pageantry. Petrarch describes the equestrian games that concluded festivities celebrating the capture of Candia. He mentions twenty-four young noblemen, all magnificently attired, and the knight in charge of them, who had been summoned from Ferrara for the occasion.[129] But by this time these carefully regulated confrontations were simply one entertainment among many, an ever-present spectacle amid numerous balls, regattas, and nautical pageants. The *concursus hastiludia et ensiludia* (tournament of jousting and fencing) still counted among the games celebrating the election of a doge.[130] Thenceforth defined solely in terms of blood and function, the aristocracy gave proof of its honor and its influence in other fields.

Thus, in the late fifteenth century, Landucci's Florentine *Diario* seems to indicate the existence of professional athletes who took part in the races and equestrian games that still punctuated the festive life of urban Italian society. In describing the life of his brother Gostanzo, the author mentions the varying fortunes of a Tuscan champion who raced in Florence, Siena, and Arezzo, earning prizes for himself and glory for his patron, Lorenzo de' Medici.[131] The quarrels that often broke out at the end of the *palio* in Siena, when the winner was declared, reveal that the games were degenerating, compromised by the influence of contradictory interests, either financial or local.

The same changes may be observed in Venetian military games. In the various cities, military exercises[132] and war games[133] were common features. But so long as social rifts set knights *(milites)* against footsoldiers *(pedites)*, and a particular prestige attended all manifestations of war on horseback, the places and manner in which training was undertaken were clearly distinct. In Milan, the *juvenes in armis* (young men in arms) gathered outside the city walls, while on the other side of the city the *milites* conducted exercises on horseback.[134] Normally military training, like war games, took place among men of equal status. This was the rule, despite occasional examples of intermixing between equestrian games and the games of city dwellers[135]—and even though the *milites* of ancient stock sometimes took part in certain war games clearly intended for the common people. They did so to recall their former military supremacy, or to use these games as a screen to promote family rivalries or oppositions between factions.[136]

As it is described in official sources, Venetian military training reproduced in part the same social rifts. In each division of the city, two *capicontrada* (regional chiefs) controlled the *duodene* in which were registered all men of an age to bear arms.[137] But only one age group practiced shooting with the crossbow. Between the ages of fifteen and thirty-five, all *giovani* were required to train on feast days, with Christmas, Good Friday, and Easter being the only exceptions.[138] However universal this obligation may have been, it was clearly specified that *quelli di povol,* men of the people, did not mingle *con li nobeli,* with nobles. The various arrangements that, in the first decades of the fourteenth century, organized training in the *ballesterius ludus* (crossbow), also provided for the repair of badly maintained *bersalia* (shooting ranges) or asked for new ranges to be created. The list of *contrade* (districts) cited proves that these areas were fairly equitably divided in the city.[139] Even so, the year 1374 marked a turning point. The Council of Ten voted for two *palia* per year to be organized, at Christmas and Easter, on the strand of San Nicolo del Lido.[140] It fixed and supervised their development; a counselor, three noblemen, and one of the *capi* (leaders) of the Council of Ten presided over the meet. Financing and prizes were regularly provided.

Only snow, pestilence, or flooding could cause these competitions to be canceled or postponed. They seemed to meet with immediate success, and several times during the fifteenth century attempts were made to schedule a third meeting, at Pentecost or on Saint Bartholomew's Day.[141] It was not until 1490, however, that three such competitions were regularly instituted.[142] In the interim, the spring *palio* slipped from Easter to Pentecost,[143] while at the end of the century the Christmas *palio* was moved to Santa Lucia's Day. There were prizes to reward the best throws, and the champions competed individually against each other. The competition was devoid of the old divisions that used to control military training, and the games did not aggravate spatial or social fragmentation. In the middle of the century, the festivals grew longer and were followed the next day by

a banquet organized by the armament officers. The aim of this banquet
was to bring together the protagonists, men and youths, following the
joust. Edicts strove vainly to control the increasing expenditure. Thirty
ducats had initially been allotted for the festival, and in 1473 fifty ducats
were spent on the Christmas *palio*.[144] Faced with this chronic deficit, the
Ten granted the sum of forty ducats, beginning in 1492; but this soon
proved inadequate.[145] In much the same way, the Council gave in on the
problem of wine sales and, to avoid the consumption of contraband wine,
authorized a sale—an exceptional circumstance.

After being well organized for decades, the *palio* underwent several
modifications at the end of the fifteenth century. First, the Council of Ten
lamented the decrease in the number of participants and regretted that
competition had become limited to a few specialists. That same day, there
was a vote rejecting a proposal to prohibit anyone who did not possess his
own crossbow from entering the games. This vote also tried to resist the
evolution in progress by maintaining the popular, universal bases of the
meet: the city's military exercises.[146] Converging signs confirm that the
competition was being modified. When the Saint Bartholomew's Day *palio*
was introduced, an order went out to publish news of its opening throughout the Terra Ferma.[147] Parallel to this, the reluctance of the nobles responsible for the event to assume their role reveals the collapse of vertical
solidarity and the obliteration of the symbolic cohesion represented by an
age cohort.[148] Perhaps the form of the meet led to this mutation, and
resulted in the original tournaments being transformed into a champion-
ship and cause for rivalry. But changes in social balances, together with
developments in the Venetian armies,[149] accelerated the metamorphosis.

Despite chronological differences in these transformations, knightly
jousting and the crossbowmen's *palio* seem to have undergone the same
evolution. At the end of the fifteenth century one can discern a radical
departure from the old sporting events. As they broke lances, the young
Tiepolo or Ziani boys exhibited the warlike virtues they or their fathers
had displayed on the battlefields of Italy or of the empire. On the lido of
San Nicolo, all the young men of the city competed together, united in
exercise and festivity according to the wishes of the Council of Ten. But

jousting became a spectacle, and the *palio* was reduced to a contest in which a few champions showed off.

The same observations may be made concerning the regatta. Even though this race between oarsmen was a part of Venetian tradition related, in its purpose and in the chronology of its first manifestations, to other forms of military exercise, its meaning was also changing. At first the nautical games were arranged during the inactivity of winter. Their military character was preserved, and in the fifteenth century the Arsenal was still providing the vessels needed for the various regattas. But clearly, maintaining well-trained teams was no longer the goal when the spectacle of the oarsmen in light boats became part of the entertainments; or when, in 1493, several women took part in these competitions.[150]

It is equally surprising to note that Venetian sources do not offer real evidence of the war of the bridges until the first years of the sixteenth century.[151] We cannot exclude the possibility of warlike or playful confrontations on bridges at the city limits during the medieval period, confrontations in which group awareness reasserted itself. While comparisons with other cities offer no proof, the frequency of battles fought with fists or pebbles—collective fights—in Siena, Perugia, or Modena must be considered. But such battles did not spread to Venice until relatively late, and thus the official form they eventually assumed—the historico-legendary dress, the fact that they were performed as local urban curiosities when foreign guests visited[152]—were correspondingly late developments. Spectacles and festivities changed during the final decades of the fifteenth century. In all accounts of them, the fights on the bridges functioned as popular entertainment, to be watched from the banks of the canal or from the windows of neighboring houses. And their folklore refers to the new urban fragmentations then taking place, to the strong socioprofessional identity found in the two neighborhoods of San Nicolo dei Mendigoli and Castello.

In these ritualized confrontations, the young men played a decisive, though not exclusive, role.[153] As a result, two successive breaks may be distinguished. The longevity of jousts, races, and other armed confrontations in Italian cities, and the seemingly stable form of these manifestations, should not obscure the reality of the changes taking place. Of course, skill in equestrian games could still be a sign of social distinction. Habits endured, even if aristocratic identity and superiority had long been based on criteria other than military worth. With the development of forms of military training or playful battles, the whole meaning of the *giovani*'s military function was perverted; occasions of group cohesion or ritual confrontation lost their significance, being transformed into spectacles and exhibitions variously appreciated by the rest of the community. Thus, during the second half of the fifteenth century, the brutality of fights on the bridges—a brutality wrongly described as recent—was condemned in Venice. First, the sharp, pointed sticks that the combatants fought with had to be blunted.[154] Next, the battles had to be fought with bare hands; finally, this war of fisticuffs *(guerra dei pugni)* was also judged too violent.

From the second half of the thirteenth century certain cities, such as Perugia, had sought to regulate these types of urban battles, in an attempt to restrict their violence and, above all, to try to eliminate the risks of budding factions. Commanded by *capitanei*, the young men's societies that played a fundamental role in organizing and developing the *ludus* were the first targets of these repressive measures. This regulatory effort did not, however, result in disarmament. In the first half of the fourteenth century, the statutes of the brotherhoods of San Stefano and San Rufino of Assisi forbade their members to "go and fight with weapons or stones" *(ire ad bactagliamentum cum armis vel lapidibus)*. Moreover, the communal statutes issued a general prohibition against these battles.[155] The attempt to eradicate these violent ludic practices seems to have met with strong resistance: narrative sources describe violent brawls in Perugia that lasted for two successive days in 1389, involving three societies of young men.[156] On the second day, despite the communal authorities' attempts to effect a reconciliation, these companies marched into the city square to avenge the first man killed. The battle of pebbles quickly degenerated. As often happened after an initial shower of stones, the combatants drew weapons of war. The struggle ended only when two of the groups joined together and ejected the third group from the square. At that point another corpse was discovered.

According to the general chronology of the forms and norms of social control already discerned, these societies were subject to stronger repression in the early fifteenth century. The statutes of San Bernardino, adopted in Perugia in 1425, totally prohibited them. The first reason given to justify such harshness was their reckless expenditure. This initial indulgence was seen as authorizing all other excesses, abuses, and crimes: luxury, adultery, sodomy, and violence. The sins that religious and secular authorities increasingly identified as those of *giovani* were thus specially favored by these "societies of war-dancers" *(societates tripudiantium)*. These fellowships had assumed a role of prime importance in the festivities that punctuated the old civic calendar. Active in the "battle games" *(ludus battaglie)*, they also organized games for other festivals, such as the game of the bull, or *ludus tauri*. All these events were now forbidden. In the street, the town square, within churches, inside houses, societies and their amusements were rigorously hunted down. Initially the authorities had targeted the brigades of young aristocrats, in their struggle against the values and lifestyles of an elite that was socially and politically in decline. But from this point on the condemnation was not so much political as moral: young men's societies were guilty of lasciviousness, license, and debauchery. Nonetheless they continued to survive, controlled to varying degrees by the urban institutions.

It is this intervention of public institutions that constituted a decisive point in the history of juvenile societies. In Assisi the company of San Vittorino, authorized to stage dances and songs on its holy patron's feast day, was received by the priors of the commune. We may then wonder about the continuity Fortini thinks he perceives between this company and the brigade led by Saint Francis. In Perugia, while the members and the lord *(podestat)* of these societies still financed the banquets at which they met, the commune granted them funds to pay for the festivities accompanying public holidays. And the spectacles, performances, banquets, and dances organized by the cities of Umbria for the Calendimaggio (May 1) or the weddings of princes were no different from the entertainments ordered in Venice by the societies of the *calƷa*.

In his now classic essay on the history of these societies, Venturi endeavors to show the weakness of the control that Venetian authorities imposed on these companies.[157] Until the late fifteenth century, he maintains, these companies do not appear to have been subject to the guidance that the Council of Ten imposed on all fraternities. The first intervention of the Ten is dated 1494, when they limited the young men's associations to twenty-five members. In the first decades of the sixteenth century, the supervision gradually increased. The statutes of new companies were thenceforth submitted for the approval of the Council. Until this apparently new departure in Venetian politics, the Signoria had intervened only to restrain the pomp and luxury of banquets and festivities, bringing the companies back into the field of sumptuary legislation. Is such an interpretation pertinent? Certainly not.

To begin with, what were these companies that fifteenth-century texts still termed *societates juvenum* (young men's societies)?[158] The first lines of the statutes of the company of the Modesti, drawn up in 1487, give immediate evidence of their very particular social composition: *"adolescentes nobilissimi, et Patritii"* (most noble adolescents, and patricians). In forming, the fraternity simply sanctioned and reinforced, within the same age cohort, the bonds of friendship and kinship and the extraordinary proximity created, beyond occasional rifts, by the aristocratic elite's almost total monopoly of fortune and power. Its statutes expressed one of the most solid ideological foundations of the patrician regime: the relative equality that united this elite. And the patrician palaces that, until the first decades of the sixteenth century, formed lines of buildings of almost equal size along the Grand Canal were meant to translate this reality into stone. *"In hac republica praestantissima quot sunt Patritii, tot fuerunt Fratres"*: In this outstanding republic some are patricians, all are brothers. The companies were therefore simply emanations of those families that, since the first third of the fifteenth century, had founded and maintained the patrician regime. We may thus point to a first chronological coincidence. These societies were formed during the very period when power tended to define, with procedures such as the Balla d'Oro, the status and identity of Venetian nobility. At the same time it was trying to discipline the *juvenes* by accelerating the start of their political careers.

A second point of intersection between public and private spheres was the role these companies played in Venice's relationships with foreign princes. When Alfonso d'Este visited the city in 1487, he was received by the company of the Potenti. The following year, for the visit of the duke of Ferrara, the Potenti organized a celebration in the hall of the Grand Council, and the Senate provided 250 ducats to finance the banquet and entertainment. In 1493, the same company was chosen to organize festivities honoring the duchess of Bari and the duchess of Ferrara: balls, regattas, and performances. Numerous other examples could be cited, such as the visits of the dukes of Mantua, Milan, and Urbino, for which the councils lent the hall of the Grand Council or other buildings, and regularly voted funding for nautical games and sea-battles.

A simple exposition of facts illumines a third point of intersection between public and private spheres. The festivities given by companies did not respect the traditional boundary between spaces for public and private entertainment. They invaded the doge's palace, the Piazza San Marco, the Grand Canal, and even the duke of Ferrara's house, where visiting foreign princes were housed. When Andrea Contarini was in Constantinople and could not attend the wedding of his sister Lucrezia to Jacobo Foscari, son of Doge Francesco Foscari, his brothers Ramperto and Jacobo wrote him letters describing the accompanying ceremonies. These letters, which give detailed descriptions of nuptial celebrations throughout the city, provide the first evidence of the active role that the companies played in them.[159]

The bridegroom's party—250 men on horseback, preceded by bugles and trumpets—assembled at San Marco. After riding around the ducal palace and the square, the cavalcade advanced as far as San Samuele. A provisional bridge of barges and planks had been erected between this point on the Grand Canal and the house of the bride, the Ca' Contarini, which was on the other bank at San Barnabà. Once the procession reached the Contarini bank, the religious phase of the ritual began in the parish church. Then the cavalcade of companions set off again: "And all on horseback, they rode all through Venice." The riders showed off their clothes, their mounts, and their skill. The part of the ceremony known as the *ductio* did not take place until after dinner. Aboard the republic's ceremonial ship, the *Bucentaur,* which was escorted by a fleet of boats, the bride was taken to the ducal palace.

Each day's celebrations ended in the doges' palace, where meals, dances, and *momarie* took place. On the second and fourth days, forty and thirty jousters, respectively, tested themselves on the Piazza San Marco. On the third day, the companions had their oarsmen row from San Marco to Santa Chiara, all along the Grand Canal. On the morning of the fourth day, the companions once again boarded their boats "to go through the city until dinnertime." The earthbound processions of the second day were intercalated between these nautical displays. Since it was connected with the dogeship, the Foscari-Contarini marriage naturally involved an extreme degree of this new commingling of public and private elements. Each of the processions began in the square and ended at the doges' palace, where Jacobo gave the banquets that every companion owed the members of his society when he married. Nevertheless, the habit of putting public space to such uses was becoming more general.

Examples of Venetian spectacles included dances and banquets on the *Bucentaur* for the arrival of Federico Gonzaga; competitions between boats; and regattas involving men and women, who raced to the Giudecca. There were also processions on the Grand Canal organized by the newly formed company of Valorosi; regattas, banquets, balls, and performances on rafts, with the duke of Urbino taking part in all these festivities.[160] The nature of these spectacles, which were still unusual in the second half of the fifteenth century, though they subsequently became more common, modified the scenes of the festivity. The evolution was a double one. The entertainments, or at least certain of the forms they took, broke with the central, unitary setting that the authorities had hitherto proposed. In the celebrations of the companies, public spaces served no longer for civic ritual but for entertainment and ostentation. Similarly, all the rafts, boats, floating stages, and mobile sets erected by the companies were part of a general evolution that imposed a facade of illusion and artifice on the city

during festivals.[161] The companies thus contributed directly to this transformation of festivities, which marked a departure from the ceremonies of
the communal city. Similarly, the entertainments proposed by all the companies during the carnival[162] reveal the force of this break, anticipating and
accompanying the modifications of the "Fat Thursday" festival during the
dogeship of Andrea Gritti.[163]

In consequence, the incidents that set councils against companions,
involving an excess of luxury and ostentation, were only minor setbacks
in the history of these particular societies. Membership in the companies,
lasting from the moment young men adopted the *calza* to the moment they
gave it up,[164] reinforced the links between *juvenes* from close lineages.
Bringing aristocratic alliances to the forefront of the urban scene, rhythmically punctuating city life with sumptuous feasts, the companies had no
need of being placed under the severe control of the Council of Ten.
Under the authority of the lord they elected, the companies united the
patrician *juvenes* for several decisive years, years in which the young men
married and entered the political arena. Doubtless their aim was to promote these transitions. Their statutes controlled the number and arrangement of banquets celebrating the companions' weddings. But the *giovani*
celebrated and sanctioned only weddings that were politically and socially
adequate. As such, these societies emanated from a private sphere that was
largely confused with the public one. They strengthened the patrician
regime by showcasing the *giovani* at the summit of the governing elite,
which basked in the glory of all the spectacles the young men organized.

Several observations are now necessary. The structures of these young
men's societies were in no way perennial, even if, in the fifteenth and early
sixteenth century, some of them proved extremely durable. There is, of
course, the apparent stability of their role in festivals, and the stability of
their common organizational model: all had a leader, equipped with the
emblems of his function; all had a system of fines and subscriptions. But
these superficial formal characteristics cannot maintain the illusion that the
associations survived through the centuries.[165] Similarly, the problems of
conserving documents do not explain the breaks and silences that keep
occurring in the history of these societies—as if, atypical institutions, they

resisted time and held together despite radical developments in the city. All evidence suggests that the meaning and function of these associations changed over time. The fifteenth-century *societates* of Assisi differed from the society Saint Francis had led. The companies of the *calza* were formed with the consolidation of the patrician regime. And the groups in Florence that temporarily banded together at the beginning of the fifteenth century to organize a few jousts were only slightly comparable to the *societates* that had existed there two centuries before.

The bonds that these associations maintained with the sociopolitical powers then in force may to some extent account for such mobility and diversity: aristocratic brigades of the thirteenth century, *potenze festeggianti* (festive powers) of the duke of Athens, Venetian companies, Florentine *potenze* recreated by the Medici. . . In the fifteenth century, the situation in Florence was clearly different from the situation in Venice. Florence was reluctant to integrate its *giovani* into political institutions. The young men's societies had only an ephemeral role, even if, during festivities or the visits of foreign guests, they assumed roles very similar to those of the companies of the *calza*.

But such considerations account only partly for the reality of these groups; they ascribe too much importance to purely functionalist criteria, thus favoring a reassuring interpretation of the history of such societies. Without a doubt, these associations saw themselves as emanations—sometimes even as instruments—of the faction or force in power.[166] Even so, they sometimes became the place and instrument of conflict. The abbey of the Stolti kept some order in Turinese life. Having quieted the uproar in the town,[167] it successfully tamed the violence of certain popular rituals, such as the charivari, and played an increased, official role in city life by organizing a number of religious festivities, and by assuming a major role in the "entrances." But it was not to be confused with an institution charged solely with pacification and social conservation. Its direct participation in late fifteenth-century violence illustrates its collisions with local authority and proves that, if it functioned as a "drive belt," it drove in both directions, from power toward the collectivity, and from the collectivity toward civic authority. As such—and there is no need to enter into a historiographic debate on the role and degree of integration of these associations in the sociopolitical fabric—it constituted, through this very ambivalence, an instrument of social regulation.[168]

The extremely smooth history of the companies of the *calza* folds into similar wrinkles if we consider that in 1459 the company of the Fedeli was formed, where "gentlemen of the people" gathered. Its members, young men of the Zon or Amadi families, came from lineages that were rich, old, and influential, although excluded from the councils. Desire to rival the patrician sons, social mimesis—yes, of course; but these were not the only reasons behind this association. The urban bourgeoisie was allied with certain noble families. In the major companies, for example—the *scuole grandi*[169]—it filled the managerial offices reserved for it. In addition, it provided the men who were indispensable to Venetian administrative structures, such as the Chancellery. But through diverse means—houses in the city, houses in Murano, religious foundations—the bourgeoisie also attempted to heighten its renown, besmirched by the fact of not belonging to the Grand Council. The formation of the company of the Fedeli was probably related to one of its attempts at self-expression. But apart from the evidence of its birth, no documentary traces of this company's activities have survived. Admittedly, the history of the first companies is relatively unknown. But in this case, the lack of information is probably attributable not so much to lacunae in the sources as to a rapid disappearance of the Fedeli, after a rather boring term of existence. During the decades in which the first *societates juvenum* were formed, their sociopolitical characteristics were not completely established. The history of this original association reveals the tensions of a society dominated by an oligarchy.

There were thus two sides to the history of young men: the violent acts, such as they appear in the judiciary archives, and the institutionalized *societates juvenum*. The two sides interacted in several respects. The societies did not serve simply to restrain the impulses of a turbulent and dangerous age cohort. The ludic, festive functions allotted them did more than discipline and integrate, under public control, rituals that would otherwise have been celebrated with greater disorder and excess. But the *giovani* were not divided into neat categories of those included in the societies and those excluded from them, as if some hypothetical line were drawn that destined some to be socialized and others to be violent. Occasionally, this apparent instrument of pacification or integration was contaminated by the conflicts.

Above all, and quite apart from this habitual relationship with society, the *giovani* spoke up whenever they could and invaded the public scene, from which they were normally excluded. This was the case in Venice, through the nocturnal events I have described. It was also the case in Florence at the time of Savonarola. When Savonarola thought that society would be reformed through children,[170] conflict broke out between little boys *(fanciulli)* and *giovani*. The task of purging the city of all its sins and ruffians fell to tiny children. Spreading through the town and its surroundings, they led the hunt so zealously that no one could resist them. The taverns were closed; games of cards and dice were vigorously opposed; all splendors, vanities, and luxuries—women's headdresses, books, paintings—were proscribed by these ferocious agents of God's order. A time of repentance began, the prelude to the reign of a new Jerusalem. Gamblers fled, women decked themselves in virtue, everyone was on guard against sin and the "abominable vice" in particular.[171] These bands of children were quick to resort to violence,[172] putting their usual weapons at God's service: battles of stones ensued, or forced collections at carnival time, levied by the children to benefit the poor. Grouped by district into four associations, the "Friar's boys" *(fanciugli del frate)* caused reigns of terror in their districts and, on days designated by Savonarola, marched in procession dressed in white, bearing olive branches—the picture of innocence.[173]

The children sang, and people thought they heard the voice of the Lord.[174] Against them stood the "young men," the "ribald men," the "scoundrels" *(giovani, ribaldi, sclerati);* the "most dissolute men, of ribald lives" *(dissolutissimi et di ribalda vita);* the "persons capable of any evil" *(persone da fare ogni male).*[175] Groups formed around a few young noblemen.[176] And these "evil companions" and "enraged ones" (*compagniacci* and *arrabiati*) sang quite a different tune: shouts, insults, bells during the night; disturbances and more bells during sermons. They would produce rotting asses' skins in church, or bless the faithful with an onion impaled on the point of a sword, thus introducing fetid smells into the sacred compounds, to pervert the holy rites and make Christ's kingdom founder in derision.[177] Although forbidden, the young men's ritual forms of violence erupted again when the procession of the four city districts degenerated into a pitched battle, with everyone throwing stones; if stones and tiles were not enough, they drew their weapons—in front of the convent of San Marco.[178]

The young men won this war, and after Savonarola's death they instituted their own reign. The chronicles then describe the infernal license of men aged thirty to thirty-five. In taverns and in brothels, the "ribald" would let all hell break loose. The "scoundrels" ruled the streets. Dressed in disguises, they sang their songs on the Piazza della Signoria or in front of the convent of San Marco. By this time the little children had also enlisted on the side of vengeance. However, it seems to me they were still furthering both God's work and the ideal purity of society when they sold pamphlets describing the "Friar's malice," or when they threw stones at Savonarola's body while it burned at the stake. In resorting to their ritual gestures of violence, they were trying to exterminate the false prophet, the Antichrist. Therefore, I do not think that the children's violence, which Savonarola had channeled for a while, broke out again after his death,[179] nor that the *fanciulli* "went over to the other side."[180] In both cases—under Savonarola, when the time of the new Jerusalem seemed to have arrived, and again during the months that followed the failure of the ordeal of fire and the death of the false prophets—the children assumed, in the same way and by their very violence, God's work.

Thus the connivance between *giovani* and children was only apparent because the former, like "furies out of hell,"[181] seem to have plunged the city into an apocalypse. Whereas the children, in one way or another, pursued the work of reform, purification, and hope that had fallen to them, the law of the *giovani* was a law of total license. In these crucial years, society's worst images of its young men seem entirely justified.

It was essentially through moral criteria, rather than biological or socioeconomic ones, that contemporaries were able to define the age and group of *giovani*. But this dark, strongly negative image that all types of fifteenth-century sources uniformly reflect was assembled only gradually. Like women—and also more than women—the *giovani* were seen as a menace and a danger. And their entire code of behavior, their excesses and disorders, simply encouraged this fearsome suspicion. The *giovani* were said to be capable and culpable of every aberration. In the chronology of these images, the final decades of the thirteenth century constituted a decisive stage. Warfare was changing radically. The dignity of knighthood was in the first stages of a long evolution that would redefine its meaning and its function. The violent acts and behavior of the old families fell subject to harsh condemnation. Though not solely the province of the aristocratic *juvenes,* the habit of violence, both in the city and on the battlefield, delimited their social and symbolic role. The new communal order condemned these roles to atrophy. At a deeper level, a whole value system was tottering, as is indicated by an analysis of the first regulatory texts of the communes, and made even clearer by the legislative and administrative apparatus put in place in the fifteenth century. What was thenceforth reproved, repressed, and regarded as the characteristic behavior of *juvenes* were the precepts that the young male elite had previously held dear: generosity and valor, ardor and ostentation. Faced with the seemingly irrepressible desires of the "unbridled ones," with this energy that threatened order because it was unchanneled, the old men who governed Venice or Florence resorted to exclusion and repression. We should not be deceived by the longevity of jousts and other warlike games. These meets changed, as did the forms of military training, festivities and entertainments generally, and also the status of the *giovani*.

The system, seemingly so closed, of tutelage and mistrust of *giovani* nonetheless developed cracks in it. Contemporaneous, for the reasons I have shown, with the emergence of the communal city, it also declined with the commune. The public roles conferred in varying degrees, temporarily or permanently, on young men in Venice, Turin, and Florence during the fifteenth century bear witness to these transformations. Charged with welcoming foreigners, with organizing festivities and displays, their associations were supposed to "bring the people no mediocre joy" *(render al Populo allegrezza non mediocre)*. They worked for the "preservation of the states" *(la conservazione delli stati)* and for "their honorableness and grandeur" *(l'honorevolezza ed grandezza loro)*.[182] Thus a real evolution was beginning. Despite conflicts that reveal the slow pace and fragile nature of this pacification, and a rhythm that varied with each city, this evolution tended to reconcile the young men with authority and reintegrate them into the community.

CHAPTER 7

EMBLEMS OF YOUTH:
YOUNG PEOPLE IN
MEDIEVAL IMAGERY

Michel Pastoureau

It is good for a man that he bear the yoke in his youth.
LAMENTATIONS 3:27 (RSV)

How did medieval imagery express the idea of youth? How did it represent this age that comes between childhood and maturity? What attributes, codes, and methods did it use to distinguish young men and women who had reached puberty but were not yet established in adult life? Did it even try to do so? And if it did, were the codes and attributes it used particular to medieval imagery, or did they derive from taxonomies or systems of representation that went beyond the bounds of the image? In either case, what can these codes and attributes teach us about the status of youth in medieval society and sensibility? What ideologies, what social or religious moralities do they express?

To try to respond to these questions is no easy exercise, not only because the strategies of the image rebel against all generalization (if not against all analysis), but also and especially because in the Middle Ages, Western culture had a concept of youth that was neither uniform nor unchanging. Even over something as traditional as the demarcation of the various ages in life—a topos inherited from the culture of antiquity— opinions could differ greatly.

WHICH AGES?

Fourteenth- and fifteenth-century theories on the subject of youth were not the same as those in the Carolingian age; and even within a particular period, the opinions of jurists did not always tally with the opinions of theologians, still less with those of doctors, encyclopedists, literary men, or poets. Life's ages were demarcated differently depending on whether one was in a monastery, a castle, a university, the law courts, a fairground, or the marketplace. Two systems are clearly contradistinguished: one recognizing four ages in life (sometimes reduced to three); the other, six (sometimes extended to seven or even eight). The first establishes correspondences with the four seasons and the four elements. Childhood is spring, youth is summer, midlife is autumn, and old age is winter. When reduced to three such periods, this system fuses childhood and youth into a single age, symbolizing the spring of life. Maturity is then compared to summer, old age to autumn, and death to winter. This system basically derived from profane culture. In the late thirteenth century, Philippe of Novaro became its poet in a treatise written in the common language, *Les Quatre Aages de l'homme*, which was imitated several times.[1]

Classification by six or seven ages, on the other hand, derived from the culture of scholars and clergymen. Inherited from the taxonomies of antiquity, and contaminated by numerical symbolism (of which medieval culture was inordinately fond), it recognized *infantia* (from birth to age seven); *pueritia* (from seven to fourteen); *adulescentia* (from fourteen to twenty-one or twenty-eight); *juventus* (from twenty-one or twenty-eight to thirty-five); *virilitas* (from thirty-five to fifty-five or sixty); and *senectus* (after fifty-five or sixty). The boundaries between these different age groups were both flexible and uncertain. Often a seventh age was added, *senies* (more than seventy), thus permitting a correspondence to be established with the number of planets, metals, colors, days of the week, ages of the world, and gifts of the Holy Ghost. Doctors and astrologers, in particular, emphasized the links uniting every age of life with a specific planet, thus protracting into the seventeenth century a code of correspondences previously used by Hippocrates. According to this code, *pueritia* was influenced by Mercury, *adulescentia* by Venus, and *juventus* by the Sun.

In peasant society, the demarcations were less speculative and less arithmetical. Besides, very few men and women knew their exact age (which may also have been the case in aristocratic society). Thus not seven but eight categories seem to have characterized communal village practices and folkloric rituals. They represent less age cohorts as such than social functions: wet nurses, children, young men and girls, newlyweds, fathers and mothers, widows and widowers, old people, dead people. Each of these categories had a specific role in the community. Young girls generally carried out purificatory and prophylactic functions (driving off demons, sorcerers, and evil spirits), while the young men had a more transgressive role, notably that of organizing festivities and rejoicing. As for the newlyweds, they were often seen as dispensers of good luck and prosperity toward the village or parish generally.

This diversity of classifications enjoyed a corresponding diversity of vocabulary. The vocabulary relative to adolescence and youth was particularly rich and flexible, both in the vernacular languages and in Latin. Between *puer* and *juvenis* came a whole range of terms and expressions: *impubes, pubes, adulescentulus(a), adulescens imberbis, puella, puer jam juventutis aetatem contingens, virguncula, virgo, juvenculus(a)* (boy not yet at puberty; boy who has reached puberty; very young man or woman; beardless young man; girl; boy already reaching the age of youth; young virgin; virgin; very young man or woman), and so on. Each author employed and articulated them in his own way. One could be a *puer* at age seven or fifteen; *virgo* at ten or twenty; *adulescens* at twelve or twenty-five. Georges Duby has shown how, in the aristocratic class of the twelfth century, the term *juvenes* described all the young men who had been dubbed knights, but were not yet married or enfeoffed. Thus the famous Guillaume le Maréchal remained a *juvenis* until he was forty-five, at which age he finally decided to take a wife.[2]

Similarly, the age required for some juridical capacity—to give evidence in court; exercise certain rights, trades, or functions; receive this or that sacrament, marry; take vows; be thrown into prison—varied with each epoch, right, and custom. There were all sorts of comings of age, connected with all sorts of impediments or dispensations. In canon law, girls could marry after the age of twelve; boys, after fourteen. Before reaching these ages, they had no legal capacity. On the other hand, until they reached the age of twenty-one (*majoritas plena, aetas perfecta*—full majority, complete age), each new year endowed young men and girls with fresh rights and capacities.[3]

Imagery had to come to terms with this diversity—this indeterminacy, even—of social, religious, and juridical classifications. But it almost always gave priority to its own discourse, which in turn managed to be supple and pluralistic, and onto which the language of texts and the taxonomies of institutions had to be grafted, without always being perfectly adapted to it. Hence the exceptional complexity of problems raised by the portrayal of youth in medieval imagery—and the need for the historian to focus his or her research on a reasonably definite and limited corpus. Like images, young people seem to resist all generalization.

WHICH YOUNG PEOPLE?

Imagery, moreover, performed its own selection. Certain young people or groups of young people were never represented; others, only rarely. Among these groups were young people from the countryside, who, like the peasant class in general, count among those conspicuously excluded from medieval iconography. To be sure, they are not totally absent—we see them in calendars, in scenes associating months with agricultural activities; but compared with young aristocrats, they constitute a very slender corpus (even if shepherds and shepherdesses became more numerous in the late Middle Ages).

The same was true, though perhaps to a lesser degree, of urban youth: the youths found in the workplace, in studios, shops, fairgrounds, or on the street; also, the youths we find in schools and universities. There is an enormous contrast between the importance and effervescence of university life after the thirteenth century, and the rarity of images depicting students—not just students engaged in typically turbulent activities, but even these simply learning or studying.

Though less few and far between, pictures of young clerics, little monks, or novices, are far from numerous. Only deacons, whose model was obviously Saint Stephen, formed fairly numerous series. But were they still "young" men?

These lacunae in iconography are historical documents in themselves. The selections performed through imagery were neither neutral nor anecdotal. They were ideological, militant, and must be studied as such. The silences of imagery are always eloquent.

Its loquacity speaks volumes too. So far as the aristocracy was concerned, medieval iconography was not quiet at all, but highly talkative. Young princes and noblemen abound, and the way in which they are represented raises all the problems relating to the depiction of youth. In particular, it helps distinguish two age groups, in which adolescents remained separate from young adults. In the world of chivalry, for example, the difference between aspiring knights or squires and young knights who have recently been invested is an essential one, which the image always takes into account. They may be very close in age, even of the same age, but they derive from two entirely different universes. The former still belong to the mobile, multiform world of *valets* (in the noble sense that Old French lent this word). Their emblematic hero was Perceval: a Perceval who has not yet been knighted, a rough-hewn, simple, frank, rather stupid adolescent, but of such an innocence that he later becomes one of the three knights chosen for the quest for the Holy Grail. The latter category is personified by the figure of Gawain, nephew of King Arthur, a more mature and courtly character, more cunning too, certainly more aware of life's difficulties. Awaiting his uncle's inheritance—Arthur and Guinevere are a sterile couple—he is not yet married or enfeoffed. This does not prevent him from making numerous female conquests, however, like most of the young knights of the Round Table.[4]

Perceval and Gawain personify two different types of aristocratic youth. Accordingly, medieval imagery treats them differently. Perceval is still almost a child; he does not possess the full panoply of clothing and military equipment needed by a knight; his gestures are awkward, his coat of arms is monochromic.[5] Gawain is already a man, in the virile sense, but still a young man who cannot aspire to the privileges and attributes of *virilitas plena;* that is, of maturity. Gawain is often presented in tandem with his uncle, King Arthur, and in showing them side by side an image could emphasize all that separates the young man from the mature man. Postures, gestures, attitudes, dimensions, colors, clothes, objects: everything may serve to distinguish uncle from nephew. It is impossible to confuse the two. The same is true of the two other uncle-nephew pairings often seen: Charlemagne and Roland, Mark and Tristan. Nephews of kings are not yet kings. They are, however, models of princely youth, courtly and valiant.

Yet the most abundant corpus of young men furnished by medieval iconography is not that of knights and princes, be they real or literary, but that of the Bible and the lives of saints. Remarkable young people abound in the Scriptures, and imagery naturally accords them a predominant place: Joseph and his brothers; David before his coronation; Jeroboam as Solomon's intendant; Daniel and the three young Hebrews cast into the blazing fiery furnace; the adolescent Saul, witness to the martyrdom of Stephen; the pharoah's daughter who saves Moses; Dinah; Thamar; Salome; sons and daughters of every description, from Adam's children to those of the New Testament, all mobilized by history, the Passion, and the parables of Christ (the prodigal son, the wise and foolish virgins, and many others).

Angels were young men of a particular type. But representations of them may constitute an almost archetypal image of youth—not from a social point of view, obviously, but from a doctrinal, even aesthetic viewpoint. As for saints, they easily constitute the most numerous group of young people, one that justifies numerical, almost statistical, research, and most of the following remarks are based on this group. Moreover, the iconography of young saints must be compared with that of divine figures shown during their life on earth. Christ and the Blessed Virgin are ever-present models—particularly Christ, who was always young in his earthly existence.

Any study of the iconography of young people in the Middle Ages must reckon with the imbalances in documentation. Not only the sociological and typological imbalances just mentioned, but also and in particular the chronological ones (there are far more images for the fourteenth and fifteenth centuries than for the high Middle Ages), and the geographical and technical ones. Each researcher uses the collection of images most familiar and accessible to him, and the choice of corpus necessarily determines the results of the study. As for the present contribution, while I examined numerous categories of images, I nonetheless gave priority to miniatures—that is, images included in books—and mainly those from France, England, and the countries of the Holy Roman Empire.

STRATEGIES OF DIFFERENTIATION

A young man is only a young man when compared with other individuals who are not, be they children or adults. That is true both of his place in society and of his place in imagery. If he is alone in an image—and cases of this are rare before the fifteenth century—the young man is the object of a particular treatment only in relation to a few transdocumentary archetypes; that is, unless the image representing him corresponds to one or more other images showing children or people of mature age. Then the images interact among themselves. In 1445 Pisanello thus poured two medals in bronze, representing the two Malatesta brothers: Sigismund, the elder, lord of Rimini (born in 1417); and Domenico, the younger, lord of Cesena (born in 1428). The two profiles complement each other: the first has all the attributes of a mature man, whereas the second, in contrast, is intended to show all the qualities that made this "New" Malatesta (as the inscription puts it) an adolescent with an as yet uncertain future. The other side of Sigismund's medal shows him dressed as a warrior, surrounded by all his heraldic and emblematic attributes, whereas on the reverse of his medal, Domenico is shown praying at the foot of a Calvary.[6]

Whatever their medium, medieval images, like those of the Renaissance, are rarely isolated images. They almost always echo other images, presented either in contrast to them or else forming a pair or sequence. Even in the case of isolated portraits from the late Middle Ages, the historian always has enough documentary sets to discern the iconographic elements that make a young man recognizable as such. Moreover, as I said before, representations of groups are far more numerous than representations of isolated individuals. This makes it easier, within the same image, to compare different age cohorts and different social categories.

To distinguish characters from each other, the simplest procedure used by medieval systems of representation was that of differentia. In a group, one person would be portrayed exactly like all the others, except for some element or point of detail (position, attitude, size, gesture, and so on).

Before the presence of any attribute or specific deictic sign, differentiae were what emphasized a person, indicating his rank or status, and helped to situate and even identify him. It was, in a sense, a matter of "minus attributes," of exceptional details.

The young man was thus distinguished from children and adults by a certain number of differentiae. The one that recurred most frequently in images was that of size: young people were larger than children but smaller than adults. A differentia of size was thus enough to isolate an age cohort. Until the late fourteenth century, in classical representations that showed the four ages of man as four differently sized figures, the smallest always represented childhood and the largest, old age. Between them came two figures of medium but unequal height: youth was smaller than maturity. When no child was present in a group, then the smallest figure embodied an adolescent or a young man. Thus, in depictions of the Three Wise Men, as associated with the three ages in life, the youngest is always the smallest figure (which in no way indicates this king was a child).[7]

Through the effect of the figures' size and height, medieval imagery managed to erect a veritable pyramid of age. The nuances of generations depicted in it are sometimes extremely subtle, and it is a pity that iconographers and art historians have not shown more interest in these problems, which they have not only ignored but also disdained.[8] The imagery contains a constant code, flexible and incisive, that was partly inherited from Greco-Roman iconography and that has occasionally extended into modern imagery.[9] It deserves more thorough study.

This code is revelatory of the ideology that subtends any representation of the different ages of man. The scale of sizes is in fact a scale of values. It underlines the power and weight of age, the respect that is its due, the power it possesses. Conversely, it makes evident the scant consideration that society and its authorities (theologians, jurists, doctors, for example) accorded childhood and adolescence. To depict old men as very large and young men as very small—when in reality men and women of eighteen to twenty are often larger than those of sixty or eighty—amounts to using imagery to proclaim a clear difference in status, be it social, theological, political, juridical, economic, or symbolic. A young man occupies a small place in an image because he occupied a small place in society.

Nonetheless, the problems and implications are not always so simple. The geometry of imagery does not always rotate round a single axis, that of the age pyramid. Another axis is frequently involved in the dimensions of figures, that of dignities and functions within the society, whatever the age in question may be: princes, potentates, and rich people were entitled to large sizes, whereas plebeians and the humble poor were not. This axis was usually preemptive. In the same painting, an old peasant would always be depicted as smaller than a young nobleman. In battle scenes, squires, sergeants, and pikemen are always represented as smaller than the knights. In banquet scenes, servants and attendants always take up less space than their masters. The problem is no longer age, but social status. This can lead to errors in interpretation: we should not mistake a small figure for a young man—or even a child!—when in fact this is a simple house servant or stable boy, a herald, a scribe, an elderly servant, a maid, or a chamber-maid.

Imagery is never realistic. It is always ideological. Thus, certain tensions sometimes arise between the axis of ages and the axis of social hierarchy (or even between other axes based on various symbolic considerations). Priorities can then have different nuances, or even be reversed. In certain cases, it is important to show that a young man really is a young man, and this may take priority over any consideration of his social or symbolic status. Thus, he will be given a small size even if he is surrounded by persons who are socially or symbolically less important. In relation to customs, this differentia may serve to emphasize and make the idea of youth more evident. The code is inverted or transgressed and assumes an almost exponential dimension (which, moreover, is a frequent process in medieval symbolic systems). The iconography of Jesus in his infancy and adolescence provides many examples. In the scene in which he appears among the doctors, he is always shown as smaller than the physicians. This is not simply because he is only twelve at the time (as Luke explicitly states, in the only gospel that describes this episode); it is, above all, because his tender age—which must thus be indicated in the image—contrasts with

1. The Three Kings, representing the three ages in life. The youngest has no beard, whereas the oldest, who leads the procession, has a long beard. Miniature from a manuscript of Origen's *Homilies* (twelfth century). Charleville, Bibliothèque Municipale, ms. 245, vol. 1, folio 198, reverse side.

2. The four ages of man, represented by four different-size figures. The youngest figure is the smallest, and the oldest, though depicted as a bearded old man, is the largest: his height and beard are iconographic attributes. Miniature from a manuscript of the Languedocian translation of Bartholomew English's *De Proprietatibus rerum*, copied and painted for Gaston Phoebus, count of Foix, circa 1350. Paris, Bibliothèque Sainte-Geneviève, ms. 1029, folio 66, reverse side. Photo: J.-L. Charmet.

3. A couple and their twenty children: Juthaël, the legendary king of Brittany, and his wife, surrounded by their offspring, who are arranged according to sex (boys on the left, girls on the right) and age (the youngest appear in the foreground). Miniature from a manuscript of *La Vie de saint Josse*, copied and painted in Brussels, circa 1450. Brussels, Bibliothèque Royale, ms. 10958, folio 2.

4. An exercise for future knights: tilting at the quintain (above, a wedding scene). Miniature from a manuscript of the *Histoire du Graal*, copied and painted in northern France circa 1285 to 1290. Paris, Bibliothèque Nationale, ms. fr. 95, folio 273. Photo: BN.

5. A dubbing ceremony. The future knights are beardless, whereas their godfathers in knighthood wear beards. Miniature from a manuscript of the *Roman de Troie* by Benoit de Sainte-Maure, copied and painted circa 1330 to 1340 (Bologna?). Paris, Bibliothèque Nationale, ms. fr. 782, folio 161. Photo: BN.

6. Three iconographic types of young girls. Miniature depicting the legend of three virgins saved from prostitution by Saint Nicholas. Manuscript from *Images de la vie du Christ et des saints*, copied and painted in the Cambrai region, circa 1280 to 1290. Paris, Bibliothèque Nationale, ms. n.a.f. 16251, folio 90, reverse side. Photo: BN.

7. Reclining figure of Prince Philippe, eldest son of the French king Louis VI, the Fat. The prince died at the age of sixteen, in 1131, after falling from his horse in a street in Paris. The memorial statue was sculpted at the request of Saint Louis in 1263–64 (its nose and scepter were restored in modern times). Basilica of Saint-Denis, north transept crossing. Photo: Paris/SPADEM.

8. Saint John, the ideal model of a young and handsome face. In keeping with the Scriptures and with tradition, medieval image makers almost always strove to emphasize John's youthfulness and to distinguish him from the other apostles. Portraying him without a beard was an effective way to do this. Miniature representing the Last Supper in a manuscript from *Images de la vie du Christ et des saints*, copied and painted in the region around Cambrai, circa 1280 to 1290. Paris, Bibliothèque Nationale, ms. n.a.f. 16251, folio 30, reverse side. Photo: BN.

9. Youthful recreation. Two young men dressed in the latest fashion (striped clothing is a sign of sartorial elegance here) are playing at quoits, while in the background a servant is preparing a meal. Miniature from the famous *Codex Manesse*,
copied and painted in Zurich circa 1300. Heidelberg, Universitätsbibliothek, Cod.
Pal. Germ. 848, folio 339.

10. The four ages of learning. The sizes of the different protagonists in this scene indicate the age and level of competence reached: we see a schoolmaster and his assistant (both brandishing impressive rods), two schoolboys learning their lessons, and two very young children. Miniature from the famous *Codex Manesse*, copied and painted in Zurich circa 1300. Heidelberg, Universitätsbibliothek, Cod. Pal. Germ. 848, folio 292, reverse side.

11 and 12. Scenes of student life at the college of Hubant in Paris, in the mid-fourteenth century. Miniatures from the *Livre des statuts du collège de Hubant*. Paris, Archives Nationales. Folio 6, reverse side: bedtime and the evening prayer; folio 7: distributing food and shoes to the poor; folio 7, reverse side: cleaning the chapel; folio 10: handing out books, being awakened by bells, caring for birds.

13, 14, and 15. Young people relegated to the margin of the image: dancing, making music, and dressing up in disguise. Marginal miniatures from a *Roman d'Alexandre* copied and painted in Flanders around 1340. Oxford, Bodleian Library, Bodley ms. 264. Folio 78: dancing and music; folio 89: choosing a "king of the hens," and nautical quintain; folio 74: charivari, mockery, and reversal of roles.

16. A tiny squire. While the knight who has just won the tournament is in the background chatting with the ladies, his squire, in the foreground, is attending to his horse. The squire's diminutive size in no way indicates that he is a child. It represents his inferior rank (emphasized by his striped clothing) and his place in the foreground (this image is divided into several planes). Here the same code expresses both social position and spatial position. Miniature from the famous *Codex Manesse*, copied and painted in Zurich circa 1300. Heidelberg, Universitätsbibliothek, Cod. Pal. Germ. 848, folio 231.

17. Young people who are not young. The small size of the musicians in the foreground does not in this case indicate that they are young; to the contrary, it emphasizes the inferior social position accorded musicians, regardless of their age. Miniature from the famous *Codex Manesse*, copied and painted in Zurich circa 1300. Heidelberg, Universitätsbibliothek, Cod. Pal. Germ. 848, folio 13.

18. A bald young man. When he witnessed the stoning of Saint Stephen, young Saul (the future Saint Paul) was only twelve, according to tradition. But rather than giving him the features of a child, the image maker chose to make him identifiable by giving him his usual iconographic attributes: baldness, in particular. Miniature depicting the stoning of Saint Stephen in a manuscript from *Images de la vie du Christ et des saints,* copied and painted in the Cambrai region, circa 1280 to 1290. Paris, Bibliothèque Nationale, ms. n.a.f. 16251, folio 76. Photo: BN.

19. The first seal of King Philippe I of France. When he ascended to the throne in 1060, Philippe was only seven years old. The royal chancellery continued to use the seal of his father, Henri I, simply changing the name *Henricus* to *Philippus* in the inscription. As for the image, it stayed exactly the same: the infant king was thus depicted on his seal—the only royal portrait to circulate throughout the kingdom—as a bearded man in the prime of life. Paris, Archives Nationales, Sceaux, D 33. Photo: Archives Nationales.

20. First seal of King Louis IX of France, engraved shortly after his coronation in November 1226. For the first time on the seal of a French monarch, a timid effort seems to have been made to indicate that the king was a young man (age twelve), and not a man of mature years. Paris, Archives Nationales, Sceaux, D 41. Photo: Archives Nationales.

21. Two young horses receiving advice from their father. For animals, too, size in an image was a matter of age and seniority. Miniature from a manuscript of the *Roman de Fauvel*, copied circa 1330. Paris, Bibliothèque Nationale, ms. fr. 571, folio 149. Photo: BN.

19

Im martzo is 14 dieser gstalt, der
Rock mit attlassen zaun: das mambs
attlas die hosen mit gelb zendl: da
fing ich an meine klaider auff zu
zaichnen

17. Jar 1 monet.

22. A most elegant young man. Portrait of Matthäus Schwarz,
son of a rich patrician of Augsburg, shown at age seventeen.
Painting (circa 1520) from the *Book of Costumes,* in which
Matthäus Schwarz had himself portrayed at different ages in
his life. Paris, Bibliothèque Nationale, ms. all. 211, folio 27,
reverse side. Photo: BN.

his knowledge and wisdom. The precocity expressed by his small size matters more than his divinity here. More accurately, it is the sign of his divinity.

THE FOREGROUND

The fact that young people were so often relegated to the very edge or margins of an image emphasizes the difficulty they had in finding a place within the space of an image (and within society), and constitutes a further type of differentia. When the image makers depicted several age cohorts, the young ones were not entitled to occupy center stage, only the periphery. Typical in this respect are representations of noble families, showing a couple accompanied by their children: the father and mother appear in the middle and the children are shown on either side, in decreased order of age. The young ones are thus pushed toward the edges of the image, both to the right and to the left, often with the girls on one side and the boys on the other. In the case of genealogical trees or treelike structures representing kinship, the younger generations are similarly relegated to the top or bottom of the image.[10]

In illuminated manuscripts from the late thirteenth century onward, an even more radical form of relegation appears: young people are expelled entirely from the space of the image as defined by its perimeter, and appear in the decorations among grotesqueries, monsters, insect feelers, and foliage. In the next century, young people's activities or excesses actually became a favorite theme of these marginalia in French, English, and Flemish illuminations. The artists enjoyed representing young men and girls at play, joking, having fun, dancing, making music, putting on fancy dress or parodying adult society. Numerous examples of this are found in the splendid *Roman d'Alexandre,* copied and painted in Bruges in 1339–40.

Social transgression and pictorial transgression thus go hand in hand here, as if, once outside the bounds of the image, youth could give free rein to all its excesses and extravagances. Viewing this mid-fourteenth-century panorama, the historian can indeed connect what is shown in these marginal scenes (marginal in terms of placement, but essential to the images' function) with the evils that prelates and theologians censured in contemporary youth: turbulence, noise, reckless expenditure, luxury, sartorial excess, debauchery, disrespect, immorality of every species and description. In these marginalia—veritable safety valves for both imagery and society—we see the habits that the sermons of bishops and the harangues of lay authorities addressed so abundantly: young people "flare up," quarrel, fall into evil ways, commit "folly with their bodies," seek "vain glory," and "insult everything and everyone."[11]

This habit of banishing young people to the periphery of a scene not only involved the height and width of an image. It could also involve a third dimension: depth. Although flat, medieval images were in fact almost always conceived, constructed, and interpreted as if structured with density; that is, formed as if on a series of planes superimposed on each other. The processes of encoding and decoding began with the most distant plane and ended with the foreground, after passing through all the intermediary planes. When persons belonging to several age cohorts were represented, old people were normally placed in the background and young people in the foreground. Until the midfourteenth century—until the time when, in Western imagery, interest in depth (later, in perspective) was beginning to prevail over interest in density[12]—it was rare for young people, and especially children, to appear anywhere but in the foreground. This was by no means a way of focusing attention on them; on the contrary, it was another means of marginalizing them, for the density of an image also had its periphery, which was the foreground.[13] And in the foreground, young people were shown as being small, not because if they were larger they would hide everything behind them, but because smallness, as we have seen, was one of the iconographic attributes of youth.

This density of planes and the reduced value of the foreground were essential characteristics of medieval systems of representation. We also find them in coats of arms—the most theorized form of imagery the Middle Ages have given us, and the one that most precisely expresses the relationships of kinship. Within the escutcheon, generations pile up on successive planes: in the background, distant ancestry is evoked, great-grandparents and grandparents; in the foreground, the plane closest to the onlooker, we find the *brisures* (breaks)—the totality of signs evoking not the family as a whole but the individual bearer of that shield. Through the use of these *brisures,* family coats of arms, sometimes very old, were reactivated, individualized, even rejuvenated. In the heraldic image, as in any image, the background represents the past and the foreground represents the present.[14] Time is registered in the density of the image; youth is seemingly thrust forward by the generations standing behind it, generations in which it is iconographically and ideologically rooted. Without a doubt, this is the furthest Western imagery has ever progressed in treating the relationship between time and space. Duration, the passing of centuries, ages, and generations, blend with depth—that is, with an element not materially present in two-dimensional geometry!

YOUTHFUL BODIES

Size and placement were not the only techniques used by medieval imagery to show that a young man was a young man. The particular representation of the body through specific codes and attributes was equally helpful in indicating or emphasizing a character's youth. Here again, the "minus attributes" were the most pertinent and recurrent. The principal ones had to do with hair and hairiness; a young man was rarely bearded; a young girl wore her hair not covered but undone or plaited. Admittedly, nothing is systematic in this field, but beards and hair often help establish distinctions in age—and thus in social status—among the characters present in the image. It is regrettable, again, that the study of these problems has been neglected by iconographers and historians. The few works we possess on the history of beards and hair in medieval society are ancient pieces of work, anecdotal or romantic, deriving from "lesser history." In any culture, hair is an essential attribute of the human person; it has a profound anthropological dimension and often plays a social role of prime importance.

For medieval image makers, to represent a beardless man and a bearded man was to represent two age groups, just as it was to oppose or associate a woman whose hair was clearly visible and a woman whose hair was hidden by a veil or a coif. A married woman did not show her hair. When worn long and visible, such hair was a sign of availability. Nevertheless, the hair of a young girl was not to be confused with a prostitute's hair. The young girl wore her hair carefully arranged, knotted and plaited, gathered together. The prostitute, who abused her hair just as she did her body, wore it floating freely, disordered and untidy. In medieval images, it is impossible to confuse the two.

Differentiae could also involve clothing and accessories, especially in images from the late Middle Ages. Numerous features served to contrast the appearance of mature adults and that of young people: a long garment as opposed to a short one; a loose garment as opposed to a close-fitting one; a traditional garment as opposed to a garment in the latest fashion; the presence or absence of some detail or element of dress—fur, braid, embroidery, and so on. However, nothing is ever systematic in this domain either. In certain images, the old custom of dressing children, young people, and mature persons all in the same way endured well into the Renaissance and even beyond. Besides, young people were distinguished more by their clothes when in a group, just as they were also differentiated by gestures, rhythm, and color. I shall develop this point later.

The way in which artists represented the body itself, its forms, structure, flesh tints, and various parts could also draw attention to the condition of youth. However, imagery was less prolix in this regard than literary, medical, and encyclopedic texts, which contained numerous descriptions of young men and girls, repeating the same clichés and value systems an infinite number of times. These epithets reveal the corporal ideology and aesthetics that permeated the entire Middle Ages: a young body was handsome, light, smooth, fresh, healthy, smiling, slender, lively, and "nimble." People tried to preserve it for as long as possible, as evidenced by numerous recipes for beauty preparations, healthy diets, and the struggle against aging.[15] Young people were neither bald nor obese nor deformed nor bent nor hunchbacked; their features were not irregular, and their skin was neither dull nor pimpled. It was immaculate, just like the monochromic arms of young knights in certain chivalrous romances, waiting to be dubbed.[16] If young people were fat or bald, twisted or lame, pockmarked or pimpled, then they were evil young people, in one way or another, since any defect in physical appearance could only be concealing a moral or social vice. For that very reason, perfect young people were angels.

Naturally, imagery expressed all this, but rather timidly. It often proved incapable of providing iconographic equivalents for the most common textual clichés applied to youthful bodies. Here, for example, is how Bartholomew English, the most widely read encyclopedist of the Middle Ages, described a typical young virgin, around 1230 to 1240: of warm and moist complexion, she was "clean in heart and body," pure "as the iris of an eye"; she was simple and "not talkative, with a fine countenance and delightfully dressed"; her soul was timid and shy, because she was "a virgin in the greenness of her age." Compared to a young man, her hair was softer and longer, her neck whiter and longer, her countenace more "cheerful," her voice higher; her words were "lively and light," and she walked with shorter steps. Of "changeable" courage, she could not "tolerate heavy toil"; she was "more compassionate and subject to delusion," but loved with greater intensity.[17]

Among these topoi, several have to do with physical appearance and could be expressed in imagery without too many problems. But this was rarely the case. Image makers preferred to proceed otherwise, instead emphasizing gestures, postures, attitudes, and placement. A young man was shown as young above all through his relation to space. Not until the late Middle Ages, and only in very ambitious or elaborate categories of imagery, did artists engage in a true play of colors, of oppositions between dullness and brilliancy, smoothness and roughness, saturation and emptiness, in such a way as to express a body's youth, freshness, suppleness, or virginity. Admittedly, examples do exist from before that time, but they involve isolated images rather than whole sets, and—apart from the case of angels, whose iconography deserves a special study[18]—they occur more in sculpture than in painting, especially in funerary sculpture. When a king or a prince died while still young, the image sculpted (or graven) on his tomb often was often intended to preserve the memory of his premature death. A fine example may be found in the abbey church of Saint-Denis on the funeral monument of prince Philippe, elder son of the French king

Louis VI, the Fat. Philippe died after falling from a horse in 1131, at the age of sixteen. In accordance with custom, he had already been crowned king while his father was alive, and he embodied all the hopes of the Capetian dynasty. His shameful death (a runaway pig—*"porcus diabolicus,"* as the abbott Suger put it—had caused the accident) was viewed as a catastrophe by Louis and his kingdom. This sentiment was preserved in a sculpture added to the tomb at the request of Saint Louis, more than a century after the event; the young prince was represented as a recumbent figure with a pure and youthful face.[19]

In other cases, however, the young prince (or princess, though this was more unusual) was shown not as having the body and features corresponding to his actual age but as being much older, for ideological reasons. A young king of twelve or fifteen who had just ascended the throne would never, for example, be represented on his seal as an adolescent of that age; on the contrary, he would be depicted in a conventional effigy endowing him with the age any king must have to govern: maturity. This was the case with the majestic seal of the young Saint Louis, the matrix of which was engraved in 1226 when he was only twelve.[20] Like a monetary portrait, a portrait on a seal was always archetypal, never "realistic," and this was sometimes still the case up until the mideighteenth century. When Otto III became emperor in 983, he was only three years old. This did not prevent the engraver of the seal from giving him the features of a bearded man in the prime of life.[21]

A SOCIETY OF NOISE AND COMMOTION

There was therefore sometimes a considerable gap between image and reality, just as there was between image and text. Not only did medieval iconography scarcely ever show the reality of a young body, but it also seldom illustrated youths' active function within society. It almost always gave youths a passive role, representing them in a set, static, almost undifferentiated manner. The discourse of the texts, no matter how repetitive and topical, was different. In texts, youths often appear noisy, turbulent, and dangerous. They created disorder, respected nothing, and transgressed social and moral order. Young people disdained established values and older people, whom they found senile. They were bumptious and quarrelsome, thought they knew everything, indulged in mad behavior of every kind, spent without reckoning, and lived in luxury and sin. They needed to be given lessons, taken down a peg, made to do useful physical exercises, taught to disdain life's pleasures and, above all, made to marry young to avoid fornication and adultery.[22]

This picture of youth, often repeated in texts of every kind from late antiquity to the dawn of the Renaissance, was not totally absent from iconography, but it is given rather short shrift there. We have to look for it in images from the late medieval period, in grotesqueries and marginalia, in misericords, in the all too rare depictions of student life, of rituals of reversal, of the carnival or the charivari, in the presentation of festivities and entertainments—even in the iconography of a certain number of vices or dishonest activities. In these sources, young people dance, play, shout, and cheat. They are seen ridiculing authority and the powers that be. And they introduce movement, rhythm, and music into imagery.

Those young people are not shown isolated but in groups, troops, even gangs. The images try to represent the cohesion of these groups and gangs plastically, through effects of fusion, tangency, and superimposition. Young people form a mass, a block, a dense body; they occupy a specific zone, taking over a whole visual plane. Far from the tranquil society of adults, they constitute an ensemble both homogenous and diversified: forms, volumes, and contours emphasize the links that bind them, whereas gestures, colors, rhythms, and surface structures (small blobs of color, checkerboards, stripes, motley colors) show the extent to which this group of young people could be the cause of noise, disorder, transgression, or violence. Gestural and chromatic diversity contrasts with plastic unity.

These diversities introduce an element of sonority into the image, and offer the historian pertinent material for studying the way in which medieval systems of representation translated the idea of noise into visual terms. Depicting musical instruments, acoustical objects, musicians and dancers, artisans at work, and men or animals bellowing is not what makes an image musical or noisy. Noise is introduced into an image first through the play of colors, then through the treatment of surfaces, and finally through contours delineating gestures, forms, and places. Contrasting colors, variegated colors, stripes; lined structures, checkered structures, striped structures, lozenge-shape structures; interrupted lines, serrated lines, wrinkled lines; plastic and chromatic echoes from one zone to another, from one plane to another: these things create rhythm, resonance, and noise. And often the fact of representing young people and youth is what gives imagery an opportunity to show how well it can perform in these domains.

Here, as always, the play of colors is essential. It must always be studied in relation to the documentary unity concerned before being compared, later on, to some contingent transdocumentary coding, or even to a more general symbology of colors. These colors never function out of context.[23] Having taken these precautions, we may reasonably ask if a color that was emblematic of youth existed in medieval culture—a color that could function as an attribute in the representation of young people. The answer is positive: green sometimes played this role.

After the Carolingian era, numerous Western texts did in fact associate youth with the color green. In the twelfth and thirteenth centuries, this association even became so strong and recurrent that heralds and several poets made green the truly *heraldic* color of youth, and especially of young men who had recently been dubbed knights. In chivalrous romances, a "green knight"—that is, a knight whose arms, banner, clothes, and caparison are all the color of green—is always a young, impetuous character, whose intrusion into an episode unfailingly provokes disorder.[24] This can be taken in a positive or a negative sense, because green, like any color, is ambivalent. Encyclopedias, allegorical literature, and treatises on heraldry not only make green the color of youth but also that of hope, love (generally, faithless love), and fortune. Taken negatively, green evokes license, disorder, misfortune, illness, poison, sometimes even the devil. Associated with yellow, it symbolizes madness or hypocrisy.[25]

Clearly, the idea of sap rising, of nature in full growth is what makes green the color of youth. And because it is the color of youth, it is also the color of hope, love, disorder, and inconstancy. However, whatever techniques, pigments, or media they used, medieval painters and tinters always had difficulty in mastering green tones. These tones are the most unstable, they have most difficulty in penetrating cloth fibres, parchment, glass paste, or metals. It is hard to fix greens, to give them consistency, and to make them limpid, luminous, and clear. Hence the relative rarity of greens in medieval imagery—and also, a possible link between chemistry and ideology: pigmentary instability could correspond to symbolic instability. Like green tones, young people were changeable, unstable, and sometimes dangerous.

Although the color green was rare in medieval imagery, it was not absent, and this same rarity could actually favor uses charged with meaning. Thus, in illuminations green was often used as a peripheral color, a marginal color, unlike red and blue, which were central colors. This explains why it was used to emphasize the inferior status or devalued character of persons attired in it. It further explains the spatial connection between this color and young people, who were also peripheral or marginal. The encoding of the image and the symbology of colors coincide in this case, associating green with youth. This association would endure long into the modern age.

CHAPTER 8

GUARDIANS OF DISORDER:
RITUALS OF YOUTHFUL
CULTURE AT THE DAWN
OF THE MODERN AGE

Norbert Schindler

In the year 1532, the Protestant pastors of Schaffhausen addressed a solemn petition to the town authorities concerning the insults inflicted on them by the populace. Among other things, they complained that:

> When our brothers try to punish such things, (as happened recently in one place), they are not sure of their lives, either in the street or in their own homes . . . The miscreants come beating drums under cover of darkness, and smear the preachers' locks with human excrement. Among other dastardly tricks, the trees the preachers have planted and nurtured at great pains and expense are cut down. In short, these bad deeds are so widespread, things could not be worse in Turkey.[1]

Anonymous attacks on people and possessions, door locks smeared with feces, fruit trees cut down—it hardly seems that reformist clergymen were appreciated for the new morality they preached. Prudent in its policy toward the Reformation, the town council offered only weak support, thus giving the reformists' adversaries every opportunity to show their hostility. But who were these adversaries whose behavior was worse than the Turks'? Were they youths acting alone, or did these attacks also involve adults?

We may well suppose that the policy introduced by the Reformers three years earlier had resulted in representatives of both age groups being united against them.[2] If adults were participating, this would add further weight to these hostile protests: it would mean things were really becoming serious. Nonetheless, the actual *forms* of protest so clearly recall the habitual practices of juvenile culture—from brutal pranks to collective reprimands—that there can be no doubt that youth took part in these "misdeeds." Could these menacing nocturnal drumrolls be attributed to anyone else? Young men were always at the service of someone waging war, and people had grown used to assuming their arrogant behavior was responsible for any form of rowdiness or similar disturbance. In fact, the next complaint submitted by the Protestant pastors of Schaffhausen in 1536–37 denounced not only the "ordinary" sins—"fornication, blasphemy, swearwords . . . gambling, drunkenness, and uproar lasting until midnight"— but also the typical nocturnal noises made by irreverent youth: "swearwords, blasphemous songs, and cries that keep everyone awake."[3] But not everything these young people did was farcical or frivolous; on the threshold of adulthood, they constantly mixed gravity with humor. The communities of the preindustrial era knew how to make use of this blend of gravity and gaiety—sometimes more effective than any form of argument—and granted them considerable freedom of action, besides making them representatives of public morality. In the charivaris, or other public reprimands punishing lapses in social morality,[4] young men acted in place of adults, and with their tacit agreement. This gave their actions the importance of adult acts while freeing them from the responsibility of roles they would have had difficulty growing used to.

Despite the freedoms granted young people, youth was a time of aspirations still dictated by the expectations of adults, and for those adults—to turn once again to the incidents in Schaffhausen—almost nothing was more serious than the depredation of fruit trees or vines, "insolently" cut down. In agrarian societies, this "outrage" was the equivalent of an open declaration of war, threatening its victims' right to live in the community. The actions of youths were connected with the adult world in a more functional manner than we can imagine today, accustomed as we are, since the upheavals among middle-class youths of the turn of the century, to recognizing that youth has its own particular perspective and experience.[5] The intensive exchanges in the sixteenth century between the two cultures—the culture of youth and the culture of adults—were made easier in that adult behavior was far less disciplined and far more "youthful" (not to say puerile)[6] than what we are used to today. Around 1539 the synod of Schaffhausen decreed that "adults should not play at carrying each other,"[7] a well-known childish pastime. In 1526 Hans Stockar, then aged thirty-five, a good burgher and future municipal magistrate, noted in his diary that during the carnival a band of "honorable" fellow citizens, obviously well known to him (including the Latin teacher from the school) had broken into his cellar at night and plundered his reserves: "They swigged two quarts of my wine, and devoured and drank everything they found, turning my house upside down. And I have to take it all as a joke! They also got my valet and my maidservant drunk, and shouted and danced."[8] The victim had to put a good face on this rather dastardly prank. It may be that Stockar was a miser who had not been very generous at some preceding festivity, or that his companions had other scores to settle with him. In any case, this invasion—which in today's courts would be condemned as aggravated theft and burglary—was simply consigned to the council records as a nocturnal disturbance, a kind of practical joke covered by the license of the carnival and which might well have been committed by young people.

At the dawn of the modern age, youth had not yet become what it is today: that period of life weighed down by pedagogy, viewed with deep distrust, and constricted by numerous instances of bureaucratic control. Only the class-stratified society of the industrial era has dramatized youth in such a way that it has become both a vehicle of hope and a latent social menace, making the transition into adulthood a phase both positive and negative, and further transforming it into a cult phenomenon.[9] In substance, today's passionate debates on youth, with their underlying or expressed fear that future generations may simply reject the heritage handed down to them, are scarcely a century old.[10] In comparison, the relatively relaxed relationship that the adult world had with its young people—despite all their escapades—at the dawn of modern times strikes us as surprising. This relationship was based not only on the concept of a well-founded hierarchy (characterized by the fact that alternatives to the norms offered were quite scarce), but also on the idea that young people should gradually become accustomed to social relationships, in a society still dominated by the familial model.[11] This was an idea of social apprenticeship linked to experience; that is, of "apprenticeship as a simple process of gaining confidence . . . in which the apprentice learns, without realizing it, the principles—including the unknown ones—of an 'art' and the art of living from those already engaged in the practice."[12] This idea was so radically denounced by the pedagogues of the Enlightenment that it seems hard, today, to connect with its tacit principles and mechanisms of socialization. Nothing is more deceptive than the idyllic appearance of a simple life; thus we should also beware of the "smooth" appearance of an implicit apprenticeship. Historico-anthropological approaches that would like to be more than mere projections of current problems into the past should interpret the juvenile culture of early modern times not as a kind of social moratorium, but as a phase of initiation and transition into adult status, analogous to ethnologists' "rites of passage." The areas of freedom that the adult world granted its young people had their place in daily living (as when young people were "masters of the night"); they promoted the formation of age cohorts and offered innumerable opportunities for self-education and self-representation within the group. The ritual activities characteristic of groups of young people in effect constituted a laboratory of practical knowledge in which the prevailing norms could be tested, and surprising social consequences could afterward be expected. At the point where playful acquisition coincided with the relativizing of dominant concepts, we find not individual procedures for interiorizing norms but mechanisms of collective apprenticeship, deriving from the dialectic between observation of the rules and the controlled infraction of those rules.

But let us first address the question of the chronological limits of youth.[13] Recent research on juvenile culture in early modern times has been stimulated by Philippe Ariès's assertion that in sixteenth- and seventeenth-century society, the borderline between childhood and youth was not yet firm, and a precise notion of what we now term "adolescence" did not yet exist.[14] On the other hand, Natalie Zemon Davis has suggested—rightly, in my opinion—that groups of young men, both in the city and in the country, had activities that offered and anticipated numerous functions of socialization, functions that educational theorists would later attribute to the adolescent phase.[15] I would now like to amplify Davis's attempt to describe early modern youth from the point of view of its group culture, its rites and customs; I shall enlarge on some historical points and enrich them through documentary material from the linguistic region of southern Germany. However, it may prove rewarding to dwell a moment on Ariès's hypotheses if we keep sight of the fact that the boundary between childhood and youth raises major difficulties in the sources, where the term *youth (Jugend)* is often employed as a synonym for childhood. Perhaps the clearest example occurs in the baptismal edicts of the sixteenth century: "Whosoever is baptized again, having already been baptized in his *youth*, our lords . . . will never let him back inside the city."[16]

Felix Platter (1536–1614), municipal doctor of the city of Basel, uses the term in the same sense when recording childhood memories in his diary: "I used to enjoy listening when stories were told, and especially, since *youth* enjoys them so much, fables and stories of Merlin."[17]

But we should bear in mind that here an old man of almost seventy is remembering events from far back in his past, in which things crowd together or even become confused. This is also the retrospective view—not simply nostalgic, but also patriarchal—of a man writing his memoirs, his gaze fixed on the carefree time of childhood and youth, which he compares with moralistic intent to the responsibilities of adulthood. And lastly, in the jargon of authorities and old men, the word *youth* was used as a generic term in the sixteenth and seventeenth centuries, to indicate all those who were not yet fully responsible for their acts.

On the other hand, in this same period the word *youth* came to be used in a sense that corresponded largely to its modern meaning, identifying youth as a distinct phase between childhood and adulthood. Thus, in a petition the Reformers drew up in 1532 to have the Basel brothel closed, we read:

> This house is nothing but a cause of corruption for youth . . . Allowances may be made for childhood, which is not yet contaminated by sin; but

the rod should always be within sight and close at hand. Above all, youth should not be forgiven for anything; on the contrary, the more it is inclined to pleasure, the more it must be held in check by punishments and discouraged from the sin of luxury.[18]

It is impossible to confuse childhood and youth here: this text is intended to save young men who have reached sexual maturity, but who are not yet married. If we change ground and take a quick look at religious pilgrimages, we reach the same conclusions: in the sixteenth and seventeenth centuries, the miracle of childhood was already held and recorded as a separate phenomenon, whereas young pilgrims were counted among adults so naturally that this provides food for thought. In the Bavarian pilgrimages, the division was made at about the age of ten.[19] We may thus suppose that in the sixteenth century, society had a keen and concrete awareness of the cultural difference between childhood and youth. For historians, however, this distinction has almost been supplanted and effaced by the neopatriarchal and authoritarian dichotomy between the emancipated and the nonemancipated, between those responsible and those "devoid of responsibility," a dichotomy that widened in the wake of the Reformers' arguments.

If, at the start of the modern age, the boundaries between childhood and youth remained flexible, this was mainly because, for most of the population, school was not yet antithetical to the workplace—a contrast typical of the modern world. It was not until obligatory schooling was instituted in the early nineteenth century that the cutoff point at age fourteen was adopted (reinforced, in Protestant regions, by the ritual of religious confirmation).[20] Then, with the end of school and the beginning of apprenticeship and entry into the workplace, the distinction between childhood and youth was clear.[21] The state-imposed necessities of school and military service began to stabilize the boundaries of youth. In contrast, the beginnings of the modern age—when school was more of a possible duty than an actual obligation for most boys and young men—were characterized more by a combination of school and apprenticeship, which took different forms at different times, and in which there was no distinct boundary between studying and work. It was common to entrust easy tasks, such as watching over animals or carrying messages, to children of five or six; in the poorer social strata children were placed as servants when they were only ten or twelve, thereby relieving the family of the burden of their keep.[22] For the children of peasants and workers, it was obvious from their earliest childhood that they would help their parents at work. The "school of life," with its implicit praxis (Bourdieu), proved more powerful than the schoolteacher. Deriving more from immersion than from education at a distance, the pedagogy of accustoming children to the adult world through small tasks in the workplace still dominated education in its early stages. It is thus difficult to fix the point where childhood ended and youth began; in fact, this depended on conditions particular to the milieu and situation in which the process of socialization and apprenticeship took place. Only in the cultivated classes do we find germinating the modern idea of youth as a moratorium; that is, as the temporary renunciation of an economic situation that is already prepared, in favor of a career and improved status in the future. This concept had its social basis in a "formative" period, devoid of material worries, which lasted several years, and which has since become familiar to us—pehaps too familiar. Childhood and youth were also confused at a conceptual level, because feudal consciousness preferred to clothe its ideas of political order beneath the familiar and concrete topoi of house and family, notions accessible to everyone. In this way, in a paternalistic perspective, childhood became the social metaphor for dependency and minority. This also explains why, in household inventories and wills, unmarried servants of fifty or sixty were considered as children, whereas it was not unusual to find young men of fifteen or sixteen confronting each other on the battlefield.

If the beginning of youth was difficult to determine, its ending, on the other hand, was clearly delimited by marriage and the establishment of a home separate and independent from the original family's, as seems normal to us today. The municipal laws of the late Middle Ages already took note of differences in mobility connected with this change in state: whereas, for married adults, the right of citizenship was linked to the obligation of residency and could be withdrawn after two years of absence, "unmarried persons could enter and leave when they wanted, without compromising their right of citizenship."[23] But even so, marital habits varied greatly according to different social classes. In the seventeenth and eighteenth centuries, for reasons based on economy and the politics of subsistence, the age of marriage tended to be deferred more and more in the lower classes—and was never reached at all in certain cases.[24] As a result, it was not the youth of the wealthier classes (as would be the case today) but the youth of the humbler strata that was swelled by the number of de facto adults aged twenty to thirty-five—and thereby gained social importance during the early modern period. If we review the well-known socioeconomic factors, we can summarize by saying that in this period of history, there was a marked awareness of youth as an independent phase of life, perceived less as a social moratorium than as a transitional phase or "rite of passage." In other words, it was conceived as a period of gradual familiarization with the adult world, and thus lacked the structure of age cohorts based on numbers, such as we have grown used to today, given the conditions of modern states. Whereas the beginning of this phase of "youth" remains rather vague, its conclusion at first sight seems clearly marked by marriage. A more attentive examination, however, indicates that this, too, was subject to the imperious social logic of subsistence.[25]

The question of the existence of youth and youthfulness at the dawn of the modern age assumes a different, more precise form only when we give serious thought to the *cultural* dimension of young people's self-definition, and consider their concept of themselves and their autonomous forms of organization. To my knowledge, no one has raised the question more radically than Natalie Zemon Davis, who sees this juvenile culture as an informal group culture, created essentially through *ritual* actions. It would be useful to contrast her idea with the narrow concepts that seek salvation in the *formalization* of social relationships. To avoid the abstraction of arbitrary limits, we need to return briefly to the problem of the distinction between childhood and youth: anxious to preserve their privileges in regard to the "little ones," groups of young people were very careful to exclude children from their activities by teasing or sharp words—and by making them submit to rites of "initiation," twilight repressions, and, if necessary, thrashings.[26]

In this different perspective, it is worth casting a fresh glance at the old historico-popular writings on youth. This literature may be described as not yet possessing a precise concept of informal cultures. But, following the juridical and constitutional teachings prevalent at the time, it clearly imagined youth as a social structure trying to represent itself through the most elaborate forms of organization possible (statutes, financial regulations, regular meetings, parades, and the like). An attempt was then made—not exactly crowned with success—to find organizational models for juvenile culture; these schemas, which corresponded to romantic illusions about the populace, had moreover to be traced back to the most venerable ritual origins possible. The Basel folklorist E. Hoffmann-Krayer sought vainly to escape this dilemma: how was one to affirm the continuity "of this venerable institution of *Knabenschaften*" (boys' societies)[27] when one disposed of only sporadic and relatively tardy pieces of evidence? In his essay "Knabenschaften und Volksjustiz in der Schweiz" (Boys' Societies and Popular Justice in Switzerland—still worth reading) he tries to get out of it by advancing the theory that "with the passage of time the organization [had] become much more relaxed . . . [had] even completely dissolved . . . either through unbridled degeneracy, or through atrophy."[28] Such cultural pessimism, typical of the era, does not reflect the crux of the problem, but shows the intensity of the expectations it aroused. The juvenile culture of the early modern period was not an association of burghers, and did not aspire to become one. This modernist parallel does not lead far, even in Switzerland, where the *Knabenschaften* assumed clear corporate forms following the increased autonomy of the villages.[29] These "brotherhoods" of young bachelors had no need to describe themselves as rigid bureaucratic organizations in order to be capable of action. They drew their social power from the principle of peer groups, and stayed united because they had known each other for a long time. A simpler social mechanism can hardly be imagined: they met regularly in the evening, in the village or town square, in small groups structured by kinship, neighborhood proximity, or friendship; they met with the members of the other, nearest groups, and discussed what was to be done. This was informally decided through the authority of the oldest members, who had some experience, and then put into action.[30] "Beginning in May, we stayed outside almost every Saturday evening, until late at night; we made bonfires, a bottle was passed round, we sang, and played the harmonica; before going back home, we carried out some plan."[31] Above all, their thoughts turned to girls, as they pondered how to attract their attention through various pranks and traditional stratagems of courtship. These customs, created to facilitate contacts with possible brides, were central to the young men's culture; in northern and central Europe they took the classic forms of nocturnal visits to the beloved.[32] These forms of organized courtship gave the young men a chance to meet members of the opposite sex, and also gave them a certain amount of control over the local marriage market, as manifested particularly in their punitive actions against "misalliances" (unions with foreigners, remarriage of widowers, even "false" and "unsuitable" matches). Everything we know on the subject indicates that the use of charivaris—a form of public reprimand gradually extended to address all manner of problems of "moral economy"—had its origins in the patriarchal surveillance exercised by young bachelors. In accordance with the endogamous practices of small communities, the bachelors collectively considered themselves guardians of the morality and honor of a village's unmarried daughters. In parts of the Grisons, it was even common practice—as in the May festivity—to assign each young girl a young man to guard her honor, in a sort of temporary trial union that combined preparation for marriage with the control of morals and a gradual education in future matrimonial roles.[33] If young men who were foreign to the community tried to court the girls, it was viewed as an "invasion," and the local boys repelled them with fierce, sometimes even brutal fights; in these cases the boys constituted an autonomous social group, and in protecting "their" girls they were thus charged with defending the honor of the entire village.[34] In 1590, a stranger from Chur and his adolescent son moved to Burglen, in Thurgau, into a house where there was a girl of marriageable age: he was immediately confronted by all the young men in the region, who gathered in front of the house shouting "very obscene" words, thus annihilating his matrimonial chances.[35] As early as 1612, the statute of the *Knabenschaft* of Tamil in the Grisons (the oldest such statute to be preserved in Switzerland) asked whether a peaceful solution to the problem of outside competition in the marriage market could be found through negotiation, and payment of a kind of ransom or tribute.[36]

The second ritual dimension that gave the juvenile culture its group structure was the prominent role it played in organizing the carnival and the various events that accompanied it, of which young people were in effect the protagonists. According to the safety-valve theory, this role offered welcome and healthy possibilities for freedom and exuberance, behavior more open to young people during this period of collective madness, when all the rules were turned upside down. At Stilfs (in the South Tyrol), the young men were known as *Hoale*—a typical rustic metaphor that compared their rebelliousness to the energies of castrated young draft bullocks, who were difficult to yoke and lead on account of their impulsiveness and excessive strength.[37] In the Rhaeto-Romanic Grisons they were known as *Matti*—madmen—for the same reason.[38] More significant, certainly, was the fact that adult society made its young men the official representatives of this "world upside down," viewing them (a view that has never been belied) as natural administrators of the rites of transformation and regeneration that the carnival staged so well. In Swiss towns, especially, there were numerous young men's associations connected with the carnival; their ironic, self-derisive forms have posed ticklish problems of interpretation for traditional historians of folklore. Many institutions had names whose mixture of serious and grotesque elements proved enigmatic, such as the "Corporation of Pigs" of Rapperswil, mentioned in documents in 1578;[39] or the "Society of the great, powerful, insurmountable Council" of Zug, as it appeared in protocols after 1608, with its falsely pompous name.[40] There was the "Parliament of Madmen" of Weinfeld, documented until 1786; every year, on Ash Wednesday, it led a procession of homage to the castle of the provost of Zurich—and organized a mock tribunal satirizing local events; there was also the "Most noble, highly reputed, particularly highly honored, and especially highly treasured Consecration Society" *(Kilbigesellschaft)* in Schwyz, with its "All-Powerful Provost of Girls" *(Maidlivogt)*.[41] These puzzles become clear when compared to the French "abbeys of youth," with their carnival-style, "world upside down" type of government—that is, "abbeys" or "kingdoms" of "bad government."[42] In all these cases the dominant order was parodied and the pretensions of power jokingly proclaimed, while at the same time the rising power of youth was demonstrated. The exercise of real functions of order and the parody of these functions always went hand in hand. That youth acquired social relevance through presiding over the events of the carnival derived mainly from the fact that the carnival, with its principle of inverting the habitual norms, also influenced the customs of the other yearly festivals, especially those occurring in winter.[43] In this way young men rose in status, becoming the organizers of festivals. The midwinter festivals, in which change was associated with the renewal and reinforcement of social relationships, became their exclusive domain.[44]

There was a third sphere of activity reserved for young men, one that extended their function as guardians of nubile girls: they were given the more general task of policing morals—not only the moral failings of young people but also those of adults. Thus, article 4 of the statutes in Tamil clearly stated that anyone who "strayed from the right path" would be officially shamed through "public ringing of the bells," and even brought back to reason, if necessary, through harsh attacks on his property and possessions. The association then defined its moral pretensions as follows: "5. When married persons quarrel and one of them leaves home and spends the night elsewhere, that person will have to pay a fine of sixteen measures of wine after agreeing to return. If they refuse, then the bells will be rung and the drums beaten, in front of everyone, according to the old custom."[45]

Matrimonial lapses were thus seen as beginning when the conjugal roof was abandoned for a certain period of time—promptly noted by the neighbors, naturally. As a preventive measure, before an act of adultery could be committed (leaving the conjugal home was considered an antecedent fact), the group of young men condemned the infraction and imposed a forfeit—the measures of wine, which they then drank together.

In addition, there was the lurking threat that conjugal disagreements would be made public through a degrading and cacophanous charivari. The social "message" was quite clear: if anyone refused, the warnings could escalate and lead to the miscreant's definitive exclusion from the community. This surveillance of mores was not limited to conjugal or sexual morality, however; the young men's censorship reached far beyond, and into many other domains. The further the control extended, the more it influenced pedantic rules of moral conformity, until it culminated in a veritable reign of petit bourgeois terror. In the nineteenth century, the statutes of the Swiss *Knabenschaften* acrimoniously prosecuted anyone who went to church unwashed and with untidy hair, or with a dirty apron, ill-cleaned shoes, or untied laces—and even punished girls who went to fetch water from the fountain without their apron, or who went for a walk without covering their hair.[46] These petty restrictions were aimed particularly at young girls subject to the control of the young men's associations; with the approach of modernity, the rules were gradually modified into a plan for communal discipline and social hygiene. The eighth article of the Consecration Society of Schwyz, dating from the early nineteenth century, declared: "When a young man has reason to complain of filth in one of the village houses, he must denounce it to the Provost of Girls, who will admonish the guilty girl, telling her she will have to improve and do better in the future."[47]

Article 10 contained a relatively poetic threat: "Young girls must return home by nine o'clock precisely. If one of them is found outside her house after nine, she will be numbered among the bats."[48]

In the period of transition to bourgeois order, the charivari once again displayed its two-faced ambivalence. During the revolutionary years, the traditional forms of justice exercised through public reprimand gave the lower classes some possibility of expressing political protest.[49] But in other circumstances, these same customs could rapidly devolve into a petit bourgeois restriction of popular culture. I should emphasize, however, that all these petty rules, all the monstrously charming and dully dogmatic pronouncements as to "good" and "bad" behavior, would eventually constitute the bourgeois idea of "decent behavior"; moreover, they all originated

in one of the elementary functions performed by the young men's associations: the control of sexuality before and after marriage.

A question naturally arises: Weren't these the wrong guardians?
Wasn't this putting the wolf among the sheep? It is a troubling question
that, in my opinion, provides a key to understanding the youth culture of
the early modern period. In fact, the young men's entire sphere of activity
was permeated by these apparent contradictions. Semiadults, officially
organizing major popular festivals? Amorous young men, acting as guardians of sexual morality? Notorious disturbers of the peace, set up as
guardians of public order? The Consecration Society expressed this paradoxical logic in a pronouncement worthy of a sybil: "No maiden shall have
an admirer, unless one should come along that she likes."[50]

The young bachelors did in fact protect "their" girls' virginity, but
only with a view to making them sacrifice it in the long run. The resolution
of this paradox is anticipated in practical terms and expressed with great
good sense in the words, "unless one should come along that she likes." A
similar tendency toward self-parody may be found in the moral judgements
administered in sixteenth- and seventeenth-century towns. We should not
be deceived by rituals of self-representation that appear to respect the
hierarchy by aping the pomp and ceremony of official power. The more
they appear to conform, the more pungently their derision undermined the
dominant complacency. It was precisely by imitating official procedures as
closely as possible that they stimulated criticism: the old historians of
folklore were struck speechless by the obscenities contained in the protocols of the seventeenth-century Tribunal of Pigs in Rapperswil. An example from the year 1631 shows how the carnivalesque spirit of the young
men's organizations carried the rituals of established power to absurd
extremes: "Hans Zuppiger was accused of having torn the wings off a
horsefly one summer, then of regretting it. He shut it up inside a bottle
and carried it solemnly to the chapel, praying that the wings would grow
back. Condemned to give two heads."[51]

The "crime" was a farce, considering that "dissecting" all manner of
captured insects and beasts was one of the country boys' favorite pastimes.
No less farcical were Zuppiger's repentance and attempt at reparation,

which ridicule the religious rituals of penitence and pilgrimage—and also the superstitious, credulous nature of the country people; the final farcical element was the fine of two "heads" of wine. This was thus a complete, deliberate parody of official justice, bordering on blasphemy; it was based on the apparent incrimination of a normal youthful peccadillo, hypocritically subjected to a "normal" trial in order to expose the twisted logic of the dominant powers to the censure of common sense. Astonishingly enough, these shocking deeds seem not to have caused a scandal at the time. As was the case with the carnival, subterranean and surprising connections existed in these "tribunals" between the real world and the world-upside-down, and these connections formed the major themes of this organized madness. Those who so overtly mocked the established order were not in fact so marginal; there was every chance that, a few years later, they would reappear resplendent in the robes of councilors and aldermen. The "incredible formalism"[52] that dominated the justice of young men was simply a faithful reflection of the official forms of justice. Even in 1810, the statutes of the *Knabenschaft* of Andeer still explicitly declared these goals: "To learn to administrate justice, civil and criminal, and . . . practice it."[53] The carnivalesque spirit of these mock tribunals transformed young men into guardians of disorder; at the same time, in a way both pleasing and direct, it allowed them to exercise their youthful freedom while simultaneously preparing for the serious business of being an adult.

I should like to add a word on the military function of the Swiss *Knabenschaften*, a role that was often idealized during the nineteenth century by enthusiastic students of military might. It is incontrovertible that, because of the decentralization of the confederation's military system, the associations' duties coincided largely with the organization of local militias. The commandants and other *capitani* organized their groups of young men according to paramilitary hierarchies;[54] but they were still far from comprising a well-regulated force in the modern sense of the term. It seems the mountain populations, especially in the beginning, kept apart from all this: they were content that their wild bands did not torment the villages but turned their unpredictable energies toward foreign soil. Forays and other pillaging expeditions into Piedmont—especially into the villages and onto the boats on Lake Constance—were frequent occurrences in the fifteenth century.[55] The conquest of Thurgau, which took place in 1460, was curious in this respect: groups of young "warriors" from Unterwalden, Lucerne, and Rapperswil assembled in Rapperswil and decided to mount an expedition against Thurgau, more or less on their own. These irregulars had no official status and thus were not authorized to engage in military action. Since the besieged cities feared their vandalism, they tried to get rid of them as quickly as possible by swearing oaths of loyalty and making diplomatic concessions. Afterward, the respective authorities of these impromptu hordes of warriors had merely to legalize the unofficial campaign, and the submission of Thurgau was thus achieved with a minimum of military expenditure.[56] The Schwabian war of 1499 also demonstrated how strongly military actions had been influenced by the habits of these youthful groups. In particular, the attackers tried to fool the enemy with daring thefts of cattle, carried out at night, thus making military deeds of skills acquired in childhood.[57]

So far as young women were concerned, we know of no organizations comparable to the *Knabenschaften*. Except for the carnivalesque customs of public reprimand (such as drawing the plough)[58] and the May auctions of girls[59]—rituals linked to the problems of marriage and the local marriage market—the sources give very few indications that can be interpreted as collective appearances and common public actions on the part of nubile girls.[60] One of the most interesting documents, the *Nuptial Ordinances* of Nuremberg in 1485, provides information that forms a decided contrast to the patriarchal customs then predominant:

> Item. . . Several maidens have invented a new custom of walking through the streets at night to make public their engagements. Such behavior is not suitable for young girls, and an honorable warning is given them: in future, for similar announcements, no virgin must venture out alone into the streets at night; they must do so in groups.[61]

It may well be that in large cities, girls appropriated a "right" enjoyed by young men and bade a noisy farewell to those among them who left the group to be married. But too little is known on this subject for us to count out possible surprises. The authorities exhibited strong allergic reactions to these encroachments on masculine privilege, encroachments that called into question the roles traditionally allotted the two sexes. Alluding to the erosion of traditional marriage customs (due to the development of pre-capitalism), Luther wrote to the prince-elector of Saxony in 1544: "We have many young men from all the provinces. The girls have grown far too bold; they run after the young men and follow them into their rooms and elsewhere, and freely offer them their love."[62] The evening walks taken by unmarried women regularly drew thunderbolts from the authorities in sixteenth-century Protestant cities.[63] Veritable gulfs of perversion yawned before the vigilant moral brigades: in 1625, in Berne, reprimands were addressed to "young men and women who . . . kissed publicly in streets and alleyways, like whores and rakes. It would not be a cause for wonder if the earth opened up and . . . swallowed these scandalous persons, who are shameless before God and before men."[64] The trysts of young people, who used to meet at night in the cemetery, also attracted the long arm of the communal authorities.[65] And in seventeenth-century Berne, an increasingly rigid official policy of separating the sexes in public places put an end to the traditional workers' market, among other things.[66] Gradually this increasingly strict concept of order confined women to the house and prevented them from appearing in public. Under such conditions there was naturally no further interest in an autonomous "group culture" of unmarried young women. At the beginning of the seventeenth century in the eastern Swiss town of Wil, the number of visits young girls could receive was limited to five per year, and only in the afternoon; the girls had to be decently dressed and meet together under strict supervision. In 1663 the town council justified the restriction by remarking that: "In meetings arranged for young people, the just wrath of God is violently aroused by vicious and sinful behavior . . . Certain young people, and girls among them, take advantage of the occasion to drink wine and take liberties incompatible with their station."[67] At about the same time, the abbott of Saint-Gall, in his capacity as lord of the city, criticized married women for their habit of assembling in taverns *(Räteschenke)* on New Year's Day, on

Fat Thursday (for the *Weiberfastnacht*), and on various other occasions, to "drink together, which is a disgrace and a bad example for their daughters."[68] He thus devoted his considerable power to ensuring that taverns were exclusively reserved for men.

One could, of course, interpret this evidence quite differently: nothing (for example) was simpler than to cloister women in their homes, where they had important tasks to perform! An edict of Berne, dated February 9, 1627, inclines to that opinion: "It is forbidden for young girls and women . . . to perform indecent songs and dances, in the evening and at night, for they should stay peacefully at home with the men of the house."[69] If we know so little about the needs and public appearances of young girls, this is largely due to a policy of mores that taxed such behavior as amoral, thus repressing it as much as possible. During the carnival, it was entirely normal for men to attack women physically; but the lords of the council reserved especially harsh condemnation for "women and young girls who were so shameless as to desire this kind of thing," or who simply responded in kind.[70] In rural culture the only places where women could meet in public were the sewing workshops, where they worked together and had some possibility of social contact; accordingly, religious authorities fought these institutions tooth and nail with every means at their disposal, using moral discrimination, sexual segregation, and stricter family supervision.[71] Under the cover of honor and decency, this policy of domestication confined women and girls to their sexual function of reproduction, to their roles as housewives and mothers, leaving them little room or freedom for attempts at public socializing. Only by comparing these moral restrictions to the natural permissiveness granted young men in their roles can we understand the young men's behavior for what it was: the privilege of a restored patriarchal system.

But what were these youthful pranks like during the early modern period, and how did they differ from those of young people today? The scar on Felix Platter's nose was probably the result of a classic prank inflicted on his mother in Liestal (near Basel) in 1539:

This must have been caused by something that occurred when my mother used to stay awake late at night sewing, with me beside her on the bench in my cradle. A few merry, irreverent young souls had stolen a death's head from the cemetery; they put a lighted candle inside, then brandished it on the end of a pole at the window near where my mother was seated. When my mother saw this dreadful spectacle she was very frightened, especially as the head fell off the pole and rolled across the room; my mother jumped up and in her haste, she probably knocked my cradle over.[72]

Frightening other people, especially women and children, has always been typical of young men's behavior: it is linked to manly rituals of fear and courage that confirm the traditional roles of the sexes and are particularly effective under cover of darkness. The love of diabolical masks exhibited during the carnival also belongs in this category: "Some young men dressed as devils, or else wrapped in shrouds, were frightening people."[73] Several carnival customs popular around Shrove Tuesday have an anthropological meaning connected to rituals of fear; the masks and other virile disguises (which the old folklorists attributed to every possible cultural heritage) actually have quite a simple explanation when placed in the context of this theater of sexual roles, in which young men could affirm their masculine identity.

Ordeals of courage were also typical of juvenile culture. As always, they expressed group pressure and the need for individual recognition; through them, the group's internal hierarchies were constantly renewed. An example occurs at the beginning of the sixteenth century, in Kaiserstuhl (Aargau). There it became so fashionable—and dangerous—to climb the bridge across the Rhine at night that in 1512 the council published the relevant punishment in the town chronicle.[74] Few young men would have attempted such a thing on their own, but the group pressure was too strong to resist. The need to prove one's courage to the group was an especially strong coercive factor in nocturnal larceny, the prestige of which increased the more often one got away with it; this logic made it easy to cross the threshold of petty crime. In 1659, several nocturnal attacks on vineyards were recorded in the upper Rhineland, where "some wicked boys tore the grapes off the vines one night; another night, they stole some wine."[75] Since, in these vinicultural regions, the actual vines were strictly protected by the state,[76] the lure of "forbidden fruit" must have been particularly potent. As a general rule, however, the excesses of "arrogant and wicked boys"[77] stopped short of criminality. When they went beyond the bounds, they did so in such a way that it was difficult for the authorities to react adequately. An edict of 1493 from Solothurn gives an idea of the miseries they inflicted:

> Whatever person causes an indecent uproar at night with his cries and songs or builds barriers across the streets with logs and shafts; whoever removes cart wheels and hides them, or throws them into fountains, that person shall be thrown into prison for a day and a night without mercy, and shall pay a fine of ten shillings to the poor.[78]

Artificial obstacles and barriers, hard to see by night in the unlit narrow streets; cartwheels removed and hidden or thrown into the fountain to subvert the daily round—all these things were symbolic rejections of established order, and emanated from another, as yet hidden power, which was just beginning to take shape. "Whatever person": the Solothurn text perfectly expresses the contrast between the authorities working by daylight and the unidentified regents of the night, while clearly perceiving their anonymity as a threat. The expression "riff-raff fleeing from the light" *(lichtscheues Gesindel)* also appears. That none of the perpetrators could be recognized was bad enough for a system based on clear identification, but the abiding worry was that the suspects might be the residents' own sons—a portent of impending disaster. "The implicit rule governing the nighttime activities of youths was that everything in the streets belonged to them."[79] The symbolic challenge to established order was manifest, above all, in attacks on the burghers' private property; whereas the material damage was often minimal, the victims' rage could be far greater, the morning after the affront. As is apparent from the statutes of the town of Zofing, in 1604, these "nocturnal felonies" *(Nachtbosheiten)* included "the destruction of, breaking of, or other damage to windows, doors, benches, etc."[80] Another such misdeed was to roll empty casks about in the narrow streets, making a great clatter;[81] the young men also used to throw stones and snowballs at doors and windows.[82] And as we read in an ordinance from Berne of 1715, they threatened "to injure many people, by throwing benches and chests about and setting large stones rolling, and also casks and ladders from the walls of churches adjacent to the houses. This is deplorable in a well-policed city, where peace and quiet well-being should dwell."[83] But it was precisely the silent pressure exerted by this respectable bourgeoisie that prompted increasingly violent protests from young men. All these demonstrative aggressions and other "acts of vandalism" were accompanied by "shouts, bellowings, wild cries, and blows on wooden chests." All this "disturbed the nightly rest and frightened many people, especially people who were ill."[84] Indignation at nocturnal uproar is as old as the hills; on the other hand, this mention of rest needed by the sick and elderly was new to the eighteenth century.[85] This shows how serious the authorities were about reinforcing their arguments when combatting these traditional forms of disturbance.

Municipal edicts against nocturnal noise began in the second half of the fifteenth century. They became noticeably more frequent during the Reformation, diminished somewhat after 1550, and then degenerated into standardized forms. Between 1493 and 1540, Solothurn alone issued nine edicts against disturbers of nocturnal peace, six of which occurred in the "hot phase" (1526 to 1535) of debates and confrontations that accompanied the Reformation.[86] In 1526 in Basel, Oekolampad had advised the council to publish an edict protecting religious services against the noise caused by young people, "so that these insolent rascals cannot enter the church and disturb people with their singing and shouting."[87] The ease of passing from traditional juvenile rowdiness to politico-religious action can be divined from the moral edict published in 1526 in Solothurn, deploring "the numerous outrages committed at night by young and older men, with shouts, insults, and damages inflicted on the worthy burghers."[88] The fact that the term *insults (Schmähung)* suddenly appears in the traditional canon should attract attention, for other sources from the same era frequently mention mocking or insulting songs.[89] Two years later, it is quite clear that "nocturnal disturbances" were, first and foremost, attacks on unpopular preachers: "Whoever screams, shouts, or utters insults against clerics or lay persons, whether outside their homes or elsewhere," was to be "thrown in prison" and punished with a fine of ten pounds.[90] Considering that these nocturnal incidents were fairly normal, the penalties were exorbitant, indicating that town councils feared these anticlerical disturbances would threaten social peace. Young men took part not only in the barely disguised ritual attacks of the carnival,[91] but also in attacks on individuals: in 1522 in Basel, a fisherman named Ullin de Rynach, son of Martin de Rynach, was punished for "helping other persons damage a priest's house at night and drag his woman outside"[92]—probably a charivari against priestly concubinage. In 1527 Claus Fry, a farmhand from Zurich, was put in prison for dragging a priest from his house one night and calling him a liar;[93] in 1532, in Riehen (near Basel), three young bachelors dismantled their pastor's door and threw it in a pond.[94] Psychological warfare was also used: in March 1529, young Lienhart Hanis warned the pastors to keep an eye on all valuable possessions, because "the trashy priests were going to be driven from their hiding place, and whether they liked it or not, it was going to happen in the next few days." He had heard men working on the grape harvest say that "it was going to be like looking for Easter eggs, like a carnival night."[95] Hostility toward preachers seems to have been at its strongest in the villages around Basel. First, there was opposition to preachers who were threatening to impose a new social discipline: in 1529, when the pastor of Benken tried in person to prevent people from singing in the tavern in the evening, those he had criticized gathered outside his house, singing and shouting; they made the "rascal" come outside, and broke one of his windows.[96] Second, the disappointed members of the rural population—who had hoped for a reduction in taxes—expressed their resentment by refusing to pay the ecclesiastical tithe and by voicing rebellion. Someone shouted that the pastor of Muttenz was "flaying the people,"[97] and another pastor was given "the smallest possible amount of corn."[98]

In this rebellious atmosphere, the young men's misdeeds passed almost unnoticed. Again in Benken, in 1530, several young men were punished for having "secretly demolished the pastor's privy closets."[99] In April 1530 in Pratteln, six young men—including three servants—"threw human excrement into the garden" of the preacher Jakob Ymelin, and "threw dung into his bower, with insulting shouts of 'Jeckli, Jeckli,' all this at night."[100] Four months later, a group of seven young men—including three apprentice weavers and a servant—led a further expedition against the detested priest. They bombarded his house with stones, and also the trees in his garden; they sewed "weeds and rotting plants" in a freshly dug piece of ground, so that "good may not be distinguished from evil."[101] They dismantled his garden gate and threw it in the horse trough; they smashed his chamber pot and demolished the woodpile, spreading "logs and wood all over the street, in front of his house."[102] In all these cases it is striking to note that the young men were acting on their own initiative, but with the tacit approval of adults. In Pratteln, the authorities did not try to find out who the troublemakers were; the father of one miscreant had even told his son that "if he were still a young lad, he would have liked to break up the priest's woodpile."[103] In Muttenz, the town magistrates were judged at the same time as the young men, because they too had taken part in the outrages inflicted on the pastor.[104]

The measures taken by the authorities against nocturnal charivaris did not amount to much: they issued threats of punishment, appealed for greater strictness on the part of the night watchmen, and exhorted parents to keep a better eye on their offspring and to "keep them at home in the evening."[105] In Rheinfelden, the oath administered to apprentice workers included the following words: "You must not make noise at night after the bell has sounded."[106] All this hardly suggests much practical success: the furious tone of the ordinances and edicts indicates, rather, that people felt helplessly exposed to the nocturnal charivaris.[107] We find ourselves wondering how much of this rhetoric was designed to soothe the feelings of the victims of these deeds. Did the authorities really intend to repress the young men's actions with all their might? The directions for carrying out municipal edicts inspire doubt: one is surprised to see that the "nocturnal disturbances" were held separate from the normal punishments and treated specially, "according to the knowledge of the mayor or the council, and according to the importance of the crime."[108] Clearly it was not in the interests of the town councilors to criminalize their own offspring on account of minor delinquencies; they were aware that youths needed breathing space. At the same time, for political reasons, they could not allow misdeeds to multiply without some attempt at punishment. They needed a judicial remedy that blended rigor and indulgence, corresponding to the playful aspects of these youthful provocations: the answer was the *Narrenhäuslein,* or "little prison," known simply as the cage *(Käfig)* in Solothurn. This was a cell reserved for short incarcerations, to be occupied by those who had offended someone's honor without committing a real crime. One was built in Augsburg in 1475 for "nocturnal prowlers, drunkards, and noisy troublemakers."[109] There is mention of another in Saint-Gall in 1533.[110] In Lucerne, Renward Cysat noted in 1575 that "the little prison for punishing evil pranksters—especially young lads—has just been finished and installed on the bridge over the Rüss . . . It has served as an example for many other towns and confederations, large and small, that have imitated the custom."[111] It is indeed remarkable that in the seventeenth century even the villages of eastern Switzerland imitated the disciplinary measures taken by city authorities. In 1672, the rural community of Mosnang asked the monastery of Saint-Gall, on whom it was territorially dependent, to "construct a small prison or cell, near the church," so that "ill-bred youths can be kept under lock and key."[112]

None of this did much good. In numerous towns the well-known conflict was renewed, as authorities struggled to contain the excesses of their young people. In Saint-Gall, the clash had begun with a municipal edict of 1508, condemning the shameful cries, rowdy processions, and undisciplined songs of adults and "young men" alike.[113] After the Reformation, when the control of morals became more strict, the council decided to combat this public exuberance and its mostly youthful protagonists by instituting a system of spies. Four such informers were appointed, who "made secret rounds at night and denounced those who sang, shouted, and indulged in similar rowdiness."[114] For poorer boys, this heightened surveillance was hardly cause for alarm; rather, it incited them to deride and defy the official norms of order and morality even more audaciously. Thus, in

1615, two young men were arrested for shouting insults and throwing excrement and trash from the height of the main gate at some monks, who were on their way to the monastery to reenact the *via crucis*.[115] A guerilla war of constant harassment ensued, waged mainly on the night watchmen and guards at the town gates, whose oath of office had required them to control nocturnal troublemakers since 1487.[116] In 1668, the council admonished them to pay more attention to the ruffians who were causing so much nocturnal damage; they were to denounce them systematically.[117] Ten years later, guards and watchmen were severely rebuked by the council, because the disorder in the streets had reached such proportions that "in some streets, every single bell pull and even the iron door knockers had been broken; the locks of shops had been twisted and wrenched with such force that in several cases, anything at all could have been opened."[118] The more strict and extensive the measures of control became, the more the conflicts escalated.[119] Fighting back seems to have been a matter of honor, and matters took a turn for the worse. At the end of the seventeenth century, we read of mocking attacks and even pitched battles taking place between the guardians of order and groups of young men from every social class.[120] In 1763, the town council of Berne was obliged "to prohibit, universally and under threat of grave penalty, attacks on constables, patrolmen, watchmen, and sentries, whether in word or deed; . . . if they were attacked with insolence and premeditation, then the guards *were ordered to defend themselves as best they could, with the weapons and bayonets* at their disposal, although they were first to identify and arrest their assailants"[121] in order to mete out the appropriate punishment. It was at just this time that the struggle over Berne's newly installed street lanterns began, mute guardians of the peace whose task was to illuminate and unmask the traditional masters of the night; the bourgeois nineteenth century greeted their arrival with enthusiasm, because it was thought that each lamp would replace a policeman[122]—a symbolic fight that has still not ended.

In the country, young men's pranks were obviously determined by the means at their disposal, but they scarcely differed in spirit from the pranks of young city dwellers. We find the same playfulness, the same

presentation of the "world upside down": cartwheels removed, carts stolen, harrows hung in trees; hay wagons and wood carts perched artistically
on farm roofs; wood piled up in front of doors; and ritual thefts, aimed
not only at cherry and plum trees, but also at the well-stocked storerooms
of certain peasants.[123] An edict issued in Glarus in 1724 noted that "many
respectable persons have cause to complain that during the night, windows
are broken and fences knocked over."[124] There was also the ritual custom
of "stealing cherries"—that notorious struggle between the adult sense of
private property (represented by the authorities) and the collective ideals
of the young, who sought to prove their valor in this "daring" adventure.
Every year between 1552 and 1856, the authorities of the canton of Glarus
published their "edict of fruits," aimed—always in vain—at preventing
thefts of "fruits or vegetables from honest people, either nuts, pears,
apples, beans, peas, beetroot, or other kinds of produce, by night or by
day, in secret or in full view of everyone."[125] Solothurn issued its first edict
forbidding the theft of fruit in 1557, revealing the numerous forms this
nocturnal larceny could take:

> Whoever . . . enters a garden, orchard, or meadow belonging to someone
> else, and crosses his fence without permission; whoever damages or
> knocks over a hedge or barrier and carries off wood, or simply fruit,
> whether cherries, apples, pears, or any other fruit, or causes light or
> severe damage, either at night or during the day, even if he does so for
> his lord, shall be publicly treated as a thief.[126]

The threatened punishment, increased two years later for "ordinary
thieves caught in the act,"[127] reveals what was at stake in this conflict: to
protect the rights of property owners, the authorities hoped to transfer
offenses of this kind from the traditional confines of youthful folly to the
domain of ordinary laws—with their corresponding penalties—against
theft. But the young men's adventures obeyed an entirely different social
logic. In the symbolic order of the village, the struggle over cherries
simply marked the permanent conflict between adults—the definers and
guardians of limits—and their rightful heirs, who had to destroy and
redefine those limits, in obedience to the logic of the renewal of generations. In these communities structured by bonds of kinship and survival

strategy, youth was not simply an "organic" guarantee of social evolution; it was also a "collectivity" that could act relatively freely, without the material divisions that encumbered the adult world. Thus, youth was able to represent the *totality* of a village far more clearly and convincingly in its actions than some tediously elected *bürgermeister*. In short, it was because the young men represented the community *socially* that adults entrusted their young men with orderly functions they could not themselves assume so convincingly; this is also the reason the war of the cherries could never end. Besides furtive petty thefts, the Swiss sources were already recording attacks carried out openly, in public. The significance of these attacks, and the provocative harshness with which young people pressed their claims against the self-interest of the property owners, become fully apparent in this chronicle from the Tirol:

> Thus they go straight to the owner of the cherry trees, wake him up, tell him some cherries have been stolen, and spur him to retaliate. If anyone tries to chase them away, they enage in scuffles and other mean tricks. For example, they might put a basket full of stones above the door of the house; when the peasant tries to go out, the stones come tumbling down on him. Or else they might coat the steps of his house with slippery mud, and put thorns and spines at the bottom. When the peasant runs down these steps he knows so well, trying to chase them, he slips and falls into the thorns. When this trick works, they begin to shout and whistle, addressing mocking remarks to the peasant who's fallen into the trap. While this buffoonery is going on, some others steal the cherries.[128]

This, therefore, was one of the ritual means of forcing somebody outside; a ritual that raised a simple case of fruit theft to the level of the "war of the cherries." Masculine provocation rituals, with their accompanying ideas of honorable retaliation, thus passed from simple confrontation[129] to a show of open conflict, the intention being to make the whole affair look farcical through carefully planned pranks. The adults of the village ended up wondering if it was really worth collaring the boys, or if it wouldn't be better simply to turn a blind eye to the "minor liberties" they took. The young fellows' attacks finally triggered a potentially explosive idea: maybe the cherries actually belonged to everyone! In agrarian society, ideas of collective property were limited to fruits growing in the wild, whereas all produce grown in fields, which required careful tending, was taboo, and if outsiders touched such produce, this was deemed an outrage. But cherry trees required relatively little work, occupying, as it were, a border zone between cultivation and nature; minor thefts therefore seemed permissible, and in imposing their "rights," the young men saw to it that boundaries remained mobile and flexible. Certain social factors may have entered into the question, albeit subliminally. Sources often mention that the spoils of the theft were offered to young girls,[130] and Swiss fruit edicts give the impression that many of the poorest villagers regularly sent their children marauding in the gardens of wealthy proprietors. In any case, receivers of stolen fruit were punished far more harshly than the thieves; in Solothurn, adults who accepted this kind of merchandise were threatened with banishment.[131] And although it is hard to determine this exactly, the boys' thefts, committed mostly in a spirit of sporting competitiveness, must also have been reflected in social tensions and in internal conflicts of the village hierarchy. "Repression and provocation go hand in hand,"[132] and it was hard to distinguish where repression ended and provocation began in the young men's daily activities. In the eighteenth century, the numerous victims of these misdeeds began to defend themselves more vigorously against the attacks.[133] This does not simply indicate that the traditional policy of repression was in decline; it also suggests a hardening of boundaries in the problematic zone in which repressive measures were employed. Taken seriously at first, the youthful charivaris were now included in a broad praxis of "daily rowdiness." Here I agree with E. P. Thompson, who maintains the importance of following the "long prehistory" of repressive conflicts,[134] while recognizing that the ritual activities of juvenile culture helped obscure it.

The Church of the Counter Reformation, with its one-dimensional ideas of order and reform, could not appreciate the libertarian elements of "implicit" popular pedagogy. To it, these boastful, noisy, dead-drunk adolescents, with their insolent manners and their brawls, who "confronted each other with knives in streets and ballrooms alike,"—

according to an inspection report of Pfalz-Neuburg[135]—were like thorns in the flesh. The Bavarian "Catholic Reformation" was not simply a matter of forcing the lower classes to attend religious services and learn Christian doctrines, to attend confession and communion; it was part of a more general "project of social discipline, carried out under the double banner of morality and the fear of God."[136] Since their attempts to instruct and convert old people proved unsuccessful, if not to say disastrous,[137] Church missionaries soon turned their attentions to children and adolescents.[138] The young people proved almost equally recalcitrant, offering active and passive resistance that ranged from finding every possible excuse for avoiding catechism classes to rowdy behavior at Mass, which had become obligatory, and to spectacular acts of protest. In Nuremberg in 1659 they rolled a large stone in front of the door of an unpopular sacristan and engaged in a pitched battle with the *Streifer* (whose job was to keep order during the divine services), hurling stones and snowballs at them.[139] At the beginning of the Counter Reformation in Bavaria, Jesuit preachers who too brutally censured the habits of the populace were subject to regular physical attacks.[140]

A typical example, drawn from a document of the time, illustrates the significant points of tension and conflict (now habitual) between youth culture and ecclesiastical discipline. Toward the end of the seventeenth century, an ecclesiastical complaint records the "indecencies being committed in certain curacies in the Stanzerthal"[141] (a valley situated on the Tyrolean side of the Arlberg); of the nine grievances, at least six involved young people. In the first place, of course, the pastor took aim at courtship as practiced in the countryside: "young people—unmarried boys and girls—behave very badly, both at night and during the day, meeting in taverns and other places reserved for the purpose; particularly scandalous and dangerous are visits to the girls, when they go walking in the streets or converse at windows [*gassen gehen, fensterlen*], on Saturday, Sunday, and on holidays." Here the ritual liberties of courtship—a crucial moment in the young bachelors' anticipation of adulthood—appear only as examples of indecency and moral decadence. Even the deliberate use of words like "scandalous places" shows how little members of the "reformed" clergy of the Counter Reformation were disposed to accept the social logic of popular culture. According to their abstract moral reasoning, anyone that tried to escape the moral control of the authorities was destined for the pillory. In the second place, therefore, they poured scorn and condemnation on popular dances, especially those held in private houses at night. They criticized the festivals the rural population held on Sundays and during the carnival: "as I myself saw . . . not only adults, adolescents, and young girls gathered to dance in the inns, but also children of eight, nine, and ten." In his moral zeal, it never occurred to the complainant that the inclusion of children in these popular dances was the most obvious proof of their innocence. For him, dancing was a uniform cause of sexual perdition; unmarried dancers are mentioned only as potential sinners. Every social misery—according to his intimate conviction—resulted from uncontrolled sexuality, and this convenient idea allowed him to continue in the same vein:

> A most pernicious custom has developed in the above-mentioned curacies, in churches and during services. Young men, already adults, stood under the porch of the church—as happened this year in Strengen—and threw snowballs at the unmarried persons inside. During the Easter holidays, some of these ne'er-do-wells brought a bag full of sawdust under the porch, and during the service they poured the contents on some women's clothes. Also, it often came about that they played under this same porch during sermons. I shall say nothing of the incessant chattering, horseplay, and other numerous indecencies committed in all the above-mentioned curacies.[142]

This particular priest was better at denunciation than at grammar; but in his pronouncements we notice the recurrent idea of the "porch" (*Vorkirche*). The term denotes not only the place through which the faithful entered the church (a social event, in a sense), but also the favorite strategic position of young lads, who could keep an eye on everyone else without being seen themselves ("The bachelors always liked to sit in the front rows of the balcony, because from there they could look down at the girls")[143]— the high point of profane interest during sacred ceremonies. In the volleys of snowballs and sawdust aimed at the girls of the community, we easily

recognize the mixture of fun and seriousness that was common in relationships between the sexes. But the clergy were not at all concerned with the
social significance of these carefree pranks: they saw only the disturbance
of the divine services and an absence of moral sense. The clergy particularly condemned the tricks young men got up to during wedding nights:
"Scarcely have the bride and groom withdrawn to rest than the young
bachelors go to the place where the marriage is being celebrated, causing
all manner of disturbances. When they find the married couple, they pick
up their bed and carry them in it all through the streets to the tavern, where
the bride and groom have to promise something."[144]

For a *Knabenschaft*, the rite of passage that was marriage formed the
apogee of its communal activities. When one of its members left to be
married, the others had to honor him as energetically as possible, and take
their leave of him with numerous practical jokes. When Felix Platter
married in 1557, he had to submit to the ritual deeds of the "lads" on the
steps of his house.[145] The act of picking up and carrying the marriage bed
through the streets to the inn is really a dramatization of the break that
marriage constituted in village life; it provides spectacular proof of the
control that young unmarried males exerted over sexuality, a control that
ended at the foot of the nuptial bed—but did not really end there. The
priests' complaints indicate nothing of this, content as they were to portray
the young men as chronic troublemakers and a permanent threat to moral
norms. And the young men had no need to be reticent; they needed only
to don the negative "role" offered by the authorities to evoke the conflict
that marked the relationship between Church and youth at the start of the
modern age. This conflict was all the more inevitable given that the youth
culture's will to self-assertion had always been fed by the joy of opposition
and the pleasure of relativizing the dominant norms through pranks and
ridicule.

The young men's recalcitrance was felt especially by the overzealous
rural priests, who tried too enthusiastically to impose the new moral rigor,
attempting to tilt in their own favor the delicate balance between government morality and the morality of the people. In 1661, in the Basel district,
a complaint was lodged that "nocturnal sallies, carousing, and vulgar

shouts are very common . . . Wicked night birds are dishonoring people and even the pastor is not safe from it."[146] When in 1724 the incumbent of Prittriching (in the district of Landsberg) used his bully pulpit to lament the "moral decadence" of his commune, the sole result was that "farm boys and knaves" gathered before the church and presbytery "to shout, sing, shriek with joy, and complain most insolently"[147]—a paradoxical echo that raises doubts as to the moral efficacy of his preachings. In confrontations of this kind with the religious authorities who sought to reform customs—and particularly with the more intransigeant among them—the bachelors' group culture was in the vanguard of resistance against this moral offensive launched like a spear from above, and defended the village culture's rights to self-definition. Its demonstrative protests gave voice to the discontent of the communes, and were designed to force the priests to adopt an attitude of compromise; if they wanted to live peacefully with their community, they would have "to conform to the needs and rules of the village, in both behavior and words."[148] The decisive weakness of the reformers was certainly their relative isolation. When in 1625 the pastor of Döpshofen (near Augsburg) wanted to prohibit dances (this was one of the war-cries of the new austerity) because dancing distracted young people from religious education, "young men came running to confront me in the presbytery, shouting and screaming. The provost let it happen, so what can we do?"[149] Abandoned by God and the earthly hierarchies, the worthy fellow could only take refuge in his sighs.

Behind these examples of *Katzenmusik*[150]—these bacchanalia of howls, catcalls, and songs—the hidden presence of adults and property owners must be suspected. Naturally, they wanted to know nothing of the matter and laughed about it to themselves—a common way, in rural culture, of approving youthful protests. We may conclude that a strong moral consensus existed; it strengthened rural hierarchies and even provided a model for acts of revolt among the peasants.[151] We should not, however, interpret the relationship between young peasants and adults as a conspiracy; it was more a matter of indulgence than incitement. The tacit agreement between young and old was generally so clear that the question

of organizing acts of protest scarcely arose. Above all, the instinctive flair
of the village boys came to the rescue when moral precepts and other rules
of bahvior were imposed from outside the community. An excellent example of the moral consensus binding the different generations in rural
culture—and of the link between the freedoms granted youth and their
preparation for future adult roles—is provided by Johann J. Bodner in his
description of the cantonal parliament of Appenzell and the young men's
parody of that event, staged the following day:

> At the beginning of the eighteenth century, the young men of Appenzell
> had the happy custom of holding a parodic assembly the day after the
> true cantonal assembly, in which they mimicked the figures, speeches, and
> customs of their magistrates and fathers, with a wonderful natural wit.
> They allowed themselves the liberty of presenting in an amusing and
> often mocking light the serious plans, counsels, and speeches that had
> been put before the assembly. They were at great pains to mock the
> failings, large and small, in expression, voice, and attitudes. When they
> noticed, in their representatives' speeches, some sophistic phrase or a
> maxim that contradicted itself, then they were merciless. It was not
> unusual for them to make resolutions and judgments that were contrary
> to the judgments and resolutions of the previous day. This license had
> been permitted for years, and doing away with it would have required all
> the activity and apparatus of government.[152]

It may seem surprising, at first sight, that the cantonal parliament—the
supreme instance of political decision making at the cantonal level—was
exposed to the criticism and mockery of its youth. Yet similar institutions
existed in the other cantons as well.[153] In these limited social units, where
everyone knew everyone else, this procedure—which may strike us as
risky—acted as a safety valve for expressing political discontent. At the
same time, this cunning expedient made sure the heirs followed every word
of the adult assemblies, thus enabling them to continue the work in their
turn. So long as politics was still closely tied to family relationships, it was
possible to familiarize tomorrow's politicians with their future duties in this
rather paradoxical way. Lastly, the fact that the "boys' tribunes" *(Kna-
bengerichte)* of the Grisons or Aargau—or even the burlesque tribunals
(Spottgerichsthöfe) held every year in Zug, Rapperswil, Weinfelden, Stans,

and Appenzell—carefully noted real follies committed in the community was simply another form of everyday politics; moreover, everyone knew that the *Knabenschaften* influenced official politics by virtue of their large numbers and concerted actions. Above all, we know of their tactics of "attempted manipulation" in the rural electoral assemblies.[154] Nor will it surprise us, as we examine complaints about disturbances (frequent, in the eighteenth century) in the venerable voting rituals, to learn that "the unspeakable tumult,"[155] outbursts, and inopportune cries with which the speakers were "interrupted or even prevented from speaking"[156] were generally imputed to the *Knabenschaften*.

Even the secret regents of popular culture did not always have complete control over their youth. The tensions between youth culture and the world of adults were already considerable. A brewer's son had only to say, "You're already almost bald, you should be a councilor, you dirty scoundrel!" to trigger a brawl that sent beer steins flying and brought blows raining.[157] This was a precarious "balance of power" that could capsize at any moment. One dark February night in Traunstein in 1644, just before midnight, the windows of twelve houses situated on the marketplace were shattered by well-aimed snowballs. The victims' immediate thought was that their local youth had done it; but the attack was on too grand a scale to be considered an act of vengeance by one sole individual. Since no one was caught, explanations remained conjectural.[158] In 1706, the bailiffs of the Saint-Gall district similarly deplored, in one of their edicts, "serious insolences and knavish tricks." In the district of Kalkbrunnen, the "rascals" had "shouted wild things in the streets by night and endangered the lives of honest people by throwing stones at them, even in their houses; not content with that, they had been so insolent as to stick libelous posters on the houses of religious persons."[159] This last remark provides another glimpse of hostility toward a detested pastor, a hostility that in this instance occasioned intervention on the part of the authorities, who threatened to "punish the offenders as soon as possible, with the full force of the law."[160]

For the established order, those still growing up represented a permanent factor of disorder and insecurity. Adults made it a principle not to get excessively involved in the affairs of youth, preferring to leave young people to settle matters among themselves. This libertarian aspect of popular culture in the early modern age seems less surprising if one considers that the normative system of rural society offered relatively few alternatives at the time. Not only did this liberal attitude give space to society's youngest members, but it also had the advantage of sparing adults certain complex problems concerning the recognition and establishment of these same young people, together with their sexual and familial implications. They therefore limited themselves to keeping an eye on the acts and inclinations of their own children, relying, for the rest, on the mechanisms of socialization that let this age group develop from within. For the adolescents, these youthful freedoms and the adventures and other pranks they planned and executed as a group represented a transversal community experience in relation to the established social hierarchies; the integrating effect of this experience was only gradually effaced by the transition into adulthood and the adoption of different roles based on property and social status.[161] The wonder and amazement with which the younger adolescents viewed the exploits of the "older ones" guaranteed continuation of the rural society's value system almost automatically, without formal education having to wag its finger.[162]

Naturally this distance between youth culture and the adult world had a reverse side composed of disagreeable surprises, such as the mass snowball throwing just mentioned. Young men had a marked preference for violence in settling rivalries and internal conflicts, as in any group culture; physical strength, skill, and daring played an essential part, and in the masculine world, social recognition literally could only be acquired at this price—as is hardly surprising. The following two examples are typical cases taken from the records of regional tribunals; they come from Siegsdorf, a market town in High Bavaria, and are dated 1616:

Adam, son of Georg Aufhaimber the blacksmith, threw a stone at Stephan Peuntner, weaver from Miesenspach, and broke his rib; he then hit and insulted him repeatedly. The attack took place at night in the street of Siegsdorf.[163]

Wolf, a servant of Pämer in Siegsdorf, stabbed Adam, servant of Wolf Sparzenreiter, in the stomach. The assault occurred at night in the middle of the street, when the paths of the two men crossed; they did not know each other.[164]

In comparison with the macabre "games" and other tests still popular in sixteenth-century towns, these two cases seem relatively harmless. During a reunion of young men that took place in Munich in 1513, it was decided one evening "to beat to death the first man they met in the street."[165] The first man to come along, however, had only one arm, and so they spared him on account of his infirmity; but the next passerby—a servant of the duke of Wirtemberg—fell victim to this "test of courage." In July 1533, a canon from Augsburg only just escaped an attempted murder perpetrated by four young men in a "test" of the same kind.[166]

The culture of young bachelors was not characterized solely by its tendency to brutality—a tendency it shared, in any case, with other group cultures.[167] We draw closer to the truth if we recognize in this tendency the play of symbolic bravado that accompanied rites of virility: acts of provocation and retaliation, stoicism during ordeals, the ability to prove one's valor. In addition, there was the idea of the division of local territory, the sense that each man owned the place in which he asserted his own presence. This idea was closely linked to control of the local marriage market, and on various occasions it resulted in "boys' wars" between neighboring country villages;[168] its function was then to represent the formation and definition of each village's identity.[169]

All this was based on the will to assert and represent one's territory, a symbology—almost a logistics—of local presence, adopted by young people and largely recognized by adults. Perhaps the most dramatic expression of the youth culture's will to assert its presence through intense demonstrations of noise—a symbolic occupation of space—was the frequent use of yodeling and other exultant cries. The meaning of these cries was clear: they expressed contented self-consciousness and well-being, an irrepressible joy at being alive, and confidence in one's own strength. These vocal acrobatics invited everyone to share in the euphoria, but at the same time declared war on those who did not wish to participate; in any case, they signaled a massive physical presence it was impossible to ignore. For the common people, who had to be the heralds of their own identity, these ringing falsetto tones were what trumpets, drums, and fanfares were for people in power. During the carnival, yodeling and other noisy manifestations of presence (little bells rung rhythmically, whips being cracked, and so on) played an essential role in the festivities; in noisily drawing attention to themselves, young people boldly announced they were ready to turn the world upside down.[170] We can only hazard conjectures as to the source of these acoustical "performances": they may have originated in imitations of animal cries, as practiced by fairground performers. It was said admiringly of a certain Maulhans (Big-Mouthed Hans), a night watchman in Messkirch in Schwabia, that he could "whinny like a horse."[171] Another, more important hypothesis involves the calls and recognition signals that cowherds and shepherds used to communicate, even across large distances, in the alpine and prealpine pastures.[172] The most important clue, however, is probably found in the arrogant behavior of young single males, in their habit of defiantly puffing out their chest when confronting the other sex and also their own companions, seen as potential rivals.[173] As for parallels in modern youth culture, we might think of the screeching of tires and gunning of engines that accompany departures from discotheques—rather than the tame folkloric yodeling now used in Alpine tourist advertisements.[174]

Clearly these cries produced the best echoes in the narrow city streets at night. In large cities this was rather a serious problem. With typical reformist pathos, a moral edict published in Augsburg in 1546 observed: "Lest God should turn his face from us, girls must no longer be courted with musical instruments, or with songs and whistles; moreover, when going to church or elsewhere, any cry, yodel, shout, speech, or song that is indecent and shameful is completely forbidden in streets and houses alike."[175] But for the governing regime, these moralizing directives soon proved inadequate. In the narrow minds of the authorities, the cries and calls of undisciplined youth seemed like a public invitation to disobey and violate the laws: a symbolic challenge to established power that needed to be firmly opposed. By means of various edicts, a merciless campaign was thus waged against the "insolence" and "loud shouts at night."[176] The local authorities knew their men far better than did the new caste of bureaucrats; thus their responses to the ever-renewed provocations often took on a characteristically resigned tone, even "in the case of weddings"—ideal occasions for the ritual shouts. "Cries and yodeling will not be allowed—as far as possible," the edicts generally added.[177] Clearly, they had few illusions as to the respect their interdictions would draw. The yodel *(Jauchzen)* remained the youths' favorite means of expressing festive jubilation, being linked to the very idea of "marriage" *(Hochzeit)* in Middle High German; above all, it was a kind of ritual farewell, a salute the bachelors gave one of their number when he abandoned youthful freedoms and settled into adult life. They could not, would not, fail to "serenade" him; the louder and more colorful their performance, the more he felt honored by his peers and companions.[178] No administrative measure could prevail against the social value of such public "rites of passage" (Van Gennep), as the executive powers were perfectly aware; in the words of one Bavarian magistrate in 1618, it was clear that "there would be neither peace nor rest from these nocturnal uproars in the streets, given that the representative of the tribunal could not spend the whole night in the street."[179]

In the course of the eighteenth century, the population increased, the hierarchical structure of society was reinforced, and the new morality really began to take root in the countryside. Only then did the first cracks began to appear in well-established coalition of young men and adults. Once again, the churches played a central role in this.[180] In the southern Tyrol, the "night butterflies" *(Nachtschwärmer)* of the Martel Valley and the "night caterpillars" *(Nachtraupen)* of Ulten (or "howlers," as they were known, on account of their loud, high-pitched charivaris) led a bitter defensive struggle against the growing disciplinary pressures exerted by priests and missionaries. This was a prolonged battle that continued into the early nineteenth century, when it forced the resignation of Pastor Josef Eberhöfer, for one—even though he was a local boy and well acquainted with the customs of local youth.[181] The draconian punishments provided by the village ordinances of Wurtemberg indicate, here again, a marked escalation in community tension:

> Whether married or unmarried, the "night butterflies" who are caught yodeling or shooting off firearms or creating other forms of uproar in the village and its surroundings, and especially outside the church, will be condemned to prison for the first offense; to forced labor for the second; but if after all this they do not better themselves and are caught a third time committing punishable offenses and disturbing the nocturnal peace, then bachelors will be sent to serve in the army, and married men thrown into prison.[182]

All things considered, the relationships between the Swiss *Knabenschaften* and their priests during the eighteenth century were by no means as harmonious as the idyllic picture painted by Caduff would have us believe.[183] To give but one example, this discord is apparent in a petition of 1767 from the synod of Glarus, denouncing the young men's misdeeds and "vile debauchery":

> We, the servants of the Church, take every possible pain to instill in adolescents and young boys the truths and duties of our Holy Religion. Often we have every hope of seeing our labors bear joyous fruit. But our work, which began so well, is in numerous cases frustrated and almost destroyed when a boy enters the so-called "associations of boys of the streets" [*gassen knaben gesellschaften*] As soon as the young boys have been admitted to holy communion, they are supposed to enroll—often against the will of their parents, even against their own will—in these associations, where they see and hear more evil than good . . . In these societies, young men learn to scorn God and his words; to rebel against their natural authorities, their professors, parents, and teachers; to waste precious time roaming about; to make their presence heard at night in streets and alleys, in a most indecent way that disturbs the rest of honest people; and they learn to set fires. If this is denied them, decent people can no longer be sure of anything and must fear the most shameful insults, even physical attacks. If the boys are given money, they spend it all very quickly—enormous sums each year—on all manner of debauched and violent deeds. In these conditions, many of them get so used to leading a dissolute life that they subsequently become regular drunkards, commit

serious sins, become bad husbands, debauched citizens, and Christians unworthy of the name on account of their scandalous behavior.[184]

Young men as the apocalyptic horsemen of bourgeois respectability? This was something new, and interestingly enough it coincided with a radical change in the "march to Näfels," an annual pilgrimmage held in the canton of Glarus to commemmorate a decisive battle with the Hapsburgs that had occurred in 1388: those who had formerly been considered mythical heroes were now viewed by the authorities simply as notorious troublemakers.[185] In the orgy of order that characterized the new, "enlightened" cult of the state, the staid bourgeois celebration honoring national heroes no longer contained a place for them.

Under the "civilizing" influence of religious morality, many leading villagers began to distance themselves from the unruly driving force in their community. The young men's associations paid an increasingly high price for their privileged status as representatives of the communal consciousness, and their actions were increasingly subject to the pressures of legitimate power. Nonetheless, the more the *Knabenschaften* were kept on the defensive, the more violent—at least, verbally violent—their tone became. The link between increased social marginalization and growing verbal radicalism becomes increasingly manifest, culminating in the vindictive, boastful folklore of the nineteenth-century *Haberfeldtreiber*.[186] At Schondorf, for example, on the Ammersee, because "the pastor had spoken up against the uproar caused by night prowlers," the village boys had "smashed his windows and totally destroyed his well . . . Then, during the sermon, these same youths had shouted out in church: 'Shut up and be quiet, priest, or else we'll do something else to you!'"[187] It is hard to imagine that these rough words, addressed to the pastor, together with threats of beating, could have met with the community's unreserved approval. Clearly, in this case the representatives of youth culture were acting only for themselves.

The history of the progressive decline of the *Knabenschaften* and *Burschenschaften* during the eighteenth and nineteenth centuries is still largely unwritten. However, it may be summarized in one simple formula:

the higher their degree of organization, the more brutal their collision with the advancing bourgeois order. This was true of both the Bavarian and Austrian *Haberfeldtreiber* and of the Swiss *Knabenschaften*. During the eighteenth century, the high court of Disentis (Grisons) had already expressed the constantly aggravated discord between the authorities and popular justice. Referring to the justice meted out by the *Knabenschaften*, they declared, "It is indisputable that these procedures, illegal in themselves, are more effective and successful than the measures taken by the authorities. Nonetheless, we must not authorize these illegal means in a civilized country—albeit a free one—even when their objective is to do good."[188]

This quotation gives some hint of the difficulty the state had in stemming the justice of the *Knabenschaften*, especially in the country; and indeed, adults continued to give local support to young men's associations until well into the nineteenth century. At the same time, an increase in social mobility began gradually to open up the closed world of the villages, and public reprimand was directed increasingly against foreigners and immigrants. This practice thus assumed the appearance of a narrow-minded xenophobia, leading to a huge rise in complaints about the arbitrary reign of terror imposed by young men's groups. In 1856 village authorities in Ems (now called Domat) sought to preserve the traditional autonomy of the local *Knabenschaft* by entrusting it with police functions in the commune's territory. The cantonal government of the Grisons naturally understood this maneuver and rescinded the commune's decision a few weeks later: police power, they warned, could not be delegated, and the privilege granted the *Knabenschaften* contravened the basic principle of egality among citizens of the commune.[189] The time of glory was now past, and the *Knabenschaft* of Ems went into mourning, burying its moral rights to the sound of a military funeral march. The young men who came after were "allowed" to busy themselves with such fundamental questions as whether their girls' pigtails were the right length.

The masked figures of the High Bavarian *Haberfeldtreiber* had grown up with the old forms of popular village justice. During the nineteenth century, these associations evolved further and further toward becoming a superregional penal organization. Operating secretly, the organization tried, through spectacular acts of popular justice, to defend the rights of the rural population against the encroachments of the modern system of state government, and against the social changes accompanying it. The reasons for its failure lay not so much in an unfavorable balance of power, nor even in the fact that it had only reactionary ideas with which to counter social revolution. The fundamental cause of its decline may be found in its attempt to translate local punitive practices into a more general political activity, thus undermining its own basis. What may have seemed morally and socially plausible in the collective life of the village proved quite inadequate when applied to the abstract principles of political debate at a national level. The old moral categories, no matter how artfully presented, no longer had any effect. To accuse judges, priests, and functionaries of corruption and immorality in the style that worked so well against other villagers only proved useless, because it was easy to demonstrate the sophistry of most of the charges.[190] With such questionable methods, these movements gradually lost the support of their own communities, whose very rights they claimed to maintain. In this ambiguous light, the resistance lost ground; the vainglorious *folklorization* of their protest, through which they attempted to compensate for the tottering consensus, could not replace politics for long.

In the early modern period, youth was and remained a haven for disorder. Only the consumer society of the twentieth century has conceived an absolutely positive idea of young people, an idea that characterizes the adult world's dream of an eternal youth. It is a sad ideal, because it represents utopia for those who have grown old, and because it threatens to enclose those who are truly young in an industrial and cultural ghetto. At the beginning of modern times, the utopia of youth still corresponded to a simpler and perhaps less distressing concept: that of the "fountain of youth" of carnival time, capable of turning the generational wheel upside down, against the laws of nature. Everything was still determined by this dual idea of the natural evolution of time, and the possibilities of regeneration inherent in it. Youth was a profoundly ambivalent concept, a transitional stage closer to adulthood than to childhood, but in which one could still hold up the mirror of irony before becoming serious. Nothing is more surprising to us than the generous indulgence adults of the time showed toward juvenile misdeeds, secure in the knowledge that it would all soon come to an end. This attitude reflected not only an awareness that the passing of generations was both necessary and natural, but also a confidence in society's future that we seem to have lost.

YOUNG NOBLES IN THE AGE OF ABSOLUTISM: PATERNAL AUTHORITY AND FREEDOM OF CHOICE IN SEVENTEENTH-CENTURY ITALY

Renata Ago

In the collective imagination of the Italians—and for anyone who has read Manzoni's *I Promessi sposi*—the episode of the nun of Monza has acquired the persuasive power of an archetype. The beginning of this episode has, I am sure, been instrumental in shaping our common historiographic sense:

> She was the youngest daughter of Prince ————, a great nobleman of Milan, who could reckon himself among the richest men in the city . . . History does not tell us exactly how many children he had; all it does is give us to understand that he destined all his younger children of either sex to the cloister, so as to leave the family fortune intact for his eldest son, whose function it was to perpetuate the family, to have children of his own, and so torture himself by tormenting them in the same way. The unhappy creature of our story was still hidden in her mother's womb when her state in life had already been irrevocably settled. All that remained to be decided was whether it was to be that of a monk or a nun, a decision for which her presence, but not her consent, was required.[1]

These few lines conjure up in the reader's mind the potent image of a world filled with convents where unfortunate creatures were cloistered against their will, without the slightest vocation; a world dominated by paternal power, by the crushing weight of family policy prevailing over individual wishes, by the total impossibility for those involved of having any say in decisions that concerned them. But was it really true that power relationships were so unfavorable to young people of both sexes? Could so brutal an impossibility of self-determination conceivably have resulted in such rare cases of rebellion as have actually been verified? The evidence collected reconstitutes fragments of reality far more complex and contradictory, which shake the certainty of our imagination, and which must all be pondered.

THE TERMS OF THE PROBLEM

It was during the sixteenth century that the system of primogeniture was adopted on a massive scale by the aristocratic families of western Europe. Although the juridical rules governing its application varied from one state to another, the great European families quickly converted to the custom, no longer dividing a patrimony among all their children, but transmitting it in toto to one son. In consequence, one sole male heir was in a position to meet the conditions necessary for finding a wife and perpetuating the name and title of his ancestors. The others were condemned to a more or less obligatory celibacy, unless a whim of fortune placed an heiress in their path, or unless they resigned themselves to marrying below their station.

Where extant sources and the present state of research allow us to calculate percentages, the figures are quite clear: after the second half of the sixteenth century, the proportion of bachelors in the aristocracy increased steadily, and in the following century, in both France and Italy, more than half the men who reached adulthood did not marry.[2] During the same period, approximately one man in three embraced the cloth. In the English aristocracy, the percentage of bachelors remained slightly lower; but even there, between the end of the seventeenth century and the beginning of the eighteenth, more than one-third of adult men did not take a wife.[3]

According to the principle of collective family responsibility, the honor or dishonor of one single family member reflected on all the others. This made it impossible to ignore the problem of the younger children, to resolve it by simply abandoning them to their fate and their ability to forge independent lives. Sons excluded from inheritance—and therefore often from marriage—had to be settled in some way, and if possible in a way that allowed them to live decently and even contribute to the family prestige. We shall examine some of these solutions presently.

If celibacy was the destiny of younger men, things hardly differed in the case of girls. One or two might receive a dowry that corresponded to their status, enabling them to make a good match. The others were even more likely than their brothers to remain single for their entire life. In Milan, during the first half of the seventeenth century, one out of two aristocratic girls entered a convent.[4] In other towns in Italy and France, the percentages of nuns and unmarried girls were lower than the Milanese figure, but not by much. In England, on the other hand, Henry VIII's closure of the convents necessarily led to a reduction in the proportion of unmarried women. But even in England there was an increased tendency in polite society to limit the number of marriages: at the start of the eighteenth century, there were twice as many spinsters as there had been a century before.[5]

The problem of the dowry seems to have been crucial to all this. Despite numerous attempts to restrain the tendency, the dowries provided or required by noble families reached very high figures, sometimes the equivalent of five years of revenue from the family patrimony.[6] Since the size of a dowry was a public demonstration of a family's importance, no family could allow it to be limited or reduced; on the contrary, the need to keep up appearances tended always to drive a dowry up. On the other hand, the sum required for entering a convent was fixed by custom and bore no relation to the social status of the novice. Certainly the figure might vary from one convent to another, according to an institution's prestige and the type of girls it intended to receive; but a study of wills shows that—at least for the richer classes—a convent was far easier to please than a future husband.

Furthermore, in families that could allow themselves to marry off only part of their progeny, birth order had diametrically opposed consequences for boys and girls. Whereas the eldest son, without exception, inherited the title and the accompanying patrimony, which placed him in a privileged position to marry and have children of his own, the eldest daughter almost always took the veil, leaving her younger sisters the pleasure or duty of taking a husband. Here again, the problem of the dowry was to blame: if a younger rather than an older daughter was destined for matrimony, this left more time for the family to accumulate the necessary sum. And if the marriage of a girl was planned to coincide approximately with that of the heir, this allowed the family to balance its finances with the incoming dowry of the elder son's wife. As boys married at a later age than girls, this calculation could involve only a younger sister.

The privileges or, in the case of girls, disadvantages of primogeniture led to ambivalent reactions on the part of those involved. At the end of the sixteenth and in the beginning of the seventeenth century certain moral treatises—and certainly at least one younger child—began contesting the principle of differentiation founded on the chronology of births. And some elder daughters, victims of a predestination that led them straight to the convent, accused their parents of "not respecting the privileges of primogeniture that, according to the Old Testament itself, deserved some advantages."[7] From the parents' point of view, however, linking privileges to the order of birth was a way of avoiding arbitrary judgments, of following an objective criterion that spared them the odious task of having to discriminate between their own children. In this regard, the testimony of an English mother is quite clear: according to her husband, she said, "I had the right to leave my possessions to whichever of my children I preferred, or else to reserve the further exercise of this right in order to keep them all respectful and obedient. But I refused to impose on them so contemptible a dependency, and decided to bequeath everything on the basis of birth alone, to avoid any temptation, in myself, to practice—and in them, to suspect—so mean a partiality."[8]

The importance of these financial matters explains why, in the private correspondence of Italian nobles of the period, references to the girls of a house (who might be daughters, sisters, or nieces) were always inextricably mingled with more or less feverish conjectures on the possibility of finding them a "decent" dowry. While they were still children, a father (and especially a more affectionate grandfather) could take pleasure in telling or being told of their witty sayings, their minor impertinences, or their rate of growth; but once they reached puberty and, with it, marriage-able age, the epistolary exchange concentrated exclusively on the financial question, which was evidently no trivial matter. And Italian parents were not alone in this respect, compared to their French, Spanish, or English counterparts. On the other hand, if a girl was not intended for matrimony, either because she did not wish it or because her parents had decided so, the alternative was clear: in Catholic countries, the only other possibility open to a young aristocratic girl was to enter a convent. In Protestant countries, there was not even that choice.[9]

For male children, the difference between Catholic and Protestant countries was of less consequence because, as we shall see, the monastery was only one of several possible solutions for disposing of younger sons. The ranks of the army and the benefits of the higher clergy were open to all young men of good family, both in reformed countries and in countries faithful to Rome. Nonetheless, a fundamental difference remained between Protestant and Catholic clergy: in the case of Catholics, the celibacy required by the Church perfectly matched the families' desire to limit marriages as much as possible.

FREEDOM OF CHOICE: THE THEORETICIANS' VIEW

These facts seem to suggest that freedom of choice for those involved was extremely limited, given that family politics and demography seemed to play a far more decisive role than personal inclinations. Yet this determinism was countered by other forces.

Numerous manuals on the art of raising children warned parents of the dangers of excessive fondness, propounding instead a pedagogy whose first object was to discipline the will of children so that they would be obedient to the will of their parents.[10] As for moral treatises, Catholic or Protestant, they all insisted on the respect due to the Fourth Commandment (Honor thy father and thy Mother), and thus on the children's duty of obedience.[11] But despite this general emphasis on obedience, Catholics and Protestants still specified (and the restriction is an important one) that the limit of obedience was defined by the "honesty" of the order received:

to disobey one's father was a mortal sin, except when he ordered an act contrary to God's will and the teachings of religion. The Catholics, for their part, extended this condition to include the specific respect owed the spiritual magistracy of the Church, thus anticipating the possibility of a conflict between paternal authority and the authority of spiritual advisers. In this way, the general pedagogy of obedience was translated into a particular pedagogy of obedience to the Church and its ministers.[12]

When the pedagogic thinking of Renaissance humanism advised parents to limit fond behavior toward their children, it was for the children's good: "Indulgence in parents," wrote Juan Luis Vives, Mary Tudor's tutor, "is the source, in our century, of moral corruption in young people and their intractable character."[13] But this adult duty of self-control also required parents not to take advantage of their children's subordinate position by directing them toward "situations" or careers not suited to them, to the sole end of satisfying their own pride or greed. "Greedy father," exclaimed one French preacher, "shall you give this wretched girl to this rich man! . . . You shall answer to God for this innocent victim, whom you so cruelly sacrifice to your greed and your ambition."[14] At the end of the sixteenth century, much of the debate focused on marriage and the question of the free consent of those betrothed; but for Petrarch and the first humanists, a more general reflection on an individual's "vocation" was involved—on the relationship between his natural inclination and his duty to family and community.[15] In the wake of humanists of the fourteenth and fifteenth centuries, sixteenth-century pedagogues such as Erasmus, Vives, or the Spanish doctor Juan Huarte agreed that if everyone assumed the duties most suited to his nature, the order of civil life could only benefit. As Erasmus put it, "The key to human happiness is for everyone to devote himself fully to what he is naturally inclined."[16]

The idea was an old one: it goes back at least as far as Cicero, who deplored the paradoxical fact that the fundamental choices in life are made "on the threshold of youth, when the faculty of judgment is at its weakest"; in youth, a person was seen as largely lacking in the experience that could help him to decide, while possessing, on the other hand, lively passions that could propel him toward erroneous goals. It was thus necessary for "everyone to be well acquainted with his own talents and prove a perspicacious judge of his qualities and defects," in order to be drawn along not by futile desires but by "the rules of one's nature"—given that it was perfectly useless to oppose them and to pursue a goal for which one was not made.[17] From Petrarch to Erasmus, the theme was taken up more than once, anticipating the introspective reflection of Montaigne and Charron. Charron speaks explicitly of "vocation": we must, he writes, "choose a vocation for which we are adapted; that is, our natural inclination must be fitting, and able to apply to it willingly . . . For to go against one's own nature is to tempt God and to spit at heaven, to prepare oneself for a task only to prove unable to do it."[18]

Turning from literary men to pedagogues, and especially to preachers, we find that this emphasis on the need for introspection and personal responsibility on the part of young people is tempered by the importance attached to fathers and educators, and their duty to intervene. Here is what a seventeenth-century French preacher said, expressing ideas already shared by many:

> Do not surrender . . . your children's destiny to the first impulses of ardent youth, which must always be held in suspicion. You must guard not only against some ill-governed passion that might cause them to make bad decisions, which reason always disavows when it regains control— and which it often disavows only when it is too late; you must also make sure that the inconstancy ever to be feared in young people does not cause them to make the right decision, for the same capriciousness that led them to make it out of impetuosity may lead them to abandon it out of disgust.[19]

Thus a heavy burden of responsibility fell on the shoulders of fathers, who could not and were not supposed to contemplate their children's futures with serenity:

> No human lives are long enough to foresee the thousand troublesome incidents that will befall them in some situations and will not befall them in others. You intend a son to choose the bar, because he seems moderate; but you fail to notice, in all this moderation, a basic pliancy that puts him at the mercy of anyone who wants to take control of his mind . . . You

think a daughter is suitable for the cloister, because she seems docile; but you fail to see that this docility stems from a laziness that will make the observances of religious life intolerable to her . . . You imagine that another son will be happy in a situation in which you see nothing, you say, that can cause him pain; but you do not foresee the thousand events, regardless of temperament, nature, and even prudence, that will fill his life with sorrow.[20]

At the heart of these Catholic sermons was always the question, deemed fundamental by the Church, of securing freedom of choice in regard to marriage and the priesthood—against the will of fathers if need be. The conjugal state and the ecclesiastical state were so diametrically opposed, so mutually exclusive, that the concern with free choice focused on this polarity without considering what further developments might take place in either situation. The second sermon quoted here concludes with the idea that since we cannot see the future, we should "Let God act, who does see it." In the same spirit, the first preacher warned: "But do not, in the guise of guarding against caprices or passions, take the liberty of opposing true vocations; and although it is your duty to test those vocations, do not transform, as many do, a useful test into a dangerous temptation."[21]

In the Protestant world, reflection on society had followed a different course. For Luther and Calvin, there was no vocation without predestination: it was God who chose, and man had no choice but to respond correctly to the divine call. But several generations later, we find Protestant preachers also calling for the introspection and individualized attitudes—a guarantee of general felicity—dear to humanist thought.[22]

In his *Treatise on Vocations*, published in 1602, William Perkin wrote that "every man must choose himself an appropriate vocation as his goal; which means that every vocation must be adapted to the man, and every man to his vocation."[23] Parents had the duty of guiding their children's choices by carefully studying their inclinations and their natural gifts. We find the same point of view expressed by Richard Baxter, who warns: "Consider what you and your children are most suited for, in mind as in body. For the same vocation can be a blessing for one man and ruination for another."[24] Both authors consider it useful for persons outside the family, such as magistrates, pastors, and teachers, to help and advise young people in their choices. But neither seems to foresee the possibility of a conflict with parents, in the course of which a higher authority might replace the authority of the father.

Is it therefore fair to think that on the one hand Catholic youths were supported by the Church, and on the other, Protestant youths were abandoned to the arbitrary power of fathers? The evidence at our disposal would seem to confirm this contrast.

THE EDUCATION OF GIRLS

The destiny of Gertrude, Manzoni's fictitious nun, was determined even before her birth, and as the convent seemed the natural conclusion to her stay on earth, "Dolls dressed as nuns were the first toys to be put into her hands, then holy pictures representing nuns, such presents always being given with warm recommendations to treasure them as something precious, and with a 'Lovely, eh?' in a tone of affirmation and interrogation."[25] Even so, the private correspondence of certain aristocratic Italian families suggests a rather less "specialized" upbringing. During the first months of a child's life, even the distinction between boys and girls seems not to have mattered much. Newborn babes were described and praised with the same adjectives and after the same themes, regardless of their sex.[26] But as soon as the infants began to walk and speak we note the appearance of diminutives such as *ometto* or *donnina* (little man, little woman); and remarks or jokes about clothes, accessories, and behavior appropriate to men or women begin insistently to emphasize the difference between the sexes. Speaking of his granddaughter, who was three or four, Sperone Speroni, an aristocrat from Padua and a man of considerable culture, wrote to his daughter: "Tell Signora Vighetta [the little girl] that if she agrees to walk quietly like a lady and not jump about like a lunatic, I'm pleased she's wearing shoes and I'll bring her a fine pair."[27] What this letter indicates, and many others like it from Speroni, from Orazio Spada, and from other noble grandfathers, is that in daily life, the difference between the sexes was permanently emphasized, especially in matters of outward appearance and manners. On the other hand, when character and moral qualities were involved, the "little men" and "little women" do not seem to have been viewed very differently; little girls were not expected to display more sweetness or modesty, nor the little boys more courage. Speroni declares he found one of his "diabolical" little granddaughters "very appealing,"[28] while Orazio Spada, conversely, appreciated the grace and elegance of his grandson Alessandro as much as he did the astuteness, not to say the impertinence, of his granddaughter Lulla. "Don Alessandro Mattei wanted me to watch the first lesson in the five steps given him by his dancing master, and it was wonderful to see how graceful he was," he remarked, in a letter written slightly after one in which he made these comments on the behavior of his granddaughter: "Now that Lulla is well again, the house is filled with her chatter. She comes to pester me and says she wants to stay with me, then constantly repeats that if I don't want to touch her she knows it's to avoid infecting the little Mattei boy."[29]

So long as the children were small and lived at home, the level of attention granted them by their parents and grandparents does not seem to have followed a hierarchy of gender. But when the girls went to a convent to be educated, they disappeared from family correspondence, reappearing only—and even then only indirectly—when the long negotiations necessary for their marriage began. Not that the girls were forgotten by their parents, or that their brothers loved them any the less: if they were not featured in correspondence, it was because they were not causing any problems. Sometimes we find brief references to their health, as in this letter from Prince Borghese: "Yesterday morning I went to Campomarzo, and found the little girls very well, as merry as can be; it's incredible to see how relaxed Nanna has become, how happy she seems, how gracefully I heard her play the tabour and her little guitar."[30] But as I have said, it was mainly when complications arose that attention turned toward the girls.

In January 1668 the three Ottoboni brothers—Agostino, Giovanni Battista, and Pietro—all noblemen of Venice, decided that the time had come to marry Chiara, daughter of the eldest. Pietro lived in Rome and the two others lived in Venice (as did Chiara), and an abundant correspondence flowed between the two cities until March 1670, when an agreement was finally concluded.[31] Meanwhile, in her convent in Venice, the young girl fretted, grew impatient, even began to grieve; but the only person to describe her in these terms was another woman, her paternal aunt, Caterina Agazzi Ottoboni:

> Signora Chiara is all melancholy and does not look well. I often visit her to console her. Signor Agostino is constantly telling her, "In another week, you'll be engaged," and when she needs something he replies, "I'm not going shopping for you because in a week you'll be engaged"—which torments her, because she sees the others becoming engaged without so many words, while she sees no end to this confusing wait; naturally she does not tell me all this, but Your Eminence can imagine what she is thinking to herself, poor little thing.[32]

As for her father and her uncles, they never spoke of her, but only of her dowry: how to find it, what sums to pay in cash, which suitors presented themselves, which withdrew, which should be sounded out, which should be forgotten. . . It would be unjust to conclude that they saw her only as an object of exchange and that they had no concern for her feelings: we know that her father went to see her, that he tried to reassure her; and her uncle in Rome kept informed of her physical and moral state through the letters of Caterina Agazzi Ottoboni. The young girl's feelings were therefore not irrelevent. But they were nonetheless not a subject for a correspondence centered on the difficult and very concrete problem of how to find her a good match without having to pay an exorbitant dowry.

Like all their contemporaries, the Ottoboni brothers wrote to each other mainly to resolve practical matters having to do with concerns that were often pressing and that required the efforts of several family members. Only a few occasionally took advantage of this correspondence to communicate or analyze feelings. And only those with a taste for literature, like Sperone Speroni, used letters to more complex, and thus more intimate, ends. For the others, there was no great difference between business letters and letters to the family.

This was certainly true of the Florentine Filippo Corsini, who also had to grapple with the problem of finding a match for a girl whose guardian he was.[33] The young girl had shown a strong aversion to the idea of entering a convent, but it was feared that she was in less than perfect health and that certain gynecological problems made her unsuitable for having children. In such circumstances, giving her in marriage was a risky business, for there was always the chance that the husband's family might return her to her relatives "unmarriageable and unmarried."[34] The poor child was thus a source of numerous worries for her tutor and guardian, Corsini, who wrote to his brother asking for advice. Corsini was not given to chatter, and his letters were for the most part short missives that went straight to the point. It was thus hardly surprising that he said nothing about the young girl's state of mind. Yet her refusal to enter a convent seems to have been accepted without opposition, despite the problems this caused Corsini. As Sperone Speroni explains, girls of fragile health with some physical defect were difficult to place, because "to marry them off, one has to spend a lot."[35] This language of accountancy should not deceive us, however: the same Speroni recognized that "lame girls are their parents' daughters, just as the healthy ones are."[36]

I shall have more to say about the respect that was in fact accorded to girls' wishes. For now, we should note that the life of an adolescent girl followed a path so well worn it claimed attention only in exceptional cases. Whether she wanted to be married or to take the veil, and whether or not someone else decided this for her, the convent education she received prepared her equally well for both situations. If she wanted to take the veil, it remained only to choose the convent, which would probably be one with which the family had particular ties. A little account book belonging to Prince Camillo Pamphilij, in which were noted "sums paid for my daughters Maria and Caterina at the convent of Santa Marta in Rome" (where the girls were being educated), shows that the transition into nunhood could take place with no break in continuity, in the same convent where the girls were educated: at a certain moment, in the account book, Maria became Suor Prudenza, Sister Prudence, but nothing else seemed to change, since the sum to be paid remained the same.[37]

If, on the other hand, a girl chose to marry, parents were confronted with a difficult decision—the only one that really posed a problem. From among all the potential husbands, they had to choose the best match, and be able to surmount the obstacles that invariably arose in such dealings before an agreement was concluded.

As we have seen, this process could go on for years. But in all the accounts of discussions, hesitations, and withdrawals there is never any question of the future wife's "natural inclinations," nor of finding her a husband most suited to her behavior and character. Anyone in search of a wife wanted her to be of good family, richly dowered, beautiful, in good health, and well brought up, and procured himself all available information on the subject.[38] Anyone in search of a husband for his daughter seems to have been content with rather vaguer criteria: the candidate had to be of noble family, not too demanding financially, and preferably young. But no one seems to have thought to inquire whether his character was suited to that of the future spouse. The same was true of countries supposedly more "modern" than Italy. As late as 1740, the author of a *Letter of Genteel and Moral Advice to a Young Lady* still advised girls to seek in their future husbands "a virtuous character, an adequate intelligence, a calm temperament, a solid patrimony, and a comely exterior"[39]—no mention of a character compatible with hers, or "natural inclinations" that complemented hers. On the subject of choosing a husband, the humanists' pronouncements seem to have been without effect.

Historians have traditionally thought, especially in the case of Italy, that this uniformly gray prospect for girls could be enlivened only by the exercise of ardent piety. It is thus most satifying to discover that some aristocratic girls received a slightly less mortifying education. I am thinking of a text unearthed in the archives of the Santacroce family in Rome, in which Gian Vicenzo Gravina established a curriculum for Isabella Vecchiarelli Santacroce[40]—and even of the discovery that in 1705 young Flaminia Borghese received the same education, at home, as her brother Camillo, and that her progress in classics was such that she could write to reassure her father, in Latin, that she was ardently studying Greek: *"exercitationes linguae graecae numquam intermitto"*[41] (I never leave off doing my exercises in the Greek language).

THE EDUCATION OF BOYS

Despite the case of Flaminia Borghese and several other young women, the formative years for boys approaching adulthood were altogether more exciting.

Even for boys, however, education was relatively undifferentiated in the initial stages: future fathers, soldiers, and priests were all treated and raised in the same way until the end of their adolescence.

As we have seen, in small children exuberance and vitality were qualities that were "lovable" and loved, and not only in Italy.[42] But as the years went by and the young boys began venturing outside the family circle, grace and vivacity had to give way to new norms of behavior: the dominant values thenceforth instilled in boys were modesty and obedience. When Orazio Spada asked the "master of pages" about the behavior of *cavaliere* Alviano, his son, who was being raised at the court of the grand duke of Tuscany, it was to learn if the adolescent was "obedient, modest, deferential, devoted, polite, if he studied, and learned; if he tried to acquire virtues, and which one he was most inclined toward."[43] In writing to another of his sons, Fabrizio, a young priest at the University of Perugia, the father recommended he lead a "retired" life, that he avoid "forming friendships with other students," that he be "humble and reserved" with everyone—before adding, in conclusion: "I remind you to be modest not only in your outward behavior, but also in your speech, and to remember that you are the youngest."[44] A few years later the same Orazio Spada sent one of his sons to Paris to stay with his uncle, an apostolic nuncio, and congratulated himself on this prudent choice: "You were right to choose that style of clothes for Guido, and yet he writes to his mother saying he would have liked finery; but it's better this way, and not simply to demonstrate modesty."[45] A few months later the father wrote again: "I don't want Guido to cut a figure in society, it's too soon . . . Please satisfy me on this point, for I know what I'm doing and why I'm arranging things this way."[46]

Orazio Spada came from a family closely connected to the Roman Curia, and in emphasizing the values of modesty and polite reserve, his speech probably reflects the values of the upper ecclesiastical spheres of the pontifical court. All through Europe, courtiers and magistrates played a part in refining manners, a role strengthened in Rome by the presence of the Church and its preachings against aristocratic haughtiness, which it wanted to replace with milder behavior. Among Roman aristocrats, born and raised in families teeming with cardinals and prelates, the code of ethics propounded by the high clergy was in a good position to combat the ancient code of chivalry. Thus adolescents were taught to avoid any cause for an "engagement," or matter of honor; they were taught to live withdrawn lives, to dress "modestly," and to go nowhere unless accompanied by a preceptor or a servant promoted to the role of governor. These recommendations applied not only to boys who were to follow an ecclesiastical career but also to young pages destined for military glory, as is shown by these instructions written in 1647 for two young men of seventeen and nineteen: the boys were being sent by their uncles to Germany, to join the regiment of their brother, a captain in the imperial army:

> Count Michele has just left the seminary and Count Giuseppe will leave his position as a page when his brother arrives in Bavaria, where it is hoped that both, when they arrive, for their own benefit and to please their uncles, will prove docile, well mannered, and obedient to their governor . . . who will take particular care to see that they lead Christian lives, that they fear God and go to confession . . . and take communion . . . and behave politely and modestly with everyone . . . abstaining from gambling or any other activity darkened by the shadow of vice, but devoting themselves instead to studying military matters, mathematics, and disciplines worthy of a gentleman.[47]

This reminder of the need for modesty in young noblemen was not in itself original; such exhortations formed an obligatory passage in every pedagogical treatise. "Modesty is fitting for children, and especially for children of the aristocracy," Erasmus had written.[48] But it is interesting to note that recommendations of this kind were thenceforth adopted by parents and family members, who apparently were not concerned solely with the moral aspects of the question. On the contrary, considerations as to the social merits of modest behavior seem clearly to have prevailed over ethical considerations.

In pedagogical treatises, modesty was viewed as an antidote to one of the most reprehensible of "vices" in both children and aristocrats: pride. Protestants agreed with Catholics on this point, though arguing from different premises: "Indeed, in all children there is . . . an obstinacy and firmness of soul that comes from innate pride, and these qualities must first of all be bent and overcome," wrote a Protestant preacher.[49]

In the recommendations made by parents, the objective was far more practical. Their constant exhortations to lead a withdrawn life; never to go out alone; always to be accompanied by an adult relative, a tutor, or a trusted servant, show how much they feared the danger—more concrete than moral—that their child might go astray. A boy might associate with bad companions, who would tarnish his reputation and that of his family; he ran the risk of losing at gambling, of being robbed, even of falling into some trap that might lead to the obligation of a secret marriage. Adolescent boys were morally fragile, constantly exposed to the risk of perdition. Self-control, deemed a most virile quality, was still being acquired, still uncertain. All this likened them in some degree to women, and so it is hardly surprising that they were advised to adopt the feminine virtues of modesty and reserve, and that they were subject to the same surveillance as girls. This was one of the reasons the custom of sending boys away to school spread so rapidly in the seventeenth century.[50]

As we know, the institution of boarding schools for boys was largely the work of the Jesuits, and toward 1650 the network of their establishments spread all through Catholic Europe. Their success was based largely on the "political content" of the instruction: the Jesuits' educational program fully answered the demands of the noble families who sent them their sons. In Italy, as in France or Spain, boarding schools were able to provide true professional training, as well as a general education for gentlemen. The boys studied Latin, philosophy, and theology; but almost all the schools contained "academies" to which only "the cleverest, the best, the most advanced in science, belles lettres and other noble arts" were admitted. There, they could learn foreign languages, music, drawing, and take lessons in dancing, fencing, and so forth.[51]

Furthermore, boarding school offered guarantees that an education would succeed. Pedagogical treatises often emphasized the danger of educating sons at home, of entrusting them simply to the ministrations of a tutor, for there was often the risk of harmful contacts with servants, and tutors were not always up to their task. As a French prelate explained:

> Education in the home has many other drawbacks. It feeds the children's vanity: they see themselves as issuing from a better family, because they hear their parents and servants saying so; their ideas shrink in the limited circle of their father's and mother's conversation. In short, I prefer the education of schools to education at home, because in schools there are both friends and superiors to correct one; these friends forgive no absurd or pretentious foible; they accustom one to the scrutiny of others and prepare the mind for a diversity of moods, customs, and characters.[52]

When the institution of boarding school began to be widespread, more and more young noblemen went to spend at least a few years at one. This did not, however, mean that private tutors were entirely abandoned. Here again, primogeniture played a part, and study of the school for noblemen in Bologna has shown that the older and younger sons did not approach school in the same way. The eldest sons went there at a more advanced age, having been educated for several years at home by private instructors; often, they left the institution without taking the final exams.[53] In their case, boarding school served more to refine their education as gentlemen than to give them complete training. As future heads of families, they had to be able to hold their position in society and manage the family fortune; there was no question of their having to make their way in a profession. Their younger brothers, in contrast, entered college at an earlier age, completed a full program of study, and then enrolled in far greater numbers at the University of Bologna.[54] Once in possession of their degree "in both laws" (civil and canon), they could actually aspire to an honorable and profitable career in the magistracy—all the more desirable in that the rules of succession had favored their older brothers.

Sometimes, regardless of questions of primogeniture, the actual atmosphere of family life necessitated sending a child to school. If he were to continue to live among brothers and sisters who were much younger or older, and whose occupations were correspondingly different from his, it would be far harder to make him concentrate fully on his studies. Better, in that case, to send him away to school.[55]

Boarding school, moreover, was not the only alternative to private education. There were also schools for pages in almost all the European and Italian courts. Another possibility was to enter the novitiates found in monasteries. Yet boarding schools, schools for pages, and novitiates were not interchangeable: the choice of one or other such institution clearly presupposed the career an adolescent was intended for. Being a page meant preparing for a military career either in some army or in a chivalrous order such as the Knights of Malta. Boarding school, on the other hand, led to the life of an accomplished gentleman, or else toward a doctorate in law or a prelacy, all of which required the same basic education. As for the monachal novitiate, this choice implied that the young student would eventually take vows and enter the religious order to which the novitiate belonged.

From a certain point of view, the "grand tour" can also be considered as a specialized stage in the educational process. Only the very richest families could manage to send more than one son abroad; the others had to be content with dispatching just the eldest on his travels. In foreign courts and in the salons of the local aristocracy, the future head of a family could perfect his knowledge of the world, of politics, and of diverse European customs. But traveling abroad could also take the form of a true voyage of study at some reputable institution. This latter aspect of the "grand tour," and the fact that almost all male children spent some time at school, show that it was then thought desirable to give all boys some minimal instruction, not just those who had to find a profession: even future gentlemen, and not simply aspiring prelates, found it useful to have learned some Latin.

The education acquired in the course of a grand tour, however, was closer to the training of a future officer than to that of a potential magistrate. Marco Antonio Borghese, who traveled through Europe between 1682 and 1683, went to see the great projects being launched by engineers, such as the Canal du Midi in France, which connected the Atlantic to the Mediterranean; he also visited fortifications and parade grounds.[56] In 1702 Bartolomeo Corsini went to Paris to study "mathematics."[57] Two other young Borghese princes, who passed through London in 1751, "visited the large manufacturing houses for their entertainment, where they discovered at one and the same time the theory and practice behind the wealth of nations."[58] Prince Pamphilij, however, who was more of a bigot, bluntly declared: "I absolutely do not want them to go to England, where they stand only to lose."[59] But since our traditional image of the grand tour is the one given by Laurence Sterne and all the young Englishmen who set off in search of France and Italy, the Italians' interest in technical matters comes as a pleasant surprise.

OPTIONS AND ATTITUDES

If girls had only two possible destinies to choose between, boys had at least four options. As one of their preliminary choices had to be made when they were twelve or thirteen, parents and relatives would have to scrutinize a young boy's character most carefully before making an informed decision. But this initial decision often turned out not to be definitive, for luck, or the interplay of different wishes, could force adults to change their plans—not that this necessarily changed their view of the problem. Considerations of familial status (was it better to have a magistrate or an officer of the imperial army in the family?) were obviously of prime importance. But for the boy to do well, would it not be better if he showed some aptitude for the career being chosen for him? We have seen that manuals of pedagogy insisted on this point, and the actual practices of many families show that the idea was shared by fathers, mothers, uncles, tutors, and everyone who cared about the young boy's future.

In his *Libri della famiglia,* the great Florentine architect and humanist Leon Battista Alberti (1404–1472) described the extreme care his own parents had taken in deciding on the education and the kind of life appropriate for their sons, so that each one might pursue his "genius."[60] An echo of Alberti's work may still be seen in the autobiography of Cardinal Franciotto, who was born at Lucca in 1592: "[My father] reflected that since all his children . . . had adequately shown their particular genius and abilities, he wanted, in his foresight, to find an application for them that would suit each one." Thus the eldest was destined for "public affairs"; the third son, to continue the family line; and the second, Marco Antonio, "for the studies and training of a cleric." In consequence, "since all of them followed their father's wishes respectfully, not only did they meet with proportionate success, but they received even more benefits from God."[61]

A *vita,* or autobiography, it may be objected, is as "controlled" a text as a moral treatise. Closer to reality and its contradictions are the letters exchanged by families, and this is the type of source we should turn to when seeking proof of practices like those described by Alberti and Cardinal Franciotto. Here again, the correspondence of the Spada family is exemplary. The house had six sons, and the qualities and defects of each were carefully weighed before it was decided what would be the best path for him to follow. The eldest, Bernardino, was obviously observed the most attentively. As his uncles, who were powerful ecclesiasts, wrote:

> We are allowing our nephew, Marquis Bernardino, to travel to Spain, even though the house . . . is rather short of money at the present time. This will allow him to acquire further embellishments and enrich himself through seeing the world, and enable us to assess with what habits and economy he will govern himself, since it is up to his parents and to us, his uncles, to apply his person to some undertaking, or else to place the charge of family affairs into the hands of other, more responsible nephews or great-nephews.[62]

For his part, the father addressed his own recommendations to the young marquis:

> Your journey to Spain will provide the Cardinal and Father Virgil, our uncles, with an opportunity to give careful consideration to their decisions concerning your person, and to form an idea of the quality of your brain;

it is thus absolutely necessary (since during your stay in Rome, your lack of diligence made you lose, rather than acquire, their esteem) to use this journey to recover the lost ground, for you will thus have an opportunity to advance along the path suited to your vocation.[63]

At this stage, the powerful uncles had "not yet decided if they should direct him toward the priesthood or to secular life";[64] but finally, despite a timid indication from the young man that he would like to take holy orders, "they refused him the priesthood because it seems he has not a sufficiently firm and applied brain."[65]

The second son, Alviano, was robust and full of life. He "learned little from his studies because he did not apply himself," but he did show an aptitude for military life. He was therefore sent to be a page at the court of the grand duke of Tuscany, which greatly pleased his father: "I'm delighted that Alviano is going to Florence, because he's wasting his time in Rome; he'll make a man of himself in Florence, and when someone has enthusiasm God always helps him to succeed."[66] The third son, Fabrizio, was of delicate constitution and seemed an ideal candidate for a career in the Curia and the splendors of cardinalship, as did the last of the six sons, Bartolomeo, who was sent to boarding school in Parma. "You must remember," wrote his father, "that you yourself said you wanted to make your way in the priesthood, and I thank God he gave you this desire and inclination, because you could not set yourself a more glorious goal than that which must be reached means of virtue; but these means must be well ordered, and show no caprice."[67]

A similar evaluation of individual desires and their compatibility with family requirements took place in the case of other Spada boys from the Romagna branch of the family: Gioseppe, who had been a page for four years at the court of the elector of Bavaria, wanted to obtain advancement in a less "puerile" career, or else embark on a military career, whichever "seemed better" to his tutors. They told him they would "leave the choice up to him, depending on which profession he felt drawn to." But he did have a brother, Michele, who "although in a seminary in Rome, by virtue of his age, bodily size, and inclinations, was proving more suited for the profession of arms than for studying." Accordingly, "if Gioseppe [wants] to exchange his position at court for Michele's position, and go to the seminary, tell him that Michele is ready to make the change and I am ready to beg His Highness to substitute one for the other. And if he does not want to go back to the seminary in Rome, we'll find him another one; but if he's ready to stay at court for a few more years, and behave well, then we'll think about stimulating his talent for the things he proves most suited for."[68]

As appears from this letter, boys did not always have very clear ideas, as was only natural at their young age. It was thus not very hard to influence them to make the "right" choice. Bernardino Spada would have liked to become a Jesuit, but they had only to send him to the country for a while "to remove that idea from his head . . . considering this was only the result of a slight melancholy following the changes in our family caused by the death of our uncle the cardinal, rather than by a true vocation."[69]

Bartolomeo Corsini, too, showed some inclination for the ecclesiastical life, but when his father arranged a good marriage for him he agreed to it at once and with good grace. His mother, who had been very worried about the whole business, expressed her relief that they had not "thwarted a vocation, which turned out to be unfounded, for in truth I was very apprehensive."[70]

As a young man, Orazio Spada himself had had to change course rapidly. A brilliant student, he had been destined for the priesthood when the sudden death of his only brother forced him to return to the secular state and take a wife.[71]

Conversely, Pietro Ottoboni had dreamed of marriage for a while, and had even embarked on a half-secret venture; but suddenly he retreated and took "the virtuous decision to devote himself only to his studies . . . and make no plans for himself without the knowledge of his elders."[72]

Girolamo Pamphilij, in contrast, who declared he felt "so cruel a repugnance for ecclesiastical life that I shall never embrace it for anything in the world," effectively resisted all paternal pressure.[73] On the whole, however, the facility with which boys changed their "vocation" suggests that ultimately they were rather indifferent to their future condition. It is clear that the idea of marriage neither strongly attracted nor greatly revolted them, and the same was true of unmarried life, whether ecclesiastical or military. In the end Orazio Spada had proved very happy with his engagement, as can be seen from this letter:

> My signora Maria, although from Rome, is not like other Roman women, conceited, lazy, of little worth . . . I am very happy, and although I have only seen her once, furtively, and only know her through what I have heard, God knows I love her tenderly and would tear my heart out to please her . . . I am dying of love, only because I know I love her, and without knowing if I deserve to be loved by her . . . And yet you know, because I told you, that I have few affections, and do not become so enamored of people as to change my nature.[74]

Yet the same Orazio had agreed very willingly to the other possible choice, that of completing his studies and entering the Curia, as appears from this memento given him when he was leaving for the university:

> The reason you are being sent to study is because you are being trained in law in order to follow the Court, and in the footsteps of our uncle the cardinal. You have studied rhetoric, logic, physics, Greek, and French . . . But I think it would be useful for you to continue your studies of rhetoric . . . for literature is as important as law for someone wishing to become a prelate, and the functions require fluency in Latin . . . I would like you to study theology, but superficially, because your career will not be that of a theologian . . . Such studies can prove very useful, for among prelates, few are learned . . . and this is a great advantage for someone who is.[75]

In contrast, other young men seem to have shown a greater aversion for marriage and to have chosen the ecclesiastical state. Some of them even took advantage of their age and seniority over a younger brother to avoid it. Giuseppe Tomaso, for example, was a Sicilian aristocrat who, compared with his young brother, was "completely opposite in temperament, all gravity and strength of mind, and so dominated him whenever these subjects were broached, that if Don Ferdinando opened his mouth to refuse the marriage, the other (who perhaps had some interest in avoiding it) opened his eyes so wide and intimidated him so much that the poor boy hunched his shoulders."[76] There was also the case of Camillo Cybo who, with his brother's death, suddenly became the eldest son and was thus in a position to leave the ecclesiastical state and marry; he preferred, however, to leave this pleasure and responsibility to his third brother and continue on the path he had chosen.

It is hard for us to gauge the sincerity of these religious vocations, at once so numerous and automatic, linked as they were to the order of birth. But we do know that an ecclesiastical career could satisfy other needs that, being less intimate, were thus better documented. At the beginning of his autobiography, Cybo explains that he had always had an irresistible vocation for the priesthood; but in the rest of the text, the reader is hard put to find the slightest trace of so ardent a faith: what drew him to the Roman Curia was politics, not concern for his soul.[77] Other boys, fascinated by learning, might choose to enter a religious order to devote themselves more fully to their studies and to maintain a relationship with other scholars—something quite impossible for a gentleman grappling with the family patrimony. For many, marriage seems merely to have been a tedious duty, to which they submitted "so as not to leave the house without posterity."[78]

Despite these examples, matrimony must nonetheless have had its attractions, since cases exist of young people defying parental authority in order to be married. But managing family business was doubtless also a burden and responsibility that caused many to reflect. It was no accident that when people described the ideal virtues of a wife, she was supposed to be active and efficient: "I swear to you that . . . what she will lack is time, and not the will to work,"[79] wrote Orazio Spada of Maria Veralli. When Giovanni Battista Pamphilij fell hopelessly in love with Violante Facchinetti, it was because she corresponded—according to what he had been told—to the wishes he had expressed: "I would like a wife who can help me in running the house and in domestic tasks, as I should like to entrust that responsibility to her."[80] Although having a wife could be extremely pleasant (as various texts leave us to understand), "running the house" was still a thankless and exhausting job, for even if the patrimony was enormous, receipts and expenditures still had to be balanced. Even the most prudent heads of households were continually assailed by financial problems—and by creditors who were so bold as to threaten them with arrest. Many properties were saddled with fideicommissary clauses that did not leave much room in which to maneuver: management was limited to controlling intake and expenditure, and all too often the idea of disposing of ready money for investments or innovations seemed an impossible dream. In other words, managing the family patrimony was certainly no way to make a fortune.

In other periods of history, Italian patricians grew rich through commerce or finance. But after the second half of the sixteenth century, aristocratic ideology and the state of the international market made those two paths less practicable. At the same time, the development of state bureaucracy had increased the number of attractive public offices and corresponding careers in the service of a prince. Clearly, therefore, the different institutional configurations of the Italian states and the diverse economic and political powers of the different aristocracies influenced the choices made by families and led to a regional differentiation in the choice of careers: the king of Spain, lord of the two Sicilies, of Sardinia, Milan, and the Praesidia certainly had more to offer than the grand duke of Tuscany. But in addition to the possibility of serving a prince, there was also the possibility of serving the pope which, because of its international character, attracted and absorbed, albeit to varying degrees, all the heirs of the Italian nobility.[81] To accede to papal offices, and ultimately to the purple robes of cardinalship, one had first to embrace the ecclesiastical condition and thus take vows of celibacy. Careers in the Roman priesthood thus corresponded perfectly to the needs of families who had adopted the principle of primogeniture: not only did this prevent the younger sons from marrying, but it also provided revenues that enriched the entire family. Entering the Roman Curia meant entering the world of politics; it meant sharing in the administration of a power that exceeded the limits of Italy and its states, and it meant being rewarded in the form of ecclesiastical benefits, some of which were princely. In terms of family affection, the renunciation was not drastic, because nephews compensated for the sons a prelate did not have. In terms of power and status, a career in the Curia could raise a man above his own relatives and make him the true

head of the family—even if, officially, his elder brother had the title. Not
surpisingly, therefore, these careers proved attractive, so much so that
some men renounced the privileges of primogeniture to embark on them.

To understand the specific appeal that marriage or celibacy held for
young men, we have to proceed by hypothesis. To attempt to reconstruct
the motivations of girls is an even more uncertain venture. Here again,
the story of the nun of Monza may lead us into error: the abuse of paternal
power was the exception, not the rule. At the same time, what must have
been fairly common were the subtler maneuvres needed to convince the
girls, to obtain their consent to a state that, while not very attractive, was
not absolutely repulsive either—at least, not for aristocratic girls. In a
polemical text from the first half of the seventeenth century, a Venetian
nun wrote that at least one-third of her cosisters had allowed themselves
to be cloistered without a true vocation.[82] As for those who entered the
convent voluntarily, we still need to understand what they were seeking in
the religious life, beyond—or besides—an ardent religious vocation we
can only rarely apprehend. Certain girls had so interiorized the social norm
that they spontaneously proposed entering a convent to relieve their parents and relatives of the burden of providing for them: "I was fifteen or
sixteen when I became a nun," said one young girl from Udine, "and I did
so voluntarily, because I had several sisters and I thought it necessary."[83]
A lame granddaughter of Speroni did the same thing,[84] and so did Galileo's
daughters, because they were illegitimate.[85] Analogous examples may be
found among the Catholics in Germany, where girls who were illegitimate,
or in delicate health, chose the cloister as a refuge.[86]

For a noble girl whose character was more imperious, the convent
could, moreover, represent the possibility of a career culminating—if she
became an abbess or a mother superior—in the exercise of real power.
Such power would initially be of an economic nature, having to do with
managing the convent's property. But convents were often real centers of
political influence, sometimes even of political power, as is proved by
various documents from centers throughout Catholic Europe.[87]

Of the attractions of being a wife we know still less, for even now the
written testimony left by young brides or mothers has scarcely been stud-

ied. Some of the girls mentioned in the preceding correspondence manifested a real desire to be married; but as I pointed out, the families spoke
little of the girls' "inclinations"—all their letters tell us is that they had
"no taste for becoming a nun." Giulia Speroni wept when her daughter
decided to take the veil, indicating that in her eyes it was preferable to lead
a conjugal life.[88] But numerous young widows would not have remarried
had they not been urged to do so by their relatives.

To view marriage and nunhood as diametrically opposed is, however,
an erroneous modern tendency. For girls of that period, convent life was
more a matter of continuity than an alternative to life within the four walls
of the home or in the secular world. All aristocratic girls spent at least
several years of their youth in a convent, and even after their marriage
they maintained close relationships with the institution and its speaking
room, where they frequently visited cloistered female relatives. For widows and unhappily married women, the convent was a place of refuge:
there, without having to take the veil, they could live decently despite
having a small income, flee the power of an abusive husband and family,
or escape from tedious gossip.[89] Seclusion in a convent did not interrupt all
contact with the outer world or with one's family, as is shown by numerous
texts, including the correspondence between Galileo and his daughter
Maria Celeste, a sister in a convent at the gates of Florence.[90]

Bishops were often aware that the vocation of their nuns was not
necessarily carved in granite, and were ready to make concessions that
could make life more pleasant for them. In 1619, the patriarch of Venice
wrote to the Senate of the republic:

> In regard to their daily life, their obedience, and their clothing, I have
> always allowed them as much leeway as possible within the limits of
> honesty and good example . . . and this was to bring, if not solace, then
> at least a little less desolation into their lives, reflecting that since they are
> from aristocratic families, raised and nurtured with the utmost delicacy
> and respect, it would fall to them to govern and command the world,
> were they of the other sex. If they have enclosed themselves within these
> walls, it was not out of piety but because their families urged them, thus
> offering their freedom—so dear to those who lack the use of reason—not

only to God, but also to their country, the world, and to their closest
relatives. I have often thought that if the two thousand or more noble
girls living shut up in the convents of this city as if in a public depot had
been willing or able to dispose of themselves in some other way, what
confusion, what damage, what disorder . . .[91]

In the majority of cases, therefore, parents could count on young
people to interiorize their family's interests, and to adhere spontaneously
to the destiny chosen for them. Thus we cannot really speak of paternal
tyranny, or of true coercion. But it would also be an exaggeration to say
that parents had respect for their children. Were this really the case, parents
would have accepted decisions contrary to their own plans and wishes,
whereas in fact they did everything to discourage them. In the examples
we have just seen, there was no conflict, either because the young people's
choices coincided with the demands of the family, or because, in any case,
their decisions did not threaten the family's long-term objectives, since
brothers (Gioseppe and Michele Spada) or sisters made compensatory
choices.

REBELLIONS

Occasionally, however, sons or daughters tried to force their parents' hand,
confronting them with an accomplished fact that did not eliminate the
conflict but shifted and modified its terms. The accomplished fact was
usually a secret marriage—I have found no trace of anyone secretly taking
vows—and this was by no means rare. But the fact that the union took
place without parental consent or knowledge did not necessarily mean it
was a misalliance. On the contrary, the young woman was usually from an
aristocratic family, and the obstacle to the marriage was not social distance,
but rather the fact that the boy's parents had someone else in mind, that
the boy himself was too young, or that his father intended him to remain
single. Respect for the vocation of marriage was rarely carried to the point
of allowing full freedom of choice in the matter. Admittedly, our modern
tendency to contrast arranged marriages and marriages of love is anachronistic in some ways: fathers who arranged marriages for their sons or
daughters were not necessarily tyrants who put their own interests before

their children's happiness. Quite the reverse: as a late seventeenth-century moralist remarked, if it was unjust to force children into a marriage that could not make them happy, it would have been equally inhuman to abandon them to the inconstancy of their age and fail to help them make a choice that determined whether their lives would be happy or unhappy.[92] Even Luther was of this opinion, and devoted a treatise to the question.[93]

Reservations against ill-assorted arranged unions did not emanate solely from religious authorities, either Catholic or Protestant. On this point young people also had medical science on their side, which maintained that mutual attraction between husband and wife was an indispensable condition for the fertility of their union:

> The most frequent cause of sterility, as Paré and Liébault explained and Mauriceau confirmed in his treatise of 1668, was the woman's lack of pleasure during intercourse; in this situation not only did she produce no seed of her own, but also a clenching of the uterine orifice caused her to reject the seed of the male. Fathers who ignored the warnings of science and experience and forced daughters to marry against their will were guilty in the eyes of nature itself.[94]

An echo of this position is heard in the remark made by the Roman aristocrat who declared that "a succession is better assured when inclination, and not interest, makes a marriage."[95]

Nevertheless, the recommendations of theologians and the warnings of doctors did not eliminate all cause for disagreement, and clandestine marriages were the scourge of parents throughout Europe.

The fact that such unions were not necessarily mismatches requires further comment. At least in Italy, where girls were carefully guarded, not only was the bride's family frequently aware of the plan, it also often acted as an accomplice: otherwise, the "plot" would have failed. The expedient the young people resorted to was always the same: they appeared before a priest, who was more or less in league with them, and expressed a mutual wish to become man and wife. That is what Camillo Pamphilij and a young Austrian woman tried to do in Vienna, before the apostolic nuncio, but in their case the maneuver failed.[96] However, a few decades earlier, in Rome, the father of this same Camillo had married, against his mother's will,

Violante Facchinetti, an aristocrat from Lucca.[97] In Paris, the marchese Patrizi succeeded in secretly exchanging rings with a young English-woman; but in France such escapades were not taken lightly, and as soon as news of this got out, the young couple was arrested. The girl was put in a convent, and the boy sent back to his family in Italy.[98] In Rome, Camillo Borghese left the familial palace in secret to wed Agnese Colonna, and the two fugitives resurfaced in Venice.[99] But it was in Faenza—still inside the Papal States—that the most revealing episode occurred.[100] Paolo Spada had learned from a third party that his son, age sixteen, was in love and was planning to marry quickly. As Paolo related in his memoirs: "Next morning, his mother and I went to see him while he was still in bed . . . and told him we had woken him to talk to him directly." His matrimonial project, they said, was not reasonable. And if it was really necessary to "introduce a new wife into the family, then they had to proceed according to the normal customs of the house and speak to Giacomo Filippo, the elder brother, first, to see if he wanted to reserve this right, or if he agreed to yield it to his brother." Moreover, the young woman was twenty-one and the boy only sixteen, a "disproportion" that seemed truly excessive. "Our boy made no answer to these arguments, made very gently and in the presence of his mother, who was very helpful to me." The father then suggested his son leave Faenza, where he had fallen in with "bad acquain-tances," and go to some other Italian town, to "study well" and learn "riding, and other exercises suitable for a young gentleman," or that he stay with his father to learn how "family and domestic business was conducted"; then he asked him "to think carefully and let me know his decision when he had made it." After this interview, the boy "went all through the house, telling men and women, servants and members of the household, that my speech had been that of a loving father," as several of them afterward said, and "in particular the wife of our ———, an hon-orable and truthful woman in whom he had confided, as one does with members of the household." Nevertheless, one fine day young Spada sent an emissary to tell his father he was firmly resolved to marry the person in question and would not return home that night. Two days later, he was found at the house of Camillo Severoli, a cousin of the bride, "surrounded by followers and companions of Camillo, relatives and servants of the young woman's house . . . and was earnestly negotiating the matter with the family of his future bride, both orally and in writing." Next day, Francesco Spada and Signorita Severoli met in church before the officiating priest: they uttered the ritual words, obtained the nuptial blessing, and the marriage was recorded by a complicitous notary.

According to his parents, the boy had "allowed himself to be subverted and seduced into disobeying his father and taking a wife." The disobedient groom, on the other hand, maintained "constantly that he had contracted this alliance of his own accord, without being influenced by anyone."[101] At this juncture the civil and ecclesiastical authorities intervened in the person of the cardinal-legate, representing the pope. The cardinal had the boy cloistered in a Capuchin monastery for three weeks, to ascertain whether he had acted of his own free will or not. Then he wrote to Rome: "As for the marriage, it must follow the course determined by the young man, for I shall take great care that none of the parties involved influences his free judgment. But I have given orders for the notary instrumental in this marriage to be thrown into prison, and I mean to punish him as responsible for this new manner of proceeding, for such schemes, put into practice, may gravely disturb the republic with their bad example."[102] The marriage was finally declared valid, and the couple lived long and happily and had many children.

THE REBELS' ALLIES

The cardinal-legate's letter shows that the Church did not automatically ally itself with paternal authority. At the Council of Trent, French bishops had insisted—vainly—that parental consent should be included among the conditions of validity for the sacrament of marriage. While it condemned marriages contracted without parental knowledge on account of their dire consequences, the solution adopted in November 1563 nonetheless considered them valid: from the point of view of dogma and jurisprudence, the *consensus parentum* was a desirable but not "essential" requirement.[103] Furthermore, the decision taken at Trent allowed that failure to respect provisions concerning the publicity of a marriage (publication of banns, presence of witnesses, presence of the parish priest of the bride and groom) did not affect consent—the first component of the sacrament—as much as it did the "competency" of the contracting parties and, hence, the juridical value of the contract. In the case of a secret marriage, consent was "ineffective" but could not be considered nonexistent. This explains the position of the cardinal-legate who recognized at least a possibility of free choice in young Spada's attempt, and thus ordered a thorough investigation.

Thus the doctrine of the Council of Trent lent itself to interpretations that favored rebellious young people. Its influence was particularly strong in Italy, because in the different states of the Italian peninsula, at least until the second half of the eighteenth century, ecclesiastical tribunals had jurisdiction over marriages, and no civil power was able to claim the slightest competence—even jointly—in this domain.[104] In consequence, the will of the bride and groom, and therefore clandestine marriages, were far better protected there than elsewhere. This explains why families were so careful to keep their children, even the boys, under strict supervision. Seen in this light, the words of the man charged with accompanying Marco Antonio Borghese on his travels through Europe are quite revealing: leaving Paris—the trusted fellow wrote—would put an end to "excessive expenses, and also the fear of dangers resulting from the freedom one has in this country to converse with ladies; already I feel reborn, and am beginning to forget the apprehensions that until now have tormented me."[105]

There was another aspect of the problem, proper to Italy. For its patricians, the Church was in no way an external institution, opposed to the family: all the great houses counted at least one ecclesiastical dignitary among their members.[106] Thus the conflict between family demands and canonical law often took place inside the home, between brothers, fathers, and uncles. These potential debates between people of the same generation (constituting, it has been said,[107] the fundamental line of attrition of families of the ancien régime) also involved women, mothers being the first and principal allies of their children. In keeping with the stereotype, Italian women were indeed fond and indulgent mothers, ever ready to "spoil" their children, and especially to assume their traditional role as mediator.[108] The marchesa Maria Veralli Spada, for example, was "particularly pensive," torn as she was between the desire to please her son and the necessity of not irritating his father with demands for money, considering it was "normally her task to intervene between father and son, and convinced as she was that on her depended not only the goodwill of the marchese, but also of our uncles."[109] Money, in fact, together with vocation, were the main causes of tension between fathers and mothers, even more so than between fathers and sons. The correspondence between Lucrezia Rinuccini and Cardinal Lorenzo Corsini, her brother-in-law, turns constantly on the two themes of paternal authority and defense of the sons' right to be treated with respect, including their right to an adequate allowance.[110]

In the case of more overt rebellions on the part of young people, mothers were again the first to be called on to effect a reconciliation. We have seen how Paolo Spada considered his wife's presence a guarantee of equity during his early morning talk with his son. And in the case of secret marriages, like those of young Patrizi or Pamphilij, mothers and ecclesiastical uncles were the first to be informed, so that they might delay as long as possible the inevitable explosion of paternal rage.

As has gradually become apparent, the mothers' most trusty and powerful allies were their ecclesiastical brothers-in-law. This was generally true for any woman in conflict with her husband, her original family, or her family by marriage; whether in the institution itself or in one of its members, such women sought the support and protection that, on principle, the Church was ready to afford them. Within the family, the dynamics of this practice were only slightly more complicated.

If he attained a position of importance, an ecclesiastic actually became the true head of his family. The first lady of the house, his brother's wife, was thus in close and permanent contact with him on all manner of business, from marriage contracts to restoring the family palazzo. The two had in common that fact that they were not bound by the formal obligations of the official head of the family, and could thus move more freely in regard to the personal contacts and informal relationships that had to do with so many imortant questions: matrimonial prospects, social calls, political maneuvers. In addition, the lady and the prelate did not have the responsibility of dealing with the family patrimony, which fell to the eldest son; it was his duty to manage possessions that were largely inalienable, at least in principle, because of the numerous fideicommissary clauses. The head of the family had the formal honor of managing this fortune properly, and was always burdened with the responsibility of his sons' success. In the genealogical vision proper to these families, each generation was simply a link in a chain they hoped would be infinite, and everything they received, in terms of wealth and prestige, had to be handed on intact— better still, increased—to the heirs: that was how a gentleman's worth was measured.

Wives and prelates both enriched their families (she through her dowry, he through his ecclesiastical revenue), but in patrilineal thinking, they were not responsible for managing that wealth, at least not formally; nor were they responsible for the failings of their sons, as is shown by the following example. Antonio Ottoboni, a young Venetian aristocrat, was a perfect paradigm of dissipation: although married and freed from paternal authority, he nevertheless continued to lose heavily at gambling, chase after women, and run up debts for his family after squandering his wife's dowry. The only person who could come to his aid was his uncle, a cardinal, who was the only one to have revenue outside the family patrimony. And in fact that is what the cardinal did, at least for several years. The prestige of the Ottoboni family was not enhanced by this situation, but in the eyes of the outer world, the blame was not equally shared: whereas "Signor Agostino [Antonio's father] was still accused of having let his son do what he did, and few deemed him worthy of consideration or praised his way of doing things," the cardinal continued to enjoy general respect.[111]

The religious aspect was clearly present in this definition of the ecclesiastic's position in the family. For although imbued with aristocratic ideology, he had still received a formal education and studied canonical law. Both his culture and his professional duty, therefore, disposed him to defend the freedom of choice of young men for whom he was not responsible within the lineage. Young Italians from great houses thus had potent allies, and did not have far to go to find them.

FRANCE

Like Italy, France was a Catholic country; but the configuration and distribution of authority between family, Church, and state nonetheless produced widely differing results. Here again, what was at stake was the freedom to choose the "condition" for which one felt most inclined, and therefore the possibility of taking a wife or husband even without parental consent.

We have seen how the French bishops at Trent asked for parental consent to be included among the clauses rendering a marriage valid, and that the council did not adopt their proposal. But the decision taken at Trent was not accepted in France, and after an edict issued in 1566 by Henri II concerning the marriage of sons, legislation and jurisprudence constantly increased the penalties for clandestine marriages (even going so far as to seek the death penalty), thus increasing the fathers' power over their children.[112]

The edict of 1566 declared "only" that sons who had contracted a secret marriage could be disinherited. But an ordinance of 1579 introduced the "crime of seduction," by which "those who have been found guilty of seducing sons or daughters who are under the age of twenty-five, on pretext of marriage . . . without the knowledge, consent, or liking of fathers, mothers, and tutors, will be punished by death."[113] Subsequent legislation continued to intensify the sanctions, making them automatic and independent of parental complaints. Moreover, according to the French tribunals, marriages contracted in secret had to be considered null and void in both civil and canonical law, since consent obtained through "seduction" violated the requirements of "freedom."[114]

In contrast with civil jurisprudence, the clergy persisted in upholding the decree of the Council of Trent concerning the conditions of validity of the marriage sacrament and thus the "inessential" nature of parental consent. This led to a certain amount of tension between ecclesiastical authorities and families. While preachers and authors of moral treatises continued to insist on a child's duty to obey his or her parents, they also emphasized, after the beginning of the seventeenth century, the obligation of fathers to consider the inclinations of their children. "Parents sin gravely if they marry their sons or daughters against their will, as do those who make their daughters lead a religious life," we read, for example, in a summa of moral theology published in 1624.[115]

From one treatise to another, references became increasingly specific: Richelieu condemned not only fathers who created obstacles to the religious or matrimonial callings of young people, but also fathers who "marry them to persons they cannot love." A guide for conscientious self-examination, written in 1713, asked parents: "Didn't you force your son to contract a marriage with a girl for whom he felt an aversion, even though you could see they would be very ill-matched?"[116]

As might be expected, the alliance between priest and the wife so typical of Italian families—at least, according to Michelet—reasserted itself in this context in connection with the rights of children.[117] This was especially true since the aristocratic families of France also counted numerous clerics in their ranks: in the seventeenth century, approximately one-third of the brothers of dukes and peers were members of the clergy. If the proportion tended to decline in the following century, this was mainly because the major families had begun drastically reducing the number of births and, increasingly, dukes and peers had no other brothers.[118]

But in France, parental authority had at its disposal means that did not exist in Italy, where ecclesiastical jurisprudence had sole discretion in marriages. Thanks to the actions of civil tribunals, French fathers could count on the power to enforce their will in regard their sons' decisions. Even so, it sometimes happened that legal proceedings intended to uphold paternal authority turned to the children's advantage. A son could appeal to the tribunals, asking to be freed from the authority of a tyrannical father, for several reasons: because the father refused to consent to a perfectly "suitable" marriage, or because he wanted the son to take orders against his will, or because he meant to disinherit him, and so on.[119] In the eighteenth century, the requests of young aristocrats seem to have received increased attention. The absolute power of French fathers thus found its limits in the authority of the state, rather than that of the Church: in civil rather than canonical law.

ENGLAND

In upperclass English society of the first half of the sixteenth century, before Henry VIII's reforms, the behavior of fathers toward their children was much the same as on the Continent. If they were harsh, the same harshness was found in France and Italy; and if, on the other hand, they were indulgent, the two other countries also had a tradition of affectionate behavior toward their children, quite removed from the coldness and brutality we read about in some accounts. In the fifteenth century Matteo Palmieri, author of a moral treatise, observed: "I don't want them to be beaten, those boys whose father or master is trying to make them good."[120] The same opinion was expressed by Erasmus and also Sir Thomas More, who wrote in these terms to his son:

> I have never been able to bear hearing you cry. And you know how many times I've kissed you and how few times I've used the whip. The whip has always served to back up threats, but used as lightly as a pen. I always used it on you gently and hesitantly, so that painful blows would not disfigure your tender bottom. It is a brutal man, unworthy of the name of father, who declares he does not cry when his children weep.[121]

An almost identical idea appears in a letter from Sperone Speroni to the superior at his graddaughter's convent: "Kind words and love, rather than threats and blows, are more effective in making her do better . . . I too, when she was four or five, gave her a few, but it cost me a great effort and more pain than it caused her; and afterward I took her aside and hugged her and gave her a little present, and she was happy."[122]

But the Reformation brought about major changes in England. Whereas Catholic priests, being celibate, could effect a neutral mediation, Protestant preachers laid repeated emphasis on the spiritual authority of fathers as heads of families. This authority was exercised exclusively, without competition from other "fathers"—ecclesiastics invested with authority outside the domain of the family. This greatly strengthened the "persuasive" powers of Protestant fathers who, for their part, proved extremely aware of their responsibilities, and ready to use force to help their children make the right choices; in other words, to make them obey their will. As Lord Mountgarret wrote to his eldest son:

I am told you are possessed by a wretched blindness in your wish to marry, and thus to ruin by this one unfortunate deed both the lady and yourself, destroying (as far as you can) all my plans for you and our house. My son, in the name of the bonds of nature and duty that bind you to me, I command you not to follow so desperate a course, because it is a thing I detest and abhor. Place these words in the depths of your heart, and you will read in mine an indignation that is stronger than if they were even harsher . . . Do not lack a son's obedience in a matter of such grave importance to me and to our family. Let this prevent you from rushing to your ruin . . . If it does not, I shall act in such a way that punishment strikes whomever it justly should.[123]

It is hardly surprising, therefore, that Protestant theologians considered paternal consent essential to a marriage's validity. In England, however, where secret marriages were also under the jurisdiction of the Church, there was no legal pretext for declaring them null and void. In the second half of the seventeenth century, the spread of the successional customs known as "strict settlement" made it almost impossible to disinherit rebellious children;[124] not until 1735 did the Marriage Act finally and precisely regulate the conditions of validity in marriages, making paternal consent indispensable for minors of less than twenty-one years. But until that date, and even afterward for boys (for in England it was especially rare for them to marry as minors), although the power of fathers was strengthened by the Protestant theology that gave them spiritual authority over their families, young Englishmen still had the possibility of escaping from this authority without incurring the legal sanctions they would face in France. And in other Protestant countries, such as the German states, parents did not have the legal power to ask for a secret marriage to be anulled if it had been consummated and if those concerned persisted in their intention. But it was often possible to disinherit the rebels or at least to reduce their legitimate inheritance.[125]

Many historians of family life consider the period we have just dealt with to be the darkest in the history of relationships between fathers and sons.[126] According to them, the revival of Roman law, the Protestant Reformation, and the birth of absolutism greatly strengthened the author-

ity of fathers, who were thus able to behave like veritable tyrants without
having to fear reprisals. But as we have seen, reality was often different:
fathers had numerous other means for imposing their will, and imperious
self-assertion was not necessarily the best, nor the one most often used.

Moreover, the choice between marriage and celibacy did not always
have the dramatically antithetical nature we ascribe to it today. On the
contrary, the attractions of either state were rarely so strong as to provoke
irremediable conflicts between the young men involved and their families:
in such cases, the use of persuasion, rather than coercion, to guide the
children in their choices was more reasonable and certainly more effective.

Far from being hasty despots, the fathers we have studied seem, on the
contrary, to have devoted a considerable amount of time and money to
educating their children, and to deciding on the state or career best suited
to them. But this was true only for boys, since personal inclinations were
of particular importance in choosing a career. When it came to choosing
husbands for the girls, their desires were not taken into account, and other
considerations prevailed.

The phenomenon of clandestine marriages proves that transition into
adulthood was not always smooth and free of tension. The happy conclusions of some of these episodes should not make us forget that rebelling
against paternal authority was a risky business: the miscreants were subject
to serious punishments, made harsher by the fact that the authority dispensing them identified with paternal authority. Only in cases in which
"fathers" of another kind claimed the right to intervene and protect or
sanction the children's choice did young aristocrats have some possibility
of turning the resulting juridical conflict to their advantage.

Rather than pondering this authoritarian-liberal antithesis, we should
probably consider the aspects of persuasion and mediation. From this point
of view, the case of Italy—and in Italy, the case of Rome—is in a sense
paradigmatic of the role played by ecclesiastics, either as members of the
Church, or as individuals taking part in family conflicts. The Catholic
clergy was composed of celibates—that is, of persons marginally situated
in regard to "lineage," for which they were not "responsible"; it would be
interesting to compare their behavior with that of the Anglican clerics,

who also had full jurisdiction in matrimonial matters, but who were, in contrast, married men with children. Like the upper strata of the Italian clergy, the clergy of France,[127] England,[128] and Spain[129] were composed, in varying degrees, of younger sons of the nobility. However, differences in juridical systems led to a different division of authority between elder and younger sons, between the head of an aristocratic family and the member of an institution that claimed the right to intervene in questions of paternal power. From the end of the sixteenth century, the growing involvement of the state further complicated relationships, making our customary distinctions between Catholics and Protestants seem too generic and simplistic. This heightened complexity should be the subject of future study, since it is now clear that in every era tyrannical fathers may coexist with more affectionate and liberal parents: for historians to continue to erect or correct a chronology of paternal love is therefore rather meaningless.

NOTES

CONTRIBUTORS

INDEX

NOTES

1 INTRODUCTION

1. Charivari: "originally C., the etymology of which is doubtful, meant a hubbub of noises produced by whistling, howling, singing, and the clattering of pans, kettles, etc., which in the middle ages was raised on the occasion of an unequal marriage or the marriage of a widow, and which did not cease until money was paid to make peace. The C. was frequently characterised by violence and the singing of indecent verses, and in the 14th. c. attempts were frequently made to put it down by the Church." *The Globe Encyclopaedia*, ed. John M. Ross (London: J. S. Virtue, 1894), vol. 2, p. 97. See, in the present volume, the essay by Norbert Schindler, and some references in the chapter by Elisabeth Crouzet-Pavan. (Trans. note.)

2. Camisard rebellion: French Protestant revolt in the Cévennes in the early eighteenth century, prompted by the persecutions that followed the revocation of the Edict of Nantes. (Trans. note.)

3. *Compagnonnage:* semi-secret organizations of journeymen and artisans. There is no precise equivalent for the word in English. (Trans. note.)

2 IMAGES OF YOUNG PEOPLE IN THE GREEK CITY-STATE

1. Plato, *Laws*, I, 64b–c; quotation from Thomas L. Pangle, trans. and ed., *The Laws of Plato* (New York: Basic Books, 1980), p. 21.

2. Ibid., I, 639b; see Kenneth Dover, *Greek Homosexuality* (Cambridge, Mass.: 1978), p. 226; G. R. Morrow, *Plato's Cretan City* (Princeton: 1960), p. 301.

3. Plato, *Laws*, I, 643c (Pangle, p. 23).

4. Ibid., I, 643e (Pangle, p. 24).

5. H. Jeanmaire, *Couroi et Courètes: Essai sur l'éducation spartiate et les rites d'adolescence dans l'Antiquité hellénique* (Lille: 1939), pp. ii–iii.

6. M. I. Finley, *The World of Odysseus* (New York: Meridian, 1959), pp. 17–28.

7. Jeanmaire spells *kouros* and *kouroi* with a *c*.

8. Jeanmaire, *Couroi et Courètes*, p. 29.

9. Ibid., pp. 85–89.

10. Ibid., p. 107.

11. Ibid., pp. 115–144.

12. K. O. Müller, *Geschichte Hellenistischer Stämme und Städte: Die Dorier* (Breslau: 1844). See also the historiographic analysis by H. Patzer, *Die griechische Knabenliebe* (Wiesbaden: 1982).

13. E. Bethe, "Die dorische Knabenliebe, ihre Ethik und Idee," *Rheinisches Museum* 62 (1907): 438–475.

14. Müller, *Geschichte Hellenisticher Stämme*, p. 285.

15. Ibid., p. 289.

16. See E. Will, *Doriens et Ioniens: Essai sur la valeur du critère ethnique appliqué à l'histoire de la civilisation grecque* (Paris: 1956).

17. Bethe, "Die dorische Knabenliebe."

18. Ibid., p. 447.

19. Werner Jaeger, *Christianity and Greek Paideia*, vol. 1 (Oxford: Oxford University Press, 1969). H. I. Marrou, *Histoire de l'éducation dans l'Antiquité* (Paris: 1965); English edition, *A History of Education in Antiquity* (New York: Sheed and Ward, 1956).

20. Jaeger, *Paideia*, pp. 237–238.

21. Marrou, *A History of Education*, p. 480, note 5.

22. Ibid., p. 51.

23. Dover, *Greek Homosexuality*.

24. Strabo X, 4, 20. Quotation from *The Geography of Strabo*, trans. Horace Leonard Jones (Cambridge, Mass.: Harvard University Press, 1961), p. 155.

25. Jeanmaire, *Couroi et Courètes*, pp. 450–460; H. Van Effenterre, *La Crète et le Monde Grec de Platon à Polybe* (Paris: 1948), pp. 86–88; R. F. Willets, *Aristocratic Society in Ancient Crete* (London: 1957), p. 37; A. Brelich, *Paides e Parthenoi* (Rome: 1969), pp. 197–207; B. Sergent, *L'Homosexualité dans la mythologie grecque* (Paris: 1984), p. 17; B. Sergent, *L'Homosexualité initiatique dans l'Europe ancienne* (Paris: 1986), pp. 52–74.

26. Jeanmaire, *Couroi et Courètes*.

27. Strabo, X, 4, 21 (Jones, *The Geography*, p. 156).

28. A. Yoshida, "Sur quelques couples de la fable grecque," *Revue des Etudes Anciennes* 67 (1965): 33–41; Sergent, *L'homosexualité initiatique*, p. 253.

29. Jeanmaire, *Couroi et Courètes*, p. 547; see also Brelich, *Paides e Parthenoi*, pp. 191–207.

30. Xenophon, *The Spartan Constitution*, II, 14; Plutarch, *Lycurgus*, 17, I.

31. P. Cartledge, "The Politics of Spartan Pederasty," *Proceedings of the Cambridge Philological Society* 207 (1981): 17–36.

32. C. Pélékidis, *Histoire de l'éphébie attique des origines à 31 av. J.-C.* (Paris: 1962), pp. 7–8.

33. Ibid., p. 78.

34. P. Vidal-Naquet, "Retour au chasseur noir," in *Mélanges P. Levêque 2* (Paris: 1989), pp. 387–412.

35. L. Grasberger, *Erziehung und Unterricht im klassischen Altertum mit besonderer Rücksicht auf die Bedurfnisse der Gegenwart nach der Quellen dargestellt,* 3 vols. (Würzburg: 1864–1880).

36. P. Roussel, "Etudes sur le principe d'ancienneté dans le monde hellénique du Vᵉ siècle av. J.-C. à l'époque romaine," in *Mémoire de l'Académie,* vol. 43, part 2 (Paris: 1942).

37. Aristotle, *Politics,* VII 13, 3, 1332 b 36, quoted in Roussel, "Etudes sur le principe d'ancienneté," p. 47; English quotation from Aristotle, *Politics,* trans. H. Packham (reprint; Cambridge, Mass.: Harvard University Press, 1977), p. 603.

38. Hesiod, fragment 220; see Roussel, "Etudes sur le principe d'ancienneté," p. 81.

39. Plato, *Laws,* III, 694c (Pangle, p. 79).

40. Ibid., I, 626a–b (Pangle, p. 4). Concerning this problem, see G. E. Morrow, *Plato's Cretan City* (Princeton: 1960), pp. 297–325, and M. Piérart, *Platon et la Cité grecque: Théorie et réalité dans la constitution des "Lois"* (Brussels: 1974), pp. 355–385.

41. Plato, *Laws,* I, 631c (Pangle, p. 10).

42. Ibid., I, 633a (Pangle, p. 12).

43. Ibid., VI, 760b (Pangle, p. 146); P. Vidal-Naquet, *Le Chasseur noir* (Paris: 1981), pp. 300–301; English edition, *The Black Hunter: Forms of Thought and Forms of Society in the Greek World* (Baltimore: Johns Hopkins University Press, 1986).

44. Plato, *Laws,* VI, 760c (Pangle, p. 146).

45. Ibid., VI, 763b (Pangle, pp. 149–150).

46. For more about the *krypteia,* see Piérart, *Platon et la Cité grecque,* p. 281; also J.-P. Vernant, "Entre la honte et la gloire, l'identité du jeune Spartiate," in *L'Individu, la Mort, l'Amour: Soi-même et l'autre en Grèce ancienne* (Paris: 1989), pp. 173–206. Translated as *Mortals and Immortals: Collected Essays,* ed. Froma I. Zeitlin (Princeton: Princeton University Press, 1992).

47. Plato, *Laws,* II, 666e (Pangle, p. 48).

48. G. Koch-Harnack, *Knabenliebe und Tiergeschenk: Ihre Bedeutung im Päderastischen Erziehungsystem Athens* (Berlin: 1983).

49. Plato, *Laws,* I, 633 b–c (Pangle, p. 12)

50. See above.

51. Following the order of the chapters of the *Laws,* from 811 to 812.

52. Plato, *Laws,* VII, 822d (Pangle, p. 215).

53. Ibid., VII, 823b (Pangle, pp. 215–216).

54. Ibid., VII, 824a (Pangle, p. 217).

55. Ibid.
56. Ibid., VII, 796a (Pangle, p. 184).
57. Ibid., VII, 804d (Pangle, p. 194).
58. Ibid.
59. Xenophon, *Memorabilia*, III, X, 1, in *The Anabasis and the Memorabilia of Socrates*, trans. J. S. Watson (London: Bell and Daldy, 1871), p. 454; see E. Keuls, *Plato and Greek Painting* (Leiden: 1978).
60. Xenophon, *Memorabilia*, III, X, 2 (Watson, p. 454).
61. Ibid., III, X, 3 (Watson, p. 455).
62. Ibid., III, X, 5 (Watson, p. 455).
63. Pindar, Third Nemean Ode, lines 74–99, in Roy Arthur Swanson, trans. and ed., *Pindar's Odes* (New York: Bobbs-Merrill, 1974), p. 140 (lines 43–57).
64. H. W. Pleket, "Zur Soziologie des Antiken Sports," *Mededelingen van het Nederlands Instituut te Rome* 36 (1974): 57–87, pp. 60–66 in particular.
65. F. Lissarrague, *Un flot d'images: Une esthétique du banquet grec* (Paris: 1987), p. 132; trans. by Andrew Szegedy-Maszak as *The Aesthetics of the Greek Banquet: Images of Wine and Ritual* (Princeton: Princeton University Press, 1990). See also the ingenious interpretation by C. Calame in "Apprendre à lire, apprendre à chanter: L'inférence énonciative dans une image grècque," *La Part de l'oeil* 5 (1989): 45–53.
66. *Palatine Anthology*, XII, 208; Jesper Svenbro, *Phrasikleia: Anthropologie de la lecture en Grèce ancienne* (Paris: 1988), pp. 217–218; English edition, *Phrasikleia: An Anthropology of Reading in Ancient Greece*, trans. Janet E. Lloyd (Ithaca: Cornell University Press, 1992).
67. The theme still existed, however; see fig. 3.
68. C. Calame, *Les Choeurs des jeunes filles en Grèce archaïque* (Rome: 1977); English edition, *Choruses of Young Women in Ancient Greece: Their Mythology, Religious and Social Functions*, trans. Janice Orion and Derek Collins (Lanham, Md.: Rowman and Littlefield, 1994).
69. L. Bruit-Zaidman, "Les filles de Pandore: Femmes et rituels dans les cités," in G. Duby and M. Perrot, eds., *Histoire des femmes*, I: *L'Antiquité*, ed. P. Schmitt-Pantel (Paris: 1990), pp. 363–403; English edition, *A History of Women in the West*, vol. 1 (Cambrige, Mass.: Harvard University Press, 1991).
70. On the role of women in Greek athleticism, see B. Spears, "A Perspective on the History of Women's Sport in Ancient Greece," *Journal of Sport History* 11, no. 2, special issue, *Ancient Athletics and Ancient History* (1984): 32–47; and G. Arrigoni, "Donne e sport nel mondo greco: Religione e società," in G. Arrigoni, ed., *Le donne in Grecia* (Rome-Bari, 1985), pp. 55–102.
71. Plato, *Laws*, II, 653b–654a (Pangle, pp. 32–33).
72. C. Bérard, "La chasseresse traquée: Cynégétique et érotique," in *Kanon, Festschrift Ernst Berger* (Basel: 1988), pp. 280–284.

73. C. Bérard, "L'impossible femme athlète," in *Annali dell'Istituto universitario orientale di Napoli* (1986), pp. 195–202.

3 ROMAN YOUTH

1. See, in this order, Livy 1, 6, 3; Dionysius of Halicarnassus I, 85, 2; Plutarch, *Life of Romulus* 9, 2. English quotations from Livy, *The Early History of Rome*, trans. Aubrey de Sélincourt (London: Penguin Books, 1971), p. 39; Dionysius of Halicarnassus, *Roman Antiquities*, trans. Earnest Cary (Cambridge, Mass.: Harvard University Press, 1960), vol. 1, p. 293; Plutarch, *The Lives*, trans. John Dryden (New York: Modern Library, 1932), p. 29.

2. See Plutarch, *Life of Romulus* 9, 3. Also the commentary and parallels with the asylum provided by C. Ampolo in Plutarch, *Le vite di Teseo e di Romolo*, ed. C. Ampolo (Milan: 1988), pp. 293–294. For an English edition, see *The Lives*, trans. Dryden. On the origins of the city, see E. J. Bickerman, "Origines gentium," *Classical Philology* 47 (1952): 65.

3. A. Fraschetti, "I re latini e le selve del Lazio," in *Giornate di studio in onore di Santao Mazzarino* (Catania: April, 21–24 1988), soon to be published in *Quaderni catanesi di studi classici e medievali*.

4. For more about Faunus, see the excellent analysis by Georges Dumézil in *La Religion romaine archaïque*, 2nd ed. (Paris: 1977), p., 350 ff.; English edition, *Archaic Roman Religion*, trans. Philip Krapp (Chicago: Chicago University Press, 1970). See also A. Brelich, *Tre variazioni romane sul tema delle origini*, 2nd ed. (Rome: 1976), p. 57 ff. On the twins' passion for hunting, see Livy 1, 4, 8. On possible connections with the Greek world, see P. Vidal-Naquet, *Le Chasseur noir: formes de pensées et formes de société dans le monde grec* (Paris: 1981), p. 151 ff.; English edition, *The Black Hunter: Forms of Thought and Forms of Society in the Greek World* (Baltimore: Johns Hopkins University Press, 1986). Also, by the same author, "Le cru, l'enfant grec et le cuit," in Jacques Le Goff and Pierre Nora, eds., *Faire de l'histoire III* (Paris: 1974), p. 137; English edition, *Constructing the Past: Essays in Historical Methodology* (Cambridge: Cambridge University Press, 1985); the same essay was republished in *The Black Hunter*. For information on the physical exercises of young people and the "young men's spectacle," see below, notes 5 and 49. The arming of young Celts in 21 A.D. is mentioned in Tacitus, *Annals*, 3, 43, 2; quotation from Tacitus, *The Annals of Imperial Rome*, trans. Michael Grant (Harmondsworth: Penguin Books, 1979), p. 140.

5. The episode occurs in Ovid, *Fasti* 2, 361 ff. For young men's gymnastic exercises, see M. Della Corte, *Juventus* (Arpino: 1924), p. 14 ff.; M. Jaczynowska, *Les associations de la jeunesse romaine sous le Haut-Empire* (Wrocław: 1978), p. 50; J.-P. Neraudau, *La Jeunesse dans la littérature et les institutions de la Rome*

républicaine (Paris: 1979), pp. 112–123. Neraudau contains an important reference to Cicero, *Pro Caelio,* suggesting that at the beginning of the first century B.C., young men still exercised on the Campus Martius dressed in tunics
—an implicit defense of their *fama* (reputation) and their *pudicitia* (modesty).

6. See especially J. Scheid, "La spartizione a Roma," *Studi storici* 25 (1984): 945.

7. The episodes of the founding of Rome and the murder of Remus are described,
   naturally, in Livy 1, 6, 4 and Livy 7, 2, 3; Dionysius of Halicarnassus I, 86–87;
   Plutarch, *Life of Romulus* 9, 4–7 and 10, 1–3.

8. From the Greek word meaning "cause," an *aition* was a mythical explanation
   of a religious ritual. The myths that claim to illuminate these causes are known
   as "etiological myths." (Trans. note.)

   The bibliography for Remus's murder is obviously vast and reflects many
   different points of view. I suggest R. Schilling, "Romulus l'élu et Remus le
   réprouvé," *Revue des études latines* 38 (1961): 182, republished in *Rites, cultes,
   dieux de Rome* (Paris: 1979), p. 103; M. Benabou, "Remus, le mur et la mort,"
   AION Archeologia e storia antica 6 (1981): 103; J. N. Bremmer, "Romulus, Remus
   and the Foundation of Rome," in J. N. Bremmer and N. Horsfall, eds., *Roman
   Myth and Mythography,* University of London, Institute of Classical Studies,
   Bulletin Supplement 52 (1987): 25.

9. Plutarch, *Life of Romulus,* 21, 6 (*The Lives,* Dryden, p. 39). For parallel documentation on the Lupercalia, see A. Fraschetti, "Antonio e Cesare ai Lupercalia," in F. M. Gales and G. Grotanelli, eds., *Soprannaturale e potere nel mondo
   antico e nelle società tradizionali* (Milan: 1985), p. 164. This contains references
   to previous studies.

10. Sufficient information on the connections between ritual purity and fertility is
    provided in M. Delcourt, *Stérilités mystérieuses et Naissances maléfiques dans
    l'Antiquité classique,* 2nd ed. (Paris: 1986).

11. See the description of the grotto Lupercal given in Dionysius of Halicarnassus
    I, 2, 3–5. All materials relevant to this grotto have been collected in Marbach,
    RE XIII, 2 (1927), col. 1815–1816; see also S. B. Platner and T. Ashby, *A
    Topographical Dictionary of Ancient Rome* (Oxford: 1929), p. 321. For literary
    documentation of the Lupercal's Arcadian sources, see, for example, F. Blömer's
    commentary on P. Ovidius Naso, *Die Fasten,* vol. 2 (Berlin: 1958), pp. 101–
    103.

12. Remarks concerning the two groups of Luperci are found in M. Corsano,
    "*Sodalitas* et gentilité dans l'ensemble lupercal," *Revue d'histoire des religions* 91
    (1977): 137. For the etymology of the word "Luperci" see Fraschetti, "Antonio
    e Cesare," p. 27. On Romulus's laughter, see Ovid, *Fasti* 2, 377–378 and Verius
    Maximus, 2, 3, 9.

13. For information on the Luperci's "nudity," see the judicious remarks by
    D. Porte, "Note sur les 'luperci nudi' dans l'Italie pré-romaine at la Rome

républicaine," in *Mélanges offerts à J. Heurgon,* vol. 2 (Rome: 1976), p. 817, in connection with A. W. J. Holleman, "Ovid and the Lupercalia," *Historia* 22 (1973): 260.

14. Plautus, *Poenulus,* lines 522–523. See also, several centuries later, *Historia Augusta, Alexander Severus,* 42, 2. G. Piccaluga offers a different point of view on the Luperci's run in "L'aspetto agonistico dei Lupercalia," *Studi e Materiali di storia delle religioni* 33 (1962): 51. On *celeritas* and *gravitas,* see G. Dumézil, *Mitra-Varuna: Essais sur deux représentations indo-européennes de la souveraineté,* 5th ed. (Paris: 1948), p. 38 ff.; English edition, *Mitra-Varuna: An Essay on Two Indo-European Representations of Sovereignty,* trans. Derek Coltman (New York: Zone Books, 1988). On *gravitas* see, by the same author, *Idées romaines,* 2nd ed. (Paris: 1969), p. 142 ff.

15. I am referring here, of course, to Vidal-Naquet, *The Black Hunter.*

16. See Cicero, *Pro Caelio,* XI, 26. See also, for example, A. W. J. Holleman, "Cicero on the luperci," *Antiquité classique* 54 (1975): 198. On the *aition* of the festival, and the connection with Juno Lucina, see Ovid, *Fasti* 2, 425 ff. As to the Luperci seen as as "human herds" and "goats," I am obviously combining Varro, *Sulla lingua Latina,* 6, 34, and Paulus Festus p. 49, Lindsay.

17. For this episode generally, see Livy 1, 35–36; Dionysius of Halicarnassus II, 19–22. On the *crimen perduellionis,* see B. Santalucia, "Osservazioni sui 'duumviri perduellionis' e sul procedimento duumvirale," in *Du châtiment dans la cité: Supplices corporels et peine de mort dans le monde antique* (Rome: 1984), p. 439. See also E. Cantarella, *I supplizi capitali in Grecia e a Roma* (Milan: 1991), p. 171 ff.

18. On Ianus Curiatius, see G. Capdeville, "Les épithètes cultuelles de Janus," *Mélanges de l'Ecole française de Rome* 85 (1973): 428. On the problematic issue of the *tigillum sororium* and the epithet describing Juno, see G. Dumézil, *Horace et les Curiaces* (Paris: 1942), p. 89 ff., and, for another point of view, especially in regard to Juno Sororia, see H. J. Rose, "Mana in Greece and Rome," *Harvard Theological Review* 42 (1946): 165.

19. The zone of the Carinae and the site of the *tigillum sororium* are discussed in F. Coarelli, *Il Foro romano* vol. 1, *Periodo arcaico* (Rome: 1983), p. 11 ff. Coarelli also analyzes the meaning of walking under the beam. For the expiatory sacrifices previously performed by Horatius's father, see Livy 1, 26, 13.

20. Dionysius of Halicarnassus IV, 15, 5 (Cary, vol. 2, p. 319). The Lucius Piso quoted by Dionysius is, of course, Lucius Calpurnius Piso, consul in 133 B.C. (fr. 14 in *Historicum Romanorum fragmenta,* ed. Peter).

21. For a general treatment of the problem, see Varro in Censorinus, *On the Birthday;* Isidor of Seville, *Etymologies,* 11, 12, and *Differentiarum libri,* 2, 75. See also Neraudau, *La Jeunesse,* p. 91 ff.

22. The bibliography on this topic being particularly vast, I mention only

Y. Thomas, "A Rome, pères citoyens et cité de pères," in *Histoire de la famille*, vol. 1 (Paris: 1986), p. 195; also, by the same author, "Droit domestique et droit politique à Rome: Remarque sur le pécule et les *honores* des fils de famille," *Mélanges de l'Ecole française de Rome: Antiquité* 94 (1982): 527, and "Vitae necisque potestas: Le père, la cité, la mort," in *Du châtiment dans la cité*, p. 499.

23. On the conflicts between fathers and sons, see below, section entitled "Young and Old."

24. For information on the physical and social condition of women, consult Neraudau, *La Jeunesse*, p. 101. For the general condition of women in Rome, see the essays by Y. Thomas, A. Rousselle, J. Scheid, and M. Alexandre in G. Duby and M. Perrot, eds., *Histoire des femmes*, vol. 1, *L'Antiquité* (Paris: Plon, 1991); English edition, *A History of Women* ed. P. S. Pantel, trans. A. Goldhammer (Cambridge, Mass.: Harvard University Press, 1992). Among previous works, there is also S. B. Pomeroy, *Donne in Atene e Roma*, Italian trans. (Turin: 1978), p. 160 ff.; E. Cantarella, *L'ambiguo malanno: Condizione e immagine della donna nell'antichità greca e romana* (Rome: 1981), p. 132 ff., English ed., *Pandora's Daughters: The Role and Status of Women in Greek and Roman Antiquity*, trans. M. B. Fant (Baltimore: Johns Hopkins University Press, 1987); and, lastly, C. Petrocelli, "Studiare le donne antiche," *Aufidus* 11–12 (1990): 197.

25. For a definition of *univira*, see J. Straub, "Calpurnia univira," in *Regeneratio Imperii* (Darmstadt: 1972), p. 350.

26. For the *feriale cumanum*, see *Inscriptiones Italiae* XIII, 2, p. 279; refer generally to A. Fraschetti, *Roma e il principe* (Rome-Bari: 1990), p. 22 ff.

27. In regard to the virile toga, see Neraudau, *La Jeunesse*, p. 147 ff.; also F. Dupont, *La Vie quotidienne du citoyen romain sous la République* (Paris: 1994), p. 240 ff. On the *tunica recta*, see Paulus Festus pp. 342 and 364, Lindsay; Pliny the Elder, *Natural History*, 8, 194. On the *bulla*, see Persius 5, 31 and Plutarch, *Roman Questions*, 101. On the honors received by Gaius and Lucius Caesar, see Augustus, *Res gestae* 14, 1, and also Cassius Dio Cocceianus, 55, 9, 10.

28. The young men's procession to the Capitol is described in Servius, *Commentary on the Eclogues*, 4, 48–49. For the Capitoline cult of Juventas referred to by Camillus, see Livy 5, 54, 7 and 1, 55, 3–4 (when Tarquin the Proud wanted to "liberate" the Capitol through *exaugurationes*, only the temple of Terminus was at issue). The altar dedicated to Juventas is mentioned in Pliny the Elder, *Natural History*, 35–108, and Platner and Ashby, *A Topographical Dictionary*, pp. 308–309.

29. The entire documentation concerning the temple of Juventas has been collected in Platner and Ashby, *A Topographical Dictionary*, p. 308. The lectisternium of 218 B.C. is mentioned in Livy 21, 62, 9. For a discussion of Roman religion

during the second Punic War, see in particular Dumézil, *La religion romaine archaïque*, p. 457 ff.; English edition: *Archaic Roman Religion*, trans. Philip Krapp, vol. 2 (Chicago: University of Chicago Press, 1970), p. 476.

30. On the subject of Augustus's virile toga, see *Inscriptiones Italiae*, XIII, 2, p. 279; also the documentation collected by J. Gagé, *Res gestae divi Augusti* (new edition, Paris: 1977), p. 183. On the addition of an extra day, October 19, to the marble calendar of Antium, see *Inscriptiones Italiae*, XIII, 2, p. 209, and also the remarks by M. A. Cavallero, *Spese e spettacoli* (Bonn: 1984); for Tiberius, see *Inscriptiones Italiae*, XIII, 2, p. 448; for Virgil, *Vita Vergilii*, p. 52, ed. Reifer and Scheid; for the son of Cassius, Caesar's murderer, see Plutarch, *Life of Brutus*, 14.

31. Ovid, *Fasti* 3, lines 771–788.

32. See Neraudau, *La Jeunesse*, p. 149 ff.; M. Torelli, *Lavinio e Roma: Riti iniziatici e matrimonio tra archeologia a storia* (Rome: 1984), p. 28.

33. It is in this same sense that we should interpret the only reliable evidence of a case in which the virile toga was adopted on the day of the Liberalia. It involved the son of Quintus Cicero, according to the wish expressed by his uncle in Laodicea in 50 B.C.: Cicero, *Letters to Atticus*, 6, 1, 12: *"Quinto togam puram Liberalibus logitabam dare; mandavit enim pater."* For the sacrifice to Liber on the Capitol, see the documentation by A. Degrassi in *Inscriptiones Italiae*, XIII, 2, p. 425.

34. For information on clothing, see L. Sensi, *"Ornatus* e status sociale delle donne romane,"* Annali della facoltà di Lettere e Filosofia di Perugia. Sez. Studi classici* 18 N., S. 4 (1981): 55 ff. On familial strategies and the resulting marriages, see J. Andreau and H. Bruhns, eds., *Parentés et stratégies familiales dans l'antiquité romaine* (Rome: 1990).

35. See Dumézil, *Horace et le Curiaces*, p. 10 ff.; by the same author, *Heur et malheur du guerrier* (Paris: 1969); J.-P. Morel, "Sur quelques aspects de la jeunesse à Rome," in *L'Italie pré-romaine et la Rome républicaine*, vol. 2, p. 674 ff.; and Neraudau, *La Jeunesse*, p. 249 ff.

36. The episode is narrated at length in Livy, 8, 30–35; see V. Basanoff, "Le conflit entre 'pater' et 'eques' chez Tite-Live," *Annuaire de l'Ecole pratique des hautes études: Section Sciences religieuses* (1947–48): 3. On Quintus Fabius Massimus Rullianus's creation of the *transvectio equitum*, see below in this section on the military.

37. For Livy's reference to Lucius Giunius Brutus and Titus Manlius Torquatus, see 8, 34, 2–3; on the duel fought by Titus Manlius Torquatus, see Livy 8, 9–10. See also the analysis and comparison provided by J.-P. Neraudau, "L'exploit de Titus Manlius Torquatus (Livy VII 9, 6–10) (Réflexion sur la 'juventus' archaïque chez Tite-Live)," in *L'Italie pré-romaine et la Rome républicaine*, vol. 2, p. 685 ff.

38. This episode is narrated by Livy, 8, 7; see especially Maurizio Bettini, *Antropologia e cultura romana* (Rome: 1986), p. 20 (with the comparison already mentioned); English edition, *Anthropology and Roman Kinship: Kinship, Time, Images of the Soul,* trans. John van Sickle (Baltimore: Johns Hopkins University Press, 1991).

39. On the combination of the Lupercalia and the transvectio equitum, see Valerius Maximus, 2, 3, 9. On the *transvectio equitum,* consult S. Weinstock, *RE,* VI, 1 (1937), col. 2178 ff.; H. H. Scullard, *Festivals and Ceremonies of the Roman Republic* (London: 1981), pp. 164–165; S. Demougin, *L'Ordre équestre sous les Julio-Claudiens* (Rome: 1988), p. 150 ff.

40. See Paul Veyne, "Iconographie de la 'transvectio equitum' et des Lupercales,' *Revue des études anciennes* 62 (1960): 100.

41. On the creation of the *celeres,* following that of the Senate, see Dionysius of Halicarnassus II, 13; Livy 1, 15, 8, and Plutarch, *Life of Romulus* 26, 2–3 (for their part in Romulus's transformation from king to tyrant). As for the relationship between *celeres* and knights in the archaic period, the debate betwen A. Alföldi and A. Momigliano has been analyzed by Neraudau in *La Jeunesse,* p. 259 ff.; see also I. Ilari, "I 'celeres' e il problema del 'equitatus' in epoca arcaica," *Rivista italiana per le scienze giuridiche,* s. III, 25 (1971): 117. For the pain and alarm felt by the *romana pubes* at the death of Romulus, see Livy 1, 16, 2.

42. On the episode involving Titus Manlius and his father Imperiosus and also the attitudes of the three Manlii, consult particularly Bettini, *Anthropology and Roman Kinship* (with bibliography).

43. Tacitus, *Annals,* 1, 19–10; on the *paternus inimicus,* see F. Hinard, "'Paternus inimicus': Sur une expression de Cicéron," in *Mélanges Wuilleumier* (Paris: 1980), p. 197. On actions brought by sons in defense of the honor of their dead fathers, as "family vengeance," see J. M. David, "Sfida o vendetta, minaccia o ricatto: L'accusa pubblica nelle mani dei giovani alla fine della repubblica," in E. Pellizer and N. Zorzetti, eds., *La paura dei padri nella società antica e medievale* (Rome-Bari: 1983), p. 101.

44. See, obviously, Y. Thomas, "Paura dei padri e violenza dei figli: Immagini retoriche e norme di diritto," in Pellizer and Zorzetti, *La paura dei padre,* p. 115 (with the documentation it includes). On the *peculium* of sons, see Thomas, "Droit domestique et droit politique à Rome," ibid., p. 527 ff.

45. See the sources listed in note 22.

46. On Gaius and Lucius Caesar, *principes juventutis,* see Morel, *Sur quelques aspects de la jeunesse,* p. 671; Neraudau, *La Jeunesse,* p. 370; Demougin, *L'Ordre équestre,* pp. 259–260. On Gaius Caesar, "already designated a princeps," and the cenotaph in Pisa, see *ILS* 140. On the 300 *principes juventutis Romanae* mentioned by Mucius Scaevola, see Livy 2, 12, 15. For Cicero and his identical designation of

Domitius Aenobarbus, Curio, and Brutus, see, respectively, Cicero, *2 Verr.*, 1, 139; *Against Vatinius*, 24; and *Letters to His Familiars*, 2, 11, 3.

47. On the organizations of *juvenes* in Rome and their connection with the *regiones* and the *vici*, see S. Paniera, "Tra epigrafia e topografia," *Archeologica Classica* 22 (1970): 131. As for the associations of *juvenes* in the western provinces under the empire, all materials have been collected by Jaczynowska in *Les associations de la jeunesse*, (with bibliography). On the role of young men during military crises, see, for example, J. Gagé, "Les organisations de 'juvenes' en Italie et an Afrique du début du IIIe siècle au 'Bellum Aquileiense' (238 A.D.)" in *Historia* 19 (1970): 232.

48. On the *vereiia*, see A. La Regina, "Appunti su entità etniche e strutture istituzionali nel Sannio antico," *AION Archeologia e storia antica* 3 (1981): 134. See also G. Tagliamonte, "Alcune considerazioni sull'istuto italico della vereiia," in *Pdp* 44 (1989), p. 361. For the dedication to Marcus Valerius of Lanuvium, consult *CIL* XIV 2121. On the epitaph of Lucius Sulpicius Clemens, "praetor of youth" in Nepi, see *CIL* XI 3215. For Sutri, see *CIL* XI 3256, with discussion of whether the inscription should be interpreted as pr(aetor) juvenum or pr(aefectus) juvenum; a preference for the former appears in Jaczynowska, *Les associations de la jeunesse*, p. 44. See also, in general, the same author's "L'organisation des 'collegia juvenum' au temps du Haut-Empire romain," in *Gesellschaft und Recht in griechisch-römischen Altertum*, vol. 2 (Berlin: 1969), p. 95. On derivation and "borrowings" between Roman and Italic magistratures, in a kind of Italic cultural koine, the basic work is S. Mazzarino, *Dalla monarchia alle stato reppublicano*, 2nd ed. (Milan: 1991); an introduction by A. Fraschetti touches on the problem: see p. xi ff.

49. On the *lusus juvenum*, see Della Corte, *Juventus*, p. 29 ff.; Jaczynowska, *Les associations de la jeunesse*, p. 44 ff. On Nero's creation of the *juvenalia*, see Tacitus, *Annals*, 14, 15; Cassius Dio Cocceianus, 62, 19; Suetonius, *Life of Nero*, 11, 1; see also J.-P. Morel, "Pantomimus allectus inter iuvenes," *Hommages à M. Renard*, vol. 2 (Brussels: 1969), pp. 528–538; also by Morel, "La 'juventus' et les origines du théâtre romain (Livy, VII, 2); (Valerius Maximus, II, 4, 4)," *Revue des études latines* 47 (1969): 208; Cavallaro, *Spese e spettacoli*, pp. 68–70, with notes 107–108. On the *lusus Troiae*, see Scheid, *Annuaire de l'Ecole pratique des hautes études: Section Sciences religieuses* (1987–88): 284 ff.

50. On the social composition of the associations, see Jaczynowska, *Les associations de la jeunesse*, p. 27 ff., and see her discussion of the analyses by M. Rostovsev ("Römische Bleitesserae: Ein Beitrag zur Sozial-und Wirtschaftsgeschichte der römischen Kaiserzeit," *Klio* supplement 3 [1905]: 84), in which there is a list of gods chosen as protective divinities by the young men's associations (p. 55 ff.).

51. On the electoral "posters" of Pompei, see Della Corte, *Juventus*, p. 24 ff., and

by the same author, *Case e abitanti di Pompei* (Naples: 1965). For general consultation, see M. Jaczynowska, "Les organisations des *juvenes* et l'aristocratie municipale au temps de l'Empire romain," in *Recherches sur les structures sociales dans l'Antiquité classique* (Paris: 1970), p. 265. A list of the goals attributed to various clubs can be found in Morel, *Sur quelques aspects de la jeunesse,* pp. 668–670 (with bibliography). The "dangerous" potential of young men is also mentioned in a famous passage from Callistratus, *Digest,* 48, 19, 28, 3.

4   THE WORLDS OF JEWISH YOUTH IN EUROPE, 1300–1800

This chapter was originally written in English.

1. C. M. Cipolla, ed., *The Fontana Economic History of Europe,* vol. 2, *The Sixteenth and Seventeenth Centuries* (London: 1974), p. 7.

2. S. W. Baron, *The Jewish Community: Its History and Structure to the American Revolution,* vol. 2, (Philadelphia: 1942), p. 175; T. M. Endelman, *The Jews of Georgian England 1714–1830* (Philadelphia: 1979), p. 188.

3. For Lithuania, see S. Dubnow, ed., *Pinkas ha-Medinah* (Berlin: 1925), pp. 8, 91; Baron, *The Jewish Community,* vol. 2, p. 310. For Minz's decree, see R. Bonfil, "Aspects of the Social and Spiritual Life of the Jews in the Venetian Territories at the Beginning of the Sixteenth Century" (in Hebrew), *Zion* 41 (1976): pp. 71, 90–93.

4. See N. Roth, "The Ages of Man in Two Medieval Hebrew Poems," *Hebrew Studies* 24 (1983): 41–44, with its own translation. Although it is claimed there (p. 41) that the poem was never previously translated, see the elegant (but not very precise) rendition into Victorian English by Nina Davis in *Jewish Quarterly Review* 11 (1898–99): 565–568.

5. Israel al-Nakawa, *Menorat ha-Maor,* quoted in S. Assaf, *Mekorot le-Toledot ha-Hinnukh be-Yisrael,* vol. 2 (Tel Aviv: 1925–1942), p. 64. Assaf's collection, though nominally devoted only to the history of education, contains an abundance of source material on the lives of young people over several centuries.

6. Joseph Hahn Nordlingen, *Yosif Omet*̣ (Frankfurt: 1928), p. 279; Elijah ha-Kohen, *Shevet Musar* (Constantinople: 1712), chapter 14.

7. See Samuel Uceda, *Midrash Shmuel* (Venice: 1579), 230b. By 1801 Uceda's commentary had appeared (in Lemberg) in its seventh edition. The poem had earlier been published for liturgical use in the 1572 Venice edition of the prayer book *(Mah*̣*zor)* according to the Sephardic rite, and there it may have come to Uceda's attention. On the numerous publications of the poem, see I. Davidson, *Thesaurus of Medieval Poetry* (in Hebrew), 4. vols. and supplement (reprint, New York: 1970), no. 853. Davidson, however, fails to mention the poem's appearance in the various editions of Uceda's commentary.

8. See *Pirke Aboth,* trans. R. T. Herford (New York: 1930), v. 24: "At five years old (one is ready) for the scripture, at ten years for the Mishnah, at thirteen for

the commandments, at fifteen for the Talmud, at eighteen for marriage, at twenty for pursuit (of righteousness), at thirty for full strength, at fifty for counsel, at sixty for old age."

9. See the discussion of the poem in L. Low, *Die Lebensalter in der jüdischen Literatur* (Szegedin: 1875), p. 37, as well as in Roth, "The Ages of Man." The latter also discusses the erroneous attribution to ibn Ezra.

10. Compare the translation in H. Danby, *The Mishna* (Oxford: 1933), p. 458: "At twenty for pursuing (a calling)," and note the medieval commentary of R. Menahem ha-Meiri (d. 1316), who suggests that it means pursuit of a wife. See his "Bet ha-Behira" in *Avot* (Jerusalem: 1964), p. 101. Although eighteen is recommended earlier in the passage as the optimal age for marriage, according to Meiri's understanding if one has reached twenty and is still a bachelor, one should run to marry and hesitate no longer "so as not to become mired in evil thoughts and disgraceful actions." On the perception of the unmarried as being helplessly mired in evil thoughts, see below.

11. The Hebrew original is available most conveniently in H. Schirmann, ed., *Ha-Shira ha-'Ivrit be-Sefarad uve-Provence*, vol. 1 (Jerusalem–Tel Aviv: 1971), no. 260.

12. Shem Tov ibn Falaquera (d. 1295). See Roth, "The Ages of Man," p. 41.

13. As cited by his son, Rabbi Jacob b. Asher, *Tur Hoshen Mishpat*, no. 235. Note also the interesting testimony of his other son, Rabbi Judah, in I. Abrahams, ed., *Hebrew Ethical Wills* (Philadelphia: 1926), p. 186.

14. Two proponents of such a ban were Rabbi Abba Mari, known as Astruc of Lunel, a resident of Montpellier, and Don Crescas Vidal, a native of Barcelona and scion of one of its most distinguished families, who was then residing in Perpignan. A critical text of the former's proposal, in his *Minhat Kenaot*, now appears in H. Dimitrovsky, *Teshuvot ha-Rashba*, vol. 1 (Jerusalem: 1990), pp. 227–228. Excerpts are quoted also in B. Z. Dinur, *Yisrael ba-Gola*, vol. 2 (Tel Aviv–Jerusalem: 1969), p. 243. The epistle of Crescas Vidal to Rabbi Solomon ibn Adret on this matter is quoted and discussed in Y. Beer, *History of the Jew in Christian Spain*, vol. 1, trans. L. Schoffman (Philadelphia: 1961), p. 293. See also the letter sent to Montpellier by Rabbi Solomon and the leaders of the community of Barcelona, ibid., p. 295. The final text of the ban, however, issued in Barcelona in 1305, prohibited such studies to those under twenty-five.

15. See D. Herlihy, "The Generation in Medieval History," *Viator* 5 (1974): 353 and the sources cited there.

16. A steep fine of ten ducats was set for the offending woman. See D. Carpi, ed., *Minutes Book of the Council of the Jewish Community of Padua* (in Hebrew), 2 vols. (Jerusalem: 1973–1979), vol. 1, p. 369; vol. 2, p. 467.

17. P. S. Wiggins, ed. and trans., *The Satires of Ludovico Ariosto: A Renaissance Autobiography* (Ohio: 1976), Satire V, pp. 134–135 *("quella età che 'l furor cessa presto al voler, presto al pentirse poi.")* D. Ruderman, "The Founding of a *Gemilut Hasidim* society in Ferrara in 1515," *AJS Review* 1 (1976): 263.

18. Jewish Theological Seminary of America, New York, ms. 8594, 27r (1654). It was not unknown for women, especially among the poor, to be engaged for the first time at the age of thirty. See the case in the Italian Piedmont in Y. Boksenboim, ed., *Letters of Jewish Teachers* (in Hebrew) (Tel Aviv: 1985), p. 382.

19. Quoted by I. Halperin, *East European Jewry: Historical Studies* (in Hebrew) (Jerusalem: 1968), p. 307.

20. Ibid., pp. 293–295. See also M. Balaban, *Le-Toledor ha-Tenuah ha-Frankit*, vol. 2 (Tel Aviv: 1935), pp. 288–289.

21. Halperin, *East European Jewry*, pp. 291–300. Even boys, such as the young Solomon Maimon, would sometimes marry at that age. See Solomon Maimon, "An Autobiography," in L. W. Schwarz, ed., *Memoirs of My People* (New York: 1943), p. 201.

22. See I. Epstein, *The "Responsa" of Rabbi Solomon ben Adreth of Barcelona (1235–1310) as a Source of the History of Spain* (London: 1925), pp. 81–82, and, especially, A. A. Newman, *The Jews in Spain: Their Social, Political and Cultural Life during the Middle Ages*, vol. 2 (Philadelphia: 1942), p. 22: "Marriages between Jewish children were customary in all European countries in the Middle Ages. Certainly, in Spain in the thirteenth and fourteen centuries, child marriages were matters of everyday occurrence and excited no comment." Compare also the remarks of Baron, *The Jewish Community*, vol. 2, pp. 310–311.

23. See M. Balaban, "Die Krakauer Judengemeinde Ordnung von 1595 und ihre Nachtrage," *Jahrbuch der jüdisch-literarischen Gesellschaft* 10 (1912): 345; H. H. Ben-Sasson, *Hagut ve-Hanhaga* (Jerusalem: 1959), pp. 156–157.

24. M. Benayahu and G. Laras, "The Appointment of 'Health Officers' in Cremona in 1575" (in Hebrew) ed. S. Simonsohn, *Michael* 1 (1973): 98–99; Y. Boksenboim, ed., *Minutes Book of the Jewish Community of Verona* (in Hebrew), vol. 3 (Tel Aviv: 1989–1990), p. 189. Contrast the Valladolid (Castile) decrees of 1432, which prohibited those fifteen or older from wearing luxurious clothes of gold thread. See L. Finkelstein, *Jewish Self-Government in the Middle Ages* (New York: 1924), p. 374.

25. See S. Simonsohn, *History of the Jews in the Duchy of Mantua* (Jerusalem: 1977), pp. 532, 535, and 543 note 113.

26. *Seder Mishpetei Hevrat Bikur Holim . . . Mantova* (Mantua: 1792), 4a–b, pars. 10–11. On the age of ten as representing a turning point, and for the implicit recognition of ages ten to thirteen as representing an intermediate age, note also the sumptuary regulations of Cavaillon, discussed by A. Mossé, *Histoire des Juifs d'Avignon et du Comtat Venaissin* (Paris: 1934), p. 171.

27. R. Judah b. Leib, *Omer me-Yehudah* (1790), quoted in Assaf, *Mekorot* vol. 1, p. 219. Among the Jews of England at that time, it has been noted, even in families in which the father kept a small shop or was an artisan, "it was rare to

educate children past the age of eleven or twelve." See Endelman, *The Jews of Georgian England,* p. 188.

28. Assaf, *Mekorot,* vol. 4, p. 65. On the policy of requiring education until the age of thirteen, see I. Rivkind, *Bar Mitzvah: A Study in Jewish Cultural History* (in Hebrew) (New York: 1942), p. 23, as well as the sources cited by H. Pollack, *Jewish Folkways in Germanic Lands (1648–1806): Studies in Aspects of Daily Life* (Cambridge, Mass.: 1971), p. 239 note 46. In midseventeenth-century Moravia, for example, it was stipulated explicitly that even those youths unsuited to learning were to remain in school until that age, and could not be put to work or sent into service before then even if they were orphans. See I. Halperin, ed., *Constitutiones Congressus Generalis Judaeorum Moraviensium* (in Hebrew and Yiddish) (Jerusalem: 1952), pp. 6–7. See also Assaf, *Mekorot,* vol. 1, p. 136; vol. 4, pp. 76–78.

29. See the Spanish will of 1327 in Assaf, *Mekorot,* vol. 2, p. 60.

30. See Balaban, "Die Krakauer Judengemeinde Ordnung von 1595," and Assaf, *Mekorot,* vol. 1, pp. 98–99.

31. See Carpi, *Minutes Book,* vol. 2, pp. 313, 376–377, 415. On the use and threat of the whip in early modern Jewish education, even for older students, see also E. Horowitz, "The Way We Were: Jewish Life in the Middle Ages," *Jewish History* 1 (1986): 81–82.

32. Boksenboim, *Minutes Book of the Jewish Community of Verona,* vol. 3, p. 313.

33. Assaf, *Mekorot,* vol. 2, pp. 148–149 and 160; and A. Ya'ari, "Educational Regulations of the Verona Community (1714)" (in Hebrew), *Kiryat Sefer* 32 (1957): 505–506. For compulsory education until the age of sixteen in eighteenth-century Ferrara, see Assaf, *Mekorot,* vol. 2, p. 200.

34. Assaf, *Mekorot,* vol. 2, p. 55; Simonsohn, *Mantua,* pp. 590–599.

35. A. Susskind, *Yesod ve-Shoresh ha-'Avoda* (1782), quoted in Assaf, *Mekorot,* vol. 4, p. 145.

36. A. Cahen, "Enseignement obligatoire édicté par la communauté israélite de Metz," *Revue des études juives* 2 (1881): 304. See also Baron, *The Jewish Community,* vol. 2, p. 175, and Assaf, *Mekorot,* vol. 1, p. 152. Fourteen was also the age until which Jewish males were obliged to pursue education in Hesse in 1690. See Pollack, *Jewish Folkways,* p. 57; Assaf, *Mekorot,* vol. 1, p. 151.

37. Elliott Horowitz, "A Jewish Youth Confraternity in Seventeenth-Century Italy," *Italia* 5 (1985): 36 ff.; Boksenboim, *Minutes Book of the Jewish Community of Verona,* vol. 3, p. 369.

38. Boksenboim, *Minutes Book of the Jewish Community of Verona,* vol. 3, p. 369. Only those youths under twenty whose tutors could vouch for their ability to lead the prayers properly were permitted to do so—provided that their tutors remained by their side.

39. See D. Kaufmann, "Jewish Ethical Wills: Texts and Additions," *Jewish Quarterly Review*, o.s. 4 (1891–92): 339.

40. Ibid., vol. 2., p. 470; Carpi, *Minutes Book*, vol. 1, pp. 334–335.

41. Baron, *The Jewish Community*, vol. 2, p. 38. On the requirement of marriage for holding various offices, see also pp. 40, 45, 91–92, 104, 175.

42. The view of Rabbi Asher is quoted by his son in *Tur, Even ha-Ezer*, vol. 1. For the testimony of Isserles, see his comments in *Shulkhan arukh, Even ha-Ezer*.

43. F. M. Misson, *A New Voyage to Italy*, vol. 2 (London: 1739), p. 137 ff. On the Jerusalem ordinance, see, for example, Baron, *The Jewish Community*, vol. 2, p. 38; L. M. Epstein, *Sex Laws and Customs in Judaism* (reprint, New York: 1967), p. 141.

44. For Berukhim see S. Schecter, *Studies in Judaism, Second Series* (Philadelphia: 1908), p. 298; L. Fine, ed., *Safed Spirituality* (New York: 1984), p. 52. For J. H. Nordlingen, see *Yosif Ometz*, p. 282; Assaf, *Mekorot*, vol. 2, p. 83.

45. J. Katz, *Tradition and Crisis: Jewish Society at the End of the Middle Ages* (Glencoe: 1961), p. 139; see also p. 141. Note the instance of Simon von Geldern who, in 1736, considered himself too young, at fourteen, for marriage even though he had been offered a substantial dowry. See the excerpt from his autobiography in Schwartz, *Memoirs of My People*, p. 152.

46. Y. Boksenboim, *Letters of Jewish Teachers*, p. 303.

47. A. Toaff, *Il vino e la carne: Una comunità ebraica nel Medioevo* (Bologna: 1989), p. 33; E. Horowitz, "Jewish Confraternities in Seventeenth-Century Verona: A Study in the Social History of Piety," (Ph.D. diss., Yale University, 1982), p. 38.

48. For the former, see Mossé, *Histoire*, p. 142, and for the latter, I. Levitats, *The Jewish Community in Russia, 1772–1844* (New York: 1943), p. 112.

49. See the examples mentioned in Jacob Rader Marcus, *Communal Sick-Care in the German Ghetto* Cincinnati: Hebrew Union College Press, 1947), pp. 98–99, 147. Regarding the case of Ostroh (Stanicz) in Moravia, see H. Flesch in *Jahrbuch der jüdisch-literarischen Gesellschaft* 19 (1928): 27.

50. On the requirement of one year of marriage for admission into the Worms burial society in the 1720s, see A. Unna, ed., *Register of Statutes of the Protocols . . .* (Jerusalem: 1960), pp. 6, 37, 50. On two years of marriage or more, see Halperin, *Constitutiones*, p. 45; Assaf, *Mekorot*, vol. 1, p. 142; Baron, *The Jewish Community*, vol. 2, pp. 38, 92.

51. S. W. Baron, *Social and Religious History of the Jews*, vol. 2 (New York: 1937), p. 112.

52. See I. Abrahams, *Jewish Life in the Middle Ages* (Philadelphia: 1896), p. 107; E. Cohen and E. Horowitz, "In Search of the Sacred: Jews, Christians, and Rituals of Marriage in the Later Middle Ages," *Journal of Medieval and Renaissance Studies* 20 (1990): 241–242 and the sources cited there.

53. See I. Epstein, *The Responsa of Rabbi Simon b. Zemeh Duran* . . . (London: 1930), p. 58 and the responsum cited there, note 10.

54. See J. Katz, "Marriage and Sexual Life among the Jews at the Close of the Middle Ages" (in Hebrew), *Zion* 10 (1944–45): 24.

55. Meir Poppers, *Or Zedikkim* (Hamburg: 1960), p. 39. See also Assaf, *Mekorot*, vol. 1, p. 182.

56. *Minute Book*, Ms. Jerusalem, 4_o 553, 69r (1694). On the connection between marriage and one's standing in the community, see also S. Simonsohn, "The Communal Registers of Verona" (in Hebrew), *Kiryat Sefer* 35 (1959–60): 133, 250.

57. Broadside dated June 30, 1682, Archivo di Stato Verona, A. A. Comune, Proclame e stampe reg. no. 213 c. 410. I thank Professor Y. Yerushalmi for giving me a photograph of this document.

58. Boksenbeim, *Minutes Book of the Jewish Community of Verona*, vol. 1, pp. 148–149, 152.

59. Asher b. Yehiel, Comentary (on Nedarim 37a); Azariah Figo, *Binah le-Ittim* (Lemberg: 1858), sermon 13, p. 74.

60. Quoted in Assaf, *Mekorot*, vol. 1, pp. 76–77. For other comments and policies reflecting the dangers of the street, see pp. 112, 188, 286.

61. *Sefer ha-Hinnukh*, ed. C. Chavel (Jerusalem: 1962). On youthful roaming of the streets on the holidays, compare the comments of Levi's Italian contemporary, Immanuel of Rome, *The Cantos of Immanuel of Rome* (in Hebrew), ed. D. Jarden, vol. 2 (Jerusalem: 1957), p. 489 (canto no. 27).

62. Joseph Karo, *Responsa Avkat Rokhel* (Leipzig: 1859), no. 206. See the comments on this responsum by C. Roth in I. Abrahams, *Jewish Life in the Middle Ages* (revised edition, London: 1932), p. 405 note 4, and correct Manissa for Magnesia. On the Sabbath *after* Purim as a special occasion for youthful exuberance and role reversal, see below.

63. See E. Horowitz, "The Rite to Be Reckless: On the Perpetration and Interpretation of Purim Violence," *Poetics Today* 15 (1994).

64. B. Wachstein, *Urkunden und Akten ʒur Geschichte der Juden in Eisenstadt* (Vienna: 1926), pp. 148–149; Endelman, *Georgian England*, pp. 230–231.

65. I. Rivkind, "A Responsum from R. Moses Provençal on Ball Games" (in Hebrew), *Tarbiʒ* 4 (1933): especially 372; Carpi, *Minutes Book*, vol. 1, pp. 81, 113. On youth and ball playing, see also M. A. Shulvass, *The Jews in the World of the Renaissance*, trans. E. I. Kose (Leiden and Chicago: 1973), p. 176.

66. Nordlingen, *Yosif Ometʒ*, p. 140. For earlier testimony concerning the tendency of Ashkenazic yeshiva students to drink excessively, see M. Güdemann, *Ha-Torah veha-Hayyim be-Arʒot ha-Ma'arav bi-Mei ha-Beinavim*, vol. 3 (Warsaw: 1897–1899), p. 70 (Hebrew trans. of original German, *Geschichte des Erʒiehungswesens und der Kultur der abenlänischen Juden während des Mittelalters*, 3 vols.).

67. See Assaf, *Mekorot*, vol. 1, pp. 121–122 and the sources cited there, as well as Pollack, *Jewish Folkways*, pp. 189–190.

68. See Güdemann, *Ha-Torah*, vol. 3, p. 69; Assaf, *Mekorot*, vol. 1, pp. 30, 111, 118; vol. 4, p. 94; Shulvass, *The Jews in the World of the Renaissance*, p. 176; Horowitz, "A Jewish Youth Confraternity," pp. 44–45.

69. Carpi, *Minutes Book*, vol. 2, p. 361. On the attempt of a sixteenth-century Italian rabbi to justify, on the basis of Jewish sources, the custom of making "rough music" in the case of a widow's remarriage, see Cohen and Horowitz, "In Search of the Sacred," pp. 246–247.

70. The document was published by D. Kaufmann in *Kobeẕ 'al Yad* (Berlin: 1895), p. 6, and is paraphrased in Assaf, *Mekorot*, vol. 1, p. 150.

71. Y. Boksenboim, ed., *Letters of the Rieti Family* (in Hebrew) (Tel Aviv: 1987), nos. 251–252.

72. To Rabbi Mordecai's failure to acknowledge in these accepted ways the particular bond of their kinship, Lattes responded by asking: "Are you from an elevated family and is mine inferior to yours . . . or is your wife refusing to sleep with you?" See Boksenboim, *Letters of Jewish Teachers*, no. 146. In 1603 Simone de Sacerdoti of Alessandria had still not received from his wife's family the entire sum promised as dowry, although by then she had born him three sons. Nonetheless, he was kind enough to leave her the entire sum (350 ducats) in his will. See S. Simonsohn, ed., *The Jews in the Duchy of Milan* (Jerusalem: 1982–1986), pp. 2057–2058.

73. M. Jaffe, *Levush Ateret Zahav* (Kraków: 1594), 192: 3; I. Horowitz, *Shne Luhot ha-Berit* (Amsterdam: 1698).

74. A. Levy, *Die Memoiren des Ascher Levy . . . (1598–1635)*, ed. M. Ginsburger (Berlin: 1913), pp. 7, 11. Early in the eighteenth century, Rabbi Jacob Emden (b. 1697) had a similar experience upon his marriage in Breslau to the granddaughter of Rabbi Naphtali Katz (d. 1719), one of the great rabbis of the day. He had been promised a dowry of 1,000 thalers and received at least 200 less. See J. Emden, *Megillat Sefer*, ed. A. Bick (Jerusalem: 1979), pp. 60–63.

75. M. R. Cohen, trans. and ed., *The Autobiography of a Seventeenth-Century Venetian Rabbi: Leon Modena's "Life of Judah"* (Princeton: 1988), pp. 107–108, 114–115; E. Horowitz, "The Dowering of Brides in the Ghetto of Venice: Between Tradition and Change, Ideals and Reality" (in Hebrew), *Tarbiẕ* 56 (1987): 360–365.

76. On engagements in Italy, which frequently lasted between eighteen and twenty-four months and sometimes longer, see E. Horowitz, "The Dowering of Brides," pp. 357–358. For examples in Ashkenazic society, see that of Asher Levy cited above (note 74) as well as those in B. Z. Abrahams, ed., *The Life of Gluckel of Hameln, (1646–1724) . . .* (New York: 1963), pp. 118–137.

77. *Regolatione della fraterna del K. K. Levantini per maritar Donzelle* (Venice: 1689), p. 25.

78. S. Dubnow, ed., *Pinkas ha-Medinah* . . . (Berlin: 1925), pp. 9, 20; Baron, *The Jewish Community*, vol. 2, pp. 332–333; Ben-Sasson, *Hagut ve-Hanhaga*, p. 157.

79. See D. Avron, *Acta Electorum Communitatis Judaeorum Posnaniensium* (in Hebrew) (Jerusalem: 1967), pp. 1, 15, 151; M. Grunwald, "Die Statuten der Hamburg-Altonaer Gemeinde von 1726," *Mitteilungen der Gesellschaft für jüdische Volkskunde* 11 (1903): 31–32; Pollack, *Jewish Folkways*, p. 32.

80. *Regolatione* (1869), p. 38. On wills, see, for example, the one of 1642 from Verona published by C. Roth, "The Will of a Jewish Businesswoman of the Seventeenth Century" (in Hebrew), *Zion* 2 (1937): 127, 132, and that of Samson Wertheimer of Vienna (1717), published in J. Taglicht, *Nächtlässe der Wiener Juden im 17. und 18. Jahrhundert* (Vienna: 1917), p. 24. On organizing the wedding festivities, see the 1694 regulation from Metz cited in Abrahams, *Jewish Life*, p. 159.

81. Nordlingen, *Yosif Ometz*, pp. 279–291.

82. Ibid., pp. 285–286. He was even opposed to allowing three or more men to remain together with the maidservant, although this was clearly permitted by Jewish law, "for we have heard with our own ears of many indecent acts committed at night as a consequence of some evil men conspiring together."

83. On these meal arrangements in the European Ashkenazic communities of the time, see, for example, Assaf, *Mekorot*, vol. 1, pp. 105, 108, 119; Halperin, *Constitutiones*, index, s.v. *shabatot;* Avron, *Acta Posnansiensium*, index, s.v. *ne'arim.*

84. Nordlingen, *Yosif Ometz*, p. 290. Rabbi Joseph exhorts the householder not to interfere unnecessarily with the yeshiva student's studies, and not to impose on the young man duties beneath his dignity as a scholar—unless, however, they had so agreed in advance.

85. See the excerpt from the *Memoirs of Daniel Mendoza* (London: 1826) in Schwarz, *Memoirs of my People*, pp. 292–295, and see also Endelman, *The Jews of Georgian England*, pp. 188–189.

86. Carpi, *Minutes Book*, vol. 1, pp. 73–74, 77–78, 131. The community, for its part, promised to remain committed to finding her employment elsewhere whenever she left Rabbi Samuel's home.

87. Ibid., pp. 88–89, 193.

88. D. Herlihy and C. Klapisch-Zuber, *Tuscans and Their Families: A Study of the Florentine Catasto of 1427* (New Haven: 1985), p. 136.

89. The figures for the Jewish communities have been compiled on the basis of the data provided in R. Segre, ed., *The Jews in Piedmont*, vol. 3 (Jerusalem: 1986–1990).

90. C. M. Cipolla, *Before the Industrial Revolution: European Society and Economy, 1000–1700* (New York: 1980), pp. 78–79.

91. M. Toch, "The Jewish Community of Nuremberg in the Year 1489: Social and Demographic Structure" (in Hebrew), *Zion* 45 (1980): 65–66.

92. Figures for Alessandria and Ivrea on the basis of censuses of 1734, 1754, 1761, and 1791 are found in Segre, *The Jews in Piedmont*, vol. 3, nos 2841, 3082, 3155, 3397. Figures for Trieste are based on *Tabella delle Case Stabilite e Foresti componenti gli Ebrei abitanti in Trieste,* dated May 4, 1769, in Archivio di Stato di Trieste, supplied to me by Lois Dubin.

93. See R. Mahler, *History of the Jews in Poland* (in Hebrew) (Merhavia: 1946), pp. 284–285; G. D. Hundert, *The Jews in a Polish Private Town: The Case of Opatow in the Eighteenth Century* (Baltimore: 1992), p. 75.

94. See Hundert, *The Jews in a Polish Private Town*, pp. 72–75, who provides a rather interesting transcript of the testimony of one of these women.

95. Luzzatto's case, together with the very detailed testimony of Rachel Foa, appears in Isaac Lampronti, *Pahad Yiẓhak*, vol. 1 (Jerusalem: 1961), p. 301 ff. On the general defenselessness of maidservants and the consequences thereof, compare the comments of Simonsohn, *Mantua*, pp. 543–544 and J. J. Israel, *European Jewry in the Age of Mercantilism, 1550–1750* (Oxford: 1989), p. 201.

96. Figures based on data provided in Segre, *The Jews in Piedmont*, vol. 3, nos. 2841, 3082.

97. Simonsohn, *Mantua*, p. 546.

98. Portaleone, for example, has a maidservant respond to the ardent advances of a manservant who is exhorting her to "feel through all my goods (cf. Gen. 31:37) and touch all that is mine" with the equally resonant words, also derived from the book of Genesis (20:9): "Since I first came to know you, you have done to me things that ought not to be done." In the letters written, during the same period, by members of the Rieti family, we find an equally interesting exchange touching on the (perceived) morals of the servant class. One writer complains to his correspondent about the manservant he had sent him, who had repeatedly seduced his cook (including at least once on a Saturday morning, while the other men were in the synagogue), even after being warned to desist, eventually making her pregnant. The correspondent replied, however, that he was hardly to blame, for it was not he who had impregnated her, nor had he "instilled the burning coal of passion in her bosom, to follow after young men with ready breasts (cf. Ruth 3:10; Ezekiel 16:7)," a passion that, he strongly suggested, using equally allusive biblical language, was endemic to maidservants as a class. see J. Schirmann ed., *The First Hebrew Play: The Comedy of Betrothal* (in Hebrew) (Jerusalem: 1965), p. 38; Boksenboim, *Letters of the Rieti Family,* especially pp. 314–319.

99. *The Cantos,* ed. D. Jarden, vol. 1, p. 115, line 231. See also ibid., p. 110, line 119. On Immanuel's poetry, note Roth, *Renaissance,* pp. 46 and 89 ff.

100. *Responsa of R. Solomon Ibn Adrat* (in Hebrew), (reprint, Benei Berak: 1982), vol. 1, p. 610; vol. 4, p. 314; see also, relatedly, vol. 1, p. 628.

101. The correspondent had mentioned this in connection with his query (answered by Rabbi Asher emphatically in the negative) as to whether one prohibited from marrying a woman on account of having been suspected of illicit involvement with her was permitted to hire her for domestic service. *Responsa of R. Asher b. Yehiel* (in Hebrew), vol. 32 (reprint, Jerusalem: 1971), p. 13.

102. Note, however, Newman, *Spain,* vol. 2, p. 39, who erroneously translates Rabbi Asher's words as: "The Jewish court . . . *is* constrained to compel the man to discharge her."

103. *Responsa of R. Nissim Gerondi* (in Hebrew), ed. L. A. Feldman (Jerusalem: 1984), no. 68.

104. See Alexander Marx, "R. Joseph Arli and R. Yohanan Treves" (in Hebrew), in *Koveẓ Meda'i le-Zekher Moshe Schorr* (New York: 1945), p. 218; C. Roth, *The Jews in the Renaissance* (Philadelphia: 1959), p. 45.

105. See, especially, Roth, *The Jews in the Renaissance,* chapter 4, for the rather Burckhardtian view that "the state of sexual morality among Italian Jewry in the age of the Renaissance . . . certainly fell short of the traditional standard of perfection." What the traditional standard of perfection was, however, remains far from clear. For a critique of Roth and his excessive dependence on Burckhardt, see R. Bonfil, "The Historian's Perception of the Jews in the Italian Renaissance: Towards a Reappraisal," *Revue des études juives* 143 (1984): 59–82.

106. *Responsa of Isaac de Lattes* (in Hebrew), ed. M. Z. Friedlander (Vienna: 1860), pp. 53–56.

107. *Responsa of R. Judah Mintẓ and R. Meir Katẓenellenbogen* (in Hebrew) (Kraków: 1882), part 2, nos. 19, 33. For another instance (in 1541) of marrying off one's concubine to another after she had served both domestic and sexual functions, see Y. Boksenboim, ed., *Responsa Mattanot ba-Adam* (Tel Aviv: 1983), no. 161.

108. Solomon Maimon, *An Autobiography,* trans. J. C. Murray (London: 1888), pp. 59–60 (or see Schwarz, *Memoirs of My People,* pp. 192–193).

109. J. Reischer, *Responsa Shevut Ya'akov,* vol. 2 (1917), no. 112. See also Karz, "Marriage and Family Life," p. 37 and the sources cited in note 94.

110. See the skillful reconstruction of the case, on the basis of a responsum of Rabbi Jacob Moelin, in I. J. Tuval, *Scholars in Their Time: The Religious Leadership of German Jewry in the Late Middle Ages* (in Hebrew) (Jerusalem: 1988), pp. 115–116, 228–130.

111. Nathan and his wife remained in Frankfurt, where in 1431 their household consisted of three children and a maidservant, and where, shortly afterward, he

was appointed rabbi of the community. See ibid., pp. 23–235 for Nathan's biography after the betrothal incident.

112. See Isserlein, *Terumat ha-Deshen* (Warsaw: 1882), part 2, no. 222.

113. This requirement, however, as members of the community must have noticed, was not reinforced with any fine for the offending householder. See Wachstein, *Urkunden und Akten*, pp. 147–149.

114. Y. Bachrach, *Responsa Havot Yair* (reprint, Jerusalem: 1973), no. 196.

115. B. Weinryb, "Studies in the Communal History of Polish Jewry," *Proceedings of the American Academy of Jewish Research* 19 (1950): 40; Hebrew section, pp. 21–22.

116. The Prague decision was made in 1611. See S. Assaf, *Ha-Onashin Aharei Hatimat ha-Talmud* (Jerusalem: 1922), p. 114, and the text published by I. Rivkind in *Reshumot* 4 (1926): 351.

117. Güdemann, *Ha-Torah*, vol. 3, pp. 222–223; Assaf, *Mekorot*, vol. 1, pp. 102–103.

118. A. Marx, "A Seventeenth-Century Autobiography: A Picture of Jewish Life in Bohemia and Moravia," *Jewish Quarterly Review* 8 (1917–18): 291–292 (or see Schwarz, *Memoirs of My People*, p. 106).

119. Marx, "A Seventeen-Century Autobiography," pp. 302–303 (Schwarz, *Memoirs of My People*, pp. 113–114).

5 COURTLY CHIVALRY

1. Jean Flori, *L'Essor de la chevalerie, XIᵉ–XIIᵉ siècles* (Geneva: Droz, 1986).

2. Michel Zink, *Le Moyen Age: Littérature française* (Nancy: Presses Universitaires de Nancy, 1990), p. 44; English edition, *Medieval French Literature: An Introduction*, trans. Jeff Rider (Binghamton, N.Y.: Center for Medieval and Renaissance Texts and Studies, 1995).

3. Dominique Barthélémy, "Note sur l'adoubement dans la France des XIᵉ et XIIᵉ siècles," in H. Dubois and M. Zink, eds., *Les Ages de la vie*, (Paris: 1989), pp. 107–117. I would like to thank the author for sending us this excellent recent study.

4. Theo Venckeleer, *Rollant li proʒ: Contribution à l'histoire de quelques qualifications laudatives en français du Moyen Age* (Paris: Champion, 1974).

5. See the numerous articles and works by Georges Duby and Léopold Genicot, particularly Georges Duby, *Les Trois Ordres ou l'Imaginaire du féodalisme* (Paris: Gallimard, 1978); English edition, *The Three Orders: Feudal Society Imagined*, trans. Arthur Goldhammer (Chicago: University of Chicago Press, 1980).

6. Flori, *L'Essor*, see p. 120 and following for an analysis and references.

7. Emphasis added. References to the *Chanson de Roland* are to the G. Moignet edition (Paris: Bordas, 1969). (Trans. note: Because of the emphasis Ms. Marchello-Nizia places on the particular uses of certain medieval words, my translations of literary passages, such as those from the *Chanson de Roland*, are

rather literal. Published translations exist of several of the chansons de geste and romances mentioned in this chapter, but their aims are often poetic rather than historical. For more aesthetically pleasing versions, the reader is referred to: *The Song of Roland,* trans. Dorothy L. Sayers [Harmondsworth: Penguin Books, 1957]; Gottfried von Strassburg, *Tristan,* trans. A. T. Hatto [Harmondsworth: Penguin Books, 1960], including the *Tristan* of Thomas; Beroul, *The Romance of Tristan,* trans. Alan S. Fedrick [Harmondsworth: Penguin Books, 1970]; Chrétien de Troyes, *Arthurian Romances* [includes "Yvain" and "Lancelot"], trans. W. W. Comfort [London: J. M. Dent, 1963].)

8. Denise McClelland, *Le Vocabulaire des "Lais" de Marie de France* (Ottawa: Ottawa University Press, 1977), p. 146 and 136.

9. Flori, *L'Essor,* p. 304 ff.

10. On this point see, Duby, *The Three Orders.* See also numerous articles by Jean Batany, including "Des trois fonctions aux trois Etats?" *Annales ESC* (1963–1965) "Du *bellator* au *chevalier* dans le schéma des trois ordres," *Actes du 10ᵉ* Congrès national des Sociétés savantes (Paris: B. N., 1978); "Mythes indo-européens ou mythes des indo-européens: le témoignage médiévale," *Annales ESC* (1985). Lastly, see Joël Grisward, *Archéologie de l'épopée médiévale: Structures trifonctionnelles et mythes indo-européens dans le cycle des Narbonnais* (Paris: Payot, 1981).

11. See Marie-Luce Chènerie, *Le Chevalier errant dans les romans arthuriens en vers des XIIᵉ et XIIIᵉ siècles* (Geneva: Droz, 1986). See also, more recently, Paul Zumthor, "De Perceval à Don Quichotte: L'espace du chevalier errant," in *Poétique* 87 (September 1991): 259–269: "Among the several hundred romances composed for public entertainment and edification in diverse European languages during the four centuries (from the twelfth to the sixteenth) in which modern civilization took shape, there are very few that do not contain at least one 'knight errant.'"

12. See Barthélémy, "Note," p. 109; id., *L'Ordre seigneurial, XIᵉ–XIIᵉ siècles* (Paris: Seuil, 1990), p. 190.

13. Jean Flori, "Sémantique et société médiévale: Le verbe *adouber* et son évolution au XIIᵉ siècle," *Annales ESC* 31, no. 2 (1976): 915–940.

14. This tapestry was probably woven in Kent, England, before the end of the eleventh century.

15. Jean-Claude Schmitt, *La Raison des gestes dans l'Occident médiéval* (Paris: Gallimard, 1990), p. 209.

16. Jean Flori, "Du nouveau sur l'adoubement des chevaliers (XIᵉ–XIIIᵉ s.)," *Le Moyen Age* 91, no. 1 (1985): 201–226.

17. Georges Duby, *Guillaume le Maréchal ou le meilleur chevalier du monde* (Paris: Fayard, 1984); English edition, *William Marshall: The Flower of Chivalry,* trans. Richard Howard (New York: Pantheon Books, 1987).

18. In one of the rare cases in which a thirteenth-century romance has a woman as
    its main character, she is disguised as a man. The *Roman de Silence* by Heldris
    of Cornwall contains a most unusual figure: following a serious disagreement
    among vassals, the king of England has made it illegal for a woman to inherit
    from her father. The Count of Cornwall therefore decides that, whatever the
    sex of the child his wife is expecting, they will say it is a boy. In fact it is a girl,
    whom they name Silentius (Silence) and bring up as a boy. In her adolescence,
    Silence is the victim of a debate between Nature and Noreture, nature and
    education. When some minstrels visit the castle, she decides to run away with
    them, still disguised as a man, and acquires a certain renown in this "unisex"
    profession. In further twists of the plot, a queen falls in love with her; finally,
    having given proof of herself in combat, she is made a knight by the king of
    France himself:

> When she was seventeen and a half
> During the feast of Pentecost
> Regardless of whom it might please or pain
> The king dubbed her a knight in Paris . . .
> Silence did brilliantly in the arena
> Tilting between two ranks of fighters at the quintain.
> Never was a woman less hesitant
> To fight in this way.
> Anyone seeing her jousting without a cape,
> Carrying her shield at her side
> Hurtling to attack
> Her lance in position
> Would have been able to say that Education
> May do much against Nature,
> When it thus transforms and trains
> A soft and tender woman.

> *A .XVII. ans e a demi*
> *Tolt droit a une Pentecoste*
> *Cui qu'il soit biel ne cui il coste,*
> *L'adoba li rois a Paris . . .*
> *Entre .II. rens a la quintainne.*
> *Ainc feme ne fu mains laniere*
> *De contoer en tel maniere.*
> *Kil ves joster sans mantel*
> *Et l'escu porter en cantiel*
> *Et faire donques l'ademise,*
> *La lance sor le faltre mise,*
> *Dire pest que Noreture*
> *Puet moult ovrer contre Nature,*
> *Quant ele aprent si et escole*
> *A tel us feme tendre et mole.*

(*Roman de Silence*, ed. Lewis Thorpe, lines 5132–5156)

19. Jean Flori, "Qu'est-ce qu'un *bacheler?* Etude de vocabulaire dans les chansons de geste du XIIe siècle," *Romania* 96 (1975): 290–314.

20. A. Stefanelli, *Der Synonymenreichtum der altfranzösischen Dichtersprache* (Vienna: 1967), p. 69.

21. Jean-Charles Payen, *Littérature française: Le Moyen Age* (Paris: Arthaud, 1984), p. 207.

22. Jean-Charles Payen, "Une poétique du génocide joyeux," *Olifant* 6 (1979): 226–236.

23. Moshe Lazar, *Amour courtois et Fin'amors dans la littérature du XIIe siècle* (Paris: Klincksieck, 1964).

24. This episode is missing in the extant fragments of the romance. But evident traces remain in both Gottfried von Strassburg, who adapted it into middle-high German around 1210, and in the *Cligès* of Chrétien de Troyes, written from an opposing point of view. See Christiane Marchello-Nizia, "L'invention du dialogue amoureux," *Masques et Déguisements dans la littérature médiévale* (Montreal and Paris: Vrin, 1988), pp. 223–231.

25. Reto R. Bezzola, *Les Origines et la Formation de la littérature courtoise en Occident (500–1200)* (Paris: Champion, 1967–68), 4 vols.

26. Edmond Faral, *Recherches sur les sources latines des contes et romans courtois* (Paris: Champion, 1913)

27. See the work by C. Stephen Jaeger, *The Origins of Courtliness: Civilizing Trends and the Formation of Courtly Ideals* (Philadelphia: University of Pennsylvania Press, 1985).

28. *De arte honeste amandi*, book II, chapter 7. On the interpretation of this text, long considered an enigma, see the recent work by Bruno Roy, *Une culture de l'équivoque* (Paris: Champion-Slatkine; Montreal: Presses Universitaires de l'University de Montréal, 1992); see chapter 4 in particular: "Un art d'aimer: pour qui?"

29. Erich Köhler, *L'Aventure chevaleresque: Idéal et réalité dans le roman courtois* (Paris: Gallimard, 1974). (Original German edition, 1956.)

30. *Chanson de Roland*, strophes 168–176; *Chanson de Guillaume* strophes 69–73; *Aliscans* strophes 13–29.

31. Jacques Ribard, *Chrétien de Troyes: Le Chevalier de la Charrette: Essai d'interprétation symbolique* (Paris: Nizet, 1972).

32. Reto Bezzola, "Les neveux," in *Mélanges . . . offerts à Jean Frappier,* vol. 1 (Geneva: Droz, 1970), pp. 88–114.

33. Christiane Marchello-Nizia, "Mort du neveu, meurtre du fils: Les cas 'Tristan,'" to appear in *Mélanges . . . offerts à Georges Duby.*

34. See Claude Lévi-Strauss, *Anthropologie structurale,* vol. 2 (Paris: Gallimard, 1973), pp. 34–35; English edition, *Structural Anthropology,* trans. Monique Layton (Chicago: University of Chicago Press, 1983).

35. Antoine de la Sale, *Jehan de Saintré* ed. J. Misrahi and Charles Knudson (Geneva: Droz, 1967).

36. Laurence Harf-Lancner, *Les fées au Moyen Age: Morgane et Mélusine* (Paris: Champion, 1984).

37. *Les lais anonymes des XIIe et XIIIe siècles* ed. P. O'Hara (Geneva: Droz, 1976).

38. See Christiane Marchello-Nizia, "Amour courtois, société masculine et figures du pouvoir," *Annales ESC* 6 (1981): 969–982. See also Duby, *Guillaume le Maréchal*, p. 59: "There were five who were jealous of Guillaume. . . All five wanted to destroy their companion, because their lord loved him too much. . . In this matter, therefore, everything hinged on love. But let's make no mistake: we are talking about men's love for each other. . . We are beginning to discover that courtly love—the love of which the troubadours and then the *trouvères* sang, the knight's love for his chosen lady—masked what was perhaps the essential; or rather, it projected onto the arena an inverted image of the essential: the amorous exchanges between warriors."

39. Galeholt gives this description of his torment: "A sickness has entered my heart that is destroying me, for I have lost the power to eat and drink and rest in bed." Asked about the nature of this ill, the hermit made this unequivocal reply: "This sickness is called the malady of love." (*Lancelot*, vol. 1, p. 38.)

40. See John Boswell, *Christianity, Social Tolerance and Homosexuality: Gay People in Western Europe from the Beginning of the Christian Era to the Fourteenth Century* (Chicago: University of Chicago Press, 1980). In texts in the vernacular, homosexuality is no sooner mentioned than it is immediately rejected and condemned.

6 A FLOWER OF EVIL

1. G. Budé, *Le Livre de l'institution du Prince* (Paris: 1547), p. 54.

2. L. B. Alberti, *I Libri della famiglia*, ed. R. Romano and A. Tenenti (Turin: 1969), pp. 23, 24, 25, for example.

3. The reader may refer to the article "Aetas" in G. Facciolati, E. Forcellini and G. Furlanetti, *Lexicon totius latinatis*, vol. 1, (Padua: 1864), pp. 137–138. For these definitions in the High Middle Ages, see P. Riché, "L'enfant dans le haut Moyen Age," *Annales de démographie historique* (1973), "Enfant et sociétés," pp. 95–98. For their validity in Renaissance Italy, see O. Niccoli, "Compagnie di bambini nell'Italia del Rinascimento," *Rivista storica italiana* 101, no. 2 (1989): 346–374.

4. To give just one significant quotation: *"E note che furono stimati seimila fanciugli o più, tutti da 5 o 6 anni insino in 16."* (It was thought there were six thousand or more boys, all aged between five or six and sixteen.) *Diario fiorentino dal 1450 al 1516 di Luca Landucci continuato da un anonimo fino al 1542* (Florence: 1883),

p. 125. English edition, *A Florentine Diary from Fourteen Fifty to Fifteen Sixteen*, trans. Alice De Rosen Jervis (New York: Ayer, 1977).

5. Thus Landucci, concerning the son of the King of Naples, writes: *"Aveva 12 o 13 anni questo garzonetto"* (This boy was twelve or thirteen). Ibid., p. 5.

6. For example, *"un garzonetto d'anni 23 in circa,"* *"giovanetto di circa 22 anni."* (A boy of about twenty-three, a young man of about twenty-two). Ibid., pp. 14, 60.

7. Archivio di Stato di Venezia (hereinafter, ASV), *Avogaria di Comun (Adv. di C.)*, Raspe, reg. 14, f. 16r.

8. Since the first edition of Philippe Ariès's book, *L'enfant et la vie familiale sous l'Ancien Régime* (Paris: 1960), numerous works have been published, including the English translation, *Centuries of Childhood: A Social History of Family Life* (New York: McGraw-Hill, 1965). From the now large bibliography, I shall cite only a certain number of works devoted mainly to childhood in the geographical region examined here: C. Klapisch-Zuber, *Women, Family and Ritual in Renaissance Italy* (Chicago: 1985), and, by the same author, *La Maison et le nom: Stratégies et rituels dans l'Italie de la Renaissance* (Paris: 1990).

9. L. Banchi, ed., *Le prediche volgari di San Bernardino da Siena dette nella piazza del campo l'anno 1427*, vol. 1 (Sienna: 1880), p. 131.

10. Ibid., vol. 3, p. 261.

11. See the analysis of emancipation by D. Herlihy and C. Klapisch, *Les Toscans et leurs familles: Une étude du catasto florentin de 1427* (Paris: 1978); English edition, *The Tuscans and Their Families: A Study of the Florentine Catasto to 1427* (New Haven: Yale University Press, 1985).

12. T. Kuehn, *Emancipation in Late Medieval Florence* (New Brunswick: 1982), pp. 51–55 and 88–89.

13. ASV, *Consiglio dei Dieci (CdX)*, Miste, reg. 11, f. 83r; or reg. 13, f. 94v.

14. Ibid., reg. 10, f. 70r. For an example of the rapidity with which this legislation was applied, see ibid., reg. 11, f. 3v.

15. Herlihy and Klapisch, *Les Toscans et leurs familles*, p. 399.

16. P. Gori, *Le feste fiorentini attraverso i secoli: Le feste per San Giovanni* (Florence: 1926), pp. 39–44.

17. M. Sanudo, *I Diarii* (Venice: 1886), vol. 13, col. 50.

18. Young men had to be eighteen to participate in the Balla d'Oro. On this problem, see J. E. Law, "Age Qualification and the Venetian Constitution: The Case of the Capello Family," *Papers of the British School at Rome* 39 (1971): 125–137.

19. Proportionately, one-fifth of registered young aristocrats.

20. Or they were elected as attorneys to one of the civil courts.

21. Here I am following the analysis by S. Chojnacki, "Political Adulthood in Fifteenth-Century Venice," *American Historical Review* 91, no. 4 (1986): 791–810.

Chojnacki links the function of the Balla d'Oro in the fifteenth century to other contemporary measures designed to protect and better define the status and identity of the dominant class.

22. Ibid., p. 805.

23. For the specific role of the relatives who helped their young kinsmen enter a political career, see S. Chojnacki, "Kinship Ties and Young Patricians in Fifteenth-Century Venice," *Renaissance Quarterly* 38 (1935): 240–270.

24. R. Trexler analyzes them the same way he analyzes other moments in the fifteenth century when the problem of young men's participation in city affairs arises: R. Trexler, *Public Life in Renaissance Florence* (New York: 1981), pp. 391–393.

25. R. Finlay, "The Venetian Republic as a Gerontocracy: Age and Politics in the Renaissance," *Journal of Medieval and Renaissance Studies* 8 (1978): 157–178.

26. For equivalent quotations by Cavalcanti and Machiavelli, see Trexler, *Public Life in Renaissance Florence*, p. 392.

27. If some of them were younger than twenty-five, others were well into their thirties. See Chojnacki, "Political Adulthood in Fifteenth-Century Venice," p. 793.

28. On problems concerning the ritualization of the coming of age, consult S. Chojnacki, "Measuring Adulthood: Adolescence and Gender in Renaissance Venice," *Journal of Family History* 17, no. 4 (1992): 371–395. The article was not available when this chapter was written.

29. Dino Compagni, *Cronica*, ed. G. Luzzatto (Turin: 1978). p. 105.

30. Domenico Morosini, *De bene instituta re publica*, ed. C. Finzi (Milan: 1969). For an analysis of this text, see G. Cozzi, "Domenico Morosini e il *De bene instituta re publica*," *Studi veneziani* 12 (1970): 405–458.

31. *Tutte le opere di Giovanni Boccaccio*, ed. V. Branca (Milan: 1976), vol. 4, *Decameron*, p. 109. Ms. Crouzet-Pavan appears to be referring to the famous story of Federigo and the falcon, Day Five, Ninth Tale, in the *Decameron;* for an English version, see the translation by G. H. McWilliam (Harmondsworth: Penguin Books, 1970), p. 464 (Trans. note).

32. G. Sercambi, *Il Novelliere*, ed. L. Rossi (Rome: 1974), vol. 2, pp. 135–136.

33. *Tables florentins: Ecrire et manger avec Franco Sacchetti*, ed. J. Brunet and O. Redon (Paris: 1984), pp. 17–18.

34. F. C. Lane, *Andrea Barbarigo, Merchant of Venice* (Baltimore: 1944); R. Delort, "Un aspect du commerce vénitien au XVème siècle: Andrea Barbarigo et le commerce des fourrures (1430–1440)," *Le Moyen Age,* 71 (1965): 29–70, 247–273.

35. *Diario fiorentino*, pp. 1–4.

36. See, for example, the introduction to *Prediche alle donne del secolo XIII*, ed. C. Casagrande (Milan: 1978), pp. xii–xiv.

37. Banchi, *Le prediche volgari*, vol. 2, p. 353: *"Cosi dico simile di voi, donne, che avete dimostrato di volermi tanto bene"* (I say this of you, ladies, that you have shown me much goodwill). Or, *"Voi donne, suore mie"* (You ladies, my sisters), vol. 2, p. 6; vol. 3, p. 184.

38. P. Villari and E. Casanova, eds., *Scelta di prediche e scritti di Fra Girolamo Savonarola con nuovi documenti intorno alla sua vita* (Florence: 1898). In English, P. Villari has published *The Life and Times of Girolamo Savonarola*, (reprint, 1969), 2 vols. (Trans. note).

39. Ibid., p. 43 for example.

40. ASV, *CdX*, Miste, reg. 19, f. 178r.

41. ASV, *Provveditori alle Pompe*, B. 3 (1459), unpaginated.

42. Ibid. (1472).

43. Ibid. (1460).

44. For the repetition and enlargement of this text (anyone over twelve forbidden to wear certain clothes, furs, pearls, silver ornaments, and so on), see ASV, *Senato*, Misti, reg. 29, ff. 143v, 144r.

45. *Juvenes habentes societates, quod in conviviis eorum faciunt cenas et pastus adeo sumptuosus*, ASV, *Provveditori alle Pompe* B. 3, (1459); ASV, *Senato*, Terra, reg. 6, f. 193v; reg. 9, f. 50v; reg. 29, ff. 196v, 197r.

46. ASV *Senato*, Terra, reg. 13, f. 103 v, for example.

47. ASV *Provveditore alle Pompe*, B. 3 (1459). For other similar exmples, see ibid. (1459).

48. Banchi, *Le prediche volgari*, vol. 3, p. 189.

49. ASV, *Senato*, Terra, reg. 4, f. 142v (1460).

50. ASV, *Provveditori alle Pompe*, B. 3 (1460).

51. ASV, *CdX*, Miste, reg. 27, f. 11v.

52. Banchi, *Le prediche volgari*, vol. 2, p. 108.

53. Ibid., vol. 2, p. 142.

54. San Bernardino reminded the *"smemorati"* and *"impaʒati"* that *"la fornicaʒione e l'andare alle meretrici è peccato mortale"* (Fornication and going to prostitutes was mortal sin), ibid., vol. 2, p. 138.

55. E. Pavan, "Police des moeurs, société et politique à Venise à la fin du Moyen Age," *Revue Historique* 536 (Oct.–Dec. 1980): 241–288; R. C. Trexler, "La prostitution à Florence au XVème siècle," in *Annales ESC* 6 (1972): 1329–1350.

56. J. Rossiaud, "Fraternités de jeunesse et niveaux de culture dans les villes du sud-est à la fin du Moyen Age," *Cahiers d'histoire*, 21, no. 1–2 (1976): 76–102; id., "Prostitution, jeunesse et société dans les villes du sud-est au XVème siècle," *Annales ESC* 2 (1976): 289–325, reprinted in *La prostitution médiévale* (Paris: 1988), chapter 2.

57. There being a large bibliography on this subject, I shall simply list some basic works, such as N. Z. Davis, *Society and Culture in Early Modern France: Eight*

Essays (Stanford: Stanford University Press, 1975); M. Grinberg, "Carnaval et société urbaine, XIVème–XVIème siècles: La royaume dans la ville," *L'Ethnologie française* 4, no. 3 (1974): 215–244; J. Le Goff and J. C. Schmitt, eds., *Le Charivari* (Paris: 1981); N. Pellegrin, *Les bachellerie: Organisations et fêtes de la jeunesse dans le Centre Ouest, XVème–XVIIIème siècle* (Poitiers: 1982); C. Ginzburg, *Storia notturna: Una decifrazione del sabba* (Turin: 1989).

58. E. Pavan, "Recherches sur la nuit vénitienne," *Journal of Medieval History* 7 (1981): 339–356; E. Crouzet-Pavan, "Violence, société et pouvoir à Venise (XIVème–XVème siècles): forme et évolution de rituels urbains," *MEFRM* 96, no. 2 (1984): 903–936.

59. ASV, *Adv. di C.*, Raspe, reg. 9, f. 23r; reg. 10, f. 37r; reg. 13, f. 39r; reg. 14, f. 47r.

60. Ibid., reg. 15, ff. 30v–31r.

61. Ibid., reg. 9, f. 51r; reg. 9, f. 99v; reg. 8, f. 80r; reg. 18, f. 42r.

62. ASV, *Quarantia Criminale*, reg. 18, f. 43r.

63. ASV, *CdX*, Miste, reg. 16, f. 111r.

64. ASV, *Adv. di C.*, Raspe, reg. 5, f. 1v.

65. Ibid., reg. 8, ff. 25rv; reg. 9, f. 61r; reg. 18, ff. 64r, 83v, 87v; reg. 20, ff. 31r, 162v. For a study of the *mattinata* and various behavior producing noise and music in Italy, see C. Klapisch-Zuber, "La *mattinata* médiévale en Italie," in Le Goff and Schmitt, *Le Charivari;* reprinted in Klapisch-Zuber, *La maison et le nom.*

66. ASV, *Adv. di C.*, Raspe, reg. 1, f. 11v.

67. For the example of Florence (institution of the Ufficiali di Notte after the magistracy of the Otto di Guardia was created), see G. Antonelli, "La magistratura degli Otto di Guardia a Firenze," in *ASI* 92 (1954): 3–40; M. Becker, "Changing Patterns of Violence and Justice in Fourteenth and Fifteenth Century Florence," *Comparative Studies in Society and History* 18 (1976): 281–295; S. K. Cohn, *The Laboring Classes in Renaissance Florence* (New York: 1980); A. Zorzi, "Aspetti e problemi della giustizia penale nella Repubblica fiorentina," *ASI* 553 (1987): 393–453 and 527–578; M. J. Rocke, "Il controllo dell'omosessualità a Firenze nel XV secolo: Gli 'Ufficiali di Notte,'" *Quaderni storici* 66, no. 3 (1987): 701–723. For the crisis in the old system, see A. Zorzi, "Contrôle social, ordre public et répression judiciare à Florence à l'époque communale: Eléments et problèmes," in *AESC* (1990): 1169–1188.

68. *Le novelle di Franco Sacchetti*, vol. 2, ed. O. Gigli (Florence: 1851), p. 11; English edition, *Tales from Sacchetti*, trans. Mary G. Steegman (London: J. M. Dent, 1908).

69. *Cronache senesi*, ed. A. Lisini and F. Iacometti, *RIS*, new ed., vol. 15, part 5 (Bologna: 1933–1934), pp. 442–451, "Cronaca senese di Agnolo di Tura del Grasso."

70. Ibid., *"E così durò la corte bandita . . . a fare onore a chi vi capita, per modo che fu*

la più nominata corte di Toscana." The Italian word *corte*, court, designated at this time an assembly of nobles and knights, on the occasion of festivities or ceremonies, during which balls and banquets, tournaments, jousts and tests of ability took place (Trans. note).

71. Here I refer the reader to two extremely valuable studies by S. Gasparri: "Note per uno studio della cavalleria in Italia," *La Cultura* 25, no. 1 (1988): 3–38, and "I rituali della cavalleria cittadina: Tradizioni militare e superiorità sociale nell'Italia del Duecento," in J. Chiffoleau, L. Martines and A. Paravicini Bagliani, eds., *Riti e Rituali nelle società medievale* (Spoleto: 1994), pp. 97–114.

72. *Chronicon Mutinense Iohannis de Baʒano (aa 1188–1363)*, ed. T. Casini, *RIS*, new ed., vol. 15, part 4 (Bologna: 1917), p. 40.

73. See, for example, the wedding in 1316 of the daughter of King Robert, in *Cronache senesi*, p. 111, "Cronaca senese . . . di autore anonimo del secolo XIV."

74. *Chronicon Parmense ab anno MXXXVIII usque ad annum MCCCXXXVIII*, ed. G. Bonazzi, *RIS*, new edition, vol. 9, part 9 (Città di Castello: 1902), p. 43.

75. Fra Adamo di Salimbene, "Chronica," ed. A. Bertani, in *Monumenta ad provincias parmensem et placentinam pertinentia* (Parma: 1857).

76. *Chronicon Parmense*, vol. 9, part 9, p. 80.

77. The unknighted sons of knights were involved: "multi ex domicellis," Gasparri, "Note per uno studio della cavalleria," p. 18.

78. Quoted in L. A. Muratori, *De spectaculis et ludis publicis Medii Aevi. Antiquitates Italicae Medii Aevi sive dissertationes, Dissertatio vigesimanona*, vol. 2 (Milan: 1739), col. 838–839.

79. See for example, the remark by Dino Compagni, *Cronica*, ed. G. Luzzatto (Turin: 1978), p. 195: *"Ma i Cavalcanti, che era potente famiglia, e circa LX uomini erano da portare arme"* (But the Cavalcanti were a powerful family, and had around sixty men able to bear arms).

80. See another remark by Compagni: *"Ma il Baschiera, che era quasi capitano, vinto più da volontà che da ragione, come giovane"* (But Baschiera, who was like a captain, was ruled more by will than reason, as a young man). Ibid., p. 145.

81. *Cronache senesi*, p. 204, "Cronaca senese di Paolo di Tommaso Montauri."

82. Thus, in Pistoia: "E mandarono fuori della città tutti li fanciulli e le fanciulle piccoli" (And they sent all the little boys and girls out of the city), *Storie pistoresi*, ed. S. Adrasto Barbi, *RIS*, new ed., vol. 11, part 5 (Citta di Castellò: 1907), p. 45.

83. Ibid., p. 110.

84. *Cronache senesi*, p. 582, "Cronaca senese di Donato di Neri."

85. Ibid., pp. 590–591.

86. Ibid., p. 711, "Cronaca senese di Paolo di Tommaso Montauri."

87. On the games, see T. Szabo, "Das Turnier in Italien," in J. Fleckenstein, ed., *Das ritterliche im Mittelalter: Beitrage ʒu einer vergleichenden Formen- und Verhal-*

tensgeschichte des Rittertums (Göttingen: 1985), pp. 344–370; A. Benvenuti Papi, "Dell'astiludio: I giochi cavallereschi tra memoria e tradizione," in *Riti e cerimoniali dei giochi cavallereschi nell'Italia medievale e moderna* (Ascoli: 1989), pp. 19–30. I was unable to consult the volume entitled *La civiltà del torneo (sec. XII–XVII): Giostre e tornei fra Medioevo ed età moderna* (Narni: 1990).

88. J.-C. Maire Vigueur, "Un jeu bien tempéré: Le *Ludus Battaglie* de Pérouse," in *Mélanges offerts à G. Duby*, vol. 2 (Aix-èn-Provence: 1992), pp. 195–208.

89. *Cronache senesi*, p. 71, "Cronaca senese di autore anonimo . . ." (1286).

90. Ibid., p. 711, "Cronaca senese di Paolo di Tommaso Montauri" (1381).

91. Compagni, *Cronica*, pp. 14, 78.

92. *Alle bocche della Piazza: Diario di un anonimo fiorentino (1381–1401)*, A. Molho and F. Sznura, eds. (Florence: 1986), pp. 54–55, 62, 74, 90, 104, 135–136, 215.

93. ASV, *C. Leggi*, B. 303, fasc. 1, f. 35r.

94. ASV, *Dieci*, Miste, reg. 9, f. 114r.

95. *Le novelle di Franco Sacchetti*, vol. 2, pp. 11–12.

96. For an analysis of the theses of Marc Bloch, who argues that nobility is truly defined and affirmed on the basis of chivalrous rites, see G. Tabacco, "Su nobiltà e cavalleria nel medioevo: Un ritorno a Marc Bloch?" *Rivista storia italiana* 91 (1979): 5–25. For a more complex interpretation of these problems, see Gasparri, "Note per uno studio della cavalleria," pp. 9–10.

97. *Cronache senesi*, pp. 590–591, "Cronaca senese di Donato di Neri."

98. *Le novelle di Franco Sacchetti*, p. 12.

99. See two passages concerning the Cerchi: *"Una famiglia che si chiamavano I Cerchi (uomini di basso stato, ma buoni mercantati e gran ricchi, e vestivano bene, e teneano molti famigli e cavalli, e aveano bella apparenza), alcuni di loro comperorono il palagio de'conti . . . i quali erano più antichi di sangue, ma non si ricchi"* (A family called Cerchi—men of low condition, but good merchants and extremely rich, well-dressed, with many family members and horses, and handsome in appearance—some of them bought the palace of the counts . . . who were of more ancient lineage, but less rich), Compagni, *Cronica*, p. 45; and on the battle of Campaldino: *"Molto bene provò messer Vieri de' Cerchi et uno suo figlio cavaliere alla costa di sé"* (Vieri de' Cerchi fought very well, and one of his sons, a knight, who fought beside him), ibid., p. 23.

100. Compagni, *Cronica*, pp. 21–23. This scene has been analyzed by F. Cardini, *Quell'antica festa crudele: Guerra et cultura dall'eta feudale alle grande rivoluzione* (Florence: 1982), p. 44.

101. Rolandinus Patavinus, *Chronica in factis et circa facta Marchiae Trivixianae (aa. ci. 1200–1262)*, ed. A. Bonardi, *RIS*, new edition (Città di Castello: 1905–1908); English edition, Rolando Patavino, *Chronicles of the Trevisan March*, trans. Joseph R. Berrigan (Lawrence, Ks.: Coronado Press, 1980). For a study of this

chronicle, see G. Arnaldi, "Studi sui cronisti della Marca trivigiana nell'eta di Ezzelino da Romano," *Studi Storici* 48–50 (Rome: 1963).

102. For an analysis of different episodes and significant behavior in this courtly war, see Gasparri, "Note per uno studio della cavalleria," pp. 12–16.

103. For the analysis of this historiographic theme, see: G. Salvemini, *Magnati e popolani in Firenze dal 1280 al 1295,* new ed. (Milan: 1966); and, by the same author, *La dignità cavalleresca nel Comune di Firenze e altri scritti,* new ed. (Milan: 1972); N. Ottokar, *Il comune di Firenze alla fine del Dugento* (reprint, Turin: 1962); S. Raveggi, M. Tarassi, D. Medici, and P. Parenti, *Ghibellini, guelfi e popolo grasso: I detentori del potere politico a Firenze nella seconda metà del Dugento* (Florence: 1978). For the other communes, see U. G. Mondolfo, *Il Populus a Siena fino alla riforma anti-magnatizia del 1277* (Genoa: 1911); G. Fasoli, "Ricerche sulla legislazione antimagnatiza nei comuni dell'alta e medi Italia," *Rivista di storia del diritto italiano* 12 (1939), republished in *Scritti e storia medievale,* F. Bocchi, A. Carile, and A. I. Pini, eds. (Bologna: 1974); E. Cristiani, *Nobiltà e popolo nel Comune di Pisa: Dalle origini del Podestariato alla Signoria dei Donoratico* (Naples: 1972).

104. A. M. Enriques, "La vendetta nella vita e nella legislazione fiorentina," *ASI,* ser. 7, 19–20 (1933): 85–146 and 167–257.

105. See, for example, the Velluti-Manelli vendetta.

106. *Storie pistoresi,* pp. 4–5.

107. Compagni, *Cronica,* pp. 48–49.

108. Ibid, p. 194.

109. See the Florentine statutes of 1322 to 1325.

110. ASV, *Collegio,* Notatorio, reg. 1, ff. 9rv.

111. ASV, *M. C.,* Pilosus, f. 23v; *M. C.,* Novella, ff. 1v, 68v; *Secreta,* capitolare dei capisestieri, f. 17v.

112. Rolandinus Patavinus, *Cronica . . . Marchie Trivixianae,* pp. 24–25.

113. For an analysis of this episode, see A. Marchesan, *Treviso medievale* (Treviso: 1923); G. Folena, "Tradizioni e cultura trobadorica nelle corti e nella città venete," in Arnaldi and Pastore Stocchi, *Storia della cultura veneta,* vol. 1, "Dalle origini al Trecento" (Vicenza: 1976), pp. 453–562; L. Bortolatto, ed., *Il Castello d'amore: Treviso e la civiltà cortese* (Treviso: 1986).

114. Rolandinus Patavinus, *Cronica . . . Marchiae Trivixianae,* book 1, pp. 22–23. For an analysis of this episode, which Rolandino presents as the last fine days of the March, before the warlike ventures of the da Romano family, see G. Arnaldi and L. Capo, "I cronisti di Venezia e della Marca Trevigiana dalle origini alla fine del secolo XIII," in Arnaldi and Pastore Stocchi, *Storia della cultura veneta,* vol. 1, pp. 403–405.

115. At the joust held in Siena in 1225, the first prize was a fine horse with silk

trappings and a steel cuirass; the second and third prizes consisted of armor. *Cronache senesi,* p. 47, "Cronaca di anonimo."

116. Ibid., p. 65.

117. See here F. Cardini, "Concetto di cavalleria e mentalità cavalleresca nei romanzi e nei cantari fiorentini," in *I ceti dirigenti nella Toscana tardo communale, Atti del III Convegno, 1980* (Florence: 1983), pp. 157–192, especially p. 173.

118. This is the hypothesis advanced by Cardini, ibid., pp. 176–177.

119. According to Giovanni Villani's own notes.

120. The society was founded by Stoldo Giacoppi de Rossi. On this lineage and the governing Guelf elite, see Raveggi and Tarassi, *Ghibellini, guelfi, e popolo grasso,* chapter 3.

121. Here I am following the life of San Tommaso da Celano, quoted in A. Fortini, *Nuova vita di San Francesco,* vol. 3 (Assisi: 1959), pp. 113–114, "Appendix: le fonti, Questioni francescane."

122. *"Propter quod multoties arguebatur a parentibus dicentibus ei, quod tam magnas expensas in se et in aliis faceret, ut non eorum filius, sed cui usdem magni principis videretur"* (On account of which his parents complained repeatedly that he would spend so much on this and other things that he would seem not to be their son, but the son of a great prince.), quoted in Fortini, *Nuova vita di San Francesco,* p. 114.

123. Compare with Guillaume le Maréchal: *"Gentillesse est nourrie en l'hôtel de largesse"* (Gentility is nurtured in the house of generosity), Georges Duby, *Guillaume le Maréchal ou le meilleur chevalier du monde* (Paris: 1984), p. 108; English edition, *William Marshall: The Flower of Chivalry,* trans. Richard Howard (New York: Pantheon Books, 1987).

124. A. Lazzarini, "La cultura delle signorie venete e i poeti di corte," in Arnaldi and Pastore Stocchi, *Storia della cultura veneta,* vol. 2, *Il Trecento* (Vicenza: 1976), pp. 477–516.

125. Muratori, *De spectaculis,* col. 840.

126. A. Limentani, "Martin da Canal et *Les estoires de Venise,*" in Arnaldi and Pastore Stocchi *Storia della cultura veneta,* vol. 1, pp. 598–599.

127. For the ventures of the da Romano family and their effect on the March, according to Rolandino, see Arnaldi and Capo, "I cronisti di Venezia," pp. 402–404.

128. Martin da Canal, *Les Estoires de Venise: Cronaca veneziana in lingua francese dalle origini al 1275,* ed. A. Limentani (Florence: 1972), p. 70.

129. F. Petrarca, *Lettere senili,* vol. 1, ed. G. Fracassetti, (Florence: 1869), IV, 3.

130. *De pompe ducatus Venetorum di A, Marini,* ed. A Segarrizzi. (Venice: 1903), "nozze Pavanello-Vittorelli." This little work was probably written at the very beginning of the fifteenth century.

131. *Diario fiorentino,* p. 50.

132. *"Ut autem a puericia melius doceantur ad bellum, singulis annis a Kalendis Ianuarii
    . . . quedam spectacula faciunt, que vulgo bataliole, sed latine convenientius bellicula
    nuncupantur"* (In order, however, to better teach the youth about war, each year
    in the month of January they held these spectacles, which in the vulgar tongue
    were called "bataliole," but more appropriately "bellicula" in Latin), *Anonymi
    Ticinensis, Liber de laudibus civitatis Ticinensis,* ed. R. Maiocchi and F. Quin-
    tavalle, *RIS,* new ed., vol. 11, part 1 (Città di Castello: 1903), pp. 25–26.
133. It is not necessary to explain the extraordinary durability of these games
    through purely functionalist criteria, such as military training.
134. The text by Galvaneus Flamma is quoted in Muratori, *De spectaculis,* col. 833.
135. Gasparri, "Note per uno studio della cavalleria," p. 33.
136. Maire Vigueur, "Un jeu," pp. 14–15, a study of the *ludus battaglie* in Perugia.
137. *A LXX annis infra et a XVI supra.*
138. The oath of the *capicontrade* is quoted in P. Molmenti, *Storia di Venezia nella
    vita privata,* vol. 1 (Trieste: 1978), pp. 507–508.
139. ASV, *Dieci,* Miste, reg. 5, f. 32r; reg. 6, ff. 24v, 132r.
140. Ibid., reg. 6, ff. 130v–131r. *Palio,* literally, is a prize given for a competition such
    as a race. A modern example is the famous *palio* of Siena, a horserace held in
    the central square. (Trans. note.).
141. Ibid., reg. 10, f. 56v; reg. 16, f. 69v.
142. Ibid., reg. 24, f. 164v.
143. No doubt due to contemporary calendrical changes in the organization of the
    maritime season. In the fifteenth century, young noblemen still often served as
    crossbowmen on Venetian vessels.
144. ASV, *Dieci,* Miste, reg. 16, f. 26r; reg. 18, f. 42v; reg. 23, f. 13r; reg. 24, f. 39r.
145. Ibid., reg. 25, ff. 97rv.
146. Ibid., reg. 24, f. 146r.
147. Ibid., reg. 24, f. 164v.
148. Ibid., reg. 25, f. 59r.
149. M. E. Mallet and J. R. Hale, *The Military Organisation of a Renaissance State:
    Venice c. 1400 to 1617* (Cambridge: 1984).
150. On the vogue of regattas, see M. Sanudo, *De origine, situ et magistratibus urbis
    Venete ovvero La città di Venetia (1493–1530),* ed. A. Caracciolo Arico (Milan:
    1980), p. 62.
151. Beyond the etymology proposed by M. Sanudo for the bridge of the San Zulian
    war, we may quote A. Caravia, *La verra antiqua dei Castellani, Canaruoli e Gnatti*
    (Venice: 1550); Anonymous, *Quattro canti in ottava rima delle Battaglie fatte sopra
    li ponit di Venezia in San Zulian, San Barnaba, Crocichieri e San Marcuola* (Venice:
    1546).
152. As, for example, during the visit of Henri III.
153. "This war . . . was formerly conducted in winter in a friendly manner, with

blunt sticks, and it was tolerated because that was how youth exercised." *Le feste e trionfi fatti dalla Serenissima Signoria di Venetia nella felice venuta di Henrico III descritti da M. Rocco Benedetti* (Venice: 1574).

154. Ibid.

155. Quoted in Fortini, *Nuova vita di San Francesco*, pp. 126–127. These societies seem to have had a territorial basis.

156. Including the company del Sasso, ibid.

157. L. Venturi, *Le compagnie della calza, Secoli XV–XVI.* Extract from *Nuovo Archivio veneto*, ed. Filippi, vol. 16, part 2, (reprint, Venice: 1983).

158. The decrees of the Senate and the Council thus quote the *"Juvenes habentes societates,"* the *"societates nobilium nostrorum"* (young men having societies; societies of our nobles). Only in 1497 do we find the first mention, in Venetian sources, of *"nobiles nostri qui sunt in societatibus a caliga"* (our nobles who are in societies of the shoe) from the name of the distinctive item of clothing, the *calza*, worn by members of these societies; Venturi, *Le compagnie della calza*, p. 49.

159. These letters have been published by F. Corner, in *Opuscula quattuor* (Venice: 1758), following the *De Francisco Duce Venetiarum*.

160. See Sanudo, *Diarii*, vol. 6, col. 154; vol. 12, col. 16; vol. 25, col. 493; vol. 27, col. 255; vol. 28, col. 299; vol. 36, col. 457–459, for different examples.

161. See, for example, A. Tenenti, "L'uso scenografico degli spazi pubblici: 1490–1510," in *Tiziano e Venezia* (Vicenza: 1980), pp. 21–26.

162. To give one example among numerous others: *"Avanti di Carnevale si debe fare una festa"* (Before the Carnival there must be festivities), Statute of the Modesti.

163. In the first decades of the sixteenth century, the governing elite no longer participated directly in the ritual of Fat Thursday (Giovedi grasso), in which a bull and twelve pigs were decapitated and their quarters immediately distributed among the nobility, to celebrate Venice's victory over the patriarch of Aquilea.

164. The company of the Modesti was valid for eight years.

165. As Fortini tends to assert, for Assisi.

166. This is how J. Rossiaud analyzes the abbeys in southwestern France.

167. Once the abbey existed, the communal council no longer renewed the prohibitions, frequently renewed in the past, against the charivari. A. Barbero, "La violenza organizzata: L'abbazia degli stolti a Torino fra quattro e cinquecento," *Bollettino storico-bibliografico subalpino* 88 (1990): 387–453.

168. The study by E. Grendi, which appeared after this text was written, shows that in Genoa the *società dei giovani* was organized alongside official cadres and social groups. In fact it allowed intergenerational bonds to form and played an active role in ceremonies. Its role diminished after the beginning of the sixteenth century, because the public authorities regained control of this ceremonial

sphere. E. Grendi, "La società dei giovani a Genova fra il 1460 e la riforma del 1528," *Quaderni storici* 8, no. 2 (1992): 509–528.

169. Large companies of flagellants who played a role of prime importance in the religious and social life of Venice.

170. *"Fece la riforma delle donne et degli fanciuli, che fu opera santissima e di grandissima importanza a tutta la città di Fiorenza"* (He reformed women and little boys, which was a most holy work of great importance to the entire city of Florence). Here I am using the chronicle of Simone Filippi, fragments of which have been published in Villari and Casanova, *Scelte di prediche*, pp. 476–477; see also *La vita del beato Ieronimo Savonarola scritta da un anonimo del secolo XVI*, ed. P. Ginori Conti (Florence: 1937). For an analysis of the role of children and adolescents, see R. C. Trexler, "Ritual in Florence: Adolescence and Salvation in the Renaissance," in C. Trinkaus and H. A. Oberman, eds., *The Pursuit of Holiness in Late Medieval and Renaissance Religion*, (Leyde: 1974), pp. 200–264.

171. *Diario fiorentino*, pp. 123–124.

172. The reader is referred here to Niccoli, *Compagnie di bambini;* for a study of violence by children in France, see D. Crouzet, *Les Guerriers de Dieu: La violence au temps des troubles de religion (vers 1525–vers 1610)*, vol. 1 (Seyssel: 1990), pp. 85–91.

173. *Diario fiorentino*, p. 124: *"Si ragunorono le schiere in 4 quartieri di Firenze, ogni quartiere ebbe la sua bandiera"* (The troops gathered in four districts of Florence, each district had its own standard); p. 127: *"e questo facevano ogni quartiere";* *"tenevano in terrore"* (and all districts did this; held in terror); Villari and Casanova, *Scelte di prediche*, p. 477.

174. *Diario fiorentino*, p. 126.

175. Villari and Casanova, *Scelte di prediche*, pp. 480, 484, 485.

176. *"Poi il fiore della gioventù firentina . . . Et perche erono ricchi et nobili si tiravano dietro gran seguito degli altri gioveni simili loro"* (Then the flower of Florentine youth . . . And because they were rich and noble they attracted behind them a great following of other young men like them), ibid., p. 484.

177. *"Fra Girolamo fece gridare: Viva Christo";* *"Tutti gridano: Viva Christo ch'è'l nostro Re"* (Friar Giralomo had them call out: Long live Christ; All call out: Long live Christ.), *Diario fiorentino*, pp. 127–128.

178. Villari and Casanova, *Scelte di prediche*, p. 486.

179. Niccoli, *Compagnie di bambini*, pp. 369–370.

180. R. C. Trexler, "De la ville à la cour: La déraison à Florence durant la République et le Grand Duché," in Le Goff and Schmitt, *Le Charivari*, p. 496.

181. Villari and Casanova, *Scelte di prediche*, p. 496.

182. Here I am quoting the statute of the Venetian company of the Accessi (1562), published by L. Venturi, which further declares: *"Che con questa . . . fosse data occasione a forestieri de raggionar del felice stato di questa città"* (With this . . .

opportunity was given foreigners to join the happy condition of our city), Venturi, *Le Compagnie della calza*, p. 129.

7 EMBLEMS OF YOUTH

1. Edition of M. de Fréville (Paris: Société des anciens texts français, 1988). On the author, see Gaston Paris, "Philippe de Novare," *Romania* 19 (1890): 99–102. On his treatise, see C. V. Langlois, *La Vie en France au Moyen Age d'après quelques moralistes du temps* (Paris: 1908), pp. 184–222.

2. Georges Duby, *Guillaume le Maréchal or le meilleur chevalier du monde* (Paris: 1984), pp. 40–46; English edition, *William Marshall: The Flower of Chivalry*, trans. Richard Howard (New York: Pantheon Books, 1987).

3. A history of ages in medieval society, examining theories, laws, and habits, would be most welcome.

4. On the character of Gawain, the embodiment of the young courtly prince who was also worldly and a seducer, see K. Busby, *Gauvain in Old French Literature* (Amsterdam: 1980), pp. 83–151. Gawain's most obvious appearance as an anti-Perceval is in the *Conte du Graal* by Chrétien de Troyes (circa 1190).

5. The question of monochromic armor attributed to young noblemen who were candidates for knighthood, or who had been dubbed for less than a year, has been examined by G. J. Brault. See *Early Blazon: Heraldic Terminology in the Twelfth and Thirteenth Centuries with Special Reference to Arthurian Literature* (Oxford: 1972), pp. 29–35. See also below, note 16.

6. On these two medals, see G. F. Hill, *A Corpus of Italian Medals of the Renaissance before Cellini* (London: 1933), numbers 33 and 35.

7. Among the exceedingly numerous studies devoted to the iconography of the Three Kings, those which deal most pertinently with this problem of the three ages are: H. Kehrer, *Die heiligen drei Könige in Literatur und Kunst*, 2 vols. (Leipzig: 1908–1909); G. Vezin, *L'Adoration et le cycle des mages* (Paris: 1950); U. Monneret de Villard, *Le Leggende orientali sui Maggi evangelici* (Rome: 1952); and G. Schiller, *Ikonographie der christlichen Kunst*, vol. 1 (Gütersloh: 1966), pp. 105–124. Abundant iconography may be found in the exhibition catalogue *800 Jahre Verehrung der heiligen drei Könige in Köln, 1164–1964* (Cologne: 1964).

8. I am thinking particularly of the reception given to F. Garnier's groundbreaking work, *Le Langage de l'image au Moyen Age*, 2 vols. (Paris: 1982–1989).

9. Notably in the engravings, which, in terms of quantity, represent by far the largest body of images that the sixteenth to eighteenth centuries have left us. Here again, I must deplore the lack of curiosity art historians have shown in studying the codes of imagery, the problem of attributes, and in studying gestures, postures, attitudes, zones, planes, and so on. They still prefer to devote themselves to biographies (sometimes hagiographies) of artists and to the study

of style and "influences," rather than to the true questions concerning the encoding and functioning of images.

10. C. Klapisch-Zuber, "La genèse des arbres généalogiques," *Cahiers du Léopard d'or* 2 (1992): 37–72.

11. O. Blanc, "Vêtement féminin, vêtement masculin à la fin du Moyen Age: Le point de vue des moralistes," *Cahiers du Léopard d'or* 1 (1989): 243–253. This corresponds, almost to the letter, to what Philippe de Novare wrote in his *Quatre Ages de l'homme* at the end of the thirteenth century. See above, note 1.

12. On these essential questions concerning codification through planes and interpretation from background to foreground, I refer to my own studies, "L'armoirie médiévale: Un image théorique," in G. Duchet-Suchaux, ed., *Iconographie médiévale: Image, texte, contexte* (Paris: 1990), pp. 122–138, and *L'Étoffe du Diable: Une histoire des rayures et des tissus rayés* (Paris: 1991), pp. 12–16 and 48–60.

13. Sometimes, but more rarely, the background plane is treated as a peripheral plane, in which minor figures, young people or "extras," are placed. I know of hardly any examples before the fourteenth century.

14. M. Pastoureau, *Figures et couleurs: Etudes sur la symbolique et la sensibilité médiévales* (Paris: 1986), pp. 115–124.

15. As is also evidenced by the prelates' and moralists' condemnations of beauty care. See M.-A. Polo de Beaulieu, "La Condamnation des soins de beauté par les prédicateurs du Moyen Age," in Centre d'études médiévales de Nice, *Les Soins de beauté: Actes du IIIe colloque international (Grasse, 26–28 avril 1985)* (Nice: 1987), pp. 297–310. See also the proceedings of the conference *Vieillesse et vieillissement au Moyen Age* (Aix-en-Provence: 1987).

16. In addition to the work by G. J. Brault cited above in note 5, see M. Pastoureau, "*De gueules plain:* Perceval et les origines des armoires de la maison d'Albret," *Revue française d'héraldique et de sigillographie* 60–61 (1990–91): 37–60.

17. *De proprietatibus rerum*, book VI, chapter 1. (These quotations were originally taken from the French translation by Jean Corbechon of the edition published in Paris in 1556, under the title *Le Grand Propriétaire de toutes choses*.)

18. The relatively numerous studies on representations of angels in art analyze problems relating to cults, theology, or iconography, and rarely consider plastic or chromatic questions. Moreover, these are for the most part old studies, often outdated by recent problems of methodology. J. Villette's *L'Ange dans l'art d'Occident du XIIe au XVIe siècle* (Paris: 1940) should now be replaced by a new study.

19. See the study of this recumbent figure by A. Erlande-Brandebourg, *Le Roi est mort: Étude sur les funérailles, les sépultures et les tombeaux des rois de France jusqu'à la fin du XXXe siècle* (Geneva: 1975), pp. 131–132.

20. Archives nationales de France (M. Dalas), *Corpus des sceaux français du Moyen Age. Tome II: Les Sceaux des rois et de régence* (Paris: 1991), p. 156, no. 76.

21. O. Posse, *Die Siegel der deutschen Kaiser und Könige von 751 ʒu 1806*, vol. 1 (Dresden: 1909), no. 40.

22. J. Rossiaud, "Prostitutions, jeunesse et société au XVᵉ siècle," *Annales ESC* (1976): 289–325; C. Gauvard, "Les jeunes à la fin du Moyen Age: Une classe d'âge," *Annales de l'Est* 1–2 (1982): 224–244.

23. M. Pastoureau, "Vers une histoire sociale des couleurs," in *Couleurs, images, symboles* (Paris: 1989), pp. 9–68, especially pp. 57–66; id., "Une histoire des couleurs est-elle possible?" *Ethnologie française* 20 (1990): 363–377.

24. G. J. Brault, *Early Blaʒon*, p. 32; Pastoureau, *Figures et couleurs*, pp. 35–49.

25. M. Pastoureau, "Formes et couleurs du désordre: Le jaune avec le vert," *Médiévales* 4 (May 1983): 62–73.

8 GUARDIANS OF DISORDER

1. H. Lieb and K. Schib, eds., "Beschwerden und Sorgen der Schaffhauser Geistlichkeit um 1540," *Schaffhauser Beiträge ʒur vaterlänische Geschichte* 48 (1971): 146 ff.

2. B. Schribner, "Reformation, Karneval und die 'verkehrte Welt,'" in *Volkskultur: Zur Wiederentdeckung des vergessenen Alltags (16.–20. Jahrhundert)* (Frankfurt-am-Main: 1984), p. 127 ff.

3. Lieb and Schib, "Beschwerden," p. 152. See also J. Wipf, *Reformationsgeschichte der Stadt Schaffhausen* (Zurich: 1929), p. 292; E. G. Rusch, "Die Schaffhauser Reformationsordnung von 1529," *Schaffhauser Beiträger ʒur Geschichte* 56 (1979): 25.

4. "'Charivari' und Rügebrauchtum in Deutschland. Forschungstand und Forschungaufgaben," in M. Scharfe, ed., *Brauchforschung* (Darmstadt: 1991), pp. 430–463.

5. U. Herrmann, "Was heisst 'Jugend'? Jugendkonzeptionen in der deutschen Sozialgeschichte," in H.-G. Wehling, ed., *Jugend, Jugendprobleme, Jugendprotest* (Stuttgart: 1982), pp. 11–27; T. von Trotha, "Zur Entstehung von Jugend," *Kölner Zeitschrift für Soʒiologie und Soʒiopsychologie* 34 (1982): 254–277; L. Roth, *Die Erfindung des Jugendlichen* (Munich: 1983); J. R. Gillis, *Geschichte der Jugend: Tradition und Wandel im Verhältnis der Altersgruppen und Generationene in Europa, von des Zweiten Hälfte des 18. Jahrhunderts bis ʒur Gegenwart* (Weinhelm: 1980), pp. 105–186; English edition, *Youth and History* (New York: 1974). See also note 9, below.

6. See P. Ariès, *L'Enfant et la Vie Familiale sous l'Ancien Régime* (Paris: 1973), p. 134 ff; *Centuries of Childhood: A Social History of Family Life* (New York: McGraw-Hill, 1965); E. Schubert, "Erspielte Ordnung: Beobachtungen zur

bäuerlichen Rechtswelt des späteren Mittelalters," *Jahrbuch für fränkische Landersforschung* 38 (1978): 51–65; C. Löhmer, *Die Welt der Kindheit im 15. Jahrhundert* (Weinheim: 1989), pp. 154 ff., 178 ff. Less reliable: E. von Künssberg, "Rechtsbrauch und Kinderspiel: Untersuchungen zur deutschen Rechtsgeschichte und Volkskunde," in *Sitzungsberichte der Heidelberger Akademie der Wissenschaften,* vol. 11, *Phil.-hist. Kl.,* supp. 7 (Heidelberg: 1920), pp. 1–64.

7. Wipf, *Reformationsgeschichte,* p. 327.

8. T. Pestalozzi-Kutter, *Kulturgeschichte des Kantons Schaffhausen und seiner Nachbargebiete im Zusammenhang der allgemeinen Kulturgeschichte* (Aarau: 1928), p. 391, note 280. A quart, or *Viertel,* was a unit of measurement for liquids, corresponding to a number of liters that varied according to the region. In Switzerland, one quart equaled fifteen liters; in this case, it equaled about thirty liters of wine (Trans. note).

9. On the origins of modern youth at the turn of the present century, see Walter Laqueur, *Die deutsche Jugendbewegung: Eine historische Studie* (Cologne: 1962); English edition, *Young Germany: A History of the German Youth Movement* (Brunswick, N.J.: Transaction Publishers, 1984). See also R. Lindner, "Bandenweisen und Klubwesen im wilhelminischen Reich und in der Weimarer Republik: Ein Beitrag zur historischen Kulturanalyse," *Geschichte und Gesellschaft* 3 (1984): 352–375; D. Peukert, *Grenzen der Sozialdisziplinierung: Aufstieg und Krise der deutschen Jugendfürsorge von 1878 bis 1932* (Cologne: 1986); id., *Jugend Zwischen Krieg und Krise: Lebenswelten von Arbeiterjungen in der Weimarer Republik* (Cologne: 1987); English edition, *The Weimar Republic,* trans. Richard Deveson (New York: Hill and Wang, 1992); id., "Die 'Halbstarken': Protestverhalten von Arbeiterjugendlichen zwischen wilheminischen Kaiserreich und Ära Adenauer," *Zeitschrift für Pädagogik* 30 (1984): 533–548; W. Bucher and K. Pohl, eds., *Schock und Schöpfung, Jugendästhetik im 20. Jarhundert,* exhibition catalogue (Darmstadt: 1986).

10. Overall view presented by Gillis, *Geschichte der Jugend,* pp. 17–47; M. Mitterauer, *Sozialgeschichte der Jugend* (Frankfurt-am-Main: 1986), especially p. 164 ff.; English edition, *A History of Youth,* trans. G. Dunphy (London: Blackwell, 1992). Still stimulating from the theoretical point of view: S. N. Eiswenstadt, "Altersgruppen und Sozialstruktur," in L. von Friedeburg, ed., *Jugend in der modernen Gesellschaft* (Cologne-Berlin: 1969), pp. 49–81.

11. N. Z. Davis, "Die aufsässige Frau," in *Humanismus, Narrenherrschaft un die Riten der Gewalt: Gesellschaft und Kultur im frühneuzeitlichen Frankreich* (Frankfurt-am-Main: 1987), p. 139; original English edition, *Society and Culture in Early Modern France: Eight Essays* (Stanford: Stanford University Press, 1975).

12. P. Bourdieu, *Esquisse d'une théorie de la pratique* (Geneva: 1972), p. 192.

13. Mitterauer, *Sozialgeschichte,* pp. 44–95.

14. Ariès, *L'Enfant et la Vie familiale*, pp. 82, 86.

15. Davis, *Humanismus*, p. 171. On this controversy, see the introduction to the second French edition of Ariès, *L'Enfant et la Vie familiale*, p. xvi ff.

16. Edict of the town council of Basel against the Baptists, dated June 2, 1526, in *Aktensammlung zur Geschichte der Basler Reformation von den Jahren 1519 bis Anfang 1534*, vol. 2, ed. E. Dürr and P. Roth (Basel: 1933), p. 337; see also pp. 355 and 635.

17. Felix Platter, *Tagebuch (Lebensbeschreibung) 1536–1567* ed. V. Lötscher (Basel: 1976), p. 59. "I was fond of marauding for fruit, like the other young ones," p. 74. Elsewhere, speaking of himself at age twelve and another friend, Platter writes: "We were both children," p. 88.

18. *Aktensammlung*, vol. 6, p. 137.

19. R. Habermas, *Wallfahrt und Aufruhr: Zur Geschichte des Wunderglaubens in der frühen Neuzeit* (Frankfurt: 1991), p. 50.

20. M. Scharfe, "Kindheit à Dieu! Konfirmation als Kulturzäsur im Lebenslauf," in K. Köstlin, ed., *Kinderkultur* (Bremen: 1987), pp. 171–182; C. Burckhardt-Seebass, *Konfirmation in Stadt und Landschaft Basel: Volkskundliche Studie zur Geschichte eines kirchlichen Festes* (Basel: 1975).

21. In the early modern period and until the eighteenth century, religious instruction for adolescents began at around age fourteen or fifteen (see R. Reith, "Zur beruflichen Sozialisation im Handwerk vom 18. bis in frühe 20. Jahrhundert: Umrisse einer Sozialgeschichte der deutschen Lehrlinge," in *Vierteljahrschrift für Sozial-und Wirtgeschichte* 76-1 (1989): 7.

22. M. Mitterauer, "Gesindedienst und Jugendphase im europäischen Vergleich," in *Geschichte und Gesellschaft* 11 (1985): 88 ff.

23. H. Parigger, ed., *Das Bamberger Stadtrecht* (Würzburg: 1983), p. 64.

24. M. Mitterauer, "Vorindustrielle Familienformen: Zur Funktionsentlastung des 'ganzen' Hauses im 17. und 18. Jahrhundert,' in M. Mitterauer, *Grundtypen alteuropäischer Sozialreformen Haus und Gemeinde im vorindustriellen Gesellschaften* (Stuttgart: 1979), p. 74 ff. and p. 93; W. Hartinger, "Bayerisches Dienstbotenleben auf dem land, vom 16. bis 18. Jahrhundert," in *Zeitschrift für bayerische Landesgeschichte* 38 (1975): 629. For general observations, see J. Schlumbohn, "Sozialstruktur und Fortpflanzung bei der ländlischen Bevölkerung Deutschlands im 18. und 19. Jahrhundert: Befunde und Erklärungsätze zu schichspezifischen Verhaltensweisen," in E. Voland, ed., *Fortpflanzung: Natur und Kultur im Wechselspiel: Versuch eines Dialogs zwischen Biologen und Sozialwissenschaftlern* (Frankfurt-am-Main: 1992), pp. 322–346.

25. D. Groh, "Strategien, Zeit und Ressourcen: Risikominimierung, Unterproduktivität und Mussepräferenz—die zentralen Kategorien von Subsistenzökonomien," in *Anthropologische Dimensionen der Geschichte* (Frankfurt-am-Main: 1992), pp. 54–113.

26. E. Strübin, *Baselbieter Volksleben: Sitte und Brauch im Kulturleben der Gegenwart* (Basel: 1967), p. 138 ff.

27. E. Hoffmann-Krayer, "Knabenschaften und Volksjustiz in der Schweiz," in P. Geiger, ed., *Kleine Schriften zur Volkstunde* (Basel: 1946), pp. 124–159 (p. 125 for this particular point).

28. Hoffmann-Krayer, "Knabenschaften und Volksjustiz," p. 125 ff.

29. G. Caduff, *Die Knabenschaften Graubündens: Eine volkskundlich-kulturhistorische Studie* (Chur: 1932), pp. 23 ff.; H. Métraux, *Schweiner Jugendleben in fünf Jahrhunderten: Geschichte und Eigenart der Jugend und ihrer Bünde im Gebiet der protestantischen deutschen Jugen und ihrer Bünde im Gebiet der protestantischen deutschen Schweiz* (Zürich: 1942), pp. 40–51.

30. Strübin, *Baselbieter Volksleben*, p. 140.

31. Ibid., p. 143.

32. K. R. V. Wikman, *Die Einleitung der Ehe: Eine vergleichlende ethno-soziologische Untersuchung über die Vorstufe der Ehe in den Sitten des schwedischen Volkstum* (Abo: 1937), especially pp. 55–162 and 369 ff.; Mitterauer, *Sozialgeschichte*, p. 171 ff.; J.-L. Flandrin, "Repression and Change in the Sexual Life of Young People in Medieval and early Modern Times," in *Journal of Family History* 2 (1977): 196–210; I. Peter, *Gasslbrauch und Gasslspruch in Osterreich* (Salzburg: 1981), especially pp. 155–187.

33. Compare with Caduff, *Die Knabenschaften Graubündens*, p. 77 ff.

34. Ibid., pp. 67–74; Strübin, *Baselbieter Volksleben*, pp. 140–142.

35. E. Menolfi, *Sanktgallische Untertanen in Thurgau: Eine sozialgeschichtliche Untersuchung über die Herrschaft Bürglen (TG) im 17. und 18. Jahrhundert* (Saint-Gall: 1980), p. 286.

36. *Schweizerisches Archiv für Volkstunde* 1 (1897): 144–147.

37. A. Dörrer, *Tiroler Fastnacht innerhalb der alpenländischen Winter- und Vorfrühlingsbräuche* (Vienna: 1949), pp. 30 ff.

38. Caduff, *Die Knabenschaften Graubündens*, p. 31.

39. C. Helbling, "Die Knabenschaften in Rapperswil," *Schweizerisches Archiv für Volkskunde* 21 (1917): 121–135.

40. Hoffmann-Krayer, "Knabenschaften und Volksjustiz," p. 132 ff.; ed., "Die Fastnachtgebräuche in der Schweiz," *Schweizerisches Archiv für Volkskunde* 1 (1897): 264–268.

41. P. Meintel, "Die Organisation der Kilbigesellschaft in Schwyz," *Schweizerisches Arch für Volkskunde* 19 (1915): 182. The *Kilbigesellschaft* was apparently a society connected with the festival of religious consecration, *Kirchweih* or *Kilbi* in Swiss dialectal variants (Trans. note).

42. Davis, *Humanismus*, pp. 106–135; Mitterauer, *Sozialgeschichte*, pp. 195–197.

43. P. Burke, *Helden, Schurken und Narren: Euerpäische Volkskultur in der frühen*

Neuzeit (Munich: 1985), p. 205 ff; original English edition: *Popular Culture in Early Modern Europe* (New York: 1975).

44. See the numerous documents collected by H. Moser, *Volksbräuche im geschichtlichen Wandel Ergebnisse aus fünfzig Jahren volkskundlicher Quellenforschung* (Munich: 1985), pp. 1–97; H. Schuhladen, "Zur Geschichte von Perchtenbräuchen im Berchtesgadener Land, in Tirol und Salzburg, vom 16. bis 19. Jahrhundert: Grundlagen zur Analyse heutigen Traditionsverständnisses," in *Bayerisches Jahrbuch für Volkskunde* (1983–84): 1–29; R. Bendix and T. Nef, *Silvesterkläuse in Urnäsch* (Saint-Gall: 1984).

45. *Schweizerisches Archiv für Volkskunde* 1 (1897): p. 146.

46. Hoffmann-Krayer, "Knabenschaften und Volksjustiz," p. 141.

47. Meintel, "Kilbigesellschaft," p. 183.

48. Ibid. The German word for *bat* is *Fledermüss,* or *Fledermaus,* apparently used metaphorically to mean "flighty" (Trans. note).

49. W. Kaschuba, *Volkskultur zwischen feudeler und bürgerlicher gesellschaftlichen Wirklichkeit* (Frankfurt: 1988), p. 166 ff., p. 203 ff.; C. Lipp, "Katzenmusiken, Krawalle und 'Weiberrevolution': Frauen im politischen protest der Revolutionsjahre," in C. Lipp, ed., *Schimpfende Weiber und patriotische Jungfrauen: Frauen im Vormärz und in der Revolution 1848–1849* (Moos and Baden-Baden: 1986), pp. 112–130.

50. Ibid., p. 182.

51. Helbling, "Knabenschaften in Rapperswil," p. 127, note 1.

52. Caduff, *Die Knabenschaften Graubündens,* p. 209.

53. Ibid., p. 207.

54. Ibid., pp. 188–194.

55. H. Maurer, *Schweizer und Schwaben: Ihre Begegnung und ihr Auseinanderleben am Bodensee im Spätmittelater* (Constance: 1991), pp. 33–50.

56. B. Meyer, "Der Thurgauer Zug von 1460," *Thurgauische Beiträge zur vaterländischen Geschichte* 97 (1960): 15–47.

57. H. G. Wackernagel, "Masken krieger und Knaben im Schwabenkriege von 1499," in H. G. Wackernagel, *Altes Volkstum der Schweiz: Gesammelte Schriften zur historischen Volkskunde* (Basel: 1956), pp. 247–249.

58. N. Schindler, "'Heiratsmüdigkeit' und Ehezwang: Zur populären Rügesitte des Pflug- und Blochziehens," in N. Schindler, *Widerspenstige Leute: Studien zur Volkskultur in der frühen Neuzeit* (Frankfurt-am-Main: 1992), pp. 174–214, 361 ff.

59. G. Korff, "'Heraus zum 1. Mai': Maibräuch zwischen Volkskultur, bürglerlicher Folklore und Arbeiterbewegung," in van Dülmen and Schindler, *Volkskultur,* p. 252 ff.

60. Compare the critical relativization in L. Roper, "Gendered Exchanges: Women and Communication in Sixteenth-Century Germany," in *Kommunikation und*

Alltag in Spätmittelalter und früher Neuzeit (Vienna: 1992). I would like to thank the author for allowing me to consult her manuscript.

61. J. Baader, ed., *Nürnberger Polizeiordnung aus dem XIII. bis XV. Jahrhundert* (Stuttgart: 1861), p. 84 (republished, Amsterdam: 1966).

62. *Works of Martin Luther: Correspondance (WA)*, vol. 10, no. 3958, p. 500 ff.

63. See Article 22 of the penitentiary ordinance of Constance, 1531, in O. Feger, ed., *Die Statutensammlung des Stadtschreibers Jörg Vögeli* (Constance: 1951), p. 58; edict of Bern, dated November 8, 1600, in H. Rennefahrt, ed., *Die Rechtsquellen des Kantons Bern*, part 1, *Das Stadtrecht von Bern*, vol. 10, *Polizei, Behördliche Fürsorge* (Aarau: 1968), p. 13.

64. See moral edict of Bern, November 3, 1625, in Rennefahrt, *Die Rechtsquellen des Kantons Bern*, part 1, vol. 6/2, *Staat und Kirche* (Aarau: 1961), p. 862.

65. Edict of 1626, in Rennefahrt, *Die Rechstquellen des Kantons Bern*, part 1, vol. 10, p. 8.

66. Ibid., p. 10 ff.

67. M. Bless-Grabher, *"Liederliche Weibsbilder, Ehrenjungen und Frauenzimmer"*: *Frauen im alten Wil* (Wil: 1986), p. 26.

68. Ibid., p. 27.

69. Rennefahrt, *Die Rechstquellen des Kantons Bern*, part 1, vol. 10, p. 14.

70. Ordinance of the Council of Uberlingen, 1555, in V. Metzger, "Die Fastnacht in Uberlingen," in *Schriften des Vereins für Geschichte des Bodensees und seiner Umgebung* 60 (1932–33): 28.

71. H. Medick, "Spinnstuben auf dem Dorf: Jugendliche Sexualkultur und Feierabendbräuch in der ländlichen Gesellschaft der frühen Neuzeit," in G. Huch, ed., *Sozialgeschichte der Freizeit Untersuchungen zum Wandel der Allragskultur in Deutschland* (Wuppertal: 1980), pp. 19–49.

72. Platter, *Tagebuch*, p. 55.

73. Ludwig Lavatar, 1569, quoted in Hoffmann-Krayer, "Die Fastnachtgebräuche," p. 57. Informative examples of role-playing by both sexes may be found in H. Moser, "Zur Geschichte der Maske in Bayern," in L. Schmidt, ed., *Masken in Mitteleuropa: Volkskundliche Beitrage zur europäischen Maskenforschung* (Vienna: 1955), p. 114 ff.

74. F. E. Welti, ed., *Die Rechstquellen des Kantons Aargau*, part 1, vol. 3, *Die Stadtrechte von Kaiserstuhl* (Aarau: 1905), no. 53, p. 66.

75. W. Merz, ed., *Die Rechtsquellen des Kantons Aargau*, part 2, vol. 2, *Die Oberämter Königsfelden, Biberstein und Kasteln* (Aarau: 1926), no. 123, p. 248.

76. "But if such a man is found at night in the vineyard, he must pay ten pounds or forfeit his hand." "Der Stadt Rheinfelden Rechte und Gewohnheiten von 1530," in Welti, *Die Rechstquellen des Kantons Aargau*, part 1, vol. 7, *Das Stadtrecht von Rheinfelden* (Aarau: 1917), p. 230.

77. Renward Cysat, *Collectanea Chronica und Denkwürdige Sachen pro Chronica Lucernensi et Helvetiae,* vol. 1, part 1, ed. J. Schmid (Lucerne: 1969), p. 131.

78. C. Studer, ed., *Die Rechstquellen des Kantons Solothurn,* vol. 2, *Mandate, Verordnungen, Satzungen des Standes Solothurn von 1435 bis 1604* (Aarau: 1987), no. 34, p. 92.

79. Daniel Fabre, "Families: Privacy versus Custom," in Philippe Ariès and E. Chartier, eds., *A History of Private Life: Passions of the Renaissance,* trans. Arthur Goldhammer (Cambridge, Mass.: Harvard University Press, 1989), p. 550.

80. Merz, *Die Rechstquellen des Kantons Aargau,* part 1, vol. 5, *Das Stadtrecht von Zofingen* (Aarau: 1914), p. 262.

81. Police rulings of Bern, May 24, 1748, in Rennefahrt, *Die Rechtsquellen des Kantons Bern,* part 1, vol. 10, p. 37.

82. An edict of 1591 in Bern. Ibid., p. 6, note 1.

83. Rennefahrt, *Die Rechtsquellen des Kantons Bern,* part 1, vol. 6/2, no. 31y, p. 962.

84. Ibid.

85. On nocturnal uproars disturbing the elderly and the sick in Zug in 1741, see E. Gruber, ed., *Die Rechtsquellen des Kantons Zug,* vol. 1, *Grund- und Territorialsherren: Stadt und Amt* (Aarau: 1971), p. 482.

86. Studer, *Rechtsquellen des Kantons Solothurn,* vol. 2, pp. 2, 92, 156, 176, 224 ff.; 228, 246 ff.; 259, 267, 291.

87. *Aktensammlung,* vol. 2, p. 376.

88. Studer, *Die Rechtsquellen des Kantons Solothurn,* vol. 2, p. 156.

89. *Aktensammlung,* vol. 2, p. 230 ff.

90. Studer, *Die Rechtsquellen des Kantons Solothurn,* p. 176.

91. Scribner, "Reformation, Karneval," pp. 117–152; N. Schindler, "Karneval, Kirche und verlehrte Welt: Zur Funktion der Lachkultur im 16. Jahrhundert," in Schindler, *Widerspenstige Leute,* p. 144 ff.

92. *Urfehde,* or "Oath sworn when renouncing vengeance," of June 18, 1522, in *Aktensammlung,* vol. 1 (Basel: 1921), p. 37.

93. *Urfehde* of February 25, 1527, in ibid., vol. 2, p. 440. For the ritual of provoking someone to emerge from hiding, see K.-S. Kramer, "Das Herausfordern aus dem Haus: Lebensbild eines Rechsbrauches," in *Bayerisches Jahrbuch für Volkskunde* (1956): 121–138; H. Heidrich, "Grenzübergänge: Das Haus und die Volkskultur in der frühen Neuzeit," in van Dülmen, *Kultur der einfachen Leute,* pp. 17–41.

94. *Urfehde,* of October 2, 1532, in *Aktensammlung,* vol. 6 (Basel: 1950), p. 141.

95. *Urfehde* of March 31, 1529, in *Aktensammlung,* vol. 3 (Basel: 1937), p. 382.

96. *Aktensammlung,* vol. 4 (Basel: 1950), p. 267.

97. *Urfehde* of January 15, 1533, in *Aktensammlung,* vol. 6, p. 220.

98. *Urfehde* of August 10, 1532, in *Aktensammlung,* vol. 6, p. 110.

99. *Urfehde* of April 3, 1530, in *Aktensammlung*, vol. 4, p. 390. See also pp. 389 and 394 ff.

100. *Urfehden* of April 5, 1530, in ibid., p. 393.

101. *Urfehden* of August 1, 1530, in ibid., p. 543.

102. Ibid., p. 544.

103. Ibid., p. 543.

104. *Urfehden* of April 5, 1530, in ibid., p. 393 ff.

105. Studer, *Die Rechtsquellen des Kantons Solothurn*, vol. 2, p. 176.

106. Welti, *Die Rechstquellen des Kantons Aargau*, part 1, vol. 7, no. 181, p. 164.

107. For other Swiss edicts against nocturnal rowdiness in the fifteenth, sixteenth, and seventeenth centuries, see the following references from the *Sammlung Schweizerischer Rechtsquellen* (quoted with abbreviated titles):

1442–1443	Rheinfelden/AG	(*Aargau*, part 1, vol. 7, p. 63 ff.)
1491	Bern	(*Bern*, part 1, vol. 10, p. 1)
1501	Rheinfelden/AG	(*Aargau*, part 1, vol. 7, p. 188 ff.)
1502	Bern	(*Bern*, part 1, vol. 10, p. 1)
1532	Lenzburg/AG	(*Aargau*, part 1, vol. 4, p. 268)
1541	Basel	(*Rechtsquellen von Basel*, ed. J. Schnell [Basel: 1856], p. 379)
1557	Bremgarten/AG	(*Aargau*, part 1, vol. 4, p. 113)
1560	Kaiserstuhl/AG	(*Aargau*, part 1, vol. 3, p. 105)
1580–1590	Bern	(*Bern*, part 1, vol. 4/2, p. 839; vol. 10
1606	Bern	(*Bern*, part 1, vol. 10, p. 20 ff.)
1636–1641	Zug	(*Zug*, vol. 1, p. 471)
1645	Baden/AG	(*Aargau*, part 1, vol. 2, p. 308)
1670	Glarus	(*Glarus*, vol. 2, p. 950 ff.)
1673	Freie Amter	(*Aargau*, part 1, vol. 8, p. 605)
1681	Kaiserstuhl/AG	(*Aargau*, part 1, vol. 3, p. 180)

108. Merz, *Die Rechtsquellen des Kantons Argau*, part 1, vol. 5, pp. 262 and 351.

109. *Die Chroniken der deutschen Städte vom 14. bis ins 16. Jahrhundert*, vol. 29 Augsburg (Preu), p. 73, note 2.

110. C. Moser-Nef, *Die freie Reichstadt und Republik St. Gallen: Geschichte ihrer Verfassung und staatsrechtlichung Entwicklung*, vol. 3 (Zurich-Leipzig: 1934), p. 777.

111. R. Cysat, *Collectanea Chronica*, section 1, vol. 1, part 1, p. 131.

112. Fr. Rothenflue, *Allgemeine Geschichte der Landschaft Toggenburg* (Niederbüren: 1886), p. 208 ff.

113. Moser-Nef, *Die freie Reichstadt*, vol. 5, p. 106, and vol. 3, p. 899.

114. Ibid., vol. 5, p. 819.

115. Ibid, p. 302.

116. Ibid., vol. 3, pp. 799 and 813.

117. Ibid., p. 803.

118. Ibid., p. 806.

119. An early example of the use of massive force by the party of order is found in G. Schwerhoff, *Köln im Kreuzverhör: Kriminalität, Herrschaft und Gesellschaft in einer frühneuzeitlichen Stadt* (Bonn: 1991), p. 306.

120. N. Schindler, "Die Entstehung der Unbarmherzigkeit: Zur Kultur und Lebensweiser der Salzburger Bettler am Ende des 17. Jahrhunderts," in Schindler, *Widerspenstige Leute*, p. 293 ff.

121. Rennefahrt, *Die Rechtquellen*, vol. 10, p. 41 (emphasis added).

122. Ibid., p. 42. See also W. Schivelbusch, *Lichtblicke: Zur Geschichte der künstlichen Lelligkeit im 19. Jahrhundert* (Frankfurt-am-Main: 1986), p. 98; English edition: *Disenchanted Night: The Industrialization of Light in the Nineteenth Century*, trans. Angela Davies (Berkeley: University of California Press, 1988).

123. Strübin, *Baselbieter Volksleben*, p. 143 ff.; Dörrer, *Tiroler Fastnacht*, p. 34 ff.

124. F. Stucki, ed., *Die Rechtsquellen der Kantons Glarus*, vol. 3 (Aarau: 1984), p. 1304.

125. Ibid., p. 1503.

126. Studer, *Die Rechtsquellen des Kantons Solothurn*, vol. 2, p. 374. See also the examples quoted by Moser-Nef, *Die freie Reichstadt*, vol. 5, pp. 108, 113, 114.

127. Studer, *Die Rechstquellen des Kantons Solothurn*, vol. 2, p. 375.

128. Dörrer, *Tiroler Fastnacht*, p. 36 ff.

129. L. Roper, "Mannlichkeit und männliche Ehre," in *Journal Geschichte* 1 (1991): 28–37.

130. Dörrer, *Tiroler Fastnacht*, p. 37; Caduff, *Die Knabenschaften Gräubundens*, p. 50.

131. Studer, *Die Rechtsquellen des Kantons Solothurn*, vol. 2, pp. 374, 375, 429.

132. Strübin, *Baselbieter Volksleben*, p. 142.

133. D. Fabre, "La famille," pp. 562 ff. See also N. Z. Davis, "Charivari, Honor and Community in Seventeenth-Century Lyon and Geneva," in J. MacAloon, ed., *Rite, Drama, Spectacle: Rehearsals toward a Theory of Cultural Performance* (Philadelphia: 1984), pp. 42–57.

134. E. P. Thompson, "'Rough Music' oder englische Katzenmusik," in E. P. Thompson, *Plebeische Kultur und moralische Okonomie: Aufsätze zur englischen Sozialgeschichte des 18. und 19. Jahrhundert*, ed. D. Groh (Frankfurt: 1980), p. 158.

135. W. Kugler, "Die Kirchenvisitation in der Superintendentur Monheim von der Reformation bis zur Gegen reformation," in *Zeitschrift für Bayerische Kirchengeschichte* 33 (1964): 58.

136. R. Beck, "Der Pfarrer und das Dorf: Konformismus und Eigensinn im Katholischen Bayern des 17./18. Jahrhunderts," in R. van Dülmen, ed., *Armut, Liebe, Ehre: Studien zur historischen Kulturforschung* (Frankfurt-am-Main: 1988), p. 135.

137. Testimony of a priest of Mögeldorf (near Nuremberg), during the pastoral

inspection of 1626: "I was recently asked to give communion to an old man of eighty. When I asked him how many Gods there were, he answered, 'Six.' So then I reminded him—since he thought himself so old as to have forgotten what little he had learned—that there was one sole God, but three persons in the Holy Trinity—whereupon he calmly replied: 'Ah, so one and three makes one; I always thought it made six!'" Quoted in K. Leder, *Kirche und Jugend in Nürnberg und seinem Landgebiet 1400 bis 1800* (Neustadt: 1973), p. 159.

138. The decision to give religious instruction to children and young people rather than adults (a change in policy generally initiated around 1600, perhaps sooner in Protestant regions) originated in a methodological error on the part of the missionaries: the adults reacted to publicly administered instruction and corrections as if they were insults and stayed away from the catechism classes. Thus in 1588 the ecclesiastical ordinance of Hohenlohe recommended not tormenting adults and old people further in regard to their knowledge of the catechism, "save on the essential points"; rather, it suggested conversing gently and patiently with them, and letting them "learn from the mouths of children . . . during public lessons." Quoted in E. Sehling, ed., *Die evangelischen Kirchenordnung des XVI. Jahrhunderts*, vol. 15 (Tübingen: 1977), p. 278. See also J. Schmidlin, *Die kirchlichen Zustände in Deutschland vor dem Dreissigjährigen Krieg*, vol. 3 (Freiburg: 1910), p. 28 ff.; R. Steinmetz, "Volksbildung in Bayern: Zur Situation und Aufklärung," in H. Gerndt et al., eds., *Dona Ethnologica Monacensia: Festschrift für L. Kretzenbacher zum 70. Geburtstag*, (Munich: 1983), p. 213; E. Hegel, *Geschichte des Erzbistmus Köln*, vol. 4 (Cologne: 1979), p. 312.

139. Leder, *Kirche und Jugend in Nürnberg*, p. 204. This type of incident—and, of course, the protection precaution against venal priests—is found in the edicts issued by the authorities. Thus, in the *Landbuch* of the Langweis district (Grisons), a new article was introduced after 1674 that declared, "it is forbidden to throw snow or stones, especially at the church or the town hall." Quoted in E. Meyer-Marthaler, ed., *Die Rechtsquellen des Kantons Graubünden*, part 2, vol. 1, *Gericht Langwies* (Aarau: 1985), p. 223.

140. S. Riezler, *Geschichte Baierns*, vol. 4 (Gotha: 1899), p. 574; F. J. Lipowsky, *Geschichte der Jesuiten in Baiern*, vol. 1 (Munich: 1816), p. 276. See also, in general, E. W. Zeeden, *Die Entstehung der Konfession: Grundlage und Formen der Konfessionsbildung im Zeitalter der Glaubenskämpfe* (Munich-Vienna: 1965), p. 103.

141. Mentioned in the parish register of the community of Flirsch (Aarlberg), Parish Archives, p. 220 ff.

142. Ibid., p. 220.

143. Strübin, *Baselbieter Volksleben*, p. 135.

144. Parish register of Flirsch (Aarlberg), Parish Archives, p. 221.

145. Platter, *Tagebuch*, p. 327.

146. Strübin, *Baselbieter Volksleben*, p. 141.

147. Quoted in Beck, *Der Pfarrer und das Dorf*, p. 136. See also pp. 133–135.

148. Ibid., p. 137.

149. Birlinger, *Aus Schwaben*, vol. 2, p. 227. For similar incidents in central Protestant Franconia, see K.-S. Kramer, "Alterer Spuren burschenschaftlichen Brauchtums in Mittelfranken," in *Jahrbuch für fränkische Landesforschung* 20 (1960): 381–383.

150. Thompson, "'Rough Music,'" pp. 131–168; Davis, *Humanismus*, pp. 106–135; J. Le Goff and J.-C. Schmitt, eds., *Le Charivari: Actes de la table ronde . . .* (Paris: 1981).

151. The fact that unmarried sons and servants of peasants were forcibly conscripted into the imperial army was a cause of the Bavarian peasant revolt of 1705–1706, a protest based on evident economic concerns. See S. Riezler and K. von Wallmenich, eds., *Akten zur Geschichte des bairischen Bauernaufstandes 1705–1706* (Munich: 1915), p. 28 ff.; C. Probst, *"Lieber bayrisch sterben": Der bayrisch Volksaufstand der Jahre 1705 und 1706* (Munich: 1978), pp. 139–180. On the role of the *Knabenschaften* in peasant revolts, see also H. G. Wackernagel, "Der Trinkelstierigkeit vom Jahre 1550," in Wackernagel, *Altes Volkstum der Schweiz*, pp. 222–243; I. Werlen, "Die Walliser Mazze: Ein Rebellionsritual," in *Zeitschrift für Volkskunde* 74 (1978): 167–197; A. Suter, *"Troublen" im Fürstbistum Basel (1726–1740): Ein Fallstudie zum bäuerlichen Widerstand im 18. Jahrhundert* (Göttingen: 1985), pp. 355–368, 198 ff.

152. Johann J. Bodmer, *Historische Erzählungen, die Denkart und Sitten der Alten zu entdecken* (Zurich: 1769), p. 237, quoted in R. Wolfram, "Der 'äussere Stand' in Bern und die Entwicklung städtischer Jungmännerverbände in der Schweiz," in R. Wolfram, *Studien zur älteren Schweizer Volkskultur. Mythos, Sozialordnung, Brauchbewusstsein* (Vienna: 1980), p. 217, note 312.

153. Hoffmann-Krayer, "Knabenschaften und Volksjustiz," pp. 133–137, 148 ff.

154. Caduff, *Die Knabenschaften Graubündens*, p. 243 ff.

155. *Die Rechtsquellen des Kantons Glarus*, vol. 3, p. 1012.

156. Ibid., p. 1013.

157. Communal archives of Traunstein, August 3, 1689, fol. 60–62.

158. Communal archives of Traunstein, AV 16, 26 (judicial hearing for the victims of February 24, 1644). Young men gladly took advantage of the fact that throwing snowballs—unlike throwing stones—was treated and punished by the authorities as a minor delinquency, even though its results were sometimes just as serious. In 1647, the young men of Augsburg bombarded the magnificent parade of nobles in their sleighs so zealously that throwing snowballs was thereafter forbidden by a decree of the Council; four policemen were assigned to control these habits and prevent future assaults. (Birlinger, *Aus Schwaben*, vol. 2, p. 23.)

159. F. Elsener, ed., *Die Rechtsquellen des Kantons St. Gallen*, part 3, *Die Rechtsquellen der Landschaft*, vol. 1 (Aarau: 1951), p. 558.

160. Ibid.

161. The egalitarian principles of these rural associations of young men have been emphasized in Davis, *Humanismus*, pp. 118 and 120; R. Muchembled, "Die Jugend und die Volkskultur im 15. Jahrhundert Flandern und Artois," in P. Dinzelbacher and H. D. Mück, eds., *Volkskultur des europäischen Spätmittelalters* (Stuttgart: 1987), pp. 35–58. In the countryside, the traditional forms of youth culture did not die out until the present century, and they were partly replaced by certain types of local associations. Research based on oral history, conducted by A. Gestrich in a working commune of Wurtemberg, emphasizes the break with tradition at the time of the First World War; see A. Gestrich, *Traditionnelle Jugendkultur und Industrialisierung: Sozialgeschichte der Jugend in einer ländlichen Arbeitgemeinde Württembergs 1800–1920* (Göttingen: 1986), pp. 101 and 115. Background material consists of the socioeconomic changes accompanying the transition to industrial factories; these changes altered the marriage market and shortened the adolescent phase by lowering the age at which people married (ibid., p. 102 ff.).

162. The persons questioned by Gestrich declared that "the absence of so many young men" during the First World War "led to the disappearance of several important traditions"; ibid., p. 115. "During the war, the younger boys missed the older ones, who would normally have instructed them in them the village subculture"; ibid., p. 101.

163. Communal archives of Traunstein, R 17/2 *Pfleggerichtsrechnungen von 1616, Amt Mieserbach*, fol. 6.

164. Ibid., fol. 7.

165. *Die Chroniken der deutschen Städte vom 14. bis 16. Jahrhundert*, vol. 25 *Augsburg: Rem*, p. 7 (reprint, Göttingen: 1966), p. 7.

166. Ibid., vol. 23, *Augsburg: Sender*, p. 358.

167. The violent aspect has been emphasized by Muchembled, *Die Jugend und die Volkskultur*, pp. 35–58; see also Schwerhoff, *Köln im Kreuzverhör*, pp. 304, 307 ff.

168. Strübin, *Baselbieter Volksleben*, pp. 29 ff., 141 ff., 146–148.

169. Mitterauer, *Sozialgeschichte der Jugend*, p. 173; Gestrich, *Traditionelle Jugendkultur und Industrialisierung*, pp. 106–111.

170. See also W. Mezger, *Narretei und Tradition: Die Rottweiler Fasnet* (Stuttgart: 1984), p. 66 ff. It is important to note the evolution of Hänsele, the central figure in the carnival of Überlingen. He is first mentioned in the early eighteenth century. That he was constantly cracking his whip must have been particularly intolerable to the ears of the staid burghers who prohibited this activity in 1789—clearly without success. Thus we read, in 1822: "Since whistling and the

noise of whips being cracked have grown so intense as to be unbearable, we find ourselves forced to forbid these insanities once again and with the greatest severity." See D. H. Stolz, "Die Fastnacht in Überlingen," in H. Bausinger, ed., *Masken zwischen Spiel und Ernst: Beiträge des Tübinger Arbeitreises für Fastnachtsforschung* (Tübingen: 1967), p. 97 ff., 103.

171. *Zimmernsche Chronik*, ed. A. Barack, vol. 3 (Stuttgart: 1869), p. 460. In Cologne, they "sang like the nightingale, neighed like horses, or brayed like a stag"; F. Irsigler and A. Lassotta, *Bettler und Gaukler, Dürnen und Henker: Randgruppen und Aussenseiter in Köln, 1300–1600* (Cologne: 1984), p. 126.

172. E. Weiss, *Volkskunde der Schweiz. Grundriss* (Erlenbach-Zurich: 1946), p. 231 ff.

173. See also Peter, *Gasslbrauch*, pp. 117–122.

174. H. Moser, "Vom Folklorismus in unserer Zeit," in H. Moser, *Volksbräuche im Geschichtlichen Wandel*, pp. 336–358.

175. "Publication of an Edict of the Council of the City of Augsburg for the Propagation of a Christian and Virtuous Life," communal archives of Augsburg, *Sammlung Anschläge und Dekrete 1490–1649*, no. 20.

176. "Rentmeisterumrittsprotkolle Oberland, Generalia vom 8. 6. 1654," communal archives of Traunstein, A XIII 6, 1, unpaginated.

177. Ibid.

178. See also Dörrer, *Tiroler Fastnacht*, p. 49 ff.

179. Letter of complaint written by Pastor Ladislaus von Törring to the town council of Traunstein, May 30, 1618, in the communal archives of Traunstein, AV 16, p. 16.

180. See also Fabre, *Die Familie*, p. 574 ff.

181. Dörrer, *Tiroler Fastnacht*, pp. 33–40, especially p. 38 ff.; R. Wolfram, "Burschenbrauchtum, Rügerichte und Katzenmusiken in Südtirol," in *Festschrift für O. Höfler zum 75. Geburtstag*, o. O.o. J, pp. 721–741, especially pp. 726 ff. and 738.

182. Paragraph 10 of the communal and village ordinance of Elchingen, Affalterwang, etc., of 1766. F. Wintterlin, ed., *Württembergische Ländliche Rechtsquellen*, vol. 1 (Stuttgart: 1910), p. 244.

183. Caduff, *Die Knabenschaften Graubündens*, pp. 179–187.

184. *Die Rechtsquellen des Kantons Glarus*, vol. 3, p. 1322 ff.

185. In an edict of April 9, 1792, we read that "during this festival many of them behaved most indecently, especially in the choir of the church, exchanging jokes and vulgar words aloud." Ibid., p. 1108. See also G. Thürer, *Kultur des alten Landes Glarus: Studie des Lebens einer eidgenössischen Demokratie im 16. Jahrhundert* (Glarus: 1936), pp. 271 and 460–463.

186. In their attempt to describe the *Haberfeldtreiben* as a traditional "Bavarian tribunal of morals" (Breibeck), historians have been deceived by skillful way that the masked figures *(Haberer)* presented themselves; that is, by their traditions of

disguise. This is particularly true of the older studies, but it may also be said of the otherwise respectable study by H. Ettenhuber, "Charivari in Bayern: Das Miesbacher Haberfeldtreiben von 1893," in van Dülmen, *Kultur der einfachen Leute*, pp. 180–207 and 250–157.

187. Quoted in Beck, *Der Pfarrer und das Dorf*, p. 136.

188. Caduff, *Die Knabenschaften Graubündens*, p. 230.

189. Ibid., p. 233 ff.

190. Ettenhuber, "Charivari in Bayern," pp. 197 ff.; Hinrichs, "'Charivari' und Rügebrauchtum," pp. 447 ff. and 451–460.

9 YOUNG NOBLES IN THE AGE OF ABSOLUTISM

1. Alessandro Manzoni, *I Promessi sposi* (Milan: 1827); English edition, *The Betrothed*, trans. Archibald Colquhoun (London: Dent, 1968), p. 120.

2. See J. P. Cooper, "Patterns of Inheritance and Settlement by Great Landowners from the Fifteenth to the Eighteenth Centuries," in J. Goody, J. Thirsk, and E. P. Thompson, eds., *Family and Inheritance: Rural Society in Western Europe 1200–1800* (Cambridge: Cambridge University Press, 1976).

3. Ibid.

4. D. Zanetti, *La Demografia del patriziato milanese nei secoli XVII, XVIII, XIX* (Pavia: University of Pavia, 1972).

5. See Cooper, "Patterns of Inheritance."

6. Ibid.

7. Quoted in F. Medioli, *L'"Inferno monacale" di Arcangelo Tarabotti* (Turin: Rosenberg and Sellier, 1990), p. 45.

8. Quoted in L. Stone, *The Family, Sex and Marriage in England 1500–1800* (London: Weidenfeld and Nicolson, 1977).

9. A few nostalgic voices were occasionally raised in favor of retreats for women only. See B. Hill, "A Refuge from Men: The Idea of a Protestant Nunnery," *Past and Present* 117 (1987).

10. See Stone, *The Family*, especially pp. 178–196; J. Revel, "L'usage des bonnes manières," in Ariès and Duby, eds., *Histoire de la vie privée*, vol. 3, *De la Renaissance aux Lumières* (Paris: Seuil, 1987); English edition, *A History of Private Life*, vol. 3, *Passions of the Renaissance*, ed. Roger Chartier, trans. Arthur Goldhammer (Cambridge, Mass.: Harvard University Press, 1989); S. Ozment, *When Fathers Ruled: Family Life in Reformation Europe* (Cambridge, Mass.: Harvard University Press, 1983), especially pp. 144–154.

11. J.-L. Flandrin, *Famille, parenté, maison, sexualité dans l'ancienne société* (Paris: Hachette, 1976); English edition, *Families in Former Times* (Cambridge: Cambridge University Press, 1979).

12. A. Prosperi, "Educare gli educatori: Il prete come professione intellettuale

nell'Italia tridentina," in *Problèmes d'histoire et d'éducation (Actes des séminaires de l'Ecole française de Rome et de l'Università di Roma—La Sapienza* (Rome: 1988), p. 138.

13. Juan Luis Vives, *De ratione studii puerilis deque vita iuventutis instituenda ac moribus studiisque corrigendis* (Basel: 1539), p. 263.

14. Quoted in Flandrin, *Famille, parenté, maison*, p. 133.

15. See R. M. Douglas, "Talent and Vocation in Humanist and Protestant Thought," in T. K. Rabb and J. E. Eigel, eds., *Action and Conviction in Early Modern Europe* (Princeton: Princeton University Press, 1968).

16. See *Opus Epistolarum Des: Erasmi Roterodami*, ed. P. S. Allen and H. M. Allen, 12 vols. (Oxford: 1906–1958), vol. 2, no. 447 (1516), pp. 63–64. See also Douglas, "Talent and Vocation," p. 264; G.-A. Pérouse, "Le Dr. Huarte de San Juan: Pédagogie et politique sous Philippe II," *Bibliothèque d'humanisme et Renaissance* 1 (1970).

17. Cicero, *De officiis (Duties)*, ed. H. Testard (Paris: Belles Lettres, 1965), pp. xxxii–117.

18. P. Charron, *De la sagesse* (Paris: Lefèvre, 1836), p. 336–338. See also Douglas, "Talent and Vocation," p. 265.

19. Quoted in Flandrin, *Famille, parenté, maison*, p. 137.

20. Ibid.

21. Ibid.

22. See Douglas, "Talent and Vocation."

23. Ibid., p. 296.

24. Ibid.

25. Manzoni, *I Promessi sposi*, p. 525. The name of the nun is given as Gertrude in the English translation, but is Marianna de Leyva in Italian and French. (Trans. note.)

26. See Renata Ago, "Farsi uomini: Giovani nobili nella Roma barocca," *Memoria* 27 (1989).

27. Sperone Speroni, "Lettere," in *Trattatisti del Cinquecento*, ed. M. Pozzi (Milan: Ricciardi, 1978), p. 801, no. 1, letter of March 26, 1557.

28. Ibid., p. 806, no. 4, letter of June 11, 1561.

29. Archivio di Stato di Roma, *Spada Veralli*, b. 614, letter of March 7, 1674, and p. 613, letter of August 1, 1673; see also Ago, "Farsi uomini."

30. Archivio Segreto Vaticano, *Carte Borghese*, b. 30, f. 2.

31. Archivio del Vicariato di Roma, *Ottoboni*, b. ZZ.

32. Ibid., letter of March 2, 1669.

33. Biblioteca dell'Accademia Nazionale dei Lincei, *Corsini*, b. 2473.

34. Ibid.

35. Speroni, "Lettere," p. 824, letter of March 3, 1576.

36. Ibid.

37. Archivio Doria Pamphilij, Rome, b. 201, cc. 419 ss.

38. The subject is frequently broached in private correspondence. See, for example, accounts of the appearance and character of several certain princesses eligible to wed the future Charles Emmanuel III of Savoy, in D. Frogo, "L'affermazione della sovranità: Famiglia e corte dei Savoia tra Cinque e Settecento," in C. Mozzarelli, ed., *"Familia" del principe e Famiglia aristocratica* (Rome: Bulzoni, 1988).

39. Quoted in Stone, *The Family*, p. 363.

40. Archivio di Stato di Roma, *Santacroce*, Inventory.

41. Archivio Segreto Vaticano, *Carte Borghese*, b. 32, f. 7.

42. See Philippe Ariès, *L'Enfant et la Vie familiale sous l'Ancien Régime* (Paris: Plon, 1960); English edition, *Centuries of Childhood: A Social History of Family Life* (New York: McGraw-Hill, 1965).

43. Archivio di Stato di Roma, *Spada Veralli*, b. 607, no date.

44. Ibid., b. 611, letter of November 17, 1660.

45. Ibid., b. 614, letter of January 31, 1674.

46. Ibid., letter of April 4, 1674.

47. Ibid., b. 454, f. 62.

48. D. Erasmi Roterodami, *De civitate morum puerilium libellus elegantissimus* (Basel: 1538), p. 175, 12–14.

49. Quoted in Stone, *The Family*, p. 179.

50. See G. P. Brizzi, *La Formazione della classe dirigente nel Sei-Settecento* (Bologna: Il Mulino, 1976); D. Roche, "Le précepteur dans la noblesse française: Instituteur priviliégié ou domestique," in *Problèmes d'histoire de l'éducation*.

51. See Brizzi, *La Formazione*, especially p. 235 ff.

52. See Roche, "Le précepteur," p. 25.

53. See Brizzi, *La Formazione*.

54. Ibid.

55. Archivio di Stato di Roma, *Spada Veralli*, b. 613, letter of October 11, 1673.

56. Archivo Segreto Vaticano, *Carte Borghese*, b. 31, f. 2.

57. Biblioteca dell'Accademia Nazionale dei Lincei, *Corsini*, b. 2473bis.

58. Archivio Segreto Vaticano, *Carte Borghese*, b. 31, f. 3.

59. Archivio Doria Pamphilij, Rome, b. 91. 85, letter of March 28, 1699.

60. Leon Battista Alberti, *Trattato della famiglia*, ed. F. C. Pellegrini and R. Spongano (Florence: Sansoni, 1946), book 1.

61. Biblioteca Apostolica Vaticana, mss. Barberiniani Latini no. 4879, c. 1, *Vita del cardinal Marco Franciotto*.

62. Archivio di Stato di Roma, *Spada Veralli*, b. 493, f. 1.

63. Ibid., f. 7.

64. Ibid., f. 11.

65. Ibid., b. 632, letter of April 6, 1661.

66. Ibid., b. 607, letter of May 21, 1658.

67. Ibid., b. 487, letter of December 20, 1673.

68. Ibid., b. 454, f. 90.

69. Ibid., b. 285, 1662.

70. Biblioteca Accademia Nazionale dei Lincei, *Corsini*, b. 2469, no date.

71. Archivio di Stato di Roma, *Spada Veralli*, b. 285, 1635–1636.

72. Archivio Vicariato di Roma, *Ottoboni*, b. DD, letter of July 31, 1683 to Pietro Ottoboni, Junior.

73. Archivio di Stato di Roma, *Santacroce*, b. 1226, letter of June 13, 1699.

74. Ibid., *Spada Veralli*, b. 459, c. 194.

75. Ibid., b. 487, c. 226.

76. See S. Cabibbo and M. Modica, *La Santa dei Tomasi: Storia di suor Maria Crocifissa (1645–1699)* (Turin: Einaudi, 1989), p. 23.

77. Biblioteca Nazionale Centrale Vittorio Emanuele II, *Gesuitico*, mss. 95–105, *Camillo Cybo, Autobiografia*.

78. Biblioteca Apostolica Vaticana, mss. Ottoboniani latini no. 3228, t. I, c. 100, letter of February 10, 1634, Marco Antonio Ottoboni to Pietro Ottoboni, Senior; see also Medioli, *L'"Inferno monacale,"* p. 116.

79. Archivio di Stato di Roma, *Spada Veralli*, b. 459, c. 194.

80. Archivio Doria Pamphilij, Rome, b. 93. 71, f. 7.

81. See Renata Ago, *Carriere e clientele nella Roma barocca* (Rome: Laterza, 1990).

82. See Medioli, *L'"Inferno monacale."*

83. Quoted in G. Zarri, "Monasteri femminili e città," in *Storia d'Italia*, Annali 9, *La Chiesa e il Potere politico*, ed. G. Chittolini and G. Miccoli (Turin: Einaudi, 1986), p. 386.

84. Speroni, "Lettere," p. 824, letter of March 3, 1576.

85. See M. Rosa, "La religiosa," in R. Villari, ed., *L'Uomo barocco* (Rome: Laterza, 1991).

86. Ozment, *When Fathers Ruled*, p. 4 ff.

87. See Zarri, "Monasteri femminili," and Ago, *Carriere*.

88. Speroni, "Lettere," p. 854, letters of February 26 and March 3, 4, and 17, 1576.

89. See Zarri, "Monasteri femminili," p. 364; C. Casanova, "Le donne come 'risorsa': Le politiche matrimoniali della famiglia Spada (sec. XVI–XVIII)," *Memoria* 21 (1987).

90. See Rosa, "La religiosa," and also Cabbibo and Modica, *La Santa dei Tomasi*. The portraits of nuns are significant here; see D. Owen Hughes, "Representing the Family: Portraits and Purposes in Early Modern Italy," *Journal of Interdisciplinary History* 18 (1986).

91. Quoted in E. Zanette, *Suor Arcangela Tarabotti, monaca del Seicento veneziano* (Venice: Istituto per la collaborazione culturale, 1960), pp. 35–36. See also Rosa, "La religiosa," especially pp. 262–263.

92. Flandrin, *Famille, parenté, maison,* p. 168.

93. See Ozment, *When Fathers Ruled,* pp. 38–40.

94. See E. Berriot-Salvadore, "The Discourse of Medicine and Science," in G. Duby and M. Perrot, eds., A. Goldhammer, trans., *A History of Women in the West,* vol. 3, *Renaissance and Enlightenment Paradoxes* (Cambridge, Mass.: Harvard University Press, 1993), p. 374.

95. Archivio di Stato di Roma, *Santacroce,* b. 1226, letter of May 17, 1698.

96. Ibid.

97. Archivio Doria Pamphilij, Rome, b. 93.71.

98. Archivio di Stato di Roma, *Spada Veralli,* b. 634, letter of March 15, 1675.

99. Archivio Segreto Vaticano, *Carte Borghese,* b. 50, f. 6.

100. Archivio di Stato di Roma, *Spada Veralli,* b. 459.

101. Ibid.

102. Ibid.

103. See the article entitled "Matrimonio" in *Enciclopedia cattolica* (Città del Vaticano: 1948–1954); see also J. Gaudemet, "Législation canonique et attitudes séculières à l'égard du lien matrimonial au XVIIe siècle," *XVIIe Siècle* (1974); G. Gozzi, "Padri, figli e matrimoni clandestini," in A. Manoukian, ed., *I Vincoli familiari in Italia: Dal secolo XI a secolo XX* (Bologna: Il Mulino, 1983); Flandrin, *Famille, parenté, maison,* p. 129.

104. See P. Ungri, *Storia del diritto di famiglia in Italia* (Bologna: Il Mulino, 1974); Gozzi, "Padri, figli."

105. Archivio Segreto Vaticano, *Carte Borghese,* b. 31, letter of February 28, 1683.

106. See Ago, *Carriere;* M. Barbagli, *Sotto lo stesso tetto: Mutamenti della famiglia in Italia dal XV al XX secolo* (Bologna: Il Mulino, 1984), pp. 312–313.

107. See A. Daumas, "Les conflits familiaux dans les milieux dominants au XVIIe siècle," *Annales ESC* 4 (1987).

108. See L. Accati, "La sposa in prestito: Soggetto collettivo, soggetto individuale e conflitto politico (1566–1759)," in *Discutendo di storia: Soggettività, ricerca, biografia* (Turin: Rosenberg and Sellier, 1990).

109. Archivio di Stato di Roma, *Spada Veralli,* b. 453, letter of May 5, 1661.

110. Biblioteca Accademia Nazionale dei Lincei, *Corsini,* b. 2469.

111. Archivio Vicariato di Roma, *Ottoboni,* b. ZZ, letter of February 23, 1668, and bb. AA, DD, passim.

112. Gaudemet, "Législation canonique"; J.-L. Flandrin, *Les Amours paysannes (XVIe–XIXe siècle)* (Paris: Gallimard, 1970), pp. 40–47.

113. Quoted in Flandrin, *Les Amours paysannes,* pp. 43–44.

114. Gaudemet, "Législation canonique"; Flandrin, *Les Amours paysannes,* pp. 131–132.

115. Quoted in Flandrin, *Familles, parenté, maison,* p. 133.

116. Ibid.

117. J. Michelet, *Le prêtre, la femme et la famille* (Paris: 1875).

118. Cooper, "Patterns of Inheritance," p. 293.

119. Quoted in Flandrin, *Les Amours paysannes*, pp. 53–57; M. Daumas, *L'affaire d'Esclans: Les conflits familiaux au XVIIe siècle* (Paris: Seuil, 1988), p. 216.

120. Quoted in N. Tamassia, *La famiglia italiana nei secoli decimoquinto e decimosesto* (Rome: Multigrafica, 1971), p. 262.

121. Quoted in Stone, *The Family*, p. 163.

122. Speroni, "Lettere," pp. 805–808, letter of April 19, 1561.

123. Quoted in Stone, *The Family*, p. 201.

124. See R. Gillis, "Conjugal Settlements: Resort to Clandestine and Common Law Marriage in England and Wales (1650–1850)," in J. Bossy, ed., *Disputes and Settlements* (Cambridge: 1983); Cooper, "Patterns of Inheritance"; Stone, *The Family*, especially p. 269.

125. See Ozment, *When Fathers Ruled*, pp. 37–39.

126. For an analysis of this subject, see L. A. Pollock, *Forgotten Children: Parent-Child Relations from 1500 to 1900* (Cambridge: Cambridge University Press, 1983).

127. D. Dinet, *Vocation et fidélité: Le recrutement des Réguliers dans les diocèses d'Auxerre, Langres et Dijon (XVIIe–XVIIIe siècle)* (Paris: Economica, 1988); M. Peronnet, "Les Evêques de l'Ancienne France (1516–1790), doctoral dissertation (thèse d'Etat), 1976.

128. I. Green, "Career Prospects and Clerical Conformity in the Early Stuart Church," *Past and Present* 90 (1981).

129. A. Dominguez Ortiz, *Las Clases privilegiadas en la España del Antiguo Régimen* (Madrid: ISTMO, 1973).

CONTRIBUTORS

RENATA AGO is Professor of Modern History at the University of Cagliari. She is the author of *Carriere e clientele nella Roma barocca* (1990) and *La feudalità nell'età moderna* (1994).

ELISABETH CROUZET-PAVAN is Professor of Medieval History at the University of Lille III. She is the author of *"Sopra le acque salse": Espaces urbains, pouvoir et société à Venise à la fin du Moyen Age* (1992) and *La mort lente de Torcello: Histoire d'une cité disparue* (1995).

AUGUSTO FRASCHETTI is Professor of Classical Economic and Social History at the University of Rome. He is the author of *Roma e i principe* (1990).

ELLIOTT HOROWITZ is Senior Lecturer in Jewish History at Bar-Ilan University, Israel.

GIOVANNI LEVI is Professor of Economic History at the University of Venice. He is the author of *Centro e periferia di uno stato assoluto* (1985).

CHRISTIANE MARCHELLO-NIZIA is University Professor at the Ecole Nationale Supérieure (Fontenay / St. Cloud). She is the author of *L'évolution du français* (1995).

MICHEL PASTOUREAU is Director of Studies at the Sorbonne's Ecole Pratique des Hautes Etudes. He is the author of *L'étoffe du diable: Une histoire des rayures et des tissus rayés* (1991) and *Rayures: Une histoire des rayures et des tissus rayés* (1995).

NORBERT SCHINDLER is Lecturer in History at the University of Basel. He is the coeditor of *Volkskultur: Zur Wiederentdeckung des vergessenen Alltags, 16.–20. Jahrhundert* (1984) and author of *Widerspenstige Leute: Studien zur Volkskultur in der frühen Neuzeit* (1992).

JEAN-CLAUDE SCHMITT is Director of Studies at the Ecole des Hautes Etudes en Sciences Sociales. He is the author of *La raison des gestes dans l'Occident médiéval* (1990) and *Les revenants: Les vivants et les morts dans la société médiévale* (1994).

ALAIN SCHNAPP is Professor of Greek Archaeology at the University of Paris I. He is the author of *La conquête du passé* (1993) and *La chasse, les jeunes et l'érotique en Grèce ancienne* (in press).

INDEX